To Nicole —
Thanks for all
your kindnesses.
Let's

Free the Animals

Free the Animals

The Amazing True Story of the
Animal Liberation Front

Ingrid Newkirk

Lantern Books
A Division of Booklight Inc.

2000
Lantern Books
One Union Square West, Suite 201
New York, NY 10003

Printed in the United States of America

Library of Congress Cataloging-in-Publication Data

Newkirk, Ingrid.
Free the animals : the amazing story of the Animal Liberation Front / Ingrid Newkirk
      p. cm.
Originally published: Chicago : Noble Press, 1992. With new prefatory material.
     ISBN 1-930051-22-0 (alk. paper)
     1. Animal experimentation—United States. 2. Animal Liberation Front. 3. Animal rights movement—United States. 4. Valerie. 5. Animal rights activists—Maryland—Biography. I. Title

     HV4930 .N49 2000
     179'.4'06073–dc21

                    00-062994

I am in earnest—I will not equivocate—I will not excuse—I will not retreat a single inch *and I will be heard.*
  —William Lloyd Garrison (1805–1879)
  The Liberator

Contents

Acknowledgments

Thanks go to PETA's Carla Bennett, *Animal Times* columnist and author of *Living In Harmony With Animals*, who helped check many details in this book. She is a very sensitive and skilled animal protectionist. Thanks go, too, to Rebecca Kurson, for caring to get this book back in print when it was sold out and still in demand.

And to all the members of the Animal Liberation Front, whose story this is and whose identities remain secret, I can only say, "The animals would thank you if only they could."

Introduction

In April 2000, I had just arrived in the United States for The Pretenders Tour 2000 when I became aware of something very disturbing. Ingrid Newkirk, the author of this book, had been in India and had overseen the making of a video documenting the illegal trade in cows made manifest by the largest leather industry in the world. Aware only that in India cows are deemed sacred and it is illegal to kill them, I was shocked—not only by this cruel trade, but by the enormity of it. The images in the video of gentle domestic creatures being forced into trucks, crushed by overcrowding, and encouraged to keep marching on bleeding hooves by having their tails broken sickened me. Still, I continued to watch as they made their way onto the black market that led them to the killing floors of the slaughterhouse.

I was glad for the opportunity while on tour to use my visibility to join the PETA protests targeting one of America's largest retailers, GAP, Inc., and its sales of Indian leather. These protests ended in the display window of GAP, Inc., in Manhattan, when Ingrid Newkirk, other PETA members, and I were arrested as a crowd of passersby cheered us on. PETA's Leather Campaign is far from over, but our protests encouraged GAP, Inc., to change some of its practices.

Sitting in the back of the police van, I experienced something that I had never known before, and that was a feeling of gratitude and deep appreciation for being in a country where such a protest is possible. After all, during the Vietnam War, people like myself were burning the flag. Now, I was happy to spend a night in jail as a conscientious objector.

Ingrid has spent many days and nights locked up for her protests, been a subject of a federal grand jury, and had her fingerprints, saliva, and handwriting samples taken by the FBI and her possessions confiscated in raids. Another protester, Rod Coronado, a Native American and animal rights campaigner, has been through even more. He is, despite a multimillion-dollar law-enforcement exercise and a dragnet of every state of the country, the only person to spend three and a half years in jail in the U.S. for the crime of destroying a mink research station. In England, where I live, animal rights prisoners are currently serving time in many jails, sometimes going on hunger strikes, in a determined effort to rectify the immoral procedures carried out against animals in laboratories, on fur farms, and in the meat trade. I salute them as the true heroes of our society.

I believe that every creature in the animal kingdom is in our dominion and that it is our inherent responsibility to cherish and protect them. Naturally, I can't complacently turn a blind eye while some nine billion animals are hacked up barbarically and unnecessarily for human consumption each year in the U.S. alone. I try to make it my business, make it perfectly clear to all, that I present myself, wherever I am and whatever I'm doing, as opposition to anyone who supports any practice whatsoever that incorporates animal abuse. By the way, I think that it is equally unacceptable to abuse humans, but, technically, there are laws protecting them. Therefore, I continue to feel, as do all of my animal rights brethren, that it is my duty to maintain a firm and visible stance at all times regarding animal issues.

The good news is that there are kind people who walk this Earth.

Yours as always,
Chrissie Hynde

Author's Note

This is the true story of how the animal liberation underground started in the United States. Every character—including each of the wonderful animals you will come to know, most of whom made it to safety—is real flesh and blood. Because the federal government retains an abiding interest in locking up anyone involved in illegally removing animals from those who legally exploit them, it has convened grand juries to investigate the often daring and successful raids that you will read about. That is why it was necessary to change the names of the people involved, as well as some details that might reveal where they lived and what they did for a living.

"Valerie" is active in the animal rights movement today, but there is no point in wondering who she is. What matters is what the liberators have accomplished, how they came together, and why, eventually, many of them went their separate ways. Understanding how some quite "ordinary" people came to break the law may change your life.

Bishop Desmond Tutu once said, "There's nothing more difficult than waking someone who is only pretending to be asleep." When the raids began, the liberationists' first duty was to wake up a sleeping public, to show people who didn't really want to know uncomfortable truths that there were atrocities being committed every day under the pretense of saving their lives and putting clothes on their backs.

The men and women who broke into laboratories and fur farms had to break down more than doors. They had to break through public resistance and apathy. They not only had to do the dirty work, but also they had to do their homework, gathering enough—often secret—information to show exactly how wonderful animals were suffering hideously and pointlessly. They had to make sure that people got enough of a peek behind the scenes to realize that the "science" was worthless and that fur was far from glamorously obtained.

Today's liberationists know that the ice has been broken. Television and newspaper stories have shown the extent of the suffering, over and over again. People know that there are kind alternatives to every cruel thing, from veggie burgers and "pleather" to virtual organs. Perhaps that's why the "new ALF" has lost patience with the foot draggers and spends scant time explaining. Determined to cause economic injury to the exploiters, ALF members burn down their emptied buildings and smash their vehicles to smithereens. Perhaps, after reading this book, you will find that you cannot blame them.

I

The First Police Raid

She doesn't look like a gangster or sound like a fanatic, although she founded the most notorious animal rights organization in America, the Animal Liberation Front. Her background may, in fact, surprise you. I shall call her Valerie, although that is not her real name. I met her in conjunction with a police raid carried out on September 11, 1981, on the Institute for Behavioral Research, a dingy warehouse laboratory in Silver Spring, Maryland, run by a psychologist and monkey experimenter named Edward Taub.

The trial and other events that followed came to be known as the case of the Silver Spring monkeys. It changed Valerie's life forever.

Valerie was twenty-three then, in her third year on the Montgomery County, Maryland, police force and one of only a handful of female officers. Her duty sergeant liked to say, teasing, that she looked more like a dancer or a model than a cop, but when she put on her uniform and pinned her shoulder-length blond hair up under her cap, she could "wrestle and reason" out on the street with the best of them.

Valerie had wanted to be a police officer as far back as she could remember. She had been an adventurous child and an athletic teenager. She liked orderliness, being outdoors, and taking charge of things she believed in. More than anything, she disliked

3

injustice no matter what shape or size it came in. She had never really wanted to continue her education, but she forced herself through two years of junior college in order to get a jump on the other applicants for the force. Her courses in criminal justice paid off at a time when police departments were being told to swallow their pride and bring in some women.

Valerie's career ambition was to replace her partner, now out on sick leave, with a police dog. The K-9 corps hadn't yet accepted a female handler, but Valerie was working on garnering enough respect from her supervisors to rock that boat.

If you'd told her then that in a few years she'd be on the other side of the law—wanted by the FBI and Interpol, labeled an international terrorist and a fugitive from justice—she'd have tried to have you committed.

That morning she answered a call from an Asian clerk in a 7-Eleven who was being harassed by two smart-aleck kids. She found the boys behind the store, breaking out the lights on the man's old Corvair with a baseball bat. When they saw her they ran.

"Police! Stop!" she yelled. They didn't even pause. She could hardly pull her service revolver on adolescents, so she ran down the alley after them, collaring the slower one as he missed his toehold in a chain-link fence. The faster one vaulted over it like a pro, turned for an instant to give her the finger, then disappeared into an apartment complex.

The now-not-so-cocky kid and Valerie sat in her squad car, catching their breath. He was about fourteen, white, and from Potomac, a wealthy D.C. suburb. Turning to him, Valerie asked, "Did you ever consider what it must be like for that man to struggle to support a family in what to him is a foreign country?" The kid stared defiantly at his high-priced sneakers, a sneer on his face. Determined to make him think before she turned him over to his parents, she pressed on. "You know, some people in this world don't need any aggravation. Not everyone has the luxury of running around looking for kicks like you."

Pointing to a photo taped to her dashboard, of a little brown-skinned girl with black hair, huge dark eyes, and a shy smile, she said, "Her name's Carmelita. Her father died in El Salvador, and her uncle works as a field laborer to keep bread on the family table." She didn't tell him that Carmelita's picture was there to remind her that there's still innocence in the world.

The little girl had originally been officer Carmen Hernandez's "project." Carmen and Valerie had been close, spending time at each other's apartments and swimming together at the YWCA. Valerie had been camping at Maho Bay on St. John when Carmen died in an off-duty accident. Val had never quite forgiven herself for not being able to persuade Carmen to go to Maho. By her calculations, they would have been scuba diving at the time the accident occurred. In memory of her friend, Valerie had assumed the small monthly payments Carmen had sent the child via an overseas aid agency.

Valerie liked kids, except, she thought, spoiled rich ones like "Mr. Cool" sitting beside her. The boy had stopped smirking momentarily, but wasn't acknowledging Valerie's lecture.

"Your parents home?" she asked.

"My mother is," said the kid.

"Then let's go talk to her." Valerie gave her intended location to the dispatcher and pulled out of the lot. She knew she had a good chance of getting the kid's mother to write a check for damages. If that happened, she'd let him go with a warning.

As they drove north, Sergeant Rick Swain's voice came over the police radio. His "10-9" call was followed by a succession of others, each officer giving the same location. All the scanner buffs sitting at home knew what Valerie knew: a search and seizure warrant was "in progress."

Warrants can be tricky. She thought of her partner, Dick Overmyer. A raid on a drug dealer's penthouse apartment a few days earlier had left him in the hospital with a bullet through the muscle tissue in his thick neck. Overmyer was overweight, overbearing, vulgar, racist, and abnormally interested in guns and anything remotely connected to them. It was a wonder he hadn't gotten himself shot before this, she mused.

Valerie hadn't exactly wept over Overmyer's recent incapacity, but she felt differently about Swain. She hoped he wasn't about to add to his war wounds. Thirtyish and field-smart, he already sported a deep and rather dashing scar on his left cheek from an encounter with a switchblade-wielding robber. He had two marriages behind him, a penchant for long hours, and a compassionate, but not naive, disposition.

Inside the warehouse, in a front office, a lab assistant in a scruffy once-white coat had been chatting with a secretary, expecting nothing out of the ordinary, when Swain's fists hit the back door. There were no patients due and things were slower than usual because Dr. Taub, the boss, was still at home shaving.

Swain heard the lab assistant cry out, "What the hell . . . " Then the police pushed open the double doors, and the youth's jaw fell. As he went through the warehouse door Swain's nose crinkled. By closing his eyes for a second or two he could identify three separate but melding smells: rose-scented air freshener, decomposing flesh, and—thanks to his stint in Vietnam—monkey droppings.

Sounds were coming from the first room on his right. They reminded him of the tiny sounds made by an abandoned baby someone once brought to the fifth district station. Only these cries were punctuated by grunts, as if someone frail were trying to climb steep stairs.

Hours earlier, acting on a tip, ABC's wildlife correspondent, Roger Caras, had been dispatched to Washington, D.C. Long in the habit of crouching behind scrub brush waiting for gecko lizards to mate, or perching precariously on a rock face watching bighorn sheep dance along with their youngsters, he and his camera crew now hid behind the trash dumpsters outside the back door of the Institute for Behavioral Research in Silver Spring. Fumes of discarded lunch remains wafted about them as they waited to capture an historic event on film.

Caras had watched Swain turn his cruiser in behind the Brookeville Road warehouse complex. He had seen the line of cars following Swain, lights flashing but sirens silent, each car carrying a contingent of officers who would soon discover how hard it is to remove the stench of long-accumulated feces from crisp uniforms.

With them came a team of deputized civilians with talents not often sought after by the police: a primate behaviorist, a veterinary technician, humane officers, and animal handlers.

When Caras saw the "black and whites," all lit up like Christmas trees, materialize in near-silence, he gave the high sign and out came the cameras.

"Damn!" said Swain softly, giving a personal sign of his own. Luckily it was hidden from the cameras by the barrel of the shotgun sticking up over his dashboard. Two civilians got out of his cruiser. One was the chief police witness, Alex Pacheco, the twenty-three-year-old college student and leader of PETA, who had spent four months undercover in the laboratory. He looked tired and nervous, and was biting his lip. The other was in his forties, thin and bearded. He was Dr. Geza Teleki, the world-renowned primatologist and one-time protégé of Jane Goodall, known internationally for his studies of tool use by the chimpanzees of the Gombe Preserve. The doctor now suffered from a parasitic disease called Black River Blindness.

In Swain's hand was a folded legal-size paper: a warrant signed the previous day by Circuit Court Judge John McAuliffe. It directed the police and their helpers to seize seventeen macaque monkeys, some with infected wounds, as well as all evidence of violations of Article 27, Section 59 et. seq. of the Annotated Code of the State of Maryland: the laws prohibiting cruelty to animals.

Valerie had always had a soft spot for animals, and she felt frustrated to be stuck in the stationhouse instead of being at the crime scene. After leaving Potomac she was called back to Silver Spring by her sergeant to interview a mugging suspect, and this she did as news of the search filtered in: officers had found dozens of dead monkeys floating among auto parts and bits of lumber in a formaldehyde-filled barrel; "the mad doctor" had used a monkey's skull for an office decoration and a monkey's severed hand on his desk for an ashtray.

7

When her shift ended at 3:30 that afternoon she went back to her apartment in a dingy two-story brownstone in Langley Park and stashed her Walther PPK in the vegetable bin in the fridge. Then she phoned Sean, her boyfriend, to tell him she'd be over so they could watch the news together. As usual, it would take him a while to get in from the garden, where he spent most of his time.

When she arrived he surprised her with a bottle of Moët et Chandon and a warm kiss.

"What happened? Did Ed McMahon call to say you'd won the sweepstakes?" she asked. He was wearing an expensive shirt and tie, but he smelled of mulch and there were bits of bark caught in his curly, reddish-brown hair. He looked like the half-Irish, half-Swedish woodsman he was, with one foot in the business world and the other in the garden.

"No, my little peach, but it's almost as good. 'Wildnear Landscaping' is official. While you were off catching crooks today, I incorporated my company and signed a deal on office space. The phones will be in by Monday, and our ads will be listed in two weeks. Give the president another kiss."

"Sean, congratulations!" She obliged his request, and he poured the champagne.

When they first met, just after Valerie graduated from rookie school, Sean had resigned his post at the Environmental Protection Agency, disillusioned with government's lip service and inaction on pesticides and environmental toxins. He combined his deep love of the outdoors with hard study of organic gardening, natural pest deterrence, and the structure of successful minihabitats. He had never known poverty, but now, thanks to the substantial trust fund he'd inherited nine years ago on his twenty-first birthday, he was well-to-do. If he couldn't save the world, he told Valerie, he could save a part of it.

"Sean, your dream has come true!"

"Not quite, Batgirl. Even the most successful independent landscaper needs his true love in one piece. Retire from fighting the evil forces of Gotham City. Come hoe with me."

"If that's a proposal, you know the answer: thank you, but no thank you. And anyway, you know I have black thumb! I either overwater or underfeed the plants you leave me in charge of. Come on now, let's watch the news."

They'd had this conversation before. She trusted Sean like a brother, she loved him, and he excited her, but she wasn't ready to marry him. She really didn't know why. Maybe she enjoyed her independence too much, or maybe she still believed what her mother had told her so many times after her parents had argued. "Perhaps," she thought, "love really is 'the dawn of marriage, and marriage the sunset of love.' "

While Sean and Val waited for Dan Rather to report the story, Sergeant Swain sat in the police station, exhausted and filthy, filling out warrant return sheets and cataloging the reams of cockroach-infested research papers removed from the lab. As he leafed through the grubby papers, it became clear that Dr. Taub had applied to do almost anything to almost any animal with grant money from almost any institution, including the Department of Defense and the Boy Scouts of America. A peaceful silence filled the room where Swain worked, only because he had threatened to throttle the next person who dared say "banana" or "zoo."

Sean punched on the TV and joined Valerie on the couch where she sat shaking her hair loose from its eight-hour confinement. Like millions of other Americans, they saw seventeen cages full of monkeys being lifted out of a dark building into sunshine. The animals were on screen for less than a minute—pathetic little creatures slightly over a foot tall, with bandaged arms or exposed, torn flesh. They looked dazzled as they blinked toward the sun. The reporter's mellifluous voice explained how this was the primates' first glimpse of natural light and first feel of fresh air since their capture in the Philippine jungles as adolescents many years earlier. Then off they went, whisked away in a rented truck bearing a ridiculously large handmade sign reading, "People for the Ethical Treatment of Animals (PETA)."

"Makes you wonder if we're civilized, doesn't it?" Sean said, putting his arm around her and almost spilling her drink.

9

"You know," Valerie said, "I was thinking today how easy it is to get hardened by police work. Those monkeys just reminded me I *can* still feel. I never want to get like Overmyer."

Sean knew she was referring to an accident she and Overmyer responded to early one morning after a heavy rain. The driver of a truck full of bricks had lost control of his vehicle. He lay vividly dead, sprawled in the road. A tiny sports car had been flattened into a strip of tangled red metal beneath the overturned truck, the wheels of which still revolved pointlessly in the air. Overmyer had walked over to the driver's body, picked up the man's arm, and said, in his best John Cameron Swayze imitation, "And the Timex. It's *still* ticking." She had laughed.

"Val," Sean's deep green eyes were understanding. "Overmyer's just weird. That was your first major sight of blood and guts. Your laughter was normal nerves, inasmuch as *anything* you deal with out there is normal. Which is why you should give it up and, as the spider said to the fly, 'come into the garden with me.' "

"And as the fly said back, 'Bug off!' " Valerie didn't want to be pressured. It irritated her and made her snap at Sean, which she instantly regretted. "Sean," she pleaded, changing the subject, "right now I feel terrible knowing I drove by that IBR warehouse hundreds of times and never had a clue about those monkeys being in there."

Sean knew she felt guilty. Valerie always did. He also knew he was pushing her, and he stopped. "With that kind of news coverage, you know, that lab should be put out of business for good," he said. "If you want to help an animal, how about asking Mikaya to adopt me a dog?"

One cold day two winters ago, Valerie had responded to a "10-80," or "robbery in progress" call. The "burglar" had turned out to be the kind that doesn't shoot back: an elderly, confused, and cold hound covered with burrs and coal dust. He had fallen through a rotten board into the cellar of an abandoned farmhouse and someone had heard him down there, bumping into the walls. Valerie pulled him out and cleaned the icicles from his whiskers.

Mikaya was the humane officer who arrived to take the dog to the shelter. In the snow she seemed radiantly black—not brown, but black like a Wellington boot. Her blue-black curls were pinned tidily behind her head. She was also very short, which gave her an advantage on the icy pavement.

Mikaya stepped down from the battered old truck, reassured the hound, and lifted him into her arms, popping him gently but matter-of-factly into a paper-lined crate.

When Valerie was back in the cruiser radioing in her departure, Mikaya came over and spotted Carmelita's picture.

"That little bundle of brown sugar's not yours?" she asked.

"Nope. She lives in El Salvador. I'm just her sponsor."

"Good for you. I grew up in a village where we had almost nothing, unless you count heat." She gave Valerie her card.

A month or so later, Valerie saw her wheeling a shopping cart through Safeway. Sean was coming over to dinner, and somehow Valerie found herself inviting Mikaya to join them.

"Should have said," Mikaya had told her that night, politely declining the chicken breasts in white wine sauce. "Vegetarian. Sorry. You get too close to animals in my line of work to eat them. I'll be most content with the other stuff, don't you mind."

She proceeded to devour the salad, potato casserole, and broccoli with almonds as if she hadn't eaten in a week.

"Sean, why haven't you snatched this fine woman up?" Mikaya asked, "She's a real good cook!"

Sean gave her an exaggerated, pained look Valerie knew well. "Val believes life is just one fool thing after another, and love is just two fool things after one another. She's against the institution. She likes living in this hovel, alone."

Mikaya clucked and shook her head. Then she discarded her napkin and pulled a book full of pictures of dogs from her oversized purse. She was looking for homes for them.

"I'm gone all day, Mikaya," Valerie said. "It wouldn't be fair to have a dog. She'd have nothing to do but stare at the walls, legs crossed, dying to go out, bored stiff. Sean has a beautiful yard. Hit him up!"

Sean promised he'd call Miki as soon as he got Wildnear going. Now was the time to make good on his promise.

"Got a dog named Mandy Sean'll flip over," Mikaya said when Valerie phoned. "She's housebroken, no hassle, one owner—a little old lady who only took her out on Sundays!"

Mikaya told Valerie she was part of the Silver Spring monkey team. Would Val like to see the monkeys? Absolutely!

"Let me tell you where they're being kept. You and Sean can meet me there, and you can go pick up Mandy."

Valerie wrote down the address and said they'd see her there.

She and Sean headed out to Rockville, a city that reminded Valerie of an exceptionally ugly movie set: one extremely long main street, the Pike, with nothing but air behind the sterile cement and brick buildings lining it. When they got to the address Mikaya had given them, they were surprised to find a charming old home in a row of boxy little houses.

"Monkeys? In *there?*" Sean raised an eyebrow.

"Well, who would have thought they were in that warehouse? Let's see."

Mikaya welcomed them. There were papers and bags of food everywhere and everyone was doing something: typing, sorting papers, stuffing envelopes, washing fruit.

"The monkeys are downstairs," Mikaya told them. "Here, slip on these lab masks. And at the bottom of the stairs you'll see a tray of blue disinfectant—slosh through it before you go into the monkeys' area."

The monkeys, many wearing fresh bandages, sat in their large wooden cages on elevated platforms. The cages were constructed of mesh on all four sides, allowing the monkeys to see each other and touch the fingertips of their fellow monkeys in the adjoining cages. Each cage contained a toy of some kind that the primates, when they weren't looking curiously around the room, were picking apart, smelling, or moving about in their hands. One enormous brown male was using his toy as a noisemaker, rubbing it back and forth across the bottom of the cage.

"Something for them to do," sighed Mikaya. "In the lab they never had anything to touch, no stimulation of any kind. They could only sit there and wait for someone to do something ugly to them."

The basement was immaculate. The monkey smell Valerie remembered from childhood visits to the zoo was missing, and the concrete was freshly scrubbed.

Mikaya introduced them to Alex Pacheco, PETA's president, whose nervous interview they had watched on television. He was as serious as he was handsome. He gave them a brief smile, but his clear dark eyes remained solemn and searched their faces. Valerie wondered why he seemed so wary of strangers.

"Don't look the monkeys in the eyes," he cautioned them. "That's a threat to them, a sign of aggression used by challenging males." He took them around the room, warning them also not to move their arms suddenly. He named each monkey as they passed, stopping at Paul's cage.

"Look at his scar tissue. It's very deep. Paul's real old—no one knows how old, of course. The dealers just snatch these little guys out of the jungles, after shooting the mothers of the younger ones or setting net traps. Paul's scars are from years of self-mutilation, digging into his own arms to stop the pain or break his own frustration."

Paul had an old face, a wrinkled neck, tired eyes, and the sort of thin shoulders you see on prisoners of war. Valerie's heart went out to him. "Kids and animals," she thought. "How can anyone be so mean . . . ."

"Next to him is Chester. He thinks he's the leader of this sorry troop, keeps an eye on everything, makes big hooting noises if you seem about to do something to any of the gang. That's Sarah next to him, she's the only female, and the only one born in captivity." Sarah wasn't playing with her toy. She was circling in her cage, stopping at the front each time to grasp her foot and bite it.

"What's wrong with her?" Valerie asked Alex.

"She has been in a cage one-third that size for eight years, ever since she was removed from her mother. She's completely neurotic. Her foot is the only thing she's ever had to play with."

"Next to her is Hard Times," Alex continued. "He has to rock back and forth like that to relieve his constant back pain. Botched surgery, we think."

"If you ask me," Mikaya piped up with disgust, "it's voodoo medicine, not science."

"You mean they've all had their backs operated on?" Sean asked. Valerie noticed he looked a little green. He had a low threshold for blood and guts. She put her arm through his for moral support.

"No. Some are what they call 'control' animals, like those over there," Alex indicated two monkeys who, as if to illustrate, were poking at each other playfully through the bars with all four hands. "Taub and his henchmen compare the surgically mutilated monkeys to the ones they haven't messed with and write down the differences. Brilliant stuff. For example, monkeys with the use of their hands can climb and pick things out of grooves in a plate. Monkeys who have disabled limbs and missing fingers can't! Here, Hard Times would love you to groom him. For a big male, he's very passive and introverted."

Alex handed Valerie a wire hairbrush. She withdrew from Sean and moved slowly toward the cage, feeling self-conscious at making the little sounds Alex had encouraged them to try. Out of the corner of her eye she could see Hard Times rocking from one foot to the other, staring at the brush. She made a slow, stroking motion with it in the air. He immediately turned sideways and cast his eyes down.

"He's accepting your offer," Mikaya smiled.

Valerie slipped the brush through the mesh and felt its metal tines meet Hard Times's skin. As she started to brush he repositioned his body so he was no longer sitting facing her, but was, instead, on all fours, like a dog, so she could groom his sides and legs. Even in that posture his pain forced him to keep moving, transferring his weight back and forth from one leg to the other.

"Just be careful. If you snag him, he may think you've attacked, and he has teeth that would make a saber-toothed tiger jealous."

"Oh, comforting," she whispered, more afraid to disturb this abused monkey than to be bitten.

"This is Billy," Alex said softly, brushing his thick dark hair off his forehead with his hand. "Dr. Taub opened up his back and cut the nerves in his spine that control his arms. He's lost the use of them both. He has to do everything with his feet, including eat his food, and of course he can't climb."

Valerie watched the tiny primate half-close his eyes as Alex's fingers massaged his atrophied limbs and rubbed under his whiskery chin. She looked up as the door opened. Lori Lehner, who owned the house, started down the stairs. Then an orange and white cat sprang past her, ran down the stairs, and jumped onto the shelving unit.

Before anyone could do anything, Billy responded. Then the others. The room was suddenly filled with the same sort of clucking sound that Alex had made to show affection. The monkeys were bobbing their heads up and down, some of them had their arms outstretched through the bars. It was unmistakable: they wanted to touch the cat.

"Sorry about that," said Lori, retrieving her cat. "These guys certainly find William attractive, but it's clearly unrequited love. He looks ready to have a stroke!"

"It's odd," Alex told Sean, who had a dazed expression a bit like William's on his face. "Primates seem to have a natural affinity for cats. In fact, zookeepers have learned that when great apes—the orangutans, gorillas, and chimpanzees—have access to outdoor enclosures, they often win the friendship of the feral cats who live on the grounds. Wild cats avoid human beings like the plague, but they walk through the bars to get their fleas picked off by six-hundred-pound apes."

"I think William would prefer a flea collar," Valerie said.

Lori returned, Williamless, and Valerie followed her over to Hard Times' cage.

"Is he your favorite?" Valerie asked.

Lori blushed. "It's awful to pick favorites after what they've all been through. But each of us does. You can't help it. I'm so hoping one of the veterinarians will come up with some way to relieve his pain.

"Tomorrow, Taub's lawyers will present their case for getting the monkeys back. They are arguing that the animals are just property, not contraband, and can't legally be held by the police. I just hope they lose."

Valerie told Lori she hoped it would all work out. Her watch said nine, and Sean and she still had to pick up the dog. Plus, she had 7:30 roll call to make in the morning, and wash still to do. They said good night to everyone. On their way out, Alex handed her a folder about the Silver Spring monkeys case.

"Please read this," he said.

Valerie assured him she would. "Sometimes," she thought, "you forget how callous people can be." Those monkeys had harmed no one; they had once had a life, and now they were reduced to confused, debilitated wrecks. Valerie was always a straightforward sort of person. She tolerated no ifs, ands, or buts in crimes of abuse and violence. She hoped they'd throw the book at Taub and that he'd get a judge who found cruelty as offensive as she did.

Mandy looked like a queen-sized version of Benji, with a thick, wiry gray coat that belied the lean frame beneath it. Unruly bangs fell over her eyes. She sat timidly between them in the front seat, head down, as if she were racking her brains for a spell that would make her invisible.

"Looks as if I still won't hear the patter of little feet around the house, unless you can get her to wear your riot boots," Sean said as they drove to his house.

"See how long this lasts!" Valerie warned. "Dogs have a habit of taking the place over once they get the lay of the land."

The next day proved her right. She drove to Sean's after work to find him on all fours, helping Mandy dig a hole, or vice versa. Earth was flying through the air, Sean was shouting encouragement and "quiet Mandy" was barking her head off. They were having a ball, and Valerie couldn't tell which of them was happier.

Her day hadn't gone well. There was the uncomfortable news that Clay Prather, a man she had locked up in her first year on the force, had given deputies the slip. Prather had it in for her, and now no one knew where he was. Two years earlier he had threatened to kill her. Prisoners make such threats from time to time, but this man's did not seem like a throwaway remark. While the judge had liked her testimony enough to send Prather to Patuxent Institute for assault with intent to kill, Prather hadn't appreciated it one bit. He had escaped while being taken back to circuit court for stabbing an inmate who had dared to speak to him in the meal line.

Tonight she decided she'd feel more relaxed in Sean's wealthy neighborhood, with its well-lit streets, than in her own low-security apartment on the "poor" side of town. Maybe tomorrow Prather would be back in custody. She fixed herself a lime juice and tonic, and sank into the couch to read the contents of the Silver Spring monkeys folder, hoping to take her mind off Prather. Alex had taken some compelling photographs, and his account, taken from his meticulous log, was gruesome reading:

In the summer of 1981, I went to IBR to apply for a job. Dr. Taub explained to me that he was surgically crippling monkeys and then monitoring the rehabilitation of their impaired limbs. He said he had no paid positions open but offered me a job as a volunteer.

When I reported for my first day of work, Taub gave me a tour. As we entered the room where the monkeys were, I was nearly overpowered by the smell. Filth was caked on the wire cages. Piles of feces covered the cage bottoms. Urine and rust encrusted almost every surface, and rat droppings and live and dead cockroaches were everywhere. Records, soiled clothes, shoes, rags, and other items were scattered helter-skelter throughout the squalid surgery room, even under the operating table.

The monkeys sat amidst this rotting stench in metal boxes just over seventeen inches wide. They had no food dishes. They picked at the pieces of broken biscuits that had fallen through the jagged cage wire into the soggy accumulations in the waste trays below.

During the following months I got to know the seventeen monkeys well. Twelve of them had surgically crippled (deafferented) limbs; these mutilations had been done when they were juveniles. Since then, they had torn or bitten off a total of thirty-nine fingers on these limbs.

Their physical and mental torture had left many of them neurotic. One of them, Domitian, seemed absolutely crazy; he attacked his arm mercilessly and masturbated constantly.

No one ever changed the monkeys' bandages, no matter how

dirty and rotten they became before they finally fell off. Pieces of yellowed, rotten bandaging stuck to the cage bottoms. I longed to blow the whistle immediately and have it all over with, but I knew it was too soon, that Taub could easily discredit me.

The next month I was assigned an experiment in which a monkey was strapped into a homemade immobilizing chair. He would be held fast at his neck, wrists, waist, and ankles. Then I was to apply "acute noxious stimuli"—pain—to various parts of his body. The pain was applied with a pair of hemostats (surgical pliers) clamped onto the monkey and locked to the tightest notch. The stimulus previously used was the open flame of a cigarette lighter.

Thankfully I was working alone, so I could feed the monkeys regularly and fabricate the data.

On the pretext of wanting to work evenings and weekends, I asked for and was given a set of keys. Now I could explore the entire place and photograph the monkeys and the filthy equipment and surroundings.

I came upon two plastic bags labeled 'Caligula' and 'Herbie' in a freezer. When I questioned Georgette Yakalis, Taub's assistant, about them, she said Caligula had begun to mutilate his own chest cavity (this is a stress-induced behavior), so after one final experiment, he had been killed. She didn't know how Herbie had died.

Several times when I was shooting photos around midnight, my heart leaped as one of the two caretakers came in. Since they weren't on a schedule and were paid $10 a day whether they came in or not, they often didn't show up at all. Often several days went by before the caretakers threw a half-scoop of monkey chow into each cage. I had markers in the chow cans which indicated these days.

I began to prepare a case for prosecution. I stopped sneaking fresh fruit to the monkeys. The food sacks, which were clearly marked with an expiration date that had come and gone four months before I started work there, contained nutritionally deficient food. Taub would surely use any improvement in the monkeys' health brought on by food I'd slipped them to defend himself.

The medicines in the laboratory refrigerator had all expired, too, some as far back as 1969.

Several times, attempting to appear casual, I suggested calling in a veterinarian to treat the most serious injuries. When Billy's arm was broken in two places, I asked repeatedly for a veterinarian, yet Billy's hideously swollen arm went untreated.

I needed expert witnesses to vouch for the charges I intended to make about the laboratory. The five people I cautiously approached were: Dr. Geza Teleki, ethologist and global expert in primatology; Dr. John McArdle, primate anatomist and former primate researcher; Dr. Ronnie Hawkins, a physician who had worked with primates in research; Donald Barnes, a lay psychologist; and Dr. Michael Fox, writer, veterinarian, and ethologist. They all went with me through the laboratory at night and then signed affidavits.

On September 8, 1981, I took these affidavits and my own, along with my notes and photographs, to the Silver Spring, Maryland, police.

By the time Valerie finished reading Alex's account, she felt angry. The photographs of screaming monkeys in restraint devices had moved her to tears, something that didn't happen often.

She picked up the photograph that upset her the most. It was the only one of Dr. Edward Taub. He was laughing, or, really, smiling—a ghastly, mocking little smile that she could still see if she closed her eyes.

Taub was standing behind the cause of his pleasure: a brown monkey strapped into a restraining chair, one arm tied to his side. Taub held out a board that had grooves cut into it in places. In some of the grooves he had placed raisins. Valerie could see that the monkey's face was contorted. He was afraid of this man in the white coat who held the food, but he desperately wanted to eat. According to the caption on the back of the photograph, he had been starved for several days.

The monkey's free arm reached out for the raisins in Taub's board, but it was futile. Where his human-like fingers should have been there were just nubs, portions of fingers or none at all. He had nothing to dig out the raisins with.

When the doorbell chimed, she got up reluctantly. She had been sitting, wondering if the whole world was filled with aggression, variations on the Clay Prather theme, and she didn't particularly want to see anybody.

Through the peephole she saw Mikaya, looking agitated and miserable. Valerie could tell that she, too, had been crying.

"Come on in. Would you like a drink?"

"No." Mikaya stepped in to the living room and sat down. "Thanks, but I need more than spirits."

"What is it?"

"The hearing was a disaster," she said. Mikaya told Valerie the news that was spreading rapidly through the animal rights movement. The assistant state's attorney assigned to prosecute the case was fresh out of school, insecure, and inexperienced. His nervousness and the pressure he was getting from the research community showed. He had been almost incoherent in his arguments before the judge.

For the defense, IBR had retained Arnold and Porter, one of the country's top firms. Three expensive lawyers in dark suits, their firm's initials embossed onto their briefcases, had argued forcefully for the return of the monkeys. The court had ruled that the animals were Taub's possessions and could not be held. He was entitled to claim them.

It got worse. Now the young state's attorney was thinking of dropping the case. Because cruelty to animals is a misdemeanor in Maryland, the prosecutor has what's called "prosecutorial discretion." No one can compel him to proceed to trial.

"Taub and his crew, they'll be showing themselves at Lori's house tomorrow morning to collect what he's calling his 'living possessions,'" said Mikaya. "He told the reporters outside the courthouse that he's going to perform a second surgery and then kill the monkeys ten days later."

She was shaking. "I've just come from seeing them. Those sweet souls are chattering and sitting there with no idea they are as good as on their way back to hell. Alex is a wreck. Val, these lousy people are undoing the most important thing that has ever happened to help lab animals in the history of this country. It's not just turning back the clock. If they take the monkeys back, the lab doors won't just be closed. They'll be sealed like a tomb.

No one has ever gotten into a filthy place like that and gotten the goods on the researchers. Taub and his friends will make damn sure no one gets into any of their little chambers of horror again."

Valerie didn't see what she could do. She was a cop, not a judge. She had no influence of any consequence.

"You've seen them." Mikaya looked at her imploringly. "They're like children. And you know the system doesn't always work. It's not working for them, and I'm not willing to sit back and let them go to the slaughter."

"What do you mean to do?" Even as Valerie asked the question, she wasn't sure she wanted to hear the answer.

Mikaya sucked in her breath, and then let out a short, sharp sigh. You could see it written on her face: was Valerie a cop or a friend?

"I know I'm taking a chance coming here, telling you this, but from the first moment I saw you, saw your little girl's picture, I knew you were all right. Those monkeys need our help. *Your* help. No one's going to know you were caught up in all this, but if you don't get involved, it may mean the difference between saving them and letting them rot. I have a plan, the only thing that gives them a chance. I can't live with myself if I don't *try*. We are going to drive those Silver Spring monkeys out of here tonight."

"Oh, Christ. See this uniform? I'm not a bus driver, I'm a cop, Mikaya." Valerie felt annoyed, flattered, miserable, angry, and like a failure, all at once.

"Yes, but would you stand by if someone was taking Carmelita away to cut her into bits?" Mikaya's black curls swung from side to side as she railed at Valerie. Her brown eyes were moist. Valerie knew what she said was true, but she couldn't entertain the idea.

"Mikaya, I can't get involved in this. I'd be thrown off the force. I'm supposed to uphold the law, not break it. You're asking me . . . "

"Val, I'm asking you to ask yourself. Does risking your job mean more to you than what's deep in your heart? What did Martin Luther King say? 'An unjust law is no law at all.' Abused animals are like abused kids, they have no rights. If no one ever cared

enough to break the law, my people would still be on sugar planta-
tions, my mama would have been sold like a bag of flour. This is
a matter for a person's conscience, not for some law.

She was making Valerie feel like a monster, as if she didn't
care. "Mikaya, I don't want to know about this."

"I'll say you never knew a thing. I promise. We have never even
talked about it. But tonight I'm getting a big furniture van and
seventeen hairy little fellas are getting the hell out of this dangerous place. If you believe it's right to let them go back to that lab,
make your call and turn us in. If you think it's wrong, please, Val,
be there. All we need is for you to park your pretty cruiser on the
street. If some nosy neighbor looks out or another cop comes by,
it'll look like we're legally moving them. Those animals need our
help. They've been through enough horror and misery and pain
for one lifetime."

Mikaya was silent then. So was Valerie. She remembered the
photograph of the doctor laughing at the deformed monkey trying
to pick up raisins with what remained of his fingers. She thought
about what her job meant to her, how proud she was to have
sweated it out through the physical training, and how much
meanness and madness she'd had to put up with to get this far.
She was good at what she did, and she was in line for a promotion.
She looked out of the bay window to see Mandy rolling on the
grass with Sean. Valerie had a good life.

Years earlier, Valerie had written a paper on Frederick
Douglass. His words came back to her now: "Those who profess
to love freedom and yet deprecate agitation are men who want
crops without plowing. This struggle may be a moral one, or it
may be physical, but it must be a struggle. Power concedes nothing without a demand. It never did and it never will."

If she didn't help, Mikaya and the monkeys could get caught.
What kind of person would allow that to happen?

While Mikaya found a driver and hastily assembled a small
crew of people willing to help, Valerie sat Sean down and told
him what she was contemplating. As she said the words she knew
she was doing the right thing. Sean took it well.

"Val, you're a woman of principle, which is why I want to marry you. That, and because your parents will kill me if I just keep fooling around with you. Plus you make a mean highball, and you cook and sew." Valerie threw a book at him.

"Sean, you fool. I may go to jail for this and you're joking as usual."

"Val, I've always seen you as a social worker, a peaceful warrior, not a power-mad gunslinger. You need to choose your own battles, not have them assigned by a dispatcher. I think this is a very courageous thing to do. And when you get out of jail you can come work at Wildnear. I'll waive our policy of not hiring felons."

Valerie knew this was about as serious as Sean was going to be. At least Mandy took her worries seriously. She came to the couch, and she and Valerie touched noses and nuzzled.

"I think I'd like to try that," Sean said, moving toward them.

"Well, go ahead, she's your dog!" Valerie teased. If I ever doubted my love for him, she thought, I shouldn't have.

All she had to do now was not get caught.

After dark the crew was dropped off, one by one, at Lori's house. Lori had taken a hint and agreed to spend the night at a friend's. When Swain came to arrest her, she would tell him in all honesty that she knew nothing about the plan.

Valerie pulled her cruiser under the oak tree outside the house next to Lori's shortly before 2:00 A.M. She had tucked her hair up under her hat and borrowed Sean's dark-framed reading glasses to make identification harder should someone peek out of their curtains. In Montgomery County, police car numbers are painted on the roofs of the vehicles to make it easy for police helicopters to identify them. There are no numbers on the sides.

The moving van was on time. All white, it stuck out like a snowball in a coal mine. At least, Val comforted herself, Mikaya had rented it from a small outfit that didn't put giant stickers on its vehicles or paint them with cute advertising slogans. Even if someone took a hard look, there wouldn't be much to remember.

To her relief, Mikaya's people moved fast and quietly. Not a leaf rustled, nothing creaked, and the monkeys were as good as gold. She wondered if they sensed this was a life-and-death adventure for them. Or perhaps the years in Taub's laboratory had all but destroyed their spirit.

Inside her cruiser, Valerie kept trying not to think that if anything went wrong these kids would be in jail when Taub came to claim the monkeys.

Chester, the dominant male, was loaded first. If he got the idea that the others were being taken away from him, he'd start screaming bloody murder. Watching anxiously from the lip of the van loading platform, he absorbed everything that was happening and seemed remarkably calm as he watched his brood coming aboard to join him.

The neighborhood slept. As the number of monkeys in the basement grew smaller, the pace increased. As each one entered the truck, Valerie became even more anxious. Would they get them all in before something went wrong?

Suddenly, the last monkey had been lifted into place and it was time to disappear. A veterinary technician Valerie had met on her visit to Lori's sat beside Billy and took his foot in her hand to comfort him. Someone reached up and closed the van door. The driver started the engine. A cloud of black smoke came out of the exhaust and smothered the sweet smell of fresh pineapples and ripe bananas that still hung in the air.

Valerie took a chance and went up to the driver's window.

"Good luck. And don't speed."

Three very young faces gave her an odd look. Did they think she was just being a cop, that she wasn't worried about them being stopped with that cargo? She handed the driver a gold and white vehicle sticker. It identified the owner as a member in good standing of the Fraternal Order of Police.

"When you stop for gas, put this on the back of the truck, on the left, at waist height. It's a good luck charm of sorts!"

"Thank you, officer," he said.

"Go!"

The truck pulled away, the driver grinding the unfamiliar gears as he tried to upshift. As much as she longed for them to put mileage between themselves and Lori's house, soon to be teeming with police, she hoped they realized that everything depended on them seeming ordinary, driving slowly, looking right.

She pulled out behind them. One block, two blocks, three blocks. It began to drizzle, and through the rain she could see the leaves on the trees lining the road begin to dance as the first pre-downpour breeze began to blow. Everything seemed enchanted. Could this work?

Maybe not. The truck was less than a mile from the highway when they heard the siren. It came from behind them. She could sense the people in the van holding their breath and swearing. She was doing the same. For three years she had heard the sound of a siren with a sense of relief. To an officer in trouble it means help on the way. Tonight she was in a new role. It was a threat, and she wished it to hell.

She dropped back without braking, letting space open up between her and the van. The street was empty. She swung her cruiser into the first alleyway and killed the lights. Her getting arrested now wouldn't help anyone. She sat in the dark, automatically and absurdly reciting the highway code section entitled, "Turning off lights to avoid police apprehension: Automatic suspension of license, twelve points."

The seconds dragged by. She waited, hoping the wailing car would turn off the road. "Please God," she prayed, "at least give it a flat tire." She wanted to hear the siren fade, but instead it got louder. Then she saw the car, its red and white top lights whirling like a carnival ride. It raced past her hiding place, making a beeline for the van. She crept forward, inching the nose of her cruiser into the street. Through the blur of water on her windshield, she could see the officer hit his brake lights as he came up to the van. The cab would be flooded with red and white light.

Carmelita had once written to her that at night she often felt very frightened. Valerie suspected Carmelita was too young to know who her enemies were, but she did know there was violence in the woods around her. Carmelita would lie awake and pray that the jungle spirits would make her family invisible to their enemies. Every morning, when she heard her family moving about at sunrise, she knew she had succeeded. Right now, the monkeys needed some of that same magic on their side.

Then . . . they got it. As suddenly as it had come into view, the cruiser was past the van and regaining speed. Within seconds it had vanished in a sheet of misty spray.

"Must be after some other monkey thieves," Valerie thought. Looking down, she saw her hands were shaking. "Oh, real tough," she told herself.

The van kept going, its occupants giddy at the close call. The Silver Spring monkeys were on their way to Florida.

That night the monkeys camped deep in the countryside, their guardians tucked into tents while they slept under the stars, enjoying the night sounds and the warm breeze. In South Carolina they caught flying insects, holding them between their fingers in amazement; in Georgia they picked the Spanish moss that draped over the sides of their cages.

When the troop reached Florida, the monkeys were amazed to find sand beneath their wire cage floors. They spent hours running their fingers through it, digging in it with sticks, and making happy smacking sounds. One morning their guardians awoke to a ruckus and found Adidas and Sisyphus jumping up and down, trying to attract the attention of wild pigs rooting around the campsite behind their protector's house.

While the monkeys played, all hell broke loose in Maryland. Taub and his white-coated assistants arrived at Lori's house with a police escort, but no one answered the door. The place was as quiet as a grave and the basement windows were covered with cardboard. It took Swain all of two seconds to determine what had happened.

"Looks as if someone's thrown a monkeywrench into your plans, no pun intended, Doc," he told the red-faced experimenter.

After a stormy closed meeting, the State declared that without the "physical evidence," there could be no case against Taub. (More for show than anything else, Lori was arrested and strip-searched. "Where did they think I had the monkeys hidden?" Lori asked in a televised interview. With no real evidence against her and no confessions forthcoming, she had to be released.)

Mikaya kept her distance and Valerie kept a low profile. Her ears were tuned for any news of sightings of the monkeys or of Clay Prather. None came: the good guys and the bad had all disappeared from police view.

Meanwhile, Swain had a bright idea. Word was put out to the humane community that if the monkeys could be made to reappear, no questions asked, the State would arrest Taub and charge him with cruelty. He would have to stand trial in open court. And there would be a hearing at which experts from the humane community could testify as to why the court should not return the monkey victims to their abuser. The State would also appoint a new, experienced prosecutor. If this offer was refused, the search for the monkeys was to escalate with the cooperation of the state police, while Taub would be free to pursue more experiments.

The activists had no choice. The Silver Spring monkeys would be blazing a trail, one that could ultimately affect the lives of millions of other animals. Five days after the offer, Chester and his troop were back in Lori's basement under twenty-four-hour police protection. Valerie found herself chewing her fingernails, something she hadn't done since high school.

Like most cops, Valerie dreamed often of the encounters she had on the street. She had the first of her "monkey dreams" the night the monkeys returned. In her cop dreams, she usually prevailed, but this was different: a nightmare of panic and helplessness, of the power of absolute evil. She was a prisoner. Strapped down to a hospital gurney, she kept trying to undo the straps, knowing she had only moments in which to escape.

Somehow she managed to work her arms free. She could hear a man coming. Desperately she reached for the latches that closed the locks on her waist and leg straps. Her knuckles and wrists ached as she worked frantically to undo the straps. Nothing was working. She looked down. Her fingers were missing, bleeding, useless.

She began crying for help, but no one could hear her. Clay

Prather leaned over the gurney and dangled a tray in front of her. On it were bloody fingers mixed with fruit.

When she awoke, her heart was pounding. Relieved, she realized that it had been just a dream. Then, another realization hit home: for the monkeys it was no dream. It was a real-life nightmare that, for a moment, she had shared.

Swain made good on his word. The State brought in Roger Galvin, a tough prosecutor from the Major Offenses Bureau, who described himself as "an old goat" although he couldn't have been much over thirty. He let the humane society and PETA people know from the start that he wouldn't tolerate what they no longer wished to hear called "monkey business."

"I have never been interested in animals, and I believe in animal research, but I'll do my job," he told Alex as he chain-smoked his way through packs of Carltons.

On her day off, Valerie took a seat in the gallery. She was impressed not only by what Galvin said, but also by how he moved across the courtroom. Dressed in a gray three-piece suit, as his solid frame marched from the witness box to the bench, she was reminded of a powerful silverback gorilla she had seen on a *National Geographic* special, defending his territory against marauders. Galvin gave her hope. Perhaps, she thought, he really can protect Hard Times and the other monkeys from Taub.

The trial took two long weeks. Taub never took the stand. The presiding judge, recognizing his historical role, praised science in general, apparently for the benefit of the gathered press, then pronounced Taub "guilty as charged" of six counts. Valerie was relieved, but despite this success, she couldn't shake the nagging feeling that the monkeys were still in trouble.

She was right. Revelry in the PETA camp and the prosecutor's office was short-lived. Within thirty days, Taub's high-priced attorneys had appealed the verdict. There was to be a trial *de novo*: a jury would hear the case, but would not know that Taub had already been convicted. The first trial had been practice, and now Taub, although worried sick and showing it, knew where he needed to work hardest on his defense. He called in the heavies from the research community.

They came from California, Alabama, even the Mayo Clinic, to tell the court how marvelous a laboratory Taub ran, how well the animals were treated, and how important to humankind his experiments could be. The judge threatened PETA members with eviction if the groaning from the gallery got any louder.

After each glowing report, Roger Galvin would ask, "Have you ever been to the Institute for Behavioral Research? Have you examined the animals in question? Have you looked at the police photographs of conditions inside this laboratory?" And to each question the witnesses would reluctantly answer, "No."

Nothing could have kept Valerie from the trial on her day off. She wanted to be there, just once, when Taub faced his accusers, to hear the evidence with her own ears.

The judge recognized her and nodded as she took her seat on the wooden bench behind the attorneys' tables. Valerie knew the judge was wondering which side she was on, the "bride's" side or the "groom's." Trained to be poker-faced in court, she didn't dare do anything as obvious as shake her head or grimace when Taub's lawyers spoke, but she nevertheless managed to let the judge see her nod her approval as Galvin berated his first hostile witness. University of Pennsylvania psychologist and animal experimenter Adrian Morrison was describing Taub's experiments so glowingly that one might think Taub was on the threshold of enabling the lame to play tennis again.

Galvin showed Morrison police photographs of the filthy lab interior, where toilet bowl deodorants had been hung along the walls to mask the smell, and cockroaches and rat droppings covered the shelves. Valerie had been listening to the witnesses but watching Taub. Appalled at what he had done to these animals, she searched his face for clues to his insensitivity. Instead, she saw something else.

"Watch Taub," she whispered to Sean, who sat by her side.

Taub was behaving very strangely. Sitting flanked on either side by attorneys, he had started to wipe absentmindedly at the table in front of him with his pocket handkerchief. He was working away at it now, almost scrubbing at the wood, oblivious to the proceedings going on around him.

"Like Lady Macbeth trying to wash the blood out," Sean whispered back.

Several other people had noticed and attention was beginning to wander from the witness box. A young juror was trying not to giggle. The judge called for a bench conference and turned on the sound machine as the attorneys came up to chat with him. When they returned, Edgar Brenner, the lead defense counsel, leaned over and whispered a few words in Taub's ear. Taub stopped scrubbing.

Morrison declared from the witness box that the cockroach infestation provided "a good source of ambient protein" for the monkeys. Valerie's heart filled with dread. Juries, she knew, sometimes defied logic. They might buy lies and ignore the truth. If they did so now the monkeys were doomed.

Morrison's friend, Peter Hand, another University of Pennsylvania experimenter, took the stand next. The prosecutor reminded him that Taub had allowed animal waste to pile up so high in the cages that the monkeys themselves threw it to the floor, where it lay covered so thick with mold that it resembled a cake with icing on the top.

"There was nothing wrong with leaving it there," Hand declared, leaning toward the jury and smiling knowledgeably. "Monkeys are filthy critters. Not much more than defecating machines!"

This was almost too much for Dr. Shirley McGreal, the president of the International Primate Protection League. She choked audibly at Hand's remarks.

"If there's nothing wrong with letting urine and feces pile up, this civilization has wasted an awful lot of money on sewer systems," said Galvin icily.

It was easy to see that he too was sick of hearing scientists take the stand every day to tell what he knew were lies. He'd also learned he could count on the PETA volunteers to drop everything when he needed something—a blood sample run to the lab, or a primate vet at midnight.

During the break, Val saw Morrison and Hand standing by a potted palm, giving advice to Taub while his wife listened. Although estranged from her husband, Mrs. Taub was dressed up and being paraded about, a prop used by the defense attorneys to give Taub a solid, family-man image before the jury. Taub had lost weight and the strain he was under showed on his face. He kept smiling wanly at Alex, who ignored him. Valerie could almost feel sorry for him, but not quite.

"Yech," Valerie said to Alex in the hall during a break. "What slimy characters."

"They're all just fighting to stay on research welfare." Alex was philosophical. Jeff Diner, a researcher with the Animal Welfare Institute, came up. "You know what you get when a scientist gives a toxic substance to a rat?"

"Yes, a paper! Old joke, Jeff," said Alex. "But I guess it's appropriate for today. Publish or perish. This is about money and careers to them, while we're fighting to expose the big lie."

Jeff wandered off to get some quotes from Galvin for the article he was writing for the *AWI Quarterly*. Valerie couldn't share his ability to take the case in stride. She had spent enough time in court to sense how weak the thread was on which the monkeys' futures hung.

"Guilty!" Miki shrieked over the phone a few evenings later. "They found him guilty!"

The jury had been instructed that it could not find against Taub if the untreated injuries to the animals occurred in the arms with severed nerves. Nevertheless, the jury had been determined to convict and had found a way.

With nothing to lose, Taub appealed the case immediately to the highest court. Valerie knew that appeals invariably weaken the state's case and she was fearful. She didn't have long to wait.

The verdict came like a bolt from the blue. Without hearing a shred of evidence, the Court of Appeals overturned the lower courts' rulings. An experimenter receiving federal grant monies, the judges opined, did not have to obey the Maryland state anti-cruelty statute! Fuming, Valerie asked, "Any other statutes they can ignore—littering, mayhem, arson?" To suggest that a group of people was above the law because they received National Institutes of Health subsidies was preposterous. She knew that the decision had been about politics, not about justice. Taub was out of a job, but off the hook. What he'd do next had everyone guessing.

Meanwhile, the court had to do something with the monkeys: according to the terms that were set, they would not go back to Taub but were to be handed over to the NIH. No one had any notion then that the monkeys would remain imprisoned in isolation cages in a legal limbo, and that it would be eight more years before PETA's case for their custody would reach the United States Supreme Court.

"Out of the frying pan, into the fire, I'm afraid," Alex lamented.

Valerie was a bit blunter. "The system stinks," she said.

The night the monkeys left Lori's basement for NIH, Valerie raced home to change out of her uniform and then went to see them off. Dozens of people had gathered, holding candles flickering in the dark, to catch the last glimpse of the animals they had seen on television for weeks. Everyone sensed that some of them would never come out alive.

Valerie noticed Swain's new wife standing by the truck. She had tears in her eyes. Valerie looked away to avoid embarrassing her. Mikaya explained quietly, "She started coming to see them because he was always over here, making sure they didn't disappear again. Now she's all upset about them—especially Brooks, one of the control monkeys who likes her a lot."

In the midst of all this, Valerie noticed that one of Taub's assistants, Georgette Yakalis, was making a scene. Someone had tried to strangle her, she said, pinning her to the floor and choking her as she was supervising the loading. Her face was scarlet and she was out of breath.

"Not according to the duty officer downstairs, Miss," Swain said, looking right through her. "If you want to go swear out a warrant, you'll have to name someone. The officer tells me he didn't see anything."

"She tried to strangle me, then she ran off. That jerk officer

deliberately let her go. Do you hear me, I want her arrested."
Yakalis' voice was squeaky with emotion. She was struggling to re-
gain her composure, but no one was paying any attention. Swain
walked away. Like the rest of the assembly, he recognized her as
the woman Alex Pacheco had identified as using surgical clamps
to the tightest notch on Domitian's testicles when he was
strapped into the restraining chair.

As the truck door closed on the Silver Spring monkeys, Valerie
forgot monkey protocol and looked Chester squarely in the eyes.
He stared straight back at her, worry etched onto his face. Her
naive illusions about animal experiments had been shattered by
the horrors uncovered, and by the force of the researchers' opposition to legal efforts to clean them up. She was growing angrier and
angrier at what she now knew happened, in the name of science,
to millions of innocent animals like Chester, Billy, and the other
monkeys.

She had already decided what she was going to do. Mikaya had
been bringing animal rights magazines and books to her for
months. She had learned about the British underground group,
the Animal Liberation Front. The thought of their existence and
their work excited her. From somewhere deep in her heart and
her psyche, Valerie had felt emerging a passionate interest in the
philosophy of animal rights. She felt ashamed and stupid to ever
have thought patronizingly of animals. They weren't "cute." They
were thinking, independent beings whose very existence was
threatened by human domination and human encroachment.

She not only thought about animals in labs and traps, but also
about her childhood relationship with her dog, Holly. Holly
hadn't just been a "good dog," but a friend, another individual
caught with her and her sister Lettie in a family that provided
their basic needs, sometimes understanding them and sometimes
not. Simple interactions with Holly that once had seemed unremarkable and "normal" now seemed offensive and unforgivable.
Had Holly ever been "allowed" to be herself or had it always been
"here, Holly," "down, Holly," "come, Holly," "Holly, sit?"

She knew no one other than Mikaya who would understand
the transformation she was experiencing. She thought of calling

Lettie, then decided against it. Her sister was a traditionalist and new ideas frightened her. Lettie would probably think she'd been captured by cultists and call an emergency family meeting. She would keep her thoughts to herself for now.

Valerie had the address of the ALF Supporters' Group in London. She knew they could teach her how to get animals out of American laboratories, and she wanted that more than she'd ever wanted anything before.

She and Sean talked about it every day after she finished work, and often late into the night. When Valerie first broached the idea to him, he shut his eyes tightly and winced. Then he slowly shook his head, opened his eyes, and, with a trace of the gentle, philosophical smile Valerie found irresistible, said, "You're not kidding are you? You're really willing to give everything up for this?"

"Sean, I know exactly what I'm getting into! And the bottom line is this sick feeling I get when I think of doing nothing or just writing an irate letter once in a while. I can't go through the rest of my life *not* getting involved. I don't know why, but *nothing* has ever moved me, spoken to me, as much as the abuse of these animals."

Sean recognized there was no turning her back. It was clear that Valerie had thought through the possible consequences of her actions and was undeterred. He told her what he was beginning to realize was the truth. "Val, I'll worry like crazy about you, but it can't be worse than the way I worry about you patrolling that damned cement jungle day in and day out. I know you well enough to know you have to do what you feel you must."

Her flight to England was booked. The ticket had been cheaper than she expected, even for the "off-season." Her leave slip sat, approved, in the glove compartment of her cruiser. Valerie began counting the days.

2

The European Connection: Boot Camp for Activists

Heathrow was shrouded in a lumpy fog, despite all the assurances from Valerie's travel agent that London's fog had always really been smog, and that English smog had gone the way of horse-drawn carriages since the advent of smokeless coal years earlier. Too wound up to sleep, she had been playing chess with herself on a little pocket set that was a gift from her father. Her mind drifted back to the days when she and he battled it out on the beautiful hand-tooled chess board he had acquired during the war. On weekends, they would be so wrapped up in their game that they refused to come to the table for meals, much to Valerie's mother's annoyance. "Stickwithitness means more to us than food," he would say, winking at Val.

There was a sudden bump. One look out of the window made her stow the chess set and hope the pilot had surrendered to technology and turned over his controls to the computer. The jumbo jet bounced around as if determined to put the plane's welds and rivets to the test, then sank quickly through the gray clouds and banged unceremoniously onto the tarmac immediately below.

As the air brakes kicked in, huge brown rabbits, presumably long deafened by the noise of the jets, glanced up casually from the verge of the runway where they sat munching wet grass.

"Welcome to London," announced a flight attendant. "Our pilot is a far better flyer than he is a driver, so please remain seated

35

with your seat belt fastened until he has brought the plane to a screeching halt at the terminal. Thank you."

Passing through customs was uneventful. Valerie forged a path through the expectant crowd awaiting relatives and friends, and followed the blue and red signs to the Underground.

As she reached the Piccadilly Line platform, the backdraft from a departing train blew out of the tunnel, plastering stray pages of newspapers against the sooty tiled walls. Listening to someone playing the saxophone in a distant tunnel, she waited for the next train, and remembered that her mother had told her how, every night during the Blitz of World War II, Londoners had fled down here, abandoning their homes to the bombs. Valerie's mother's parents had lived in the south of England then—they emigrated when Valerie's grandfather got a job with a New York shipping firm—and her mother had told her stories of how city children had been sent to country farms to escape the trauma and devastation of war. Valerie had often looked at the old photos of her grandparents holding her mother's hand outside St. Paul's Cathedral, or waving from the old potting shed at the bottom of their garden.

Valerie's eyes fell on the ads pasted on the other side of the tracks: kids in short pants and school caps were being waved off to school after a hearty breakfast of "Weetabix," and a lion and a unicorn advertised "Somerset's best apple cider." Then she saw it. A huge poster of a black and white dog beneath the legend, "Three animals die every second in British labs." Below that, in red letters, "Help us stop this cruelty. Join the British Union for the Abolition of Vivisection." She had landed in the bastion of animal rights activism.

The Underground train rattled noisily along to Kings Cross station, a few early commuters dangling by one hand from the straps. At Kings Cross, she hailed a black Daimler taxi to the Carlisle Hotel. As apprehensive as she felt about the success of the trip, she was certainly primed for intrigue, and England seemed the perfect setting. The wet streets were gunmetal gray, the buildings black with the soot of centuries. It didn't feel silly to imagine MI5 agents, the collars pulled up high on their mackintosh jackets, waiting on a bench by the Thames to intercept a spy.

The Carlisle was a four-story rowhouse surrounded by pointed, wrought-iron railings of the type once used to impale the heads of traitors to the Crown. Inside, it was full of heavy furniture that looked like leftovers from a garage sale and awash with the smells of fried bacon, pipe tobacco, and the musty books that filled the shelves along the drawing room wall.

"Overnight from across the pond, are you?" queried the vast and pleasant woman behind the front desk. "Take a nap, then come down and have a nice cup of tea, duckie. Don't fret about forms and whatnot now. Just get yourself settled." She handed over a key, and Valerie made her way up the steep stairs, glad not to have any heavy luggage.

She sank into the big old bed, but her brain refused to shut itself off. She was thinking ahead to an eleven o'clock appointment at the British Union for the Abolition of Vivisection (BUAV) offices. BUAV's executive director, Kim Stallwood,[1] had agreed to let Val interview him about the parliamentary process. He thought she was writing an article about animal protection in the U.K. She didn't give a hoot about legislation, but according to *The Liberator*, the ALF Supporters' Group used the same address as BUAV. That's where she hoped to begin her search for the founder of the British liberationist movement, Ronnie Lee. She knew he was out of jail, but that's all she knew.

There was a little sink in the corner of the room. Next to it was a water "geezer" and scribbled instructions for its use. Dutifully, she inserted a five-pence piece and received, in return, a burst of hot water. Just like camping in your room, she thought. If there's a recession, the Holiday Inn could pick up some tips from the British. Feeling a little fresher, she went downstairs to the dining room.

After a "nice cup o' 'ot tea" and toast spread thick with quince

---

[1] In 1986, after the passage of the Animals (Scientific Procedures) Act and several exploratory trips to the U.S., Kim Stallwood left BUAV to become PETA's executive director.

jam, Valerie filled out the hotel forms and then wandered into the lounge. The papers were full of news of the coal miners' strikes, complete with pictures of minivans of roving, vigilante miners, pithead confrontations, and picketers hurling insults at helmeted police constables.

When the mantlepiece clock chimed ten, she made her way to BUAV. Outside the hotel, the smell of gasoline and motor oils mixed with the smell of the old houses, wet yew hedges, and geranium bushes that lined the road. It wasn't cold but it was raining again, and even though BUAV was no more than a few minutes' walk from the Angel Islington Underground station, Valerie was glad to have packed a long raincoat and waterproof shoes. With each step, she felt more exhilarated about embarking on her chosen adventure.

The historic anti-vivisection group was housed inside a modern, stark white, three-story warehouse. Kim Stallwood's desk was strewn with political manifestos and government white papers. A poster advertising the Threepenny Opera was taped to the wall above him, next to a silly drawing of a filthy, unshaven man with a cigarette dangling from one side of his mouth, saying to no one in particular, "Waiter, I'll have the BROWN rice with that."

Kim was in his mid-twenties, a vigorous Labour Party supporter and a fervent champion of the British working class as well as of the animals. After taking a catering course, he had worked for a summer in a chicken slaughterhouse. He said that listening to the screams of the birds as they headed to the knife had saddened and revolted him. So he had abandoned catering and joined the animal rights movement. Now he was working to get Parliament to pass a bill toughening up controls over Britain's individually licensed experimenters, and specifically outlawing the infamous Draize rabbit-blinding test, as well as smoking and alcohol tests on animals. He was meeting lots of expected opposition, both from private research corporations and what he called the "Tory Gories."

Kim needed Valerie's help. Did she have any idea how he could get information about the U.S. military's use of animals in warfare experiments?

"They do cooperative projects with our military lot at Porton Down," he told her. "That much we do know. But everything is classified. Here, take a gander at this. It arrived in last week's mail, no return address."

Kim showed Valerie a British government paper describing the effects of explosives on animals. Pigs and dogs were being exposed at various distances to blasts from seventy pounds of high explosives placed in the ground beneath their cages at a distance of thirteen feet. In other experiments, "to determine the psychological effects of blast impact," monkeys were exposed to blasts from charges of gelignite at distances of six to fourteen feet. The primates were held fast in steel cylinders and changes in their heart rhythms, blood pressure, and other bodily functions were recorded by electrodes implanted under their skin, or, in the case of two monkeys, screwed into their skulls.

Valerie offered to do the only thing she could think of—turn the paper over to PETA. Perhaps they could file a Freedom of Information Act request.

Kim was polite, but harried. Valerie felt guilty taking his time under false pretenses. As soon as she could, she posed the question that she had been longing to ask. She noticed her mouth seemed dry as the words came tumbling out.

"I'd like to interview Ronnie Lee, too, but I haven't a clue where to find him," Valerie said.

"He thinks we're all wet, you know," Kim answered. Valerie looked blank. "Thinks there's only one way to go: direct action, animal liberation," Kim shook his head wearily. "Thinks what I do, what BUAV does, is a waste of bloody time the animals can't afford. If you ask me, the animals need everything. Still, for the moment anyway, we let his volunteers have an office down the corridor because he has no income, and who knows which of us is right. He got out of the 'nick' a few weeks ago, so he's probably in today, sorting things out. I'll give him a tinkle, if you like?"

She held her breath. Was it to be this easy? Kim picked up the receiver of the bulky black phone. When he hung up, he reached for his coat and umbrella.

"Ronnie's popped down the pub for lunch. I go past it to the post office, if you'd like me to take you."

They put on their coats and walked the few blocks to the "Rose and Crown." There was a large "No Dogs Allowed" sign on the pretty, etched-glass door. Apparently, the world's number-one animal liberationist was holed up in the only pub in London that didn't allow dogs.

It was just after noon and the saloon was full of smoke, laughter, and the noise of a jukebox competing with the noise of hungry people glad to have left their "lorries," their market stalls, or their blue-collar jobs for a sandwich and a couple of pints of bitter. "Solid working-class refuge, not for white-collar bourgies," Kim shouted over the noise. "They're segregated in the lounge in the next room, paying an extra penny a pint for the privilege. You are witnessing the ongoing class wars of our green and pleasant land!"

Valerie was embarrassed to realize that she had envisioned Ronnie as an Indiana Jones type—tall, muscular, commanding. When Kim introduced her to the unremarkable man sitting alone at the little wooden table in the window, she thought at first he might be pulling her leg.

Ronnie Lee's wire-rimmed, National Health-issue glasses gave him a serious, shy look, and although he was no more than thirty, his hair was thinning on top. Here was a gentle, almost frail, individual, physically slight and personally unassuming, with a very ordinary but peaceful, bearded face. In Hollywood, they would have put a robe on him and cast him as a monk. The blue work-shirt he wore looked like prison issue and she wondered if he'd smuggled it out.

Kim waved goodbye and Valerie wished him luck. Ronnie Lee nodded, but said nothing. Valerie could feel the animosity between the two men. Now, what was she going to say to him, she wondered? Hello, I'm a cop from the States, would you mind telling me how you commit felonies? With two stints in prison, each for several years, and the ever-looming prospect of more "time," he'd doubtless had enough of cops for one lifetime. It would be a miracle, she thought, if at this stage he opened up to anyone.

"Pint?" Lee asked, when their pocket of silence amid the back-slapping din became too much to ignore.

"Sure, but please let me pay." The pound note Valerie held out was seized a little too quickly to count for polite behavior. She reminded herself that this man robbed labs, not banks, and that Kim had told her Lee lived on the "dole," British welfare.

"Lager and lime, then?"

"Fine, thank you," Valerie smiled at him, trying to get him to warm to her. When he stood up she saw he was quite short. By the time he had elbowed his way into the barmaid's line of sight, secured two peculiar, green-tinted beers, and returned to the table, Valerie had made up her mind to tell him the truth.

Lee listened, saying nothing, without the slightest flicker of expression passing over his face. Valerie could feel him summing her up, checking her eyes for the truth or falsity of what she was saying.

"Give me your wallet, please," he said when she finished.

"Sure." Valerie pulled it out of her back pocket, immediately wishing it wasn't leather. Was he going to take *all* her money, she wondered.

Lee extracted the wallet's contents and scrutinized each item: a driver's license, a Fraternal Order of Police membership card, credit cards, travelers' checks, a fortune cookie slip that read, "Time is precious, but truth is more precious than time," and a ridiculous drawing of Sean blowing kisses that had been hidden for her to find at a more opportune moment.

As Lee carefully returned everything to its place, including Valerie's money, she wondered what he had been looking for.

"Take your parka off, please, and stand up as if you're looking out the window," he said. "Lift your shirt up over your stomach and turn around all the way, then sit down."

Mikaya had once told Valerie that when Jane Goodall and Dian Fossey had asked the world's greatest anthropologist, Richard Leakey, if he would accept them as his students and allow them to go off into the jungles of Africa to study chimpanzees and gorillas, he had told them to go away and have their appendixes out. Only when they showed him their scars would he speak to them. Valerie was getting off lightly.

She did what he asked. As she raised her shirt, the elderly man at the next table nudged his friend, wiggled his eyebrows, and gave her a lecherous wink. She smiled back, finished her pirouette in as dignified a manner as possible, and resumed her seat.

"Wanted to see if you were wired for sound," Lee explained. "How long are you here for?"

"Thirteen days, not counting today."

"Well, you're in luck. There's a course starting the day after tomorrow. If you want in, I'll fix you up."

"Are you kidding? Of course I do!"

Lee told Valerie which station to go to, which train to take, and what to pack. She would be met.

"How do you know you can trust me?" she asked him.

"I don't," he said matter-of-factly. "But it really doesn't matter. You couldn't prove that the training's meant for anything in particular. It's not illegal to exercise and study tactical theory. If you use it, you're genuine. If you don't, the animals aren't any further behind."

She hadn't thought of it that way. She was impressed by this practical man who had spent long and lonely years in a prison cell, often in solitary confinement, waiting for his freedom to run ALF raids again. He knew he had nothing to fear from her. Valerie thanked him and offered him her hand. He didn't move.

"What you do is our handshake," he said. He wasn't rude, that was just the way it was. "Please understand, I can't be seen publicly doing something that looks like sealing a deal. Well, good luck."

Lee almost smiled, but not quite. Then he was gone. Valerie sat alone at the table for a few minutes, not quite believing it could be so simple. Or maybe Ronnie Lee had been stringing her along. She would soon find out.

The next morning Valerie was headed for the north of England aboard a swaying train packed with schoolchildren whose felt hats, satchels, and hockey sticks filled the overhead racks. Feeling like Gulliver in Lilliput, she moved to relative peace in another compartment, playing chess again or watching out of the window as the train swayed through the countryside and clanged through railroad crossings. Now and then she spotted storybook ponds complete with preening ducks, women pushing prams, and grocery delivery men pedaling along, their trouser bottoms fastened into bicycle clips. Back in the country, lush green farms separated by thick hedgerows stretched to the horizon. It seemed an unlikely setting for an underground army of militant liberationists.

A few hours later she stepped down onto the station platform at Little Riding.

"Nice to meet you." An athletic woman about Valerie's own age, good-looking in a boyish way, with brown hair cut very, very short, had come right up to meet her. The woman had what Valerie guessed was a northern accent, heavy on the "ah's."

"Let me clue you in on the ground rules right off," she said. "You can call me M. We only use initials here. You're V. Don't forget. Questions not allowed are those that would give away your name, where you're from, or what you do. No personal details allowed. Ronnie will link people to others on an as-needed basis. In fact, that's the key. All information's on an as-needed basis. No one discusses important things just to chat. That way we're all protected. Understand?"

Valerie nodded.

"Remember," M continued, "if you ever feel guilty for not including someone in your secrets, the ultimate kindness to those closest to you is not to give them information they don't need to have and which others may try to extract from them in most unpleasant ways. If the coppers nab them, it's best if they really don't know anything. That spares the agony. Get it? Got it? Good!"

They climbed into her Morris Mini Minor and took off for parts unknown. A couple of miles out of the station, M pulled off the road behind a barn, sending two chickens scurrying.

"Oh, dear!" she said. "Hardly the thing! Anyway, out you come. I have to make sure you're not wired."

Valerie knew the routine now, and lifted up her shirt and turned all the way around.

"Fine. Now, turn out your pockets, please, all of them. Then I must go through your kit."

That done, Valerie was invited to resume her seat. As they drove into the countryside, past huge haystacks and old farm buildings, Valerie learned more of the rules and the vocabulary. Actions are "parties," participants "guests," targets "clubs" or "offices." The person arranging the raid is the "birthday girl," or the "groom," and the animals to be rescued are "cakes," "floral arrangements," "lawn chairs," and so on, depending on their size. With proper planning and what M called "a dollop of pluck and a pound of luck," the "catering truck" takes them all away to safety.

There was no drinking at the camp. Nothing was to be written down. There would be no use of a phone, even if you could find one, which M said was unlikely. Anyone taking drugs would be tossed out, although with all bags searched coming in, it was very doubtful that had ever happened.

"It's pretty rough living, but probably not as bad as Parris Island, your Marine training place!" M grinned.

"I made it through police academy, so I think I'll survive," Valerie reassured her, only to be slapped down.

"No one wants to hear about your background," M snapped.

"Sorry about that. I'll do better." Valerie realized it might have come as a shock to M that she was a cop, but if so she had shown nothing.

"Cheer up. You'll get used to it. Or we'll feed you to the vivs!"

They were deep into the countryside when M stopped again and took a black cotton scarf out of the glove compartment.

"Put this on, will you?" she said.

Valerie took the scarf and began to tie it around her neck.

"No," M laughed, "Over your eyes, please! Then scrunch yourself down on the car floor so that if anyone passes us, they won't see you."

Feeling a bit like a fool, Valerie did as she was told. The rest of the journey became progressively more uncomfortable as the two began to bounce their way along what Valerie guessed were rut-riddled country lanes.

M stopped once more and, as best Valerie could tell, opened a gate. Valerie heard the metal scrape along the dirt as the gate was pulled open and then shut. The lock clicked back into place. They drove on for another five minutes or so. Valerie listened for other traffic but heard none. Despite the bumps, she felt happy inhaling the smell of fresh grasses that filtered through the vent. Then they stopped.

"You can take your blindfold off now," M gave her permission.

Valerie did as she was told and found herself looking at a series of low, brick mounds. Some sort of fortified buildings, embedded in the earth with only their topknots sticking up out of the soil, they were long abandoned and weed-covered. Wheatgrass poked its way out of the observation slats that were the only openings in the brickwork. Everything looked surreal, wild and desolate but somehow pretty. Behind the artificial bumps was a disused airstrip; beyond it, a thick clump of green and black forest.

M pulled the car into a space between two huge thistle bushes. She threw a speckled brown and green camouflage sheet over it, and then led Valerie down some crumbling steps into the labyrinth of fortifications.

The buildings were in bad shape. Fungus grew through the ceiling in places, and the walls were crumbling around military graffiti that must have been written a quarter-century earlier. Someone had stuffed a tarpaulin into a big hole where there was ample evidence rain had been pouring in. Camping cots were arranged against the walls.

"As you can tell, no expense has been spared to maintain this fabulous suite of deluxe dwellings," declared M. "You may be asking yourself, 'Can all this be for me?' and the answer is 'Yes, it is.' Next door's the equally attractive kit room and the aptly named 'mess.' "

Valerie followed her through a dank passageway into another room roughly the same size. This one contained a camping stove, a large folding table, stacks of canned food, packages of dehydrated hiking snacks, and several wooden packing crates. There was no telling what was in them and Valerie had no intention of asking.

45

"Hello, I'm R."

Valerie hadn't heard the man come into the room and she started.

"Um . . . I'm V," she said, putting out her hand, then almost withdrawing it as she remembered Ronnie Lee's reaction when she'd tried to shake his. R shook hands and smiled. He was in his late twenties, tall, tidy-looking, and pleasant-seeming.

"I'm the electronics man. You'll be doing several sessions with me. This is K, she's your unarmed combat and physical exercise teacher."

"Hello and welcome! Sorry you missed our first hike." A woman in a dark blue track suit had joined them and pumped Valerie's arm heartily. K moved aside to accommodate the flow of people who had begun to file into the room, mostly out of breath. There were at least twenty new arrivals. Greetings were exchanged as Valerie tried to keep track of everyone's initials.

"It's okay," said K, catching Valerie's mental gymnastics. "There won't be a test. Just take the initial you're told and then invent a name that suits your own first impression of that person. It's a lot easier than remembering real names at cocktail parties!"

"Welcome, everyone." A huge bearded man, well in his forties, was making his way around the room "I'm Auntie A. I'm camp nurse. All your physical aches and pains and gripes are my domain. My door, figuratively speaking," he made a face at the passageway, "is always open. Don't forget that. And don't be shy about coming to talk to me about absolutely anything."

"All right, everyone," M's voice rose above the others. "Down the passageway, please."

Everyone dutifully filed into the assembly room. It looked the way one might imagine a classroom to look after a nuclear war. The walls had been painted long ago in burnt orange paint that had vanished in places as if seared away. Brown metal folding chairs lay neatly on their sides as if a giant gust of wind had blown them all over at once. It looked like a lonely, cold, forgotten place.

When they were settled, M began.

"You've all had the ground rules explained to you, but if you've any doubts, *don't* guess and *don't* ask each other, please. Ask your instructors. The fewer muddles we make, the more time we save, and we will need all the time we can get."

"It may disappoint you to hear what I have to say next. We are here to learn, more than any technical skill, the ability to create a team; to work in well-placed trust; to be discreet; to think, to endure, and to prevail in our actions. It doesn't sound very James Bond, I know. But it works and that's what counts.

"There will be a lot of emphasis on seeing how much you can do for each other, not how little. Any one who thinks of herself or himself first isn't going to cut the mustard and may as well leave now."

The man in the first row was holding his head to one side and looked distressed. M noticed and stopped.

"Sorry, G and V and . . . " she found the other person she had been looking for, a man with an olive complexion behind Valerie, "S. I forgot we've got the United Nations here this time. Stop me if I forget again. What I was saying is that anyone who can't operate as part of a unit should leave. You are me and I am you, and we are all in this together. OK?"

They nodded. Valerie had heard G talking to the olive-skinned man when she arrived. He was French, and she found his thick accent very charming. The other man, she guessed, was Italian. He seemed extremely shy. As M drew the group's attention to him, his face grew scarlet.

"If anyone is allergic to philosophy," M continued, "let me warn you. We're going to talk about it. No dry textbook lectures, but we will dig through the ethics and principles that compel us to act for the animals. Don't think that's highbrow or 'wally' stuff—it's not. If you don't know what's deep in your heart and your head, if you don't understand the framework for actions and the history of social change movements, you stand a fat chance of coping.

"Animal rights means more than petting the dog; it means recognizing that there is no moral basis, none, for deciding that you have basic rights and that all the other animals on the face of the earth, from oysters to chimpanzees, don't. If you are honest, and start asking yourself exactly what your reasons are for denying all the others their rights, you'll be in for a surprise. Your own habits and your own convenience are the real reasons, other than you've never really thought about it until now.

"When you leave here, you'll read Peter Singer's *Animal Liberation*, if you haven't already done so. In his writing, Singer goes into what rights really are, and decides that just as men don't need the right to an abortion and children don't need the right to shave, dogs don't need the right to vote or drive cars. What every being needs is the right to stay alive, to breathe, to escape unnecessary pain, to shelter himself or herself, to be free to move about, to love. What else do animals need? Their rights can be seen easily if we look at their nature. For example, birds have wings so they can fly, don't they? So there goes the caged bird trade!

"Once rights belonged only to white men. Every one else had to fight for theirs or someone else had to fight for them. Institutionalized children used to be used for experiments. So were prisoners of war, gypsies, the elderly, gays. Women were thought to be so stupid that 'allowing' them to vote would be akin to 'allowing asses to vote.' Blacks were thought to be 'subhuman.' Singer reminds us that when the American president Thomas Jefferson was fighting to abolish slavery, he still believed blacks had less mental capacity than whites. He just didn't believe brain power was enough of an excuse to deny them liberty. So even if people think all the other animals are bone stupid, they should take Jefferson's lead and realize that such a belief isn't enough to deprive others of their freedom.

"When you ask people why we can eat and wear and experiment on animals, they usually say it's because human beings are superior. If I'm superior to you, does that mean I can kill you for sport or make you do a dance for me? No. Weren't we always taught that might *doesn't* make right? I can make the case that I'm superior to a person in a coma or a retarded person, but that doesn't mean I can make steak and kidney pie out of them or test drain cleaner on them, does it?

"People say, 'Yeah, but animals are dumb and animals can't

speak,' as if that means any dumb individual or group or non-communicative being is fair game for exploitation. Should we start making leather furniture out of the hard-of-hearing or those who can't pass a spelling bee? If not, then that reasoning doesn't hold up, does it? It's the same sort of rotten argument the Nazis used to justify making lampshades from the skins of Jews, or performing hideous experiments on non-Aryan children. They thought Jews were inferior and that therefore they could, with complete impunity, cause the Jews pain and suffering and deprive them of life.

"Once you start realizing we have tunnel vision when it comes to other creatures who happen not to be human, your perspectives really change. You start seeing animals as whole, social individuals whom we have deprived of everything precious to them. Animals don't belong on chains any more than we do. We're animals, too. That's a biological fact. Other animals don't deserve to be slaughtered for a passing taste, or have their feet made into key chains, any more than we do. We've got to abandon our exploitative attitudes, open our hearts and our minds, and try to undo some of the harm we've caused."

Valerie sat riveted. It was as if someone had switched on a light in a room that had always been dark for her. The materials she had read, courtesy of Mikaya, had moved and angered her and made her realize that stopping cruelty to animals mattered to her very much, enough for her to risk her career. But now, for the first time in her life, she heard someone talk about treating animals decently in a broad context, not within a framework of killing them quickly to minimize their suffering, or offering the dog a cookie for doing something "right" rather than a rolled-up newspaper for doing something "wrong." It was a revelation: a thinking doctrine that went beyond kindness, a philosophy grounded in fairness and justice for animals. M's words moved and excited Valerie. Although she didn't yet live the way this philosophy required, in her heart Valerie knew M's and Singer's beliefs were her own. She knew she would need to change herself, not just change things other people were doing, and she knew that was what she wanted.

"We're not building flash-in-the-pan heroes here," M continued, "but a long-term army of committed people who accept that they may end up in the clink. Don't think for one moment that you're too smart to be caught. You're not. The best-laid plans can go out the window with one fluke occurrence you could never possibly have planned for. It happens. Before you so much as think about being part of one of our parties, you must be prepared to rot in jail rather than implicate others. The time to think about what your mum and dad will say, what will become of your job, who's going to walk your dog, how you'll stand up to all this, is now and here, not one sunny day when you are being depended on by other people in the same boat. You shouldn't ever have to doubt your mates' commitment if they're snagged, and your arrest shouldn't give them any loss of sleep, either. Without that trust, that pact, everything can begin to crumble."

With the exception of a punk-looking girl who was intently examining the ends of her long, stringy black hair, everyone seemed genuinely engaged by M's words.

As M paused, G leaned over and touched Valerie on the shoulder.

"Where are you from, my friend?" he asked.

"Etats-Unis," Valerie's high school French came back in time for her to avoid a pause.

"I 'ave been to New York, but I dream to go west and watch the prairie dogs in the desert," G whispered genially. "'Ave you been to France?"

There was no time to answer. M began again. Valerie shook her head, "no," in G's direction.

"Now, I'm going to lead you through an arrest. I'll need two volunteers."

Valerie was curious to see how much M really knew of the world Valerie inhabited every working day. She was pleased to see that M did very well, role-playing scenarios like the "good cop, bad cop" and the "We'll go easy on you if you just tell the truth" routines. M warned how the police will try to trick their arrestee by pretending that another arrestee has already confessed, and M offered thoughtful, calm ways to deal with each experience. Every point was sensible, straightforward, undramatic.

The most important advice from M was to resist all temptation to open your mouth. No matter what. As a street cop, Valerie knew how desperately dependent on loose lips, indiscretion, and plain foolishness an officer can be when trying to piece together enough evidence to make a case or an arrest. "Convicted out of his own mouth" was the term they had used in rookie school.

"Silence is a person's best friend, remember. Don't be like the man who went before the judge to appeal his burglary convictions. The judge asked him if he had spoken to anyone out in the hallway. 'Just the people I robbed, your honor,' he said.

"In for a penny, in for a pound. Dollar, franc, lira!" said M, catching herself and smiling at the olive-skinned man. "The person who only talks about going to the party, or just lends you his car, is equally responsible in the eyes of the law as those who go to the party. Conspiracy to commit is exactly the same offense in his lordship's eyes as committing. Even one toe in the water means you got wet!"

The light was fading as M divided them up into smaller groups. Her pupils were instructed to think about and express their worst fears in case of felony arrest, then to ask themselves honestly if they could deal with them. Valerie was pleased that G, whom she had nicknamed Georges, was in her group. To break the ice, someone began teasing him that, in his country, prisoners were probably fed snails.

"Eef so," he said, melodramatically overplaying his accent, "I weel steek zem to my body and tell ze guards I have a bad eelness of giant lice. When zey take me to ze infirmary, I weel escape with zese snails to freedom!"

M raised her eyebrows at the laughter coming from G's group, but seemed pleased everyone was getting along so well. Soon the group settled down under M's gaze to some serious soul searching.

C, whom Valerie christened Crisco because of his enormous girth, was frightened of homosexual rape. How could that fear ever be put to rest? Valerie felt inadequate to the task of reassuring him. To do so would have been dishonest, she knew. She had once arrested a man for beating his wife in the parking lot of the Tasty Diner in Silver Spring. He was gang-raped the first time they let him out of his private cell into the prison "community."

The Italian man spoke softly, but his command of English was perfect. "It may help you to know that I am gay," he said to C. "It is good, given your fear, which I understand, that you are so obviously not homosexual. I am much more at risk of a sexual attack in jail than you. Also, if you will pardon me, you are not slender or very young. Those three things are your insurance."

The Italian's words were delivered with great kindness, but they did nothing to allay C's fears. "I feel like a dunce," C looked at us miserably. "I've wanted to be part of the ALF ever since my brother went to work at Pfizer labs. He's a pathologist and totally callous. He's the only person in our family that doesn't like animals. Anyway, he brought home these papers and I started leafing through them. They were all technical papers, written by him, about force-feeding digestive powders down animals' throats. There were two pictures of dogs with stomachs so bloated they looked about to explode. Those dogs' eyes were so wretched. I confronted my brother about it, but he just said, 'Grow up. It's business, Cecil.'" C caught himself too late. "Sorry," he said. "Anyway, I knew I had to do something, but I'd never thought, really thought, about whether I could deal with this fear."

One of the women put her arm around C. The group moved on. Other concerns evaporated as they were aired: people would chip in to meet mortgages; household expenses could be cut to reduce the family budget by one salary; Y, a diabetic, needed reassurance that she would receive medical care if she needed it. Even the question of a long absence from a mate seemed to be workable. With the exception of C, who looked crushed, they emerged from the session feeling pretty good.

M had spent three months in prison for her part in the rescue of pregnant beagles from a lab breeder's farm. She recounted her initial fears. "What really helped me was reading Solzhenitsyn's *Gulag Archipelago*," she said. "When I was feeling particularly deprived, I would read how the Soviet authorities would take a prisoner and put a strip of toweling through his mouth like a bit, pulling the ends over the man's shoulders, and tying them to his heels. They'd leave him like that for days. It was called 'the swan dive.'

"Or they would take a prisoner out into the hot sun and make him dig a trench to lie in with no shade and no water. Sometimes prisoners would be forced to sit on the edge of a chair or stand without being able to move or stretch all day and night."

Valerie looked over at "Crisco." His expression had not improved. M's comparisons weren't cheering him up one bit. G caught her eye and raised his eyebrow and grimaced. They were both wondering if C was going to stick it out.

"The cells were so crowded five men would have to lie on their sides and then turn over as one. The usual sentence was called 'a quarter,' meaning twenty-five years. Men would cry with joy to hear they had only received ten or eight years at hard labor. Never were they able to write to their families or receive letters.

"Everything Solzhenitsyn wrote really happened to people like me, so how could I be depressed when I would be home within a few months, I was not beaten, I had food to eat, shelter, and my own bed? There was even a prison vicar who I got to say prayers for the animals every Sunday! Life in today's jails is awfully luxurious compared to the Gulag. And think what the animals go through. I couldn't complain. And two of my cellblockmates went veggie because of what I told them!"

Next came warnings about cellmates, the "you can cry on my shoulder" police plants that London's Metropolitan Police Force uses routinely. Women who try to win your friendship by sharing their cigarette or food rations, telling you how much they "love animals," and even offering to have their mum "pop 'round to your flat and keep it nice for you while you're inside." Men who tell you how they've always wanted to smash laboratories, and could you please tell them how they could do it right.

M told the assembly true stories of infiltration attempts, some subtle and well-planned, others obvious and easy to detect, like the woman who came into the movement saying she had been an organizer with the Campaign for Nuclear Disarmament. Inquiries at CND's London office revealed that she had started volunteering there, then been pegged as a police agent. After being followed to the local detective superintendent's home, she was publicly exposed and had to be reassigned!

M warned everyone always to be on their guard. Some of the "confession extraction" ruses pulled by police were absurd. Interrogating officers telling a young arrestee that the dog he had denied pulling out of a laboratory had been injected with rabies. If he didn't seek an immediate antidote they had brought to the holding cell, he could die, they said. Valerie stopped smiling when she learned that he'd confessed and been deported back to his native Canada.

Dinner that evening was a cucumber and veggie pâté sandwich and a Cornish curry "pastie," a mildly spiced triangular pastry filled with potatoes, peas, and carrots. Not even the light from a cigarette lighter or a match was allowed, so they ate outside, their eyes adjusting to the moonlight, which cast a silvery sheen on the now-black leaves and decaying fortifications. Valerie was very happy to be there. As much as she liked many of her police colleagues, she realized that she had never experienced the sense of togetherness she felt on this "force."

The first night was to be taken as seriously as the rest. Once the group's small collection of trash was buried, they were told to lie on their backs.

"You are looking for the Big Dipper, Ursa Major," said R. "Above the two stars in the front of the bowl you will see Polaris, the North Star. And he's led many a confused raider home from a dark field. Get him, and the rest will fall into place. But in winter, when the Dipper is low on the horizon, or on a misty night, don't waste your time groping around tree trunks to find which side the moss grows on. That's an old wives' tale!"

When R finished, four trainees were chosen for nightwatch shifts, and a roster established for upcoming nights. No intruders were expected, but the exercise was designed to teach surveillance. The trainees soon learned that to doze was to fail. Early in her shift, Valerie could distract her mind from sleep by going over imaginary chess moves. Later, her palms bore the marks of her fingernails, as she dug them into her flesh to force herself to keep her eyes open. A full report of all comings and goings and the slightest sound was required, and every night the instructors made sure some things went on that only the most astute observers would catch.

They learned to gauge the passage of time without a watch, how to count away the quarter hours, and how to identify the different sounds of the badgers, foxes, and night-singing insects. In the end, only one of them, L, who wore Coke-bottle lenses in his glasses, proved he could never be anyone's lookout.

In the middle of the first night, Valerie woke and looked at her watch. It was morning in Washington. For a brief moment, she had a flash of the station house. She could see officers she knew opening their lockers, ready to go on duty. If I had not come to England, she thought, I would be there with them, preparing for another day on the streets. Then the thought faded, and she told herself that, if this didn't work out, she would be back at work, nothing gained, but nothing lost.

The first few nights Valerie slept badly, waking when someone coughed, waking because it was time to get up in Maryland, waking because her feet were freezing. She learned to sleep with her sweater wrapped around her toes and to force herself back into unconsciousness. Sometimes she dreamed of Prather, of Taub, and of the monkeys, and woke with a shudder.

Half an hour before sunrise each morning they were called out onto the pitch-black airstrip, to stretch and shiver in the cold, damp, morning air, and reach on K's command to the still-dark sky. They bent and flexed their joints obediently, wishing for all they were worth that they could crawl back into bed.

K was tough. Like the best physical fitness trainers, she knew how to push people beyond the imaginary line they draw in their minds for their own endurance. She reminded Valerie of her rookie school physical fitness instructor—a mountain of a man who didn't know the meaning of exhaustion. Unlike him, K did not have a built-in prejudice against female trainees.

Although Valerie was in good physical shape, K soon had her drenched with sweat and totally spent of energy. Valerie had felt the old twinge in her back as she pushed her spine knee-ward for sit-ups, and she had watched her wrists shake as they held the weight of her body off the asphalt. C hit the strip and stayed there on the second push-up. Valerie noticed that he hadn't moved since.

"If you think this is hard, my lads and lassies," K addressed the collapsed bodies around her, no mercy in her voice, "just wait 'til we pick up the pace. Your legs may turn to putty, but one day you'll thank me. At least tell yourself that, and it might just keep you going. Remember, you may have to outrun the boys in blue one night, so don't think you can give this up when you leave here. This is the beginning of the rest of your life!"

Unarmed combat came next. "Purely for self-defense and nothing beyond that," said K. "The ALF creed prohibits any violence to life of any kind. Locks, decapitators, electrode implanters, cages, traps are fair game. But neither man nor mouse do we hurt. If you fancy that kind of thing, call yourself something else, but don't come around here."

Someone helped C to his feet and, together, they filed into a huge chamber where it was still possible to make out the marks where rifles once lined the walls. The trainees' weary bodies littered the cavernous room and, waiting for K to start, everyone seemed acutely aware of their tired muscles and creaky bones. Valerie's body ached, but judging from the groans she overheard, she knew some of the others were hurting far more.

K, perky as when she had first greeted everyone, let them lie there while she demonstrated exercises Valerie had learned five years earlier and mostly forgotten: how to disarm an assailant, how to break away from a wrist grip, how to shake off someone who pins your arms to your sides.

K moved expertly, a well-built ballerina in combat boots. Valerie watched her intently, admiring her grace and skill, as she ducked, rotated her arms, kicked, and spun, her fluid movements making each evasive action, each unbalancing of her imaginary opponent, seem simple. Valerie knew that C didn't have a prayer and the rest of the group had a long way to go.

"Now he's holding his gun with both hands, pointing it at her face," K would call out before making her next move.

"Now, watch out! He's above you. He's got a knife!"

It took little imagination to see her attacker's weapons fly into the air. Valerie could almost hear the knife clang onto the floor as K's powerful kick knocked it from her assailant's hand.

Then came K's audience's turn. Forgetting her exhaustion, Valerie was on her feet before everyone else, eager to give it a go. They were paired, attackers and "sentries," each sequence accompanied by grunts, groans, and cries of "Sorry" as someone fell into an assailant or hit one accidentally. By the time K called, "Enough," a sea of confident, grinning faces looked back at her. They would need practice, but they were sure: no guards would get the better of them!

By this time, Valerie felt nauseous from hunger. She grabbed one of the breakfast packs—an orange, Ryvita toast, and a tiny soy sausage in a roll ("dynamite in a blanket," K called it)—and ate hungrily. Valerie's grandmother had told her that during the war no one in England could get an orange. She sat, on the verge of the old landing strip, peeling back the skin, savoring each juicy segment and thinking about the war. Was it fair to compare the battle for liberty she was about to engage in with the battle against Nazi oppression? In some ways, she thought, it was.

There was a latrine dug behind the first line of trees. To use it, you hung a red flag from a nearby branch and were assured privacy. About forty feet away was a stream to wash in. The water was so clear that the pebbles and leaves at the bottom were visible.

"Badger print," said the punky girl to Valerie, pointing to a claw mark on the patch of wet embankment. "I've found their set. We could go watch them, perhaps tonight, if it's not your turn to watch."

The heat of exercise gave way to the sudden chill of the icy water.

"I've never seen a badger. If it doesn't disturb them, I'd love to," Valerie said.

"You've never seen one? Then you definitely must." She tied her long hair up behind her head and sank her face into the water, then almost burst into laughter underwater as a tiny, brown- and green-speckled toad jumped out in front of her.

They finished their wash and walked back through the trees to camp. There was nothing to dry themselves on, and Valerie prayed she wouldn't come down with a cold. The punky girl was Q, a wildlife expert of some sort, Valerie guessed. She seemed to know everything about badgers, foxes, grouse, hedgehogs, and all the birds of the forest.

"Minks are native to Great Britain, of course," she told Valerie.

"I'm afraid I've only seen them in a coat," Valerie answered her and watched her make a face. She's probably wondering if there is any animal I've seen, Valerie thought.

"When I've learned the ropes, my friends and I are going to spring as many minks as we possibly can from farms. People think they're nasty animals, but that's only because they don't know them. Anyway, I'd be nasty if kept in a filthy, tiny cage my whole life. In nature, just like all the other animals, they only eat enough for their needs. They're not vicious killers or greedy, the way people can be."

R had everyone assembled. He stood, rubbing his thick brown beard in his hand, waiting for the two stragglers. "Come, little red riding hoods," he called as he saw them emerge into the clearing. "You are the last." As they quickly joined the group, Valerie looked around for C. He was missing.

R explained patiently how to switch doorjamb alarms by rechanneling the wires from the inside, keeping the circuit intact but bypassing the entry; how to test for a hidden alarm by wiggling the door or shattering a pane as if it has happened accidentally, then waiting, not too nearby, for a police response; how to spot motion detectors during a guided tour or on a false delivery; how to circumvent a perimeter-alarmed building by cutting a way in through the roof; how to remove glass windows without touching the alarmed window wood; and how to squeeze your oiled body through a small opening. R patiently repeated everything because his students could not take notes.

When it was time to eat again, Valerie was in great spirits. She thought how funny it would be to call her sergeant and tell him she was in England, studying how to be Robin Hood.

G caught her smile. "Share your joke?" he asked.

"Oh, that's forbidden territory, isn't it?" Valerie reminded him. "I was just thinking of how someone I know would react if he knew what I was doing here."

She found G charming. United by a common cause, they were coming to know each other as well as strangers can under such restricted circumstances. She enjoyed his stories almost as much for G's delightful, often deliberately exaggerated, accent as for content.

"I was fourteen," said G, as they stretched out on the grass that afternoon. "My friend and I, we are very, very mischievous boys. One night, we go to a place where business people store things, you know . . . "

"Warehouses," she helped him.

"Yes. My friend and I try to open the door on the roof, to look what are they putting in this place. We are saying, 'Perhaps it is gold!' " G smiled, still looking, Valerie thought, a lot like a mischievous little boy.

"We go inside and there is a surprise. Everywhere, little animals. Never 'ave I seen so many little animals. We are looking at them, they are afraid to us. We are not knowing what to do. We put a box full up of the little rat people. And we take it away."

"You took rats from a lab?" Valerie asked.

"Oui. They are big, white, beautiful girl rats. They live with me in my room. My mother, she says, 'G, it is not possible,' but she, after some days, she likes them too, because they are so clean, and very, very good. We make their name 'Les Soeurs Arabesque.' "

" 'The Graceful Sisters,' I think," Valerie told G. In the seventh grade she had chosen French over Spanish because the Spanish teacher was a grouch. In her three years on the force she had come to regret that decision. The Washington area was awash with South American refugees, but until this moment she had never had occasion to utter a word of French.

"Perhaps. Isolde, Martine, Cécile, Claudette, Jacquie. They never say a noise. They 'ave big, pink eyes, but these eyes do not see. To 'see' you or where they go, they use the noses, and the hair. . . . " G stroked his fingers out from above his mouth.

"Whiskers," Valerie helped.

"Yes, whiskers. At night, I open the door of the box and the Sisters 'ave liberty in my room. In the morning, the Sisters walk on my nose and kiss my eyes while I am sleeping. It is my first kiss from a beautiful woman and, almost, the best!"

Valerie rolled over on the soft, emerald green grass, and stared up at the sky. It was pleasant to imagine the rats playing about quietly in G's room at night while he slept.

"The Sisters are small people in a big world. Then, one day, Isolde turn over, like you now. I see a big thing (G indicated a lump or tumor) on the side of Isolde. My mother go with me to the doctor, but he says he cannot help Isolde. At the lab, the men 'ave put cancer inside her body.

"In the final days of Isolde, I make a pocket in my shirt, and sometimes Isolde ride with me. One morning, the Sisters sit on my bed. They say nothing. They are sad. I look at them and I know Isolde is dead. We cry together for our friend."

G's other rats all developed tumors. Claudette was the last to go and G buried her by a stream with the others, "so they can play in the water in their little rat people dreams." Later, G had returned to the lab, but the rooftop door had been sealed off. He looked all around the building. There were no windows and the door was solid metal. One day, he promised, he would come back and, in Isolde's memory, set all the animals free.

"So, you are here for Isolde," Valerie said.

"There is much more, my friend," G said solemnly, "but what it is I cannot tell you because we are forbidden here. If you come to France, I will show you a horrible thing. You will understand it is no child's game."

G's face was set with determination and remembrance of something he was keeping to himself. The "need to know" rule could be pretty crimping at times. Valerie wondered if everyone at camp had an Isolde or a Chester. She suspected they did.

They were back in "class" for the afternoon. R put them through cutting telephone wires, setting a fire at a power station to bring on an area black-out, and slowing down a tape recorder for a line tap. Never having been good at electronics, Valerie found it hard going and was glad when the session was over. Before it got dark the class was taught how to use walkie-talkies, then divided up into groups, each with a faulty set. The assigned task was to find out and fix whatever was wrong with each portable. They might as well have given me a 1957 Buick with a dismantled engine, Valerie thought. She sat on the grass and watched as the others tried to make their walkies work.

"What's this then, V? Not your lark, mechanics?" R came over to where she was sitting.

"No, I'm afraid I'm no Miss Fix-it," Valerie apologized.

"Not to worry. We all have our strong suits and our weak. Half the time even the best walkies don't work, since we don't have access to a power booster the way police do, and the cheap ones are next to useless. If they break on the job, you won't have time to fix them anyway. Sometimes I think we'd be better off going in with two tin cans tied to a piece of string, if that makes you feel any better."

Valerie knew that R was being kind, and she wondered if she should feel patronized instead of grateful. She had always made fun of communes and what she had seen as the dependency and comfort some people derived from being part of a group. But being at camp, among these kind, quasi-strangers, was getting to her. Her tough exterior shell had cracked open more than a hair.

"Seriously," R continued, "technical things are fine to know. But what really matters, and what you'll really need, is the determination to get a job done. Honestly, that's all." He offered Valerie his hand. She got to her feet, thanked him, and limped off stiffly in the direction of the "mess." Every bone in her body had begun to ache. By dinner time, she could count each sore muscle.

"Every other night, I'll tell you a bedtime story," M told the assembly after dinner.

"Tonight it's about the origins of our ever-growing group. It wasn't always the ALF. It started as the Band of Mercy. Ronnie formed the Band back in the early seventies. The name wasn't new. It had been used in the early 1800s, believe it or not, by the youth members of the Royal Society for the Prevention of Cruelty to Animals, but Ronnie chose it because he said it was perfect. It achieved that rare combination of kindness and militancy. What he calls 'active compassion.'

"The Band started out doing pretty small things, but small things that really buggered up the opposition. They'd go out at night and sabotage the vehicles used by foxhunters to train hounds and seed areas with captive-bred fox cubs. The Band would gum up the engines by putting treacle down the petrol lines and water in the fuel tanks. If they found the key rack in the worksheds, they'd 'borrow' all the keys. They'd stick tacks in the locks and ruin the tires, things like that. Or fill a dishwashing-liquid bottle with paint stripper and squirt it all over the vans."

"When the houndsmen went to get into their Land Rovers and Jeeps, they'd find notes on them signed by the Band of Mercy, explaining why the actions had been taken. Some of the notes included sayings from the Quaker doctrine of bearing witness, which requires those who witness atrocities against life to step in and try to stop them.

"After a while, the Band started to get more ambitious. They liked the fact that they could actually delay or even stop hunts altogether. Next, they branched out to try to stop the bloody seal hunt by burning the sealers' boats while they were moored in the Wash. That worked, too. There wasn't a hunt at all that year, just a lot of talk among the sealers who weren't sure what the hell had happened.

"Ronnie started to think about the labs next. Imperial Chemical Industries was in the news a lot, and Ronnie learned that they used massive numbers of animals in tests for everything from plastics to paints. First, the Band tore up vehicles used to move dogs and rats and guinea pigs from suppliers to toxicology test sites. Later they set the lorries and cars on fire, making them totally useless.

"Ronnie was determined to make animal torture a costly business, something insurance companies would hesitate to cover. Lots of times he succeeded, especially when he made sure the insurance companies were told exactly why the places had been targeted, and that unless those firms went into another line of business, they were likely to be torched again.

"The Band kept a running tally of roughly how much they were costing the animal-abusing industries. By the time Ronnie was caught for the first time, four years ago now, he reckons the Band had done well over three million pounds of damage. He and Cliff Goodman had already burned a lab almost to the ground in two separate actions. No one pinched them for that, but both of them got caught trying to break into a lab in Bicester. The place was surrounded by a high fence with razor-edged barbed wire at the top, but Ronnie and Cliff wore three pairs of gloves and heavy clothes and scaled it.

"The Tory papers, particularly the *Telegraph*, had been full of stories calling the Band hooligans for years, and the Crown was out for blood. Ronnie represented himself because he was afraid if he hired a barrister, the barrister would start apologizing for what Ronnie had done, and Ronnie would have none of that.

"The trial was over quickly, and even though Ronnie and Cliff were 'first-time offenders' and were only caught going in to this place, with no animals on them, they each got three years. The Toffs were very pleased. They really thought they had put paid to this type of 'hooliganism' for good and all. The guards and other prisoners at Oxford Prison had watched the news reports, seen all the Band's supporters at the trial. By and large, they turned out to be sympathetic, which was a nice surprise.

"Cliff and Ronnie were paroled out within the year, and Ronnie was at it again right off. He said he couldn't have lived with himself if he hadn't done something right away after a year's forced inaction. In prison, he read about the labor movement, women's suffrage, the abolitionist movement in the colonies, and how the slaves had risen up to claim their right to be free. All the time he was reminded of how defenseless the animals are, how de-

63

pendent on us they are to help stop their misery and pain. How they can never fight for their own freedom.

"Ronnie retired the Band during his first stint in prison, because his arrest had radicalized the animal rights movement. The name didn't seem to fit anymore. Some people had started printing up 'canceled' stickers and putting them over circus posters and hunting meet announcements; others had started breaking into labs. The time seemed right for a more militant handle, one that would rock the industries and make sons and daughters of animal traders shy away from their parents' careers. And so, children, that's how the ALF was born.

"Oh, I should mention Ronnie had a few narrow scrapes before he was pinched last time. One group that had done a lot of damage at a guinea pig breeder's place was stopped by the police. It was very late at night, and the driver managed to convince the officer that he was on holiday and lost. The policeman believed him and let him go on. And all the while, in the back of the van, there were people sitting very quietly with guinea pigs crawling about all under their clothing!

"The last time Ronnie was caught, the police came into his house 'on suspicion.' They were just hopeful, but they hit the jackpot. Ronnie's bedroom was full of rescued mice he had taken out of a lab breeder's building in Surrey. Ronnie said he could easily put up with another rotten year in prison, that's what he got, because he knew those mice would be going back to the lab and they would suffer much worse. It made him very angry that the police found them. He had watched those mice start to come around, not to be so frightened of people anymore, and he had wanted to give them a little bit of comfort in their old age."

Valerie wanted to listen to M, but her eyes closed before she could catch herself. She saw Sean and Mandy, out on the lawn, playing. When she woke, her head was resting peacefully on the shoulder of the man beside her. M was winding up her talk. Valerie looked up to see the owner of the shoulder, G, smiling.

"You sleep like an eennocent baby, V. Maybe I should tuck you in?"

"Hold on there, G," interrupted Q, as everyone got to their feet to head for their cots. "V and I are going to swing around by the stream and say good night to the badgers before we turn in. You're welcome to come, too, if you can 'zeeper your leeps.' " Yawning, G politely declined.

Together the two women picked their way through the fields in the twilight, down the embankment to the stream. In a low voice Q told Valerie about badgers' homes. "They're the most elaborate of any predator," she said. "Their maze of tunnels includes underground rooms for sleeping, eating, and storing carrion, and a latrine at least twenty feet away from the rest of the home. If food is plentiful, the youngsters stay on, and the family simply enlarges the underground quarters. Sometimes their homes sprawl over—I mean under—two or three acres.

"A badger whose mate dies will bury him or her. Badgers are some of the spunkiest fighters alive, but no match for humans' cruelty." Her soft voice took on a bitter edge. "In badger-baiting, hunters allow their hounds to dig their way into the badger's burrow or set. When he's all worn out, they drag him out for the hounds to tear apart."

At the water's edge, the women settled themselves into the huge exposed roots of a tree, about thirty feet from where Q had spotted the badger footprints earlier. They leaned against its broad trunk.

"With any luck, we're in time to see him take his evening drink, but we'll have to be quiet as mice," whispered Q. Moonbeams shimmered over the rippling water and bounced off the pale rocks nearby. Q leaned forward, watching intently. As they sat there in silence Valerie realized, to her own surprise, that the kinship she felt with this virtual stranger and the others at the camp was very strong. It was the sort of feeling she had read about but never experienced: the feeling that binds together groups of strangers who find themselves trapped in an elevator or taken hostage. Shared fate, secrecy, and a sense of adventure were the elements combining to form a bond between her and Q and G and the rest, a bond that other factors, like differences in background or other beliefs, would not be strong enough to break.

After forty minutes of silence, Q shrugged and whispered dispiritedly, "Sorry, looks like we missed—oh, wait!" One hand instinctively flew to cover her mouth as she pointed with the other at what appeared to be a big rock about twenty feet away. But the rock was moving, and soon they could make out that it wasn't a rock, but a big husky badger, at least two feet long. He was padding stealthily toward the water on short, stocky, bowed legs, which were all but hidden by a long, thick coat that swept the ground as if it were several sizes too big for him. The moonlight picked up the white stripe atop his head that linked him to his cousin, the skunk.

The women watched him slake his thirst at the stream's edge. Then he turned toward them. For a long moment he stared and sniffed the air. Then he turned again abruptly, gave a little snort, and hurried off into the darkness. Q gave a gleeful yelp. No big-game hunter had ever felt more triumphant than she. "Mission accomplished! Now let's run for our beds and sleep fast or we'll never make it through tomorrow."

The next days went by very quickly, or as G said, "on leetle centipede feet." Valerie felt her muscles getting tighter and her arms and legs gaining strength. By the second week, she was sleeping like a baby every night, dreaming about "parties," and feeling very happy about the whole thing. Prather and Taub no longer plagued her sleep.

When Valerie was given time to think, she did. Although she was not sure what she had expected, being at camp was nothing like anything she had imagined. Not that she had worried, but she had to admit that she had wondered if the place would be run by misfits and egomaniacs acting out bizarre paramilitary fantasy lives. In rookie school there had been constant one-upmanship battles. Recruits wanted to outdo each other. Those who failed were made fun of, goaded into failing, even, and instructors often took out their personal frustrations on the recruits. Yes, C had washed out here, but no one was happy about it. Here the instructors were friendly and the other trainees genuinely helpful, or at least just plain quiet and inoffensive. If there were unsavory oddballs in the group, Valerie hadn't been able to detect them. Most refreshingly, the machismo of police academy life and the blatant sexism were absolutely absent. There hadn't been a hint of weird-ness or ugly competition. The trainees wanted each other to get it right, for if one of them succeeded somewhere, all of them suc-ceeded.

It had also crossed Valerie's mind that there might be some sort of "I've seen more suffering than you can imagine" misery hanging over the group. Instead, camp was a happy, if no-nonsense, place. Coming here was like discovering she had a second family, a fam-ily whose members all accepted each other, without the skepti-cism with which her sister Lettie invariably greeted any news of Valerie's progress through life, or the tiresome worrying her mother seemed unable to escape. This family was glad to be able to spend a little time together. She felt peaceful and relaxed with these people, the way she did playing chess with her father or camping with Sean, even when her feet ached and her body craved sleep. When she fell asleep she was glad to be at camp, and wanted to wake up to another day there.

Valerie learned how to jimmy door locks, how to jam locks us-ing chrome-steel bits dipped into Liquid Metal, how to blow locks out with a pick gun, how to open locks with a keyhook made from paper clips, and how to drill locks out. She removed window glass using diamond-tipped glass cutters, and learned, with a sense of having crossed over into a parallel universe, how vital it is to dis-card the clothes and shoes worn on a party, the fibers and imprints from which can be used to link suspects to the scene of a libera-tion. Even bolt-cutter blades leave distinctive marks that can be the kiss of death if the cutters are found in a suspect's possession. Where once she had hoped to catch people using tricks like these, her allegiance had now shifted. She found herself rooting for her classmates' successes in foiling the police.

They practiced scaling walls, running through dark bramble fields with their eyes shielded from branches, and throwing them-selves expeditiously into ditches. They practiced surveillance techniques and the art of disguise, learning very simple ways to change their appearance, and simple tricks, like how always to take off all jewelry and turn out all pockets before a party to pre-vent something from being dropped. They altered license plates with picture adhesive. They learned how to send away for the birth certificate of someone in the obituary column, and use it to get a driver's license in the deceased's name, and how ("Forgive me, sergeant, for I have sinned") to disable police cars by pulling out the distributor-cap leads or cutting wires.

They studied simple coded communication methods. And, for true emergencies, they learned how any book—prechosen, different for, and known only to each contact—could be used to "talk" to each other, with page, line, and word numbers given freely over the phone when normal contact was unwise or impossible.

For Valerie, one of the most interesting courses was in how to handle animals. She had never had occasion to look for signs of injury and disease, or to handle animals of different types and conditions in the least stressful way. She knew nothing of how to administer emergency first aid to them, although the sight of blood and serious injury had never made her hesitate. Generally, Valerie learned, dogs should be walked out on leashes (her own belt made into a lasso)—it's quicker going; puppies should be placed together in a cat box and the mother should see them in hand—she'll want to follow. Cats can be injected with ketamine or acepromazine if they're agitated or scared. Once bagged, extreme care was to be taken to see they didn't suffocate. Injections into the abdomen or thigh work best. The trainees were told to avoid sedating dogs unless absolutely necessary, as dogs can be difficult to inject and pills can take an hour or longer to absorb. Worse, the animals can get woozy and howl or fall down, making them noisy, difficult, and like a sack of potatoes to move. When a dog has to be carried, Valerie was instructed to pick him up with her right hand under his tail and rump, her left under his chest and neck, keeping his head away from hers, and establishing a line of vision over his back.

In between the technical lessons and exercise periods, each raid that had ever taken place in Britain was broken down like a board game, analyzed, reviewed for its strengths and weaknesses, and reconstructed and improved on by the teams. They were beginning to feel there was nothing that would surprise them, no problem that they couldn't solve, because it had happened before and they had "lived" it in class.

Two nights before camp was to break up, the students carried out a practice run. They were driven, in the back of a curtained van, to the target—an abandoned old four-story building. Every move they made was to be critiqued and, when they screwed up, back they would go to do it again. This was their final test. Everyone was on edge.

"Expect anything," R had said. "If you've been awake for the last ten days, you'll be able to work out the plan pretty quickly. Then divide into your groups and try to anticipate problems, just as you would on a real raid. Briefings are always the key. Give it all you've got. Good luck to everyone."

Standing in the darkness, staring up at the creaky brown building before them, Valerie realized they had no clues to go on. Valerie's team had chosen as it's team leader, N, a competent-seeming, physically tough woman in her thirties. From something she had said to Y, the diabetic, and because Auntie A had asked her to help him when someone at the camp took a fall, Valerie guessed she was medically trained.

"Let's move away from here, find a safe hiding place and send three people back to do the reconnaissance," said N. Valerie felt as if she was moving slowly and awkwardly, as if on stage. "Eyes peeled. Let's go."

They hadn't moved two yards when G's arm fell on Valerie's shoulder. She followed his gaze. A car with its headlights off was moving slowly around the corner of the building, toward them.

N saw it at the same time. "Down," she half-whispered, half-shouted. As they fell flat onto their stomachs in the wet, tall grass, the car lights snapped on. They had responded in the nick of time.

The car came forward and stopped. No one moved. Valerie's face was pressed into the ground, and she could hear her heart beating. This is what it's like to be on the other side of the law, she thought. Minutes passed, then came R's voice.

"That could have cost you the whole gig," he said. "Well done. Now, get on with it."

They knew enough not to take his word for it and jump up, but N was warning everyone anyway. "Stay put," she whispered. When she was satisfied no one was watching, she gave the order to move. Two minutes later, the group was on its feet and heading, hunched over, for the little clump of bushes that would be their operational headquarters.

"I can't see a damned thing. Will you stick close to me, please?" It was L of the Coke-bottle lenses.

"Of course," Valerie told him. "Here . . . " She put the corner of her parka in his hand. "Hold that, we'll move together."

The "recon" revealed a "sleeping" guard on the ground floor, a roving guard in the building, and R's patrol. The guards were unarmed but had walkie-talkies. The instructors had said to treat the building as alarmed on the exterior perimeter, but not rigged with motion detectors. Each group would have to determine for themselves where the animals were kept, what species they were dealing with, and what condition the animals were in (descriptions were on cards in the rooms).

"If I slow you down, dump me," whispered L as he and Valerie moved out.

The scenario was a combination of several raids they knew inside-out, with some surprises thrown in. The instructors were as "up" for this as the students were, even filling the role of unexpected strangers wandering onto the scene. Tough as they intended to be, Valerie was sure they wanted every one of their trainees to graduate first time around. By dawn, thirty imaginary rabbits and four imaginary dogs had been transferred into the team's imaginary van; their team calling card had been left on the top floor, where it had turned out the imaginary animals were kept; and they had made a very pretty exit through the loading bay doors.

Police training may have given Valerie a slight edge, but alone it never would have gotten her through. Thanks to the camp, she had been taught many useful things. She had also learned the most phenomenal trick, something she never would have believed would work: the Ninja art of controlled movement. Ninja skills had always seemed to her to lie somewhere between cartoon and myth. Now she thought differently. Even in close quarters, under the right circumstances, she found she could make herself hard to find to someone searching for her. It wouldn't fool a police dog, but by modifying her breathing and angling her body carefully behind or above the searching party, Valerie was amazed to discover that she could almost disappear. It may sound crazy, she would later tell Sean, but it's true.

Valerie and G slapped their hands together when they heard their marks. They had passed; they were ready to go out into the real world.

Valerie and the others were allowed to sleep that morning, and it wasn't until supper that it really began to dawn on her that she was about to go home. Almost urgently, everyone began asking last minute questions, knowing that their heads already were almost too full of information they could not wait to apply. They had been buoyed up by lessons of other struggles, they had fortified their feelings of revulsion at animal abuse, and they had found that they were in good company. Miraculously, no one had as much as argued, let alone come to blows with anyone else. In fact, there was a feeling of camaraderie that beat anything Valerie had ever experienced before. The camp hadn't cost a nickel, she thought, but, to her, it was worth a million bucks.

Many of the people Valerie now felt close to would no doubt be thrown together on raids on this tiny island, but she doubted she would ever see any of them again. She wished very much that it were otherwise. As they hugged their goodbyes, she hoped she would at least read of her nameless friends' successes. She knew that it was also likely that, one day, she might also read of their imprisonment.

"Keep your ears tuned to France. You weel hear of us, V," said G. "We weel be een the news een no time."

Valerie climbed into M's car to retrace their journey to the railway station. In her pocket she had something forbidden: an enamel brooch G had given her "for good luck." It was of a little black-and-white dog with his head cocked to the side, as if waiting. Also completely against the rules, G's telephone number in Arles was etched into the metal.

"He is waiting for liberationists to come," G had said.

Valerie waved goodbye and put the blindfold over her eyes, like a model hostage. She knew that the experience of a lifetime was over, but another was beginning. She was no longer to be the student, but the teacher. As she bumped down the road, she was already set on resigning from the police force. Her dream to one day become a K-9 officer, she knew, would have to be abandoned. Over the last two weeks she realized that her heart belonged to more than one police dog. Her ambition had shifted. She would be a liberationist.

When they got to the station, M walked with Valerie to the platform and gave her a hug. "We want you to succeed, V," she said. "Don't waiver. Each animal you can get out is a whole life saved. Let us see results, won't you?"

"Count on it," Valerie told her.

M handed over an envelope, then left, turning briefly to wave when she reached the ticket gate. Inside the envelope Valerie found an address, marked "Send us all your news," and a card inscribed with an old text by Jeremy Bentham. Valerie read it twice before putting it into her wallet: "The day may come when the rest of animal creation may acquire those rights which could never have been withholden from them but by the hand of tyranny. The French have already discovered that the blackness of the skin is no reason why a human being should be abandoned without redress to the caprice of a tormentor.

"It may one day come to be recognized that the number of legs, the villosity of the skin, or the termination of the os sacrum are reasons equally insufficient for abandoning a sensitive being to the same fate. What else is it that should trace the insuperable line?

"The question is not, can they reason? Nor, can they talk? But can they suffer?"

Underneath, someone had written, "The poisoned dog in the laboratory, the little chicken whose beak has been seared off in the factory farm, the mouse in the trap, the hunted deer wait for you to bring this day closer. God Speed."

By the time the Kings Cross train pulled away from Little Riding, Valerie had thought through everyone she knew, making mental notes of potential members for the American ALF. What she really needed was a partner, someone to bounce ideas off, someone to strategize with, someone who felt exactly as she did. No one sprang to mind. Certainly not Sean, with his easy-going personality and his newly realized dream career. She sighed, realizing she might never be lucky enough to find someone to fit that bill.

3

The Christmas Cat Burglary

On the plane home Valerie remembered something her father once said. She was seven and they were on vacation in North Carolina. He had taken her walking along the beach at Cape Hatteras and asked her what she wanted to be when she grew up. Valerie said she wasn't sure, but that her teacher had told her that girls made good secretaries. Her father had gotten angry, and his voice had changed. He told her to look just a few yards down the beach where dozens and dozens of little sandpipers were running back and forth just steps ahead of the waves, picking up crabs and other leavings, then skittering out of the way again.

"See how they all do the same thing, honey?" he had said. "That's like most people. You can earn your living and be part of the everyday routine, and that's just fine."

When they got to the pier by their hotel, her father spoke to her again. He'd watched Valerie skipping in the waves and had hunted for treasures with her in the seaweed at the tide line, but aside from, "Here's a good shell," or something like that, he hadn't said a word since the sandpipers. Now he pointed to a big bird with a fascinating beak, sitting all by himself on the end of the pier.

"You see him, Val? He's chosen to work in a different way, diving alone, which suits his style better. There are a million different kinds of birds and they do lots of different things to get by in life. They're all important and right in their own way. You probably don't know yet what kind of bird you are. You could be a sandpiper or a pelican or a lovebird. You take your time and look at all the different things you can do and then you choose. Don't you let that teacher of yours choose for you. OK?"

Perhaps now her father's words meant more to her than they ever had before. It was time to shed one plumage for another. He could only approve.

Two days after Valerie arrived back at the police department, she handed in her resignation. She was disappointed to realize that she had been expected to leave sooner or later for marriage or pregnancy, although neither the real reason for her departure—nor the one she actually gave—fit that stereotype.

Why is it so easy, she wondered. Why am I not agonizing over this decision? All right, she rationalized, I'm young and healthy, I'm not in the poorhouse, I can manage, and if it doesn't work, it won't be the end of the earth. Still, she was throwing away her career. As much as I've wanted *that*, she thought, I want *this* more. Valerie knew exactly what she wanted to be: what her sergeant would have called a "vigilante."

"Every day people fill out applications to join the police force," she told Miki. "Even if I do my job better than most, there are thousands of good cops. If the animals had the tiniest fraction of a percentage of such a force working for them, there wouldn't be a mouse left in the labs."

Valerie's division passed the hat and presented her with a top-of-the-line police scanner from Security Services, a tiny police supply outfit run by a retired cop on a disability pension. They also arranged a going-away party for her in a room in 'Carl's Cavern,' a regular police hangout a few blocks from the Silver Spring station. There was always a small contingent of off-duty cops at Carl's, so seasoned crooks never so much as let their feet brush the pavement on Carl's side of the street.

People coming down the steep steps into the bar need a minute for their eyes to adjust to the darkness—darkness which lends much-appreciated anonymity to patrons in the mood to let their hair down. For ambience, Carl's rates zero. The place reeks of beer and cigarette smoke. The wobbly tables are covered with cheap Formica, and coasters and mirrored beer advertisements are the only decorations in the place.

Like combat soldiers, most cops seize any excuse to drink and play the fool among friends. It was clear, to Valerie's delight, that she was to remain a friend: the party was packed.

Rachel, an officer who had graduated from rookie school a year after Valerie, pulled her into a corner to talk. It was about Dick Overmyer, Valerie's former partner. He had had the bullet removed from his neck and was back out on the street before the stitches were out.

Rachel was upset. "Val, you can't leave! The sergeant says he's making that jerk my partner! Listen, you can hear him from here!" Being shot hadn't mellowed Overmyer. He could be heard hee-hawing over one of his lewd jokes from the other side of the room.

"Tune him out, Rachel. Don't let him get under your skin. If I were you, I'd come on like a ton of bricks on Day One. Tell him that if he ever lays a hand on you, or anyone else he's not supposed to, you'll turn him in."

"I hope you're right. The street's enough, without having that creep as a partner."

Before she could get back to her table, Valerie found herself lifted onto the bar. The dispatchers started an almost incomprehensible rendition of "Blue Moon." Then a cry went up.

"Hey, guys! It's the midnight shift!"

The "choir" switched gears into "Oh, the Night Has a Thousand Eyes," a drunken tribute to the shift they had been lucky enough not to pull.

Minutes later, Valerie looked up to see Rick Swain standing at her table. He looked sober and sensible, and she felt a momentary urge to confess her secret to him: if he hadn't served the Silver Spring monkeys warrant, she would never have decided to join the ALF. Valerie knew that NIH had terminated Edward Taub's grant to experiment on the Silver Spring monkeys, and that a court battle was being fought over their custody. Swain had no idea she was following the case at all. He wished her well and told her not to let her guard down until Clay Prather was "on ice." Valerie shook his hand and said she hoped she'd see him around.

It took Valerie several weeks to tidy up her personal loose ends. She traded in her car for a secondhand van, in which she installed her new scanner. She had about $2,200 in her savings account, not including the check her family had told her to expect for her twenty-fourth birthday. She could count on getting about $7,000 out of her retirement fund, and she was owed three weeks vacation pay.

Sean had offered her work, but she wanted to avoid the dependence, and she wanted to have every free moment to work on setting up an American ALF cell. If she hit a crunch, a temporary job wouldn't be hard to find. Ex-cops are always in demand for security work, and in a real pinch she supposed she could also teach English. In Washington, embassy families are willing to pay well for private lessons. Finances were not on her list of things to worry about.

Valerie's decision to leave the force added a new dimension to Sean's frustration that she wouldn't settle down. He had asked, "Are you leaving me next?" as they tried to hold Mandy still to give her a last flea bath for the year.

"Sean, don't get weird on me," she said, "We're in our fun years, remember!" They dried Mandy and then sat watching her race around the house, rubbing her head and chest on the rugs, full of joy at having survived the ordeal.

"Sean, I've got to be alone to breathe," Valerie said. They didn't see each other for some days after that.

Later in the week, when all of her personal chores were wrapped up, she asked Mikaya to come over. She was depending on her friend to find recruits for the American ALF.

"Where's your cruiser?" Miki asked when Valerie opened the door. "Are you an undercover narc now?" She twirled her hair around her finger, mimicking dreadlocks. "Dere's no ganga on me, mon," she mocked.

"Nope. I quit the force." Valerie told her, waiting for a reaction.

"You? You're kidding! You expecting?"

"Miki, you're as bad as my sergeant," Valerie reprimanded her. "Women don't only leave their jobs to have babies."

"Sorry! Didn't mean to tread on those oh-so-exposed feminist toes," Miki smiled. "So, what about you becoming a K-9 officer? Something serious must have happened."

Valerie opened a bottle of dark, Jamaican ginger beer for Miki and, as she sipped it, she told her about England and the camp.

"Does Sean know about this?" Mikaya asked.

"No," Valerie lied. "And he mustn't. People shouldn't know anything they don't need to. For their sake and everyone else's." Valerie knew that if Miki suspected she was shielding Sean, she would understand.

"Oh, Lord. I suppose I'm responsible for all this," Miki said. She shook her head, her expression somewhere between amazement and pleasure. "It's hard to believe you're doing this. All I can say is you have my vote."

"Miki, I'm going to need more than your vote. You're going to have to help make this work. I only know a couple of people that I'd even think of involving. Even then, it's a big maybe. You know everyone involved with animals."

"I can help, that's for sure," Mikaya said. "Sometimes, there's only been me to make a difference in the life of some wretched animal, and the law doesn't give me an inch. *You* know how that is."

She did know. Like every police officer, she had seen abused children whose abuse you couldn't quite prove, battered wives too scared to leave their men, old people too senile to accept help. Victims who fit neatly but cruelly into some legal loophole that extends greater rights to the abuser than to the abused. Sometimes Valerie had called social services or slipped someone a few dollars, but she knew she couldn't rescue them. Not legally.

"The first time I crossed over the line," Mikaya continued, "was with a bag-of-bones dog this guy kept chained up. She'd start to shake, and curl her tail under her legs clear up to her chin, when Sam, her owner, came near her. She'd even wet herself. Of course, none of that would count for a thing in court. Sam's wife was sympathetic but too scared of getting her own hide tanned to sign a statement.

"I called up two friends. They pulled their cars up right in front of Sam's house one evening, and pretended to have a little accident. Sam and the neighbors came out in their front yards to watch the show. I was out back, my fingers working as fast as I could, trying to undo the old, rusty chain, then running like the wind with the dog. She ran right along with me as if she'd been wondering what took me so long!

"We spayed her, and got the motor grease off her. Soon she realized no one was going to hit her again, and she started coming around. All you had to do was look in her eyes to know you had done the right thing, even if the law didn't recognize it as right."

"No one figured it was you?" Valerie asked.

"No. Sam's wife told me someone had stolen 'Princess.' I *love* the names some people give the animals they beat up! I made her promise she'd stop her husband from getting another dog."

Mikaya confessed that she'd rescued many more animals since then, and that the number of helpers she'd found had grown, too.

"I've got a bunch of fine white night crawlers!" Miki continued. "Being black can be very scary if you're moving around under a white man's trailer trying to nab his dog. On the other hand, I can blend in nicely in some neighborhoods, especially if the moon isn't out!"

Before Miki came, Valerie had made enough lasagna for a church picnic. This time, she had also made sure there were no animal bits and pieces in anything.

"There's something else I want you to help me with," Valerie confided.

"Sure, go ahead. It can't be a bigger surprise than the first request."

"Well, no. I'd just appreciate it if you'd help me get started as a vegetarian."

"You bet! I cook almost as well as I eat! You can have my best recipes. Why the switch?"

"Well, I kept thinking what you had said to me about not eating anything with a face. Then, at camp, this woman told me nauseating things about slaughterhouses, how frightened the animals act, how the stun guns don't always work, and about de-beaking and castration without anesthetics. Now I agree with you. If you care about animals, it's crazy *not* to be vegetarian."

"Well, welcome to the bean sprout brigade! I'm going to teach you to make the tastiest curries and rice dishes you'll find anywhere."

Miki still had her truck to clean and paperwork to do, so she begged an early departure. Valerie was grateful to her and no longer troubled by the illegality of what she was about to do. She hated stray worries and had put in a lot of time thinking her position through. She believed what M had said at camp, that the ALF's actions were no different than those of American abolitionists before the Civil War, when Southern slavery laws and even the U.S. Constitution said that owning human slaves was legal. Abolitionists broke those laws all the time and were damned by the press and politicians — even presidents — as danger-ous, violent terrorists. In the end, who had turned out to be morally right? The laws or the abolitionists? "Don't all animals," M had said, "human or not, feel the whip, fight the chain and the knife, and grieve for their loved ones?"

When Valerie told Miki what M had said, Miki did not flinch from the comparison. "She's right," she assured Valerie. "They thought my people couldn't feel pain the way white people do. They practiced surgeries on us and made our mothers feed white babies from the milk they made in their breasts for their own chil-dren. Our men were fitted with leather muzzles and had iron spikes locked around their necks when they bit the hand that ens-laved them. It's not *who* the victims are, it's whether the behavior changes that counts. Any fool can look at what's past and say it's wrong! Visionaries have to look at what we'll outlaw in the future."

Valerie wanted to play a part in building a more civilized world. She was not 100 percent comfortable in her new role, but she was convinced that she and Miki and M were 100 percent right. "A hundred years from now," she thought, "the idea of eat-

ing, skinning, and experimenting on animals will be seen as bar-
barous. No question."

Within six weeks Mikaya had assembled eleven ALF prospects,
and Valerie had met with and accepted all but one of them. The
first ALF cell in America had been formed, with the motto "compassion is indivisible."

Some of the faces Valerie recognized from the night the Silver
Spring monkeys had gone to Florida. They seemed stunned to see
her, and Valerie wondered if they had convinced themselves that
they had only imagined being helped by a cop that night.

Valerie went over the ground rules with every new recruit. She
let them know that information would be shared only on a need-
to-know basis, what to do in case of arrest, and the philosophy behind the actions. She didn't want any joyriders.

Next, she drove down to the Government Printing Office on
North Capitol street and picked up a U.S. Department of
Agriculture list of registered research facilities. There were over
a dozen potential targets in her own back yard.

It so happened, however, that events were to decide themselves.

One of Valerie's new cell members, Kay, a retired civil servant,
went every Wednesday night to PETA's work parties to stuff
envelopes and pick up the latest animal rights news. She told
Valerie about a rash of cat disappearances.

"That usually means a 'buncher' is working the area," Kay explained, "stealing cats to sell to labs." One of the PETA directors
had lost a Himalayan cat called Shalimar. While checking the
lost-and-found reports at local shelters, she realized that whole
neighborhoods were being cleaned out at the same time. When
she started calling people from the "lost pet" newspaper ads, she
found several people who remembered seeing a white van in the
neighborhood shortly before their animals disappeared. No one
had realized the connection until later, and no one had recorded
the vehicle's license plate.

The night before Shalimar's disappearance, the woman had
come home late from a reception and gone to bed. The next

morning, Shalimar was missing and the back door was ajar. Whether the door had been left that way by accident, or been opened in the night, was a mystery.

Everyone at PETA was chipping in to help trace Shalimar. They had combed the area, looked through storm sewers, gone house to house talking to neighbors, and interviewed mail carriers and delivery people. They had tracked neighbors to their work places in case Shalimar had jumped into someone's car. "The big fear is that Shalimar may already be in a lab," Kay said.

A friend at the Animal Welfare Institute (AWI) told Kay that a dealer with a long track record of keeping faulty records ("You can guess where he gets the animals," Kay said) held contracts with several local research facilities. He usually made his drop-offs on Wednesday mornings.

"If he's buying from bunchers," Kay said, "Shalimar may turn up on his truck."

Valerie, Kay, and two other cell members each chose a facility and started staking it out. Because Valerie lived near the D.C. line, she picked Howard University's run-down campus in an area called LeDroit Park. Kay drove a Montgomery County school bus in the afternoons, so she chose Bethesda Naval Hospital, just fifteen minutes from her house. The other two shared Georgetown University and Walter Reed Army Hospital.

Valerie set out at about five the following Wednesday morning and parked in the alley facing Howard's main medical building loading dock. She couldn't run the heater without drawing attention to the van, so the interior air became frosty as the hours went by. By noon her feet and hands were frozen and her ears were bright red from the cold. In Britain, she remembered, they called doing surveillance in the cold "pneumonia-baiting," and, despite her long johns, Valerie now knew why.

After 8:00 A.M. she could see students hurrying into the "Wings and Things" carry-out or the Subway sandwich shop across the street. The warm air inside the fast-food joints made the windows steamy. Then out they'd come, clasping paper cups of coffee against their bodies as they dashed across at the light, heads down against the chill wind. After ten the fryers got going, and the smell of greasy fish and chicken wafted into the van.

Valerie dug her fingers deep into her pockets, rubbing them against her "natural handwarmers": tiny packets of capsicum, zingiber, and brassica seeds Miki had given her. She listened to the early morning activities of the metropolitan police broadcast over her new scanner.

No white truck, or any other truck, delivered animals that morning, but when the sun came up over the gray, old building, Valerie noticed a brown dog with a barrel chest and thickset face, like a pit-bull, chained in the backyard of one of the rowhouses behind her. The dog was curled into a tiny ball, fighting the cold wind, and Valerie could see the hip and rib bones poking out of her sparse coat. She looked at least twenty pounds underweight.

By 1:00 P.M., Valerie had given up on the dealer. She ran over to the rowhouse and knocked on the door. A grubby young man in an open shirt answered. Valerie noticed that in contrast to the fresh cold air he smelled very unwashed.

"Is that your dog?" she asked.

"Yeah, why?" he said, pulling his shirt over his chest to keep out the biting wind.

"I was just passing by. She looks really thin. Maybe she's got worms or something?"

"I don't know what the fuck's wrong with her." He jerked his matted hair in the direction of the campus. "I took her over to Howard. They gave me worm medicine. You want to come inside? It's freezing out here."

"Sure, thanks," Valerie said, fascinated that he hadn't noticed his shivering dog. They sat down on a big dirty couch. The sickening smell of incense canceled out the man's body odor. Valerie could feel her fingers and toes begin to thaw in the warm room.

The room looked the way search warrant scenes used to, before the police PR people required officers to clean up after themselves. Drawers were open and the floor was littered with clothes and other belongings. A huge marijuana joint lay in the ashtray.

"Is she eating?" Valerie asked.

"Nah. Since she's had pups, she don't eat much. Never barks

neither, and she's supposed to be a watchdog." He laughed, took a roach from his pocket and lit it. When he'd taken a deep drag, he offered it to Valerie.

"No, thanks," she said, shaking her head. "The puppies are all gone?"

"Yeah. I took them over to Howard," he replied, scratching his unwashed scalp vigorously.

"Oh, they'll take animals?" Valerie asked.

"Yeah. They gave me a couple of bucks for them and for two cats I found."

"What do they do with the cats?" Valerie asked.

"Real funky stuff." He was grinning now. "All I know is they cut something in their backs. Makes them walk funny. They drag their legs around."

"Wow!" she said, trying to look impressed rather than revolted. "Which building do they do that in?"

He wiped the window with a cushion, and pointed to a four-story brick building. Valerie tried to keep him talking about this, but he'd lost interest. He was moving soon, he said, and if she was so interested in his dog, "Babe," he'd be willing to "let her go for a little coin." They settled on ten dollars and Valerie left with Babe. The dog didn't even look back as Valerie helped her into the van.

Valerie drove straight to the New York Avenue animal shelter, where a technician hoisted Babe onto the examining table, pulled back her upper lip, and showed Valerie her gums. They were chalk white.

"Probably riddled with hookworms," she said. "We'll try to fix her up, give her a warm bed."

With Babe in good hands, Valerie went back to work. She needed to get inside Howard and try to find the cat surgery unit.

That same afternoon Valerie was back on the campus, dressed in jeans and a sweatshirt, stripped of make-up, carrying a backpack over her Eisenhower jacket, and hoping to pass for a student.

The hall directory showed a listing simply for "Research" on the top floor of the building Babe's caretaker had pointed out.

Valerie took note of what departments were beneath it, then headed upstairs. There was no security in sight. The stairwell was unlocked and she slipped into it unnoticed.

Upstairs, she couldn't get any doors to open. She couldn't smell any animals or hear any sounds, human or otherwise, from within the rooms, and she couldn't see inside them. Perhaps, she thought, it was a storage area, or the kind of research done on paper.

She made her way along the floor, her frustration mounting. Then, beside the elevator, she noticed a set of double swing doors marked "No Admittance. Biohazard." That looked promising. She pushed on them, they opened, and she put her feet into the corridor on the other side.

The smell of disinfectant and medicine was unmistakable.

Valerie was no more than twenty feet inside the doors when, without warning, a middle-aged man in a white smock swung around the corner toward her, wheeling a stainless steel trolley. Valerie kept walking, trying to look harmless and friendly, but it was not going to work. The man stopped just in front of her.

"You lost?" he asked. "This is a 'no admittance' area."

"Oh, boy!" Valerie sighed, putting on her best dumb look. "I'm looking for a Dr. Cass or Cassidy. No, Cassaway, a dentist. Isn't this right?" She'd read Cassaway's name and room number on the board downstairs.

" 'Fraid not, honey. You're one floor too high. Go on down, and right where you're standing now, right below us, you'll find Dentistry."

"Thanks a lot." Valerie turned around and walked back to the elevator. What else could she do? The attendant stood with her, waiting for the doors to open. When the elevator arrived, he wheeled his trolley in beside her and they went down together.

"Thanks, again." Valerie waved to the attendant and got off, dutifully, on the third floor. It had been worthwhile to run into him after all. He had shown her exactly what she wanted to see. The two cats in carriers on his trolley were all the evidence Valerie needed to know that the American ALF had found its first target.

The Howard University campus is on the northernmost part of LeDroit Park, once the well-to-do bastion of the distinguished, hard-working African-Americans who founded Washington's first black university. Now it is a run-down neighborhood, full of rooming houses from which most people come and go too quickly to establish a sense of community.

The mood and tone of the neighborhood has changed over the years. Even in the early hours of the morning there is some activity: tired men and women getting off odd-hour shifts and walking briskly home, jobless men staggering to their flophouses from after-hours drinking and gambling joints, and sometimes young, doped-up hustlers trying to get their heads straight enough to score or sell. The occasional police cruiser glides by, not looking for trouble, usually not looking at all, but using LeDroit as a cut-through to the heavily trafficked streets beyond, where the real action—muggings, murders, and rapes—go on.

That night, as soon as it got dark, Valerie drove slowly through the campus. The lights were on in the buildings, and inside she could see blue-uniformed guards sitting at desks set up in the entranceways. Through the large windows, she watched people who entered the buildings being directed to sign the guard's ledger. There was some semblance of security, but not much.

The next evening, Valerie and Kay were back, waiting and watching, as the guards came on duty at six o'clock. Valerie was pleased to note that there were no guns hanging from the guard's belts, just a cumbersome assortment of "rent-a-cop" gear: flashlights, nightsticks, and handcuffs.

Valerie had picked Kay to help with exterior surveillance and Ginger for the inside work. Ginger was a freshman at another university, very attractive and outgoing, almost bubbly. She was the type who would have been cast as the heroine in high school plays, and she couldn't wait to act in this production. Her radicalization was born when her high school biology teacher took the top off a frog's head with a pair of ordinary scissors, and Ginger heard the frog scream. She told Valerie that she had come to believe what Hippocrates taught: that "the soul is the same in all living creatures, although the body of each is different."

Ginger parked her Volkswagen just off campus on Seventh Street, hid the keys under the driver's seat, and strolled into the medical building at about seven. She walked directly to the guard station.

"Hi," she breathed, stroking her long hair. The young man looked up, his dull expression switching to full alert.

"Would you mind if I sit here?" Ginger glowed. "My roommate's picking me up, but she doesn't get off work until eight. I'd feel much more secure if I could study here."

The guard didn't mind at all. Ginger learned that his name was Bill. She encouraged his conversation, and Bill found her interest in his job exciting.

Ginger found out all that she needed. There was a little room, not much bigger than a closet, behind the guard's station. After midnight, when the doors were locked, the older guard who replaced Bill would go there to watch his portable TV. Then he'd doze off. That explained why, when Valerie and Kay had driven by at two in the morning, and again about an hour later, the guard station had been unoccupied.

"Doesn't he ever get into trouble?" Ginger asked. "What if his boss comes along?"

"Hell, they never check," Bill told Ginger. "They're watching their own TVs at headquarters. Nothing ever happens around here, and they don't care what we do as long as we put in our eight hours."

To Bill's delight, Ginger returned every night to wait for her ride. Sometimes her "roommate" would be late. "She's so unreliable," Ginger would tell Bill. "But, what can I do? It's too cold to stand and wait for the bus, and to tell the truth I'm nervous out there at night."

"Don't you dare take the bus," Bill told her. "Crazy things can happen to young women these days. I'll front you a cab if she doesn't come."

On the eighth night, Ginger's "roommate" was later than usual. She still hadn't shown up by nine. Ginger seemed worried. She kept going to the phone, dialing a number where she knew there would be no answer, and then biting her lip.

Ten o'clock came and went. Ginger's eyes seemed glued to her watch. Still no ride. "I get off at eleven-thirty. If she's not here by then, I'll drive you home," Bill assured Ginger.

At eleven o'clock, Valerie slipped out of the surveillance van and made her way to the side door of the medical building. The street light was annoyingly effective. It made the area visible from almost a block away.

Valerie removed the metal bar she had hidden inside her coat and banged as hard as she could with it on the metal frame of the thick glass door. Then she moved rapidly away into the alley across the street.

Valerie pressed her body up against the wall and watched. No sirens sounded, no officers with whistles blowing appeared on the scene, no new lights flicked on. No one emerged from any of the buildings. There was only her own breath, making white wisps of cloud in the chill air. She was pleased to notice that she was not nervous at all.

Satisfied, Valerie moved quickly away, found Ginger's Volkswagen, drove up to the building and beeped the horn. It was sixteen minutes before Bill's shift ended.

"Did he hear me pounding on the door?" Valerie asked as soon as Ginger got into the car.

"Not a thing!" Ginger grinned.

"It sounded like a train crash out here. That old building must be solid as a rock."

Before Valerie turned the car over to Ginger and got out at the top of the parking lot to resume surveillance with Kay, she made a call. That street light had to go.

Just after 3:00 A.M., they noticed a sporty black car pull up by the side door of the target building. Miki's cousin, Damon, got out of the car a few feet away from the lamp. Taking a quick look around, he heaved a dark object at it and missed. The missile made a metallic sound as it hit the sidewalk. Damon tried again. This time the object thudded against the heavy glass, but didn't break it. Damon tried several more times, sometimes hitting the glass, but only chinking it.

"This is getting annoying," Kay said.

Damon got back into his car and drove away. The campus was quiet. About fifteen minutes later, Kay nudged Valerie. "It's round two," she said. "Here he is again!"

They watched Damon pull up, get out of his car, and look around. All clear. He reached behind his seat, pulled out a BB gun, and aimed. There was a quick "pop," then a louder one as the glass lamp cover exploded. Glass rained down onto the street and the light went out. Damon got back into his car and left.

"That's more like it!" Kay said, satisfied.

If Shalimar was being held inside Howard, Valerie was going to get her out. If her team had to break the door down, it seemed no one would hear them going in, and now their entry point was shrouded in darkness.

As much as Valerie wanted to charge in and search for Shalimar and the other cats, she had learned to be patient. If something went wrong it would be by chance, not because she hadn't done her homework. So, every night for the next two weeks, from 10:00 P.M. to 6:00 A.M., Valerie and Kay kept watch.

They talked about Thoreau ("Let your life be a counterfunction to stop the machine"), and Kay told Valerie about her mother's death from cancer. Kay tried to get her into an experimental drug study at NIH, but they wouldn't take her. "She was wasting away and had nothing to lose," Kay said. "They weren't interested. In the end, the pain was pretty bad and the doctor kept her doped up all the time. She looked so tiny lying in the bed." Kay knew that NIH spent millions giving rats cancer, and she had wanted some of that money for her mother. Valerie could hear the bitterness in her voice.

They logged every leaf that dropped in the vicinity of the target building. Cars and civilians were noted separately, police cruisers and guards got a star. Then Valerie compared each minute, looking for patterns of inactivity. There were clearly several options for days of the week, but only one really solid time slot when no one had ever crossed their line of vision: between 3:10 and 3:50 A.M.

Valerie decided to wait a few more days. The delay would take them into Christmas week, when the campus was bound to be even quieter. She wanted to give the team as much of an edge as it could get.

Meanwhile, the white truck seemed to have vanished. No one reported seeing it anymore, and the numbers of missing cats had dropped to normal levels. Whoever the thief was, he or she must have moved on to another jurisdiction. "Or slowed down for the holidays," Ginger offered.

Valerie called Otto, the young man who had driven the moving van full of Silver Spring monkeys to Florida and back, and told him her plan.

"Do you want in on this?" she asked.

"Only if you promise me that this time, if we get them out, we won't give them back," he said.

"Over my dead body," Valerie assured him.

Only a few of her new unit members were going home for the holidays or had family commitments they couldn't break, so she was set. She had two surveillance vehicle drivers (it was too risky an area to do surveillance on foot), two people to break in, four to help carry cats out, and a transfer vehicle driver, as well as someone to deliver press packs after the action, and—most importantly—a veterinarian who would examine the cats.

Then Lettie, Valerie's sister, called, and Valerie realized she had forgotten something: her father and mother and Lettie were spending Christmas in the Virgin Islands in a rented bungalow. Valerie's fifteen-year-old niece, Mimi, was scheduled to spend the holidays with her in Washington. For a moment Valerie thought of canceling, but then she thought better of it. Lettie had a hard time controlling Mimi, and Mimi and Valerie got along very well. Mimi wanted to be a cop, a skydiver, an explorer, anything she saw as a ticket out of domestic life and into adventure. Moreover, Lettie complained, Mimi seldom discussed things with her mother.

"Why not," Valerie thought. Mimi was a juvenile. She'd never be punished if she was caught, and Valerie would keep her involvement peripheral. She picked Mimi up at the airport and had a serious talk with her.

"Is this how you'd like to spend Christmas?" Valerie asked her. Would she? Mimi couldn't believe her luck!

For surveillance, Valerie was using a van belonging to one of her cell member's ex-girlfriends. It was a gaudy blue and green, with floral curtains in the windows. It had a battery pack used for camping and a small electric heater to keep Valerie and Kay's feet from freezing off. All had agreed that if they were caught, the owner would report the van stolen and get herself off the hook.

Valerie's van would never be seen on the campus. It was to be used to transport the cats to New York, where a veterinarian friend of Miki's had agreed to help do exams and fix the cats up with any emergency treatments they might need.

Every night, just before ten, Valerie drove the surveillance van into a campus parking lot on a hill just above the cat building. From there, she and Kay could see almost two full blocks in front of the target.

A few minutes after eleven, a guard would emerge from the administration building, walk over, and hook a chain across each of the two lot exits, effectively sealing the van inside until the chains were unhooked at just after 6:00 A.M. Whether he noticed the van or not, they had no idea. It seemed the cold made him concentrate only on completing his task.

In addition to the curtains along the windows on the sides and at the back, Valerie had rigged up a curtain to separate the driver's and passenger's seats from the rest of the vehicle. That way, the lookouts could sit on the hassocks she had installed in the back and see through small slits in the heavily patterned curtains without fear of being spotted.

Because there was a certain appeal to the timing more than anything else, Valerie decided to wait a few more days and enter Howard in the early hours of Christmas morning.

Mimi helped tape cardboard cat carriers together and set them up in the transport van, each with a tiny cup for water and a tiny tray of kitty litter. They stowed a gallon jug of water, packets of food, plastic trash bags, newspapers, and a first-aid kit under the front seats of the van. They bought black shoulder bags for the raiders, punching breathing holes in the fabric to ensure that the cats didn't suffocate on the way out, and loaded syringes with doses of ketamine hydrochloride, a drug used by groomers and veterinarians to put cats into a state of "disassociative anesthesia." She wanted the cats to be as relaxed as possible during their removal. Not knowing how many cats they would find, Valerie decided on thirty of everything.

By December 23, the last night of surveillance, Valerie was feeling elated. However, at 3:02 A.M., things changed when an old black Buick came rattling down the street directly in front of the medical building. The car, which had appeared at a snail's pace, stopped completely.

"I don't believe it," Valerie whispered.

"Better tonight than tomorrow night," Mimi answered.

Their eyes were glued to the driver as he got out of the car. He was dressed in flashy clothes and a black leather jacket. Two more men, perhaps in their early twenties, staggered out onto the street behind him. There was some arm waving and talking, then all three tried to push the car. It wouldn't start.

The men gave up and leaned against the car. One of them kicked the wheel base and yelled, "Shit!" then lurched over to the curb and urinated into the gutter. He seemed to be having a hard time standing up.

Two of the men started arguing, while the third looked around. His gaze fell on the van. He gestured to the other two. They stopped arguing and looked up at the van, too. Valerie and her young niece froze.

The driver dug around in the trunk of the Buick. When he found what he needed, he started walking toward the van.

"What the hell is he up to?" Mimi asked.

"It's OK. I think he's only going to try to siphon gas," Valerie told her.

The man came up the hill into the parking lot, a hose and a plastic bottle in his hand. Valerie hoped she could scare him off.

As soon as she heard the gas cap turning, Valerie let out as deep a sound as she could muster: a mean, growling sort of noise. At the same time she banged on the side of the van near the gas tank opening with her fist. The noise must have made him reel.

It was so quiet Valerie could hear the air. The man came past her window, hesitated, then walked back down the hill.

"He's gone," sighed Mimi.

Back at the car, the driver went into a huddle with his two friends. Then, he reached behind the front seat and pulled out a tire iron. He turned toward the van again and started up the hill.

"Oh, God, they're all coming." There was panic in Mimi's voice. Three large men, at least one obviously drunk or high, were heading straight for them. As a street cop, Valerie had seen enough strange behavior to guess what they were up to: they didn't care who was in the van, but they were going to "take them out."

Valerie pulled the keys out of her pocket and leapt through the curtain into the driver's seat. The driver of the Buick was about eight feet away when the ignition fired. Instead of drawing back, he lunged onto the passenger door, caught the handle, and tried to open it. Valerie accelerated and the van leapt forward. The Buick driver started to fall backward, grabbed the side mirror and held on, his face even with the passenger window. His eyes were bloodshot and glassy.

Valerie turned the wheel hard and kept her foot on the gas. She saw the driver struggle to keep his grip, then lose it and drop to the asphalt. She headed the van to the top of the lot, but even as she did so she remembered that both exits were chained shut. She and Mimi were locked inside.

"Mimi, grab the bolt-cutters out of that toolbox. Quick!"

Mimi's face was frozen and pale, but she did as Valerie asked. Below them, the driver was standing up, rubbing his thigh. He wasn't moving, but his two friends had picked up their pace and were advancing together with an ugly sense of purpose. Perched at the top of the lot, the motor running, Valerie had the momentary fantasy that this was a bullfight. She was the bull, pawing the ground, watching her assailants preparing to attack. She was certainly trapped in the arena, and she couldn't risk letting Mimi open the back door to try to cut the exit chain. The men would be upon them before then. There was only one thing she could think to do: attack first to survive.

"Hold on, Mimi. I'm going to run right at them," she told her. "If we make it, get ready to cut us out of here."

Mimi hung on to the back door as Valerie raced back down the hill, making straight for the men. Only when looking back afterward could she replay the action slowly enough in her mind to remember seeing their faces register doubt at what she intended to do, then the absolute realization that they would be hit if they didn't get out of the way. Valerie saw the bigger man pick up a rusty metal pole embedded in cement, and she saw the crazed look on his face as he hurtled it at the van. The pole tore into the grill, ripping the framework.

Valerie slammed down the gas pedal. For a split second she thought her assailants wouldn't jump clear of the van, but they did. As she turned the wheel again and raced back to the top of the lot, she could see them jumping over the exit chain and running out into the road. They slowed down only as they reached the end of the block, the driver limping after them. Valerie stopped a foot from the exit chain.

"Go!" she yelled at Mimi.

Mimi leapt out of the side door, cutters in hand. In Valerie's rearview mirror, she could see no one coming. All she could hear was her heart thumping inside her chest, and then, finally, the snap and clink of the chain breaking and falling to the pavement.

Minutes later, when they were truly away from the Howard campus, Valerie stopped the van on Georgia Avenue and looked at Mimi. Mimi leaned over from the passenger seat, put her arms around Valerie, and started to cry.

"I'm not a baby," she sniffed through the tears, "I'm just relieved it's over and we're OK."

"You're not kidding. Me, too. Let's go home and get some rest."

Valerie drove home thoughtfully. On the one hand, she felt guilty for putting Mimi in such danger. On the other hand, she told herself, Mimi had gotten a chance to see that "adventure" wasn't always fun and games, but that, in a pinch, she could defend herself. That knowledge in itself was worth a lot. Valerie knew she would have done anything to keep Mimi from getting hurt, but she also knew Lettie would never buy rationalizations. She wasn't exactly sure she bought them herself.

While Mimi slept, Valerie tried to figure out how to overcome the problems that had erupted out of the night's events. It was Christmas Eve. She needed help, but didn't really have anyone to turn to. Everyone was prepared to meet up that evening, but for now they were involved in routine holiday shopping and cooking with family members who never suspected what they would be doing after dark. Even Sean, who had no desire to get involved beyond a supporting role, had driven down to Florida with Mandy to spend Christmas with his folks. Valerie had kissed him goodbye and assured him she'd be fine.

Now, though, the surveillance van was missing some grillwork and the right front headlight was broken. Either could attract attention the ALF group didn't need. Valerie knew that police officers seize upon anything to stop a vehicle in the early hours of the morning, knowing there's a good chance that they may catch someone up to no good.

Worse, what if the three men she had successfully put to rout decided to come back—perhaps better prepared and with friends this time? The green and blue van was unmistakable.

Then there was the matter of the cut chain. Campus police would find it and the night shift might remember locking the van inside the lot for so many nights. No doubt they'd want to ask its owners some questions. Hopefully, they wouldn't connect the cut chain with the shattered street light.

At about two in the afternoon, Valerie woke Mimi up. Together they began transferring all the equipment and cat boxes out of the white van into the green and blue one. During the morning, Valerie had hammered the grillwork flat and cut off the protruding pieces of metal. A mechanic at the Texaco station nearby had helped by removing the shattered headlight glass and covering the exposed bulbs with thick cellophane. Except at close quarters, everything looked presentable. All she needed now was luck.

Quite a few people at the meeting that evening were nervous, but there were high hopes for the team's collective success. There were last minute glitches, but, amazingly, nothing serious: someone had forgotten to bring gloves, two of the pencil flashlights suddenly refused to work, and Bear, an earthy Native American activist who ran an organic vegetable farm with his wife, hadn't changed his shoes. Because he might leave a shoe imprint at the "crime scene," Valerie told Bear he had to throw his shoes away. But there he was, still in his favorite, "irreplaceable" running shoes. Bear accepted the sacrifice. For him, animal liberation was part of a far bigger picture. It was a fight to affirm the positive and to reject the subjugation and powerlessness caused by greed. He felt a kinship with all life.

By 2:45 A.M. everyone was in place. The green and blue van was a mile away from the campus, ready to accept the cats the group hoped to spirit out of Howard. Valerie's van was now being used for surveillance. It was parked on the street, not in the lot, and she noticed a shiny new chain on the lot entrance. She wished she had police-quality walkie-talkies, but without an FCC license or a contact in the business, they were out of luck. The Radio Shack specials she had bought would have to do.

In the alley, Valerie waited with Bear; Sonia, a county administrator who helped Miki find homes for problem animals; Jessica, a philosophy student from Georgetown University; Maxine, a waitress who had helped Miki "borrow" a watchdog from the car lot next to the restaurant where she worked; and Douglas, a science teacher who had stopped teaching his students dissection long before it became a national issue. Mimi was safely at home. Valerie figured that for a fifteen-year-old, she'd had enough excitement for one Christmas. If they needed help or bail money, Mimi would get the call.

"Unit test only. Unit test."

It was the signal to move, and they did, quickly padding out of the alley, across the narrow street, and up to the side door. They squashed themselves flat against the narrow strip of earth outside the entranceway, and watched Douglas go to work.

Among Douglas' hobbies was glass etching. Valerie had shown him how to apply his skills to tonight's action. He got to work immediately, attaching suction cups to the lower panel of the door, moving his scribe over the thick glass. The diamond-tipped pen crackled quietly as it ate into glass. The panel came away from the door frame with a pleasant popping sound. Moving carefully backward, Douglas placed the panel gently against the building, then stepped into the dark corridor. The raid was in progress.

With Valerie and Bear in the lead, they entered the first-floor stairwell and waited. Nothing. They moved up to the fourth floor, trying not to sound like a herd of elephants. They rested for a moment just inside the hallway door, then pushed through. The lights were on but the place was deserted. The double doors that had welcomed Valerie's earlier visit were locked. The "No Admittance" sign glared back at the visitors. If she'd only been on the other side of the law, Valerie thought, she'd have been able to get a pick gun. For now, jimmying would have to do.

The crowbar bit into the metal just below the lock and the doors crashed opened. Valerie, Bear, and the others raced down the hall, not worrying about noise now, cupping their hands against the glass and peering through the fortified wire observation windows.

"Empty," someone called. Then another room, "Empty."

All around her Valerie could hear, "Empty," "Nothing here."

Where were the cats? Had the experiment ended and the cats been killed? Had they waited too long?

"Here! Cats!" It was Jessica's voice, elated. Then, "Oh, my God!" she said, seeing their condition.

"Douglas, get that door open quick." Valerie urged.

"More over here," came Sonia's voice.

The first door was wrenched open, and they found themselves looking at two banks of steel cages, each containing a cat. Jessica started talking to them, making little reassuring noises, rubbing her gloved fingers along the cage bars.

"It's all right, pumpkins," she crooned, "It's OK, don't be scared."

The cats calmed down and started mewing back to Jessica. Some cats dragged themselves forward. They couldn't move toward her as normal cats would because they had to support all their weight on their front legs. Their hind limbs were splayed out behind them like frogs' legs.

"Sonia, how many in room 2?" Valerie called out.

Douglas and Valerie moved from cage to cage, giving each rump a quick, painless shot of ketamine.

"Sixteen," came Sonia's voice, "One dead, twelve in OK shape. Three screwed up."

"Screwed up" described what everyone in the first room was looking at. These cats had all been operated on. From the waist up they were animated beings. Below the waist, their hind legs dragged helplessly below them, lost in space. Along their backs were thick incisions that looked as if someone had started to hatchet them apart with a machete, then decided against it. Where the knife had left its thick mark, there were now stitches tied in huge black knots, making the cats look like strange Christmas presents.

A most handsome cat, snow white with one blue eye and one deep green eye, propped himself up against the door of his cage and called loudly. His shoulders were wide-set and muscular, his hair smooth and immaculate, and his purr could be heard from three cages away.

" 'Peter,' that'll be your new name. We're going to take you away and save you!" Jessica told him, kissing his pink nose through the bars.

Peter purred back.

"Any one see a longhair Himalayan?" Valerie called out hopefully as she came to the last cage in Room 1.

" 'Fraid not," came the answer from the next room.

Shalimar, the PETA cat, was nowhere to be seen.

The unit had worked out their routine. Maxine and Jessica walked behind Valerie and Douglas, gently scooping out each cat as he or she felt enough of the effect of the drug to make handling easy and untraumatic.

When they finished injecting the cats in the first room, Valerie realized she had underestimated. There were thirty-four cats in all. Each person would have to carry six cats out.

Bear held the stiff body of a once-beautiful ginger and white cat in his hands. One cat hadn't lived long enough to be rescued.

"His cage was at the end of the bank," Bear continued. "No water, no food. Maybe they plain forgot."

"You can leave him," Valerie told Bear.

"Wouldn't dream of it. I'll bury him properly on the farm, under the trees."

Everything went like clockwork. With only enough prepared ketamine shots for thirty cats, the three youngest, calmest cats went without. They didn't seem to object.

"I'll bet Peter would walk out with us," Jessica said. "I'll try putting him in my jacket." She lifted Peter to her chest. When she pulled the zipper closed again, Peter's head stuck out under her chin. Instead of struggling, he snuggled tightly against her and purred twice as loudly as he had before. He was ecstatic to be close to someone who so clearly admired him.

While the guard slept three floors below, every cage was swiftly emptied of its resident. Douglas placed a copy of *Animal Liberation* in the middle of the floor. Then the raiders were gone, cats in knapsacks over their arms and in packs on their backs.

The whole operation had taken less than forty minutes.

About twenty minutes into New Jersey, Valerie, with Maxine beside her, pulled off the Turnpike to make a call and get some coffee. The all-night diner they had seen advertised was locked up tight for the holiday. A sign on the door announced a place two miles further down the road where travelers would find "Gas pumps, coffee, clean rest rooms." Valerie headed for it.

Sure enough, there was a general store-cum-gas station ready to accept all the business in an otherwise deserted four-store town. The icy air hit the women in the face and made their ears burn as they left the van and headed into the warm store. The wind chill factor lowered the outside temperature to way below freezing. They knew they could only linger a minute or so, or the cats would start to feel the cold.

While Maxine filled the thermos with hot coffee, Valerie called Kay to let her know how many "chairs" they had removed from the "banquet hall." Then they both raced back to the van. Valerie had pulled the key out of the ignition without any trouble, but now it wouldn't go back in. She had no choice but to twist it, push it, and try not to break it off in the ignition. At last the key seemed to sink into place, but it couldn't have been seated properly. It simply wouldn't turn on. Valerie tried to work it loose again, but this time it jammed. No matter what she did, it wouldn't move forward or back, and it wouldn't come out. Valerie had been working on the key for about ten minutes and the van interior was beginning to feel very cold.

Maxine went back into the store and started making inquiries. They needed a locksmith or an auto mechanic, and they needed one now. No one listed in the local Yellow Pages for emergency service was answering the phone. Even the towing companies that had paid for boxed ads had their answering machines switched on. The store clerk tried to be helpful, but didn't think there was anyone available in the early hours of the morning on the biggest holiday of the year.

As time went by, Valerie's toes became numb. Her fingers were already purple and aching as, to no avail, she tried to coax the key to the right or left. If no help came, she and Maxine could stay in the tiny store to keep warm, but there was nowhere to put the thirty-four cats. She knew they would freeze to death in this metal shell. The situation for them was desperate. Valerie wondered if they could somehow get hold of extension cords and a portable heater. Perhaps the store clerk would let them plug a heater into his outlets. If push came to shove she was worried enough to consider calling the police station under some pretense and begging for a police tow truck to move the van into the station garage if it was heated.

"Tell the clerk we have animals in the back who are going to freeze to death if we don't get help," she directed Maxine. Maxine headed back inside. Valerie could see her talking to the clerk, wearing her best waitress smile. He was shaking his head although he had pulled out a notebook from under the cash register and was leafing through it, presumably looking for inspiration or phone numbers. Valerie flicked on the rear light and opened some of the carriers. The cats looked miserable. Shivering, they sat with their chests pulled in tightly as they tried to retain their body heat.

"I'm sorry," she said. "We're trying. Please hang in there."

When she turned back, the store clerk was on the phone and Maxine was running back to the van.

"Someone's coming," she said. "The clerk got him out of bed. He lives a couple blocks away."

"Is he a locksmith?" Valerie asked hopefully.

"No. He's a pipefitter. That's the best we can do. Whether it'll be good enough . . . " Maxine shrugged her shoulders.

Valerie sent Maxine back into the store to wait. After what seemed an age, a pickup truck pulled into the store lot and a man in a dirty flight jacket and a cap with earmuffs came over to the van. By now, as Valerie spoke, her teeth actually chattered.

"See what I can do," he said, getting into the driver's seat. He plopped his tool box on the engine housing. Valerie sat sideways in the passenger seat, unable to stop shivering, watching him. There wasn't a peep from the back of the van. She knew that if they didn't get the van moving soon these cats wouldn't make another peep ever again.

The repairman had both hands and most of his head under the steering column. He was finding all sorts of treasures up there and throwing them out onto the van floor. First a piece of bent metal, then some crumpled papers, finally a plastic sandwich bag.

Valerie didn't have to put her nose into the bag and sniff the green substance to know what it was. The van's previous owner, or perhaps the mechanic who had just serviced the van, had hidden his marijuana stash behind the wheel. Great, she thought, that's all we need!

The pipefitter seemed not to have noticed. Casually, Valerie reached down and, not thinking of anything better to do with it for the moment, stuffed the pouch into her pocket. The repairman popped his head out from under the steering wheel.

"Let's give that a try," he said. For a moment Valerie thought he meant the marijuana. Then he turned the key and the engine throbbed into action.

Maxine heard the noise and came running out of the store to join her in thanking the man whose sleep they had interrupted.

"Always a pleasure to help beautiful ladies in distress," he said, refusing the twenty dollar bill Valerie held out to him. "Now whatever you do, do not turn this ignition off until you get wherever you're going. And, if I were you, my first stop would be a dealership or an auto repair place."

"Don't you worry, we'll be careful," Maxine said.

In minutes they felt the heat blowing through the vents. Valerie pulled her socks off and rubbed her feet as Maxine took her turn at the wheel and sent them back toward the highway. As soon as they were up to speed, Valerie rolled down the window, took the pouch from her pocket, and let the green leaves blow out of it onto the road behind.

"What was that?" Maxine asked.

"Don't even ask!" Valerie said, laughing now. "That could have been our ticket to a different warm place to spend the night."

Kay had agreed to drop off a press release about the event. They'd written a rough draft, leaving blank spaces Kay had filled in after Valerie's phone call from the pay phone at the store. Miki was superstitious about doing the release in advance, but Valerie persuaded her it needed to be done or they would lose time, and timing, she knew, was everything to the press.

Holly Jensen, PETA's representative in Gainesville, Florida, and Holly's wildlife biologist friend, Cindy Bear, were camping out at the PETA office over the holidays when the materials arrived. Both women were totally committed to the philosophy of animal liberation, and hearing their statements on the air and in the print press later, Valerie had the feeling the ALF had been very lucky to have them as spokespeople for the "cat burglary."

"Surely," Jensen told a television interviewer, "the country that can send a man to the moon can find a more sophisticated way to find out how nerves work without butchering cats." She ended with a beautiful quote from Thomas Jefferson: "Until we stop harming all other living beings, we are still savages."

The next day, Kay drove into the city and called Valerie's New York number from a pay phone.

"Holly Jensen wants to show the press one of the cats," she said. "She feels that if we can show them one of Howard's victims, they'll stop being so awed by the university's claim that their precious 'science' has been interrupted."

"I'd trust her with any animal's life," Kay assured Valerie. "She doesn't want to see faces or know names, but she's willing to take the personal risk. She's a liberationist, through and through. Cindy's the same way. I believe they'd do anything to help, and they certainly want this story to be told right."

Kay's enthusiasm was contagious. Valerie agreed to the cat transfer. She had already learned that all experiences, including trips in the car, were exciting occasions for Peter, a cat who behaved more like a devoted dog. If any of the rescued cats could impress the news media, he could.

The veterinarian who examined the cats had been bewitched by Peter, too. Peter had stopped purring as the doctor's experienced hands palpated his spine.

"I can't do anything to reconnect those nerves," the vet said with disgust. "It isn't humanly possible. Whoever did this didn't have enough training or skill to know what they were doing. Call me day or night if you need anything. I'd like to undo some of the harm my colleagues have done."

Valerie returned to Washington that night with Peter. He flew back in a little carrier under her passenger seat in the main cabin. No one could see his wounds through the white plastic container, and no one suspected he was "wanted" by the police.

On December 28, 1982, *The Washington Post* ran a long article about the raid. The twelve cats who had not been operated on had indeed been purchased from the dealer AWI had talked about. They were to be "surgically impaired" after the holidays.

Howard University decried the liberation of the cats, argued over the number taken, and protested that it employs "three staff veterinarians." University spokesman Alan Hermesch told *Post* reporter Ken Ringle that cats "are routinely caged with as much food and water as they will consume." The university estimated the loss from the break-in at $2,640.

Alongside the article there appeared a photograph of Holly Jensen cradling Peter in her arms. Together, they must have won many readers' hearts.

Peter never recovered the use of his legs; like many of the Howard cats, he had to have a special protective sleeve made to prevent soreness and infection. He quickly learned how to propel himself around, and although he will never be able to jump or play like other cats, he is full of joy.

As it turned out, Shalimar had been found, safe and sound, by the time the ALF entered Howard. "How on earth was she located?" Valerie asked Miki, over a celebration meal.

"I don't know how you feel about these things, Val," Miki said, "But she was found with the help of a psychic."

"Give me a break, Miki!"

Miki shrugged. "For a radical, you can be so conservative sometimes. Even police departments use them sometimes nowadays to look for psychotic killers, you know. Anyway, someone at PETA called this woman who says she can read animals' minds, knows what they're thinking. She told them that the door had blown open the night Shalimar disappeared, and that Shalimar had crossed the road to explore in some woods. Then it had started to rain, and the rain washed out all the scents she needed to find her way back home.

"The upshot was that Shalimar was found exactly where the psychic said she'd be, about half a mile away on the other side of the woods, living under someone's house. She was very thin, very scared, and thoroughly grateful when they brought her home."

"I'd wager that this psychic's guesswork cost a pretty penny?" Valerie asked Miki, curious.

"Not a dime, Officer Skeptic. Not a dime!"

Feeling put in her place, Valerie helped herself to more vegetable steamed rice, and ate her curried chickpeas without another word.

4

A Sea Dog

The first raid had been a success! Valerie realized that pulling off this liberation felt better to her than a promotion or a raise or anything she had ever experienced as a cop. We weren't the most organized raiders in history, she thought, but we didn't do badly. Thirty-three cats were out and safe, and Americans were hearing and talking about what goes on in labs. Within twelve hours of the cat liberation at Howard, the story had made news on every radio and television station in the metropolitan area. Talk show hosts encouraged callers to vent their spleens: should the raiders be forced to "choke on a hairball?" Should they be lynched for "rating the suffering of cats over the plight of the homeless?" Or should the ALF be given an award while the experimenters were marched off to jail? Some people demanded the ALF's capture, others hoped the cats would never, ever be found.

Some newspaper reporters put work into the story. A *Post* writer discovered that the Washington Humane Society/SPCA had cited Howard repeatedly for "sanitation violations" and a failure to provide the minimum space required for animals by federal law, i.e., enough room for them to stand, sit, and turn around.

Howard countered that its facility was "accredited by the American Association of Laboratory Animal Care," a shill group originally set up to fight any "outside" regulation. Administrators produced evidence that the U.S. Department of Agriculture

(USDA) had found everything "satisfactory" inside Howard laboratories—no surprise considering the agency's track record in the Silver Spring monkeys case. (On the witness stand, the USDA inspector who inspected Taub's lab had agreed that he had not so much as counted how many primates were kept at IBR, and had "always deferred to Dr. Taub" on every aspect of the inspection.)

Although Valerie expected some calm weeks and a chance to critique this first action, it was not to be. Kay, the ALF's "mole" at PETA, had news. "Opportunity may be knocking again," Kay said as she and Valerie drove to Western Union to wire some money to New York. "A PETA volunteer seems to have come across a source you might want to interview. He knows all about the Navy's use of dogs in diving chamber experiments."

"What experiments?" Valerie asked.

"Apparently, the Navy's been using monkeys and dogs in simulated deep sea dives for about forty years. Top secret stuff. Over at the Bethesda Naval Research Institute. Gracie, the volunteer, got a call from a man she met at the Adams Morgan Community Festival. It seems this well-dressed, middle-aged man came up to her animal rights display and didn't want to go away. He just stood there, leafing through the pamphlets on the table, not really reading them, and looking awkward. She asked him if he'd like to sign up, but he said he couldn't. He was in 'a sensitive job,' but he wouldn't say what sort."

"Half the men in Washington use that line," Valerie reminded Kay.

"True," acknowledged Kay, "but, according to Gracie, this fellow wasn't a con. He seemed very upset, as if something was troubling him. After a while he asked her to write down her name and phone number, which she did. He said he might call her one day with some information that could be helpful to PETA's work. That was last spring."

"So is Gracie's mystery man in the Navy?" Valerie asked Kay.

"You got it. And what he knows is pretty hair-raising. The dogs' eardrums blow out when the pressure gauges are turned off in the chamber. All sorts of ugly stuff."

"Isn't it a bit of a coincidence that he'd call her now?" Valerie raised an eyebrow at Kay. "Perhaps he does work for the government, but in law enforcement."

"Maybe, but Gracie's judgment of people is usually pretty good. Mystery man told her that hearing about the raid on Howard helped him make up his mind. He wants to know if she can find the ALF and have them get into the Navy labs and get this one particular dog out for him!"

"What did she say?" Valerie asked Kay.

"That she had no idea how. Which is true. It was a stroke of luck that she called me. I got his number from her and told her never to mention it again. She said, 'Fine.' "

"What do you think? Shall we risk contacting him?" Valerie asked.

Kay shrugged. "I'm going to take the easy way out and leave that to you. You're the boss. I have grandchildren due for lunch, and they'll be screaming the house down if I don't get home soon and start cooking. If you need me, call."

At midday Valerie took a reluctant Mimi to the airport to catch her plane home. The cold had eased up, at least for a day or two. Driving over the Woodrow Wilson Bridge onto the Parkway, they admired the Potomac river, shining silver in the sunlight, reflecting the perfect blue sky. Here and there, people were actually out boating.

"I'll try to keep mom and grandma off your back," Mimi said when Valerie hugged her goodbye.

After Mimi had left, Valerie called Kit, the Navy man. He answered the phone on the first ring. Valerie had looked up his number in the Haines Directory before calling, just to be sure it cross-referenced to a residential listing. She didn't want to be phoning in to the FBI headquarters downtown.

Yes, he would meet her. By the Lincoln Memorial at 2:30 P.M. Alone. So much for Valerie's first opportunity to see Sean since his return from Florida.

Valerie parked her van about a quarter of a mile from the Memorial, near the Smithsonian metro stop, and walked back past the Washington Monument, where a handful of visitors stood despondently by the "Closed" sign. No bird's-eye view of the Capitol would be theirs today. The water in the Reflecting Pool was black with weed-killer, and the sign at the rim read, "Danger. Wash hands if in contact with water." Ducks who couldn't read were preening their feathers and drinking, heads tilted back into the sun with each beakful of insecticide. At the end of the walkway a man yelled at his Chesapeake Bay retriever, "Get out, Sammy, get out of there!" The dog, full of energy and completely inattentive, bounced through the shallow pool, his webbed paws padding along the bottom, enjoying the day.

Valerie made her way down to the grassy slope where the Vietnam veterans keep their twenty-four-hour-a-day vigil. At a folding table beside their army pup tent, they sat collecting signatures on a petition to Congress asking for an investigation into the whereabouts of their buddies still missing in action. Valerie signed the petition under the watchful gaze of a U.S. Park policeman who sat, mounted on a bay gelding, watching to make sure the veterans didn't violate the provisions of their permit by dozing off in the warm sun.

From the rows of American flags on the knoll, Valerie had a clear line of sight to the east steps of the Monument, where she had arranged to meet Kit. He arrived just before 2:30, dressed in his Navy uniform, as she had asked him to do. He was carrying a black briefcase.

Kit was short and about twenty pounds overweight. Valerie guessed he was in his late forties. She left him waiting there long enough to be convinced that he was unaccompanied.

"Follow me quickly, Kit," Valerie said, coming up alongside him and not slowing down. She led him down the embankment into a copse of saplings near the fountain. Although the trees were bare, they were close enough together that the pair could sit among them without being seen.

"Hi!" he said nervously, as soon as they sat on the stone wall among the trees. Kay's friend was right, Valerie thought, he does have a worried but honest face.

"Hi," Valerie answered him. "Sorry to do this, but I must ask you to open your jacket, pull up your clothes until I can see your stomach and chest, and hand me your briefcase and your wallet. I need to make sure you're not wired and that you are who you say you are."

Kit shifted uncomfortably. "Is that really necessary?" he asked politely. "I mean, I don't know who you are."

"I understand, but yes, it is." Valerie had years of practice being firm. This was like a traffic stop, or a "stop and frisk," that she'd done dozens of times. "I have everything to lose, so the odds have to shift. And I need your promise you won't attempt to find out who I am."

Kit sighed. "All right," he said. "I suppose you know what you're doing."

With some embarrassment, Kit pulled open his jacket and raised his navy sweater, shirt and undershirt up to his armpits and showed Valerie his torso and chest. Then he handed her his briefcase and his wallet. If FBI agents are this clever, she thought, I'll turn myself in. With forty minutes notice, Kit had produced a Navy uniform that fit properly, a wallet that included various credit cards in the name he had given her over the phone, a driver's license with an address that matched the one Valerie had found in the Haines, and, among his photographs, one of himself as a little boy sitting on a dock beside a curly-coated black dog.

"OK, tell me what it is you think I can help you with," Valerie said matter-of-factly.

His lips pursed into little bundles, Kit said resolutely, "I hope you have a strong stomach, because it isn't a pretty story." For two hours he told her everything he knew. On his first tour of duty, in 1952, he had been aboard a carrier in the South Sea islands, part of the post-World War II push to test weapons for a stronger U.S. arsenal. He had watched monkeys being sealed into pods in the sand, and goats and pigs strapped to the topdecks of boats, their unprotected bodies exposed to blasts of radiation. He had seen firsthand how those who survived had succumbed to the effects of the radiation. He described hollow-eyed animals, still alive, but with 90 percent of the skin burned from their bodies, animals in such pain that he could never forget. He had watched a mini-Hiroshima reenacted in peacetime on peaceful beings who had declared no war on the human race.

Eighteen years later, with those experiences a nasty memory, Kit had been transferred to Bethesda Naval Research Institute and the horror had begun all over again. Kit's position gave him access to the laboratories but no say-so. He had quietly befriended the dogs but could do nothing to save them from being strapped into solid-metal diving chambers, or from the pain and death that followed.

"The few times any of the laboratory workers have protested the animals' treatment," he told Valerie, smoothing back his thin brown hair, "they've been warned not to let their emotions interfere with their work or they could suffer repercussions. One man lost his job when he reported an animal technician for punching monkeys in the face."

It was pitch dark when they left the park. The starlings roosting above them had stopped their chattering and settled in for the night. Valerie had been so appalled by and caught up in Kit's earnest recounting of what he had witnessed that she had barely noticed the deep night coldness that had descended again on the city.

She had no doubts about Kit. He was 100 percent real. Unfortunately, so were the documents he had left with her. So were the experiences he had told her of with such feeling. She found it hard to think of society as civilized.

Kit shook hands with Valerie under the trees, and she watched him walk away toward the Tidal Basin, a career Navy man whose solid little steps were taking him back to the world he had known for thirty years. It had taken guts to contact the ALF. When he had disappeared, Valerie tucked the papers into her coat and made her way to the metro. Although she knew no one was behind her, she forced herself to follow protocol: to take the escalator down, wait fifteen minutes, and then come up again, before approaching her van. What Kit had told her affected her deeply. She knew she had to get things organized without a moment to lose.

Valerie's sleep that night was punctuated by a violent dream of dogs thrashing about on the ground. Men in uniforms laughed at her as she tried to stop the blood that spurted from the dogs' nostrils and ears as the pressure crushed their sinuses to a pulp. She argued with them, wrestled with them, and cried over the sea of mangled bodies she couldn't help.

A little after 4:00 A.M., she awoke. Kit's papers lay on the dining room table, but she couldn't look at them again. She had read and reread the cold, clinical descriptions of animal agony. She could still hear Kit's voice, when she asked him why these tests go on, year after year.

"It has nothing to do with science," he had said. "Nothing to do with animals. It has to do with funding for the command. Ask anyone: the treatment for divers suffering from the bends hasn't changed one iota in the forty years these tests have been going on. But no one would ever suggest cutting their own command's funds just because they're not finding anything new. That would mean eliminating staff. The fewer positions, the less power and prestige for the command. That's all, that's everything."

As he talked, Valerie realized that Kit was in love, in love with a little black dog who reminded him of the schnauzer in the photograph he kept in his wallet. A dog he had grown up with and still remembered as once being the center of his life. For a Navy man to express such feelings of affection for an animal would make him a laughing stock. For him to try to save that animal from impending death in a diving chamber could mean a court martial and the end of his career. He had let himself look foolish in front of her because he was desperate to help this dog, and she admired him for that.

"I've watched so many of them go to their deaths," he told Valerie. "I know this one shouldn't be any different, but that's not how I feel. I've played with him, fed him, tried to look after him. Every time his number has come up, I've moved him back in the line. But he's in bad shape. The kennel's overcrowded and he's been attacked twice, badly, by the larger dogs. I can't keep him back any longer. They're going to dive him any day now because they don't want to waste him, and I'm too attached to him to let him suffer like that."

Valerie asked Kit if "his" dog would come willingly if she went in to get him.

"He hasn't the strength to struggle. When you see him, you'll know what I mean. He's weak as a wilted flower and can't hang on much longer. He may not even be able to walk at all, because he hasn't been out of his cage the whole year he's been there."

Kit had gone through his files, explaining the tables that listed the simulated depth of the chamber drops and the number of hours, sometimes days, the dogs survived after being pulled out of the tanks. He painstakingly described how the United States military has waged an unseen war on animals for hundreds of years. How the Department of Defense (DOD) and Veterans Administration (VA), together, are the federal government's second largest user (after the National Institutes of Health) of animals, and have used dogs, cats, mules, pigs, sheep—all kinds of animals—in everything from mustard gas to radiation experiments.

The facts were all there: the military had buried monkeys alive at various distances from the Nevada nuclear test sites and left them there to be irradiated when they exploded nuclear bombs. They exploded sheep and dropped pigs off high platforms. They exposed monkeys and beagles to total-body irradiation. At the Naval Medical Institute in Maryland, rats' backs were shaved, covered with ethanol, and "flamed" for ten seconds.

Kit's briefcase contained pages and pages of paperwork detailing dog-, cat-, rat-, and monkey-drowning experiments, conducted by the Navy directly and under contract with universities far and wide. The experiments went back at least forty years.

"Since as early as 1854," the Navy Diving Dog Experiments report read, "scientists have speculated about the effect and ultimate treatment of decompression sickness in humans. Successful treatment in humans has been reported and used in various forms via the U.S. Navy Tables published in the mid-1940s.

"Dogs have been used to study the physiological effects of decompression since 1937 and anywhere from 2-100 dogs may be used in a simple experiment." Someone had typed in a cautionary note: "Be advised, findings in dogs cannot be extrapolated to man."

"Decompression experiments can involve severe pain as a result of congestion in the respiratory tract, abdominal bloating, lung hemorrhages, and ruptured spinal cords." Valerie knew from Miki about the campaigns that led twenty-three states to ban the decompression chambers used in dog pounds and shelters. They were too inhumane to be used to destroy animals, Miki had said. She continued to read:

Three Common Experiments:

1. Dogs are placed in stereotaxic devices, the skin and muscle over their nose and skull is peeled back, electrodes are inserted into the skull, and then the dogs are subjected to simulation diving. After the experiment the animals are killed with a cardiac injection of potassium chloride.

2. Animal is intubated and decompressed until decompression sickness occurs. Often the animal does not contract decompression sickness the first time and must be decompressed again, which can cause extreme pain due to the pressure injuries sustained in the first attempt. The animal is then perfused and brain, spinal cord, and heart are removed, frozen, and cut up.

3. Unanesthetized dogs are put in airtight boxes and given only pure oxygen to breathe—after 48-90 hours the dogs die spontaneously or they are killed.

Kit also included a sheet from the Diver's Action Network called "The Number and Severity of Human Cases of Decompression Sickness," reporting that "approximately 400-500 minor cases of decompression sickness or 'bends' are reported annually. The cases are all recreational and the injury is temporary. Cases that result in permanent disability or death are 'very few.' "

Valerie made a cup of tea and watched the dawn. She had never liked sleeping late, but Kit's information made it difficult to sleep at all. Kit was too timid to do the deed himself, but he had mapped it all out. He had described when and how to enter the Navy Compound and where to find the little black dog. It seemed much too simple.

At 7:30, Valerie called Sonia Karelli, the city administrator who had been part of the Howard team, and asked to meet her at the Hot Shoppes cafeteria in Bethesda.

"I'm supposed to be at work by nine," Sonia said.

"Can you take leave?" Valerie asked her. "I'm planning a small dinner party and I need your help."

"Well in that case, I suppose so. Almost everyone is still out for the holidays, including my boss."

Valerie felt relieved. To make the plan work, she needed not only Sonia's help, but that of Sonia's son, Tiger, as well. Tiger was nineteen and as big as a house, the kind of young man it's handy to have around if you're moving grand pianos, Sonia always told people. Tiger also had one of the softest hearts you could ever hope to find. His real name was Timothy, but the nickname his mother had given him when he was a toddler was macho enough to stick as he grew. Tiger's father had been killed in the service and Sonia had raised him by herself, never remarrying. Whatever she had put in her kid's breakfast cereal, it had produced a son she could be proud of.

They ordered hash browns, toast, and coffee and Valerie told Sonia what she had in mind. Sonia was delighted.

"I'll skip work any day I can get away with it for this sort of thing!" Sonia said, "Tiger's college tuition is paid by his dad's insurance, so I don't have to worry even if they fire me. As for Tiger, he'll help in a New York minute. He has football practice this afternoon, but he'll be free by the time you need him."

Before transferring into public works, Sonia had been a public relations specialist for the county's retired persons' volunteer program. Sipping coffee, she mulled over the television reporters she knew to be respectful of the plight of the elderly. Perhaps their compassion extended to animals in trouble, too. Sonia's job would be to call them, request confidentiality, and ask them to film the condition of the little dog if the ALF got him to safety. The reporters knew her well enough to give her a chance to make her case.

If what Kit had told Valerie about the dog's condition was accurate, there would be no time to get him to New York state and the veterinarian she had found there. Tiger's job would be to take the dog to the after-hours emergency veterinary clinic in Rockville and get him treated under some pretext. She knew from

Miki that emergency clinic vets are always in a rush, never expect you to be a regular client, and are too busy to ask lots of questions. If the vet confirmed the dog's condition, the ALF could give the report to PETA to use against the Navy.

"My husband would be pleased," said Sonia. "He was in the Army. You know they always want to beat Navy! Can we call the little dog 'Vanguard?' That was his unit's code name in the war."

"Absolutely!" Valerie agreed. Vanguard had a ring of success to it.

As they left the coffee shop, Valerie stopped to call a friend of hers on the force and decline his invitation to go as part of a group to a football game at RFK Stadium. Valerie was seeing less and less of her police friends, not only for security reasons (she didn't want to have to explain her comings and goings to them, of course) but because she was breaking the rules and getting close to her cell members. She knew it was a risk, but she already felt herself so drawn into friendships, particularly with Miki, Kay, Sonia, and Maxine, that she had stopped resisting.

Finding a vehicle that couldn't be traced back to her or anyone else in the unit was something Valerie had hoped to work on in the calm she expected after the Howard storm. Now there wasn't time. Ginger's Volkswagen seemed more innocuous-looking than either of the vans, so Valerie swapped vehicles with her.

Valerie stopped at a florist and bought two enormous bunches of their cheapest flowers, and propped them up on her passenger seat. Then she drove up Rockville Pike and through the main gates into the huge Navy compound. Out of sight under her collar, for good luck, she pinned the enamel dog brooch G had given her before she left camp in England.

The enthusiastic young guard in the immaculately starched uniform had seen there were no military stickers on the car. With his white-gloved hand, he motioned Valerie to a stop. She rolled down the window, flowers clearly visible.

"Yes, ma'am?" the guard bent his head and looked into the car.

"Officer," Valerie offered, crumpling her lips and trying to look as if she was bravely fighting back the tears. "My father's in the cardiac ward. I'm going to visit him."

"You go ahead, ma'am," he said, stepping back smartly and waving her through. No sensible man wants a woman in tears on his hands. As she drove on, Valerie envisioned spending the next twenty years in a military prison cell. Did they send civilians to the brig?

The Bethesda Naval Hospital, which shares its acreage with the Naval Research Institute, is where President Bush has his physicals, President Reagan had his polyps removed, and where many presidents before them have come to be examined and treated. The imposing triad of towering buildings is surrounded by smaller buildings and massive lawns, which stretch out in front and at the sides of the complex. There is a huge circular driveway, with many inroads branching off from it, and uniformed guards occupy entrance posts throughout the complex.

To reach Building A-14, her target, Valerie would have to turn away from the hospital. In her rearview mirror, she was pleased to see a stream of traffic coming in off the street, occupying the guard's attention. For the moment the gods had chosen to smile down on the ALF.

Valerie had memorized the route Kit had described so carefully. Past the helicopter pad, turn right, past the mini-reactor on the left, take the second small roadway on the right. Go through the parking lot, turn left at the bottom of the hill, and park. The back door of the building will be directly in front of you.

Valerie pulled up in the parking spot Kit had said would be safe, turned off the ignition, and sat there until the time when he said it would be best to enter the lab without being seen.

He had said that unless there was an emergency, which wasn't often, all the technicians and other staff went to lunch at noon. Valerie looked at her watch. Almost twelve minutes past twelve. Perfect. She had a good fifteen minutes to grab Vanguard and escape before they returned.

Kit had warned her to avoid, at all costs, the man in charge of the lab, a colonel. Usually he only came through the lab once or twice a week. He was a ruddy-faced cartoon figure of a military man, who called Asians "gooks," thought women should stick to their customary places, and was completely callous toward animals.

Getting out of the car, Valerie felt as if she was on center stage. After all, it was broad daylight. She had decided to wear a brown wig that made her look very ordinary, almost frumpish. It had seemed perfectly realistic when she tried it on, but now she felt sure it looked absurdly false, as if she were balancing a lampshade on her head.

Was it her imagination, or did the two men who were sitting smoking cigarettes on the hood of a car two rows up give her a long look? One was wearing a blue animal-caretaking smock. Valerie wondered if he would remember her later. Perhaps he'd try to stop her if she managed to come out of that door with Vanguard on a leash.

Valerie walked up the steps to the back door, praying Kit had remembered to prop it open. If the door were closed, she would know something was wrong. Perhaps Vanguard had already been killed or someone had decided not to go to the mess hall.

The back door to the lab was being kept ajar by a garbage can, just as Kit had promised. Valerie slipped inside and pushed the can back so the door closed behind her. Now nothing was out of place.

There was no one about. So far so good. She repeated Kit's instructions silently to herself: "Walk straight ahead, toward the front of the building. About two hundred feet ahead, you'll see a sign marked 'Level B stairs.' Go down the stairs and you'll exit into a hallway off the main kennel."

Following the directions was easy. Downstairs, she wasn't prepared for the noise of the dogs. It was almost deafening. Each bark seemed to bounce off the concrete block walls and ricochet across the long room. If six guards had shouted at her to stop, she wouldn't have heard a word. She walked down the kennel runs, at any moment expecting to feel a hand plant itself firmly on her shoulder.

"You'll find him near the end. You can't miss him." Kit had

said. "They've written 'Snuff' beside the number on the tag on his cage. That's their name for him, and their idea of a joke."

There must have been over a hundred dogs in the place. Valerie tried not to look directly at them until she was halfway down the aisle. She had read in Kit's papers exactly how these dogs were to die, and she felt she was betraying them. Now, nearing the end of the kennel, she forced herself to look into the runs.

Most were beagles, but there were also mixed-breed dogs, and a beautiful cocker spaniel. Valerie wondered why Kit hadn't mentioned her. She would certainly stick out in your mind, Valerie thought.

Some of the dogs seemed "lab bred." Never having known human affection, they cowered back in their cages when Valerie walked near them. Others came forward, barking and wagging their tails, desperate for contact.

All the dogs were crowded together, seven or eight to a ten-by-four-foot run designed to house two. Many of them were cut up. One smooth-coated dog's face was badly swollen from puncture wounds on his cheeks and around his left eye. Another's ears hung in tatters like a shredded curtain.

Kit had said that the Navy was renovating three quarters of the building. They had refused to reduce their dog inventory to accommodate the loss of space. Dog fights, he said, were an everyday occurrence, and sometimes dogs died of their wounds.

Valerie reached the end of the kennel. There was no sign of Vanguard. How could she have missed him?

The din was nerve-racking. Valerie turned around, half expecting to find the military police standing, arms crossed, waiting for her to acknowledge their presence. Relieved to find that, for the moment at least, she was the only human being in sight, she retraced her steps, peering at each cage card hanging on the run doors. Numbers, more numbers, but no sign of "Snuff."

As she passed the fourth run, out of the corner of her eye, Valerie caught sight of what looked like a patch of black wool on the ground in the far corner of the run. She stepped back and looked again. Behind the huge panting frames of five large male shepherds, who clamored for her attention by jumping at the cage door and barking, there was a dog tightly curled into a ball.

Not stopping to gauge whether the dogs were friendly or not, Valerie undid the latch and squeezed past them into the run. She wasn't sure if Vanguard was dead or alive until she bent down and, trying to keep the other dogs away, pulled him up into her arms and felt his breathing against her chest. He certainly was a bloody mess. He wouldn't be able to walk. The leash in her pocket would serve no purpose.

The other dogs were looking out of their runs as if to say, "Take me. Why aren't you taking me? What did I do wrong?"

Valerie tried to ignore them.

She made her way out again, cradling Vanguard for what she knew might be a few precious moments of nothing more than hope. She moved as fast as she dared on the damp, cement floor. Vanguard's wet coat smelled of the urine she could feel soaking through her jacket. Please let me get him out of here, she repeated, over and over again, as she took the folded plastic shoulder bag out from under her jacket and tucked him into it as quickly as she could, her hands clumsy with haste.

As she zipped the bag three-quarters closed, two weary brown eyes looked up at her. This little dog was too worn out to object or to try to comprehend.

Valerie hadn't had time to look at her watch. As the distance between her and the upstairs door shrank, she wondered how long she had taken. The door seemed a mile away down the long hall, but she was so worried that Vanguard wouldn't make it alive to the waiting car that all sense of security left her. She walked boldly. Vanguard's body seemed weightless in her arms and she could feel his shallow breathing between her heartbeats.

An absurd thought entered Valerie's head for a moment as she neared the exit: perhaps the Navy band would be playing "Hurrah for the free" in the parking lot when she opened the door. Here at least was one little being who, if she was lucky, would be free. You're going nuts, she told herself. As if in slow motion, she stepped through the door and into the brightness of the early afternoon.

The two smoking men were gone. There wasn't a soul in the parking lot. It was as if a shield separated Valerie and Vanguard from the rest of the world. Just give me a few more minutes, she prayed, as her feet moved toward Ginger's car. Once inside the vehicle, time began to behave normally again, and Valerie found herself pulling out of the parking lot.

At the stop sign behind the hospital she pulled over and lay Vanguard, still in his bag, on the floor, and covered him with her sweater. Making sure there was no one looking, she rolled down the window and tossed the flowers over the embankment. Visiting time was over.

The guard didn't give Valerie a second glance as she drove onto Rockville Pike and back into civilian traffic. Kit could have done this himself, she thought, but he wasn't the type. At least he had done more than the hundreds of people who had seen this place over the years—he had sought help.

Sonia was waiting in the Unitarian Church parking lot, several blocks away from the Navy compound, pacing back and forth beside her car.

"Val, you got him!" she almost screamed when she peered into the Volkswagen. "He's alive!"

"Just. He's hanging on by the skin of his teeth," Valerie told her, passing Vanguard's limp body into Sonia's lap as Sonia positioned herself behind the wheel. "We have to get help for him soon. Any luck with the press?"

"Two reporters I know have shown up. They're in the DGS Grocery parking lot down the street, waiting. One from Channel Five and one from Channel Nine. Plus, I called Channel Four out of the blue and asked if a reporter would meet me and they've sent someone, too."

"Oh, God, that's a bit chancy. Well, make them blow the lid off this thing, but don't take more than fifteen minutes!" Valerie called out after her.

It was her turn to pace until Sonia came back.

"All's well, except for one problem. I'll tell you about it at home," Sonia called from her car when she returned to the church. They had agreed to rest Vanguard at her house until six o'clock, when the emergency hospital opened its doors. Valerie followed her home, scared the little dog might not make it.

Once in Sonia's bedroom, Valerie tried to get the black mop of curls that was Vanguard to stand, but he didn't have the energy. His hair was missing in so many places he looked like a patchwork quilt. His body smelled of infection from the innumerable bite marks on his flanks and face. His ears smelled, too, and were thick with brown wax. His breathing was shallow. He was physically and mentally exhausted.

Sonia brought out food and water, but Vanguard seemed not to recognize it. He licked her face with his tongue as she bent over him, then his head returned to the pillows and his eyes closed.

"We should have called him Schnoodle," Sonia said. "Look at that wonderful schnauzer face and that kinky, soft poodle fur. He won't be with us too long, though, if we don't get some Miracle Mash into him."

Sonia left for the kitchen. When she came back, Valerie propped Vanguard in her lap while Sonia emptied a syringeful of grayish mush into his mouth. He wobbled like a ninety-year-old man, but let the food slide down his throat without protest.

"That's creamed brown rice, yeast, iron, molasses, B-12, and vitamin C," Sonia said. "My specialty for almost any animal in trouble. Full of goodness and easy on the stomach. God, is he a mess."

Sonia pulled the oversize pillows off her bed and put them on the carpet against the wall. They let Vanguard sink into them, then covered him with a blanket and let him sleep. He looked like a little black angel asleep on a fluffy white cloud.

"Let's hope he pulls through," Valerie said as they crept from the room.

Sonia made coffee, and they drank it at the kitchen table, surrounded by potted plants and packing crates. Sonia's specialty was homemade boysenberry wine. She had finished her holiday sales just in time to help with Howard.

"So, how did it go with the news people?" Valerie asked.

"Really well, except for one thing," said Sonia. "They were all genuinely shocked at Vanguard's condition, genuinely sympathetic. They didn't like what the Navy had already done to him, let alone what was next on his dance card. I have no doubt they'll ask the powers-that-be over there some tough questions.

"They knew I wanted anonymity and they agreed, so I'm pretty sure the only shots they took were of Vanguard, not of me. But, as I was pulling out of the lot, I saw the guy from Channel Four still shooting. I think he has my license plate on film."

"Christ, you've got to call him," Valerie told Sonia. This was a major screw-up. Why hadn't Sonia said something right away? "You have nothing to lose except a jail term. Beg him to erase the film. Promise him you'll give him an exclusive on anything the ALF does next. Promise him almost anything."

Sonia looked crushed. She had never seen Valerie so agitated. She went into the living room to call while Valerie got up and, trying to calm down, rooted around in the refrigerator for the chili and crackers Sonia had suggested for a late lunch. As she laid out the napkins and bowls, Sonia returned with a long face.

"He says he won't erase it. He's adamant." Sonia said, "What the hell do we do? If the police see my license plate on TV, they'll subpoena the tape."

Sonia chewed thoughtfully while Valerie contemplated the logistics of a break-in at the TV studio. Sonia spoke up while Valerie was lost in thought. Tiger had a friend who was majoring in television arts at the University of Baltimore, she said. Students anxious to pick up on-the-job experience often volunteered at local stations. There was a good chance he could get into the Channel Four newsroom and seize or erase the tape.

"We'll have Tiger get him on the phone as soon as he finishes taking Vanguard to the vet." Valerie could see Sonia relax a little as she placed her hopes on the plan.

At a little after five, Tiger came in from football practice. Ever polite, he shook hands across the table.

"Want some chili, honey?" his mother asked.

"That's OK, I'll get some later," Tiger told her. "How's the little guy?"

They crept into the room and put on the light. Only the pink tip of Vanguard's nose was visible over the blanket. He didn't move.

"Boy," said Tiger. "He looks really out of it. I'd better get him on over to the doc's."

"Give a false name and address, and pay cash." Valerie coached. "It shouldn't be a problem. Tell the vet the dog belongs to your roommate, who's out of town. Say you need them to write down everything that's wrong so you can explain it to your roommate when he gets back. That should fly."

Tiger was back within the hour to say that the vet had told Tiger to report his roommate to the humane society. Dr. James Hendrickson had also written a damning report. Vanguard was "suffering from scabies (mange), contagious skin inflammation, infected fight wounds, and debilitation," he wrote, estimating that the condition had become serious about four weeks earlier. Dr. Hendrickson, not in the least bit suspicious of his client's story, had also dutifully recorded Vanguard's ear tattoo number (326) on the report. The Navy was sunk.

Because of the license plate fiasco, Valerie knew it was too risky for Sonia to keep Vanguard—even temporarily. Her hopes were on "Rita Rabbit," a wildlife rehabilitator who had a large house on a parcel of land in Frederick, Maryland. Rita didn't work, unless you count feeding dozens of ever-open beaks belonging to birds who had run afoul of everything from city traffic to plate glass windows. Luckily for Vanguard, winter is the one time there aren't baby birds, baby squirrels, baby opossums, and baby you-name-them competing for Rita's attention.

Her shingle read, "Where hawks and doves live under one roof," and on Valerie's only visit to Rita's place she wondered if she'd entered the twilight zone. She and Sean had driven out on a summer evening to find Rita and her husband trying to teach young orphaned thrushes to feed. They had the light on in the bedroom and the window open. They held the baby birds at chin level, smack up against their faces. As insects flew into the room, attracted to the light, Rita and her husband stood on the bed, ready to lunge forward, mouths open, as if to swallow each bug who came near, holding aloft the boxes of open-mouthed thrush babies they were trying to persuade to mimic their "feeding" movements. It was too silly.

Valerie telephoned Rita from a gas station on Route 40.

"Rita, this is Val. Are you expecting anyone this afternoon?"

"No, we're a full house, I'm afraid."

"Could I stop by?"

"By all means."

Valerie and Sonia were there within forty minutes. Rita looked Vanguard over and shook her head.

"He'll pull through with lots of love and warmth and care." She brought out B-12 and antibiotics.

"Later," she said, "he'll have to be shaved, bathed, dried with fresh cotton, and kept warm. He's just a bone bag, an infected bone bag."

She drew a syringeful of lactated Ringers solution, parted Vanguard's matted fur, and injected the solution under his skin. He didn't move. From the refrigerator she took a pot of gravy-covered lentil roast and offered him some on a tongue depressor. He wasn't at all interested.

"I knew Navy life was rough," Rita said. "My brother used to complain about boot camp, but they didn't do this to him." She was able to get Vanguard to lick some ice water from her finger. Then he collapsed on the mattress she had placed on the floor for him and fell fast asleep. She covered him with a comforter.

That night Valerie watched the local news anxiously. There was no sign of Sonia's license plate and the reporters were sympathetic. Each station had requested permission to enter the labs and see conditions for themselves. The Navy refused to let them through the door. Now the public and the press knew the military had things to hide, and Valerie knew she *had* to go back.

Valerie figured she'd have to wait at least several days before returning to the Navy kennel. She didn't want to give them time to install security devices, but for a government bureaucracy that would take quite a while. For the moment, she guessed the place would be teeming with security personnel and an investigation would be in progress. Most likely they already knew Vanguard had disappeared during daylight hours.

As it happened, the reporters continued to pressure the Navy to see the military kennels. Three days after the raid, the Navy's public relations machine got itself in gear and invited camera crews to the facility. They had cleaned it up and reduced their dog inventory.

The camera crews rolled down the hall. Not surprisingly, one of the dogs they focused on was the beautiful golden cocker spaniel. She stood up against the cage bars and "talked" directly into the camera. From that moment on, the Navy's phones rang off the hooks. People called relatives and friends who had missing cocker spaniels, animal shelters called other animal shelters, and everybody began calling the news stations to say, "I know a cocker spaniel who was lost. I *must* know where that dog came from."

Sonia had said right after the news: "Val, I'd love to get my hands on that cocker; I know she must have belonged to someone, and maybe we could reunite her with him or her. Maybe we could get a few of the other dogs out, too."

"Let's do it!" Valerie agreed.

The next night a small group gathered in Kay's living room. Otto, the ALF's two-time driver, had bought a cheap van and "ghost" registered it in Pennsylvania, to a nonexistent person at a nonexistent address. If someone "ran" the tags, they would never pin the vehicle on its owners.

The $800 spent to buy it came out of Valerie's savings. Otto knew cars, so Valerie didn't fear they'd end up with a lemon. The van was to be kept in Otto's garage and only brought out for ALF missions, but Otto said it had a solid transmission, heavy-duty suspension, and ran like a cheetah. Kit had peeled off a "Go Navy" bumper sticker from his car for Valerie to glue onto the van's rear bumper, and given her some Navy manuals to place on the driver's side of the dashboard, where they would be visible to the gate guard.

Again, Valerie decided that women would draw less attention of the wrong kind than men for a second foray into the research facility. Since Washington was host to every embassy and military group imaginable, and innumerable security guard companies, it had been easy to pick two navy enlisted personnel female dress uniforms at Jimmy Emm's Uniform Store.

Valerie met with Kit later that night in the parking lot of the DGS grocery store. He was elated. How was Vanguard? Would he recover? He handed Valerie a poem called "Rags." "I know it's sentimental," he said, apologetically, "but read it. It sums up how little the military's use of animals has changed."

Valerie did as he asked.

We called him "Rags." He was just a cur,
But twice, on the Western Line,
That little old bunch of faithful fur
Had offered his life for mine.
And all that he got was bones and bread,
Or the leavings of soldier grub,
But he'd give his heart for a pat on the head,
Or a friendly tickle and rub.

But we mustered out, some to beer and gruel,
And some to sherry and shad,
And I went back to the Sawbones School,
Where I was still an undergrad.

One day they took us budding M.D.'s
To one of those institutes
Where they demonstrate every new disease
By means of bisected brutes.

They had one animal tacked and tied
And slit like a full-dressed fish,
With his vitals pumping away inside
As pleasant as one might wish.
I stopped to look like the rest, of course,
And the beast's eyes leveled mine
His short tail thumped with a feeble force,
And he uttered a tender whine.

It was Rags, yes, Rags! who was martyred there,
Who was quartered and crucified,

And he whined that whine which is doggish prayer
And he licked my hand—and died.
And if there's no heaven for love like that,
For such four-legged fealty—well!
If I have any choice, I tell you flat,
I'll take my chance in hell.

When she finished, Valerie told him it wasn't over: she was going back in.

"The cocker spaniel's scheduled to dive in eleven days," Kit said. "The Navy's going crazy over all the calls coming in."

Kay, the ALF's "mole" at PETA, had mobilized PETA's media person to start calling the press and urging people who had lost dogs, or knew of lost dogs matching that description, to go to the Naval facility and demand to see the cocker spaniel.

But the Navy refused entrance to everybody and stonewalled reporters. Kit had hijacked a memo in which the Navy had outlined its strategy. If someone came forward who could prove ownership of the cocker spaniel, the Navy's position was to hold out. There was other news, too.

"The Navy has some cockamamie idea that Vanguard wasn't stolen from the kennel but from the infirmary," he said. "When Vanguard left that afternoon I tried to buy you some time by putting a note on his cage saying he'd been transferred to the infirmary. They took it to be the truth! Now they've moved two dogs *from* the infirmary *to* the kennel area for safekeeping."

It seemed too stupid to be true. Like the old joke about military intelligence being a contradiction in terms.

"Why were they in the infirmary in the first place?" Valerie asked.

"Well, the paperwork on their cages says they've had their legs broken and an infectious agent—some sort of bacterial warfare stuff—injected into their bones. Both of them are wearing heavy metal anklets, like pipes, over their joints, so they can't move without crying out."

"My God, are they being cared for?"

"No, not one bit. They were just dumped on the cement floor

and left there. They each have to get a separate run, so the dogs they displaced were put in other already crowded runs."

"Are there any new security measures at the kennel?" Valerie grilled him.

"No, none."

Perhaps the job wouldn't be so hard after all.

The Navy Medical Research Center sits directly across the highway from the National Institutes of Health. The DGS grocery store, where Valerie and Kit rendezvoused, is a little to the north of it. To the south is a Holiday Inn, where government and military visitors often stay. This building, Valerie discovered, had a parking lot in the back where a van could be parked near an upper entranceway and be within feet of the interior hallway.

Bear and his wife, Bobbie, were to take the rescued dogs to an animal sanctuary in the South. But first the press would have the story.

Bobbie walked into the hotel, saying she was from the apartment building next door.

"They're exterminating," she said, "and I can't breathe." She paid cash for a room and requested that it be in the back, so she "can watch my house."

The ALF's press contacts were growing, thanks to Kay's ears and eyes at PETA. A reporter from a magazine called *Midnight Express* had linked up with them, and she and a photographer joined Bobbie in the room to see if the mission was successful.

At lunchtime Valerie and Sonia, in freshly ironed uniforms, drove into the Navy compound. The gate guard waved, and they waved back, smiling. The technicians had already gone to eat. This time Kit had propped the door open with a little sliver of wood.

As she walked with Valerie toward the door, Sonia told her she felt as if a spotlight were on them. Doing jobs in the daytime was a peculiar experience. It was hard not to believe the whole world was watching. In the hall, a man with a trash can on wheels said "hi" to them as they walked briskly by, their heels clicking on the bare tile. Although this was only Valerie's second time in the building, it seemed routine to her. Through the double doors she went, Sonia in tow, and down into the din of the kennel. Valerie made a beeline for the third cage on the left where the little cocker spaniel had been, but she wasn't there. Valerie raced up and down the kennel runs, trying to find her, but only dogs of other sizes and colors looked back at her.

"Good boy! Good boy! Yes, yes, yes, we know." Valerie patted here, patted there, and allowed the dogs to nuzzle her fingers as she raced down the aisle. There was no cocker spaniel in the room, but by the back wall on the right were two dogs with metal pipes around their legs. They were both much bigger than Vanguard.

Sonia and Valerie looked at one another, wondering if they could lift the dogs. They certainly couldn't walk. Would they scream when they were picked up? How far could they carry them without dropping them?

"Vegan power," said Valerie. She reached in and picked up the bigger dog. Groaning under his weight, she staggered out of the run as Sonia held the gate for her.

"This won't work," Valerie said, dropping to her knees with the dog after a few steps. "We need a cart."

In the alcove just outside the door, Valerie had seen a cart stacked high with containers of dog food. She and Sonia heaved the fifty-pound sacks off the shelves. Thank God for spit and polish, Sonia thought: the cart's wheels were smooth as silk, and it slid quickly along the kennel floor.

The women grabbed some towels from the bin at the kennel doorway, and with them made a bed for the dogs to lie on. Together, gently, they lifted the dogs up and laid them side by side on the cart. The big brown dog whimpered, but that was all. Valerie wished they had something to sedate him with. Each bump must have been misery, but the dogs didn't complain or thrash about. They just lay there, submissive and accepting of whatever was done to them.

Having run into the man with the trashcan, Valerie knew they couldn't go back up the steps. They had to find the service elevator and hope it was working. She and Sonia turned and twisted through the labyrinth, trying to keep their sense of direction, hoping the freight elevator was beside the back door.

It was. Valerie pressed the button with her gloved finger and prayed. There was a huge clanking sound, then a rattle and a clunk. The elevator was descending. "Let's hope there's no one in it," she whispered to Sonia.

"Oh, God," Sonia breathed.

As they waited, Valerie read the sign on the door next to the elevator shaft: "Walk-In Freezer." She left Sonia with the cart, opened the door and stepped into the chilled air, saying nothing. It was a body freezer, a giant meat locker of sorts. And the meat inside it was the bodies of dogs used up in Navy experiments.

Valerie looked at the body laid out on the metal rack closest to the door. It was shiny and golden. The eyes were open and dull as marbles. Valerie was staring at a dead cocker spaniel. She slipped the military ID tag off the dog's neck and touched the cold fur. Rigor mortis had set in.

"Come on, come on," Sonia whispered from outside the freezer. The elevator had arrived. Valerie squeezed the tag into her pocket and ran out to join her.

Up they went. The bulky doors opened and they were standing in the sunlight at the loading dock. Valerie was red with anger. The cocker, who had a chance, was now gone.

The ramp down to the parking lot was too steep. The dogs would slide off the cart. There was nothing to do but pick them up and carry them to the van. As Valerie wrapped her arms around the brown dog's shoulders, a deep voice said, "Wait a minute."

The women froze.

Valerie turned to see a tall, muscular man in a dress uniform standing behind her. He appeared to be in his early forties, and his brown eyes held hers intently. After a moment that seemed like a lifetime, he said, "Sorry to startle you. I'll help you with those dogs."

With that, he placed his big square hands under the brown dog and gently lifted him, carried him to the van, and set him down on the comforters they had spread out in it. Then, just as effortlessly, he carried over the other dog and placed her next to the first one.

"There you go," he said.

Out of the corner of Valerie's eye, she saw the color start to return to Sonia's face, although her mouth was still open. Her expression made Valerie think of the tropical fish who seem to gape at you through the glass in pet store aquariums.

"Would you like me to put that cart anywhere for you?" the man asked. He was brushing the kennel dirt from his once-immaculately white shirt.

"Uh, no," Valerie said, noticing that her voice sounded annoyingly shaky. "A technician will get it. Thank you so much for your help."

"Not at all. I was glad to do it, especially since I love animals," he said with a broad, friendly smile. "Oh, no," Valerie thought, "he wants to chat."

Sonia was now in the front seat of the van. "Goodbye, and thanks," she called back to him from the window.

"Yes, thanks again, we must get going," Valerie said, walking backward toward the driver's seat. The man's eyes held hers for another long moment, then he waved farewell, turned, and headed toward the parking lot.

Valerie didn't want Sonia to go on wondering about the cocker. As they drove, she told her what she had seen. Sonia's heart had been set on that dog. "The bastards," she said softly. "The filthy bastards."

They had four minutes to compose themselves before going past the sentry post. If the guards stopped the car or looked down into the van, they would see two large dogs lying there with big clanky pieces of metal over their legs.

"Let's shape up," Valerie said. "Think positive!"

Then it was over. After two little waves and flirtatious smiles they were once again in the real world. Fifteen minutes later they were sitting in the Holiday Inn with Judy Calixto, the *Midnight Express* writer, and two very tired dogs savoring every moment on the motel Beautyrests.

On a more personal note, I became involved in this incident myself not long after the dogs were liberated. At 9:30 P.M. that night I was working at the PETA office, which at that time was headquartered in my apartment, when I received a call from a woman I later learned was Bobbie. She identified herself as an ALF member by using the code words PETA had been given. Could I come to the Holiday Inn to see something interesting that had to do with the Navy case? And did I know anyone sympathetic at the *Post* whom I could invite, too?

"There's a *Post* reporter writing a piece on the animal rights movement," I answered, although I explained that I had no idea where he stood on the issues. I was asked to call him regardless. Bobbie gave me a room number but instructed me not to give it to the *Post* reporter. I was to meet him in the lobby and bring him up with me. This I did.

Besides the Holiday Inn upstairs back parking lot that the ALF had found, there is the "regular" one fronting on Wisconsin Avenue. Pulling into that lot, I noticed a young man standing near one of the pillars there. He had a pencil and pad of paper and appeared to be writing down license numbers. It crossed my mind that he must be with hotel security checking to see if anyone had parked illegally.

Since I had met George Brady,[1] the *Post* reporter, earlier that week, I recognized him as soon as he walked into the foyer. I told him exactly what the caller had told me, and we went upstairs to the room. The *Midnight Express* reporter was packing up. She and her cameraman wished everyone well as they left. The ALF women were wearing wigs, glasses, and baggy clothing that disguised their build.

We had only been in the room for about ten minutes when we heard the prearranged number of taps on the door that told Valerie that Bear was ready to pick up the dogs for their trip south. No one answered the door; Bear didn't expect them to. Sonia's voice was filled with emotion as she told Brady and me that

---

[1]This is not his real name.

the cocker spaniel was dead and that the Navy had moved up his diving schedule to be sure he couldn't be claimed.

Brady was unimpressed. He finished the interview and left the room. I left, too, stopping in the women's room to wash my hands after petting the dogs' clammy coats. Valerie hadn't trusted Brady from the moment he walked in. She and Sonia immediately checked the hallway and then, with Bear's help, carried the dogs out to the truck.

What Valerie didn't know was that just as I pulled out of the public parking lot, I noticed Brady sitting in a car with the young man I had seen copying down license plate numbers. The two were parked in the shadows across the street from the hotel. I couldn't see what they were doing, but I was suspicious. What were they waiting for? I wondered if they had called the police.

Pretending not to see them, I pulled out of the parking lot and drove away. After two blocks, I circled back, cut off my lights, and sat watching them from the corner.

A minute later, I saw a van pull cautiously out into the road and onto Wisconsin Avenue toward the beltway. Brady's car pulled out to follow.

I realized that the van entering the roadway must be the vehicle carrying the dogs to safety. I also realized what Brady was up to, and that *I* was responsible for bringing him there. I started my car, sped up, and, when I had brought the car alongside that of Brady and his friend, gestured for them to pull over to the side of the road. They were startled but they kept going, trying to keep the van in sight. Their goal was clear: they planned to unmask the ALF.

I accelerated, cutting in front of Brady and swerving over into his lane. Brady screeched to a stop, backed up, and cut over into the other lane. My ex-husband raced cars and taught me to autocross, so I am no slouch at the wheel. I swung over to block that lane. Both cars swerved and braked again. I jumped out and raced to Brady's car. He already had his window down, allowing me to put my face close to his and yell,

"Leave them alone!"

"You're part of this, aren't you?" Brady shouted, red-faced and almost spitting. "You're trying to let them get away." He backed up his car and swung out to the left to avoid mine, but I ran in front of his car and put my hands on his hood.

"You'll have to run me over first," I bellowed at him. Brady could see that I meant it. In a rage, he flew from his car and confronted me. There we stood, a Washington *Post* reporter and the leader of a national animal rights organization, seething at each other. It was ludicrous. We were blocking the road. Several drivers being delayed honked their horns.

Bear and Bobbie were long gone, oblivious to the disturbance behind them. Fuming, Brady turned on his heel and got back into his car, and I returned to mine. I knew he would never find them now.[2]

As for Valerie, she never saw the other two dogs again, but for the following Christmas she received a special gift: a photo of Vanguard wearing a trucker's hat that goes really well with his white goatee. After his rescue, Rita shaved him to make his mange treatment easier to apply, and his hair grew back fluffy. He looks more like a poodle than a schnauzer now.

The ALF gave the Navy dogs' tags to PETA in the hope they could be traced. The cocker spaniel's records and those of the two dogs with the broken legs never checked out. The cocker had been bought by a U.S. Department of Agriculture registered Class B dealer—a person licensed to acquire animals from various sources for resale to laboratories. The dealer acquired the dog from a pound in Ohio, but the pound's records proved a dead end. They didn't list whether he'd been a stray or once had an owner.

Vanguard's trail did lead back to his front door, although it took many turns getting there. The Navy had acquired him from the Army. He had been "stationed" at Walter Reed Army Medical Center for about a year. Perhaps he picked up his mange there.

---

[2]That night, I called the *Post* and spoke with Brady's supervisor. She was curt and dismissive of my complaint that Brady had broken his promise not to attempt to identify the ALF members he was to meet. "He's entitled to go after a bigger story than the one you offered him," she said.

The Army had acquired Vanguard from an organization called Environmental Distributors, another Class B dog-dealing operation in South Carolina. Environmental Distributors had bought him from a small-town sheriff who ran a dog pound. The sheriff had picked him up from a family that owned eight other dogs.

PETA sent somebody to see Vanguard's original owners and tell them what had become of their dog. The woman who came to the door was unconcerned. "We just had too many," she said.

5

The Heart

W ithin a week of their liberation, the Navy dogs were getting help from a new quarter. Donald Barnes, the Washington, D.C., director of the National Anti-Vivisection Society, had picked up the ball in the case and was running with it. Barnes knew "the enemy" well because he had once been part of the military machine: as a civilian employee, he had irradiated monkeys for over a decade at Brooks Air Force Base in San Antonio, Texas. Somehow his sensitivity to animal suffering had not diminished, but grown.

Now Barnes fired off letters to the Secretary of Defense, the U.S. Navy Commander in Bethesda, the U.S. Department of Agriculture, and the newspapers, demanding an explanation for Vanguard's condition and the death of the cocker spaniel, and an end to the diving experiments. There is no question that his pressure was being felt; the only question was how the Navy would react. Melvyn R. Paisley, assistant secretary of the Navy, made a decision: there would be a command inquiry.

In February of 1983, Valerie called a meeting of all the participants in the Howard University action. She and the cell had learned a few things from their first "party." Now they needed to get better organized.

Valerie's savings account was still in good shape, and she had the time necessary to do scouting, but the cell needed more than that. They needed another van, safe houses for the animals, medical supplies, and contacts within the animal groups so they could learn of potential targets. Most of all, Valerie knew, they needed someone technically proficient.

One useful lead came out of the meeting. Bear remembered that when he and his wife lived in New Jersey, his landlord was mixed up in some "funny business." He told them once that he could get blank drivers' licenses. Valerie asked Bear to try to get in touch with him.

A month went by before Bear called her back to say he'd found his old landlord. "He's sending us two blanks in the mail. I'm going to the typewriter store to pick up a ball that does a computer print script. We'll need that to type in the codes."

The licenses arrived within a few days. They were from New York, which at that time didn't require a photo. If only my sergeant could see me now, Valerie thought, as she trimmed the plastic card edges to make the IDs fit into her wallet. It pained her sometimes to realize that she had lost almost all contact with her friends on the force. It was one thing to shield your own family from the truth for their own sakes. It was another to lie to your friends to protect yourself.

By the third week in March, Valerie's relationship with her family was strained. Although she had never been very close to her mother and sister, she could tell over the phone that they were unhappy with her. Her mother had replaced her old anxiety—that Valerie would be gunned down in cold blood while on duty—with a new one. There was gentle probing. Had Valerie left the police department because she was in some sort of trouble? What was she doing with herself? If she didn't have a job, why couldn't she come spend a few weeks with her parents?

Valerie decided to spend a little time at her parents' house to ease the tension. Her mother was relieved to be able to look her over in the flesh. "Ah," Valerie could feel her saying to Lettie, "she seems all right. No sign of drug or alcohol abuse, still coherent, doesn't seem pregnant or distraught."

Valerie reminded her father of what he had said about the birds on the beach at Cape Hatteras when she was very small. "Dad, you were right. I'm just going through a molt. Don't worry. I'm happy and I'm doing what's right for me."

That put him at ease, and he sided with her. At week's end, Valerie's family felt comfortable in the belief that she was working for Sean, going to landscaping shows. Her absences from home would be covered. She felt no guilt at misleading them. The important thing in her mind was that they not worry. After all, there was nothing they could do to make her new career any less risky.

A package came from England that summer every two months or so, addressed to the post office box Valerie had secured in another name. The news was mind-boggling. The ALF had embarked on a campaign called "Make Each Day Count for Freedom," replacing the big, planned raids in which large numbers of animals were rescued and "homed" with smaller actions that required very little planning and no special skills. It was a political move designed to scare off insurance companies and corporate backers, and directly target those whose livelihoods depended on animal exploitation.

Anyone with a brick, or a ball bearing and slingshot, could play. Butchers' and furriers' windows were put out all over London, Coventry, Bath—in fact, in every big city. Groups of teenagers stood casually in shop doorways, cracking jokes and sharing bags of vinegary, hot "chips." Behind them, someone would be busily gluing the door locks shut.

Delivery vehicles used by the meat trade, furriers, and dealers were the subjects of "Operation Van-dalism." There seemed to be no safe place to park. Overnight, the vans were decorated with spray paint or had "Meat is Murder" scrawled onto their sides with etching fluid. Freezer trucks carrying meat were attacked with paint stripper, and their windshields and side windows broken out with hammers.

Scotland Yard, which had begun maintaining files on the ALF in 1978, couldn't keep up. An employee of the Guy Salmon car company in Surrey, a company owned by a man who rode to hounds with the Old Surrey and Burstow foxhunt, made it known to the ALF that the company was hiring out unmarked vehicles to the police for use by the squad assigned to bust the ALF. Eleven brand-new Jaguar cars were decorated with paint stripper, costing the company over $100,000 in damages.

There was also news of several small-scale liberations: rats and mice rescued from experimentation at Lancaster and Morecombe College, with the slogan 'Rats Have Rights' painted on the doors; chickens and mice carried out of a Ministry of Agriculture lab in Cumbria; activists wearing diving equipment releasing thousands of rainbow trout into a lake from a close-confinement slaughter operation at the Kingsmead Fish Farm at Horton. Tuck and Sons in Battlesbridge, Essex, from which the ALF had previously liberated pigs and rodents bred for experimentation, found its new alarm system foiled—activists used a brace and bit and a pruning saw to cut a hole in the middle of the main door, bypassing the alarm system. They caused over $20,000 worth of damage to the administration offices and removed letterhead and invoices, which they later used to cancel supplies and services, even insurance policies, and to write damaging letters to clients.

In an action against Brocades Laboratories in Braintree, Essex, the ALF used crowbars to dismantle a brick wall. They entered the building and removed rabbits, guinea pigs, chickens, and research files that were released to the press.

Lord Houghton had told the British Parliament, "In this field, as in many others, if moderate leadership bears fruit, extremism can be contained: if it does not, then more militant action follows. It is those who say 'No' to demands for moderate change who have to pay the higher price in the end."

Although he had made the case that the young militants were "not rapists or muggers," by Christmas, 1984, over 200 British ALF members had been arrested, and twenty had been jailed.

In the U.S., Valerie's ALF unit was organized but idle, although not for lack of trying to find jobs. After a good start, several targets had not panned out despite a lot of work, and Valerie was beginning to wonder if she had been overly ambitious. Was the American ALF just a flash in the pan? Had she quit her job for nothing?

To add to all this, Prather was still out there somewhere on the loose, and presumably he still wanted to kill her. It wasn't possible for her to leave her apartment or Sean's house, or anywhere, without always being aware of that fact. As nonchalant as she tried to be about it, she knew from other officers who had gone through similar experiences that it wore you down, knowing in the back of your mind that your life was in danger. Valerie began to sleep badly, and her dreams returned: she watched from her restraint chair, helpless, as a grinning man cut monkeys' backs open or performed other nasty deeds.

Valerie felt frustrated. Her anxiety at not being able to pull the ALF together, the Prather problem, the strain of juggling her family and dismissing her old friends, all began to take a toll on her relationship with Sean. They had been spending more time together since the second Navy raid, and Sean was as stable, funny, and pleasant to be with as ever. He was calmly confident that, given time, Wildnear would be a stunning success. Valerie wished she had as much confidence in her own work.

She realized just how stressed she really was one evening after they had been to see a play called *Sleuth* at the Kennedy Center. The Terrace Garden was open and they decided to stop for a drink before driving home. Sean chose a table overlooking the Potomac and ordered a bottle of muscadet. He started joking that they should demand three-quarters of their ticket money back because one actor had played four parts.

The sun had gone down long ago, but the moon was full and bright, a silver sphere suspended in the violet sky beyond them, lighting up the Potomac River. Everything was perfect, so perfect that Valerie found herself overcome with a feeling of being absolutely spoiled. The inequity of her lot compared to that of animals in laboratories and slaughterhouses struck her like a ton of bricks. She felt too guilty and too miserable to just sit there, drinking her wine as if all was right with the world. Tears started flowing down her cheeks.

Sean was stunned. Valerie had snapped at him lately for no apparent reason, but her moodiness hadn't struck him as something lasting. He came around to Valerie's chair and put his arm around her. That only seemed to make things worse. The more pampered she felt, the more miserable she envisioned the animals' situation was in contrast.

"Sean," she said, eventually. "I'm sorry. I'm having trouble seeing the world in the same way I used to. I've taken a peek behind the facade into a chamber of horrors. No, a million chambers of horrors. I've given up my old life, my family, my friends. When I'm doing something to stop the pain, just a little of it, for a few animals—for one animal—it's like getting a shot of anesthesia. But, when I'm not helping, when I'm not getting my drug, I feel lower than low."

Sean drove Valerie back to her apartment. They didn't talk. He kissed her on the forehead, and told her to call him if she needed him. "I wish I needed him," she thought, "but right now I need a target, a lead, a fix." As a cop she'd had the authority she needed to resolve each problem the dispatcher sent her way. Things didn't drag on from day to day. She missed the camaraderie of the force and its formula of instant solutions for everything from disorderly conduct to murder. She was painfully aware that she had lost her power to arrest abusers; she felt less like an enforcer than like an impotent observer.

Three days later, two things happened: one good and one extraordinary. First, Valerie received a letter from Ronnie Lee, or someone in Ronnie's shop. It wasn't signed. The letter contained a list of people, all on the West Coast, and the simple message, "Can you check these people out? They may be useful."

Valerie had sent the ALF Supporters' Group in Islington all the press cuttings and news releases from the Christmas Cat Burglary and the Navy rescues. Ronnie must have felt it was time to give her some help. The letter cheered her up immensely, and she began to plan her trip west. It would take a chunk out of her savings, but it might mean expansion and the chance to locate more promising targets.

With the Navy's investigation of the disappearance of "their" dogs intensifying, it would be good to do something a world away on the West Coast. It would keep the authorities guessing, and experimenters on the West Coast were less likely to be on the alert for a raid.

She was not prepared for the next turn of events.

On an errand, Valerie had driven to Annapolis, a town settled back in the time of King James and home of the Naval Academy. Unlike many port towns, Annapolis is clean, quaint, and composed of narrow, cobblestone streets lined with picturesque little rowhouses that sell for more per square foot than a Mercedes-Benz. It has English inns and Irish pubs, an open-air market, and a pretty pavilion overlooking the harbor where tourists and residents mingle to buy exotic teas, drink foreign beers, and shop for polished wood and brass ornaments made from the salvaged remains of old sailing vessels.

With difficulty, Valerie found a parking spot outside a marine supply store and strolled off to do some shopping. A little later, loaded down with her purchases, she stopped into the Old Angler to get a snack before the drive home. The waiter showed her to a table and left her to peruse the menu. All Valerie had eaten that day was a bagel, and she was famished. She was wondering if they served anything other than shellfish when she heard a deep, pleasant voice.

"Do you mind if I join you?" it said.

Valerie looked up, straight into the tanned face and warm eyes of the man who had helped her lift the Navy dogs into the van. He was dressed casually in an open-necked white shirt with the sleeves rolled up, a yellow sweater, and a pair of faded denim jeans. His deep green eyes were full of kindness and strength. For a second time she felt herself drawn to him, not afraid of him.

"What are you doing here?" Valerie asked.

"I'm buying parts for my boat. May I join you?" he asked again. He wasn't pushy, just pleasantly persistent.

"All right," she heard herself respond.

He must have been about six-four. As he lowered his massive frame into the little wooden chair, Valerie smelled the faintest hint of shaving cream.

"There's nothing to worry about," he said, his voice inexplicably soothing. "If you're interested, I'll tell you exactly who I am and what I do. I won't ask anything of you."

"For some reason," Valerie told him truthfully, "I'm not worried by you. Perhaps that's foolish, but we'll see, won't we?"

"My name is Josh," said the Navy man. "Would you mind if we got sandwiches and ate them somewhere more private?"

"No, that's probably better," she answered, and they did.

That first afternoon, Josh drove Valerie to Bay Ridge, a private residential community with a deserted shoreline just outside Annapolis. Josh took her arm and helped her negotiate the rickety steps onto the tiny beach of a sheltered cove at the curve of the bay. They sat, facing the water, their backs against the grassy sand bank, eating lettuce and tomato sandwiches and talking.

Josh told Valerie about himself. When she first saw him outside Building A-14 it was his last week in the U.S. Navy. He had been on his way to his retirement luncheon at the Officer's Mess.

"I'm planning to move to Ft. Lauderdale in July to be with my true love," he said.

"Oh, your wife's already there?"

"No. I've been divorced ten years. I'm talking about the *Gypsy Gull*. She looks something like that one." He pointed to one of the boats moored nearby. "After twenty-five years as a naval officer, I have more salt water in my veins than blood."

Josh's father had owned and operated a commercial seabed exploration project, so Josh grew up around boats. His father taught him how to sail and take apart an engine almost before he was old enough to read, and he had gone to sea for the first time in the boiler room of a merchant ship when he was sixteen. At nineteen he had earned an engineering degree, and at twenty he joined the Navy as a noncommissioned officer. When Vietnam escalated into all-out war, Josh was sent there as part of mine-sweeping operations in the Gulf of Tonkin.

"We used dolphins in the Gulf," Josh said, looking out at the waves. "No one knows that to this day. The Navy had just begun to capture them, along with orcas, 'killer whales.' They sent skiffs out with teams of men to net whole families of dolphins in the Atlantic. They kept the young ones, even ones still living on their mothers' milk. They wanted to see how trainable they were for underwater missions, planting and detecting mines, that sort of thing. They strapped things to their chests to get them used to carrying detonators and explosives.

"Some died because the first harnesses the Navy made didn't fit properly. They would get snagged on things underwater. The dolphins wouldn't be able to break themselves free to come up to breathe, so they'd drown. Others were found dead in their tanks aboard ship. The Navy couldn't make out what had killed them. The autopsies never showed disease or injury, nothing. I think they died because they had lost everything they loved, their families, their life in the ocean. Their real cause of death was what Chief Seattle called 'a great loneliness of spirit.' "

"Jacques Cousteau says dolphins commit suicide in captivity," Valerie told Josh.

"I'm sure he's right," Josh said. "I think they die of stress. One day the lid will blow off the dolphin project and I'd like to be part of it."[1] Besides being an electronics expert, Josh was a master mechanic. Could he possibly be the person she needed to get past security systems? He obviously had the prerequisites of concern for animals, talent, and intelligence. Valerie's mind was racing. Would he be willing to get involved, take risks, even break the law? Could he be trusted implicitly? She needed to do a background check on him the first chance she got.

Josh looked at Valerie and smiled. "Cheer up, I don't mean to depress you. Look, the good part is that I'm now a free agent. I was ready to do some serious sailing, take my boat and head for the Seychelles Islands, but I haven't stopped thinking about you since that day." Josh stopped, embarrassed.

"What I mean is I'm ready to help," he continued, fidgeting with a crab shell he had picked up from the sand. "I knew exactly what you were doing when I helped you put those dogs into the

[1]Ric O'Barry has written an excellent book about the military and commercial abuses of dolphins called *Behind the Dolphin Smile*.

147

van. What I didn't suspect was that your uniform was bogus! I've spent three months trying to track you down on base."

Feeling awkward, Valerie asked Josh to give her his wallet.

"Josh, stand up for a minute, and do me a favor."

"Sure," he said, getting to his feet with a questioning look.

"Pull your shirt up."

He smiled. "This isn't exactly what I had in mind for us, at least not here."

She shook her head. "No, just do it. And then turn and show me your back."

Unhesitatingly, Josh pulled his shirt over his head. There was no mistaking what great shape he was in. Besides feeling grateful to him for his help with the dogs, there was another feeling at work—an attraction Valerie couldn't ignore. She felt herself going red as she looked over his muscular body.

"You can put your shirt back on, now," Valerie said, conscious that she sounded idiotically like an examining room nurse.

Josh's wallet contained the usual assortment of credit cards, a receipt from a boating goods store, a boat registration card, a driver's license, a U.S. Navy security pass, a PX pass, money, a picture of his family on the deck of his father's ship, and a little blue plastic packet.

"That's a condom," Josh said, quickly. "We were all given them in 1966 before we shipped out for Tonkin. Navy people keep stupid things."

According to the information in his wallet, Josh was thirty-eight, he was living minutes from where they were sitting, and he was indeed divorced.

They walked along the shore, into the breeze, then holed up to talk some more under a jetty. As they walked, Valerie realized she no longer felt depressed. In the last couple of hours she felt as if she'd been given the best present in the world. She wanted to know everything about this man.

"When you're at sea," Josh told her, "you begin to wonder what possible attraction the 'civilized world' has. How we can have torn down trees and mined the hills to build shopping malls, airports, and office buildings. On a boat, you reclaim your rightful place as a speck between the sky and water. You tune in to the sounds and moods of the sea, to the colors and scent of the heavens at night, to the signs of storms and swells. The fishes and turtles and birds are the only living beings you meet, yet they seem more complete, more whole and self-sufficient, than the artificial, dependent robots most of humanity has become."

Josh lost his father when he was fourteen. On the way back from the funeral, a truck hit the car in which he and his mother were being taken home. Josh and the driver were thrown clear, but his mother suffered massive brain damage and ended up in an institution.

"I visited her as often as I was allowed," Josh told Valerie, "but I was a kid, and when I made a fuss about the way she was treated, the staff wouldn't listen to me. My mother was nothing more to those people than a bothersome, dirty thing to be stored and ignored. When she died, I was glad for her. That experience made me bitter at first. Then, in Vietnam, I realized that it had influenced me in a positive way. Some of the men in my outfit saw the people whose villages they bombed as stupid, or a pain in the neck, almost as caricatures. I saw them as real people in trouble, suffering and not being able to communicate their needs to us. What happened to my mother made me look at the dolphins in a different way, too. Not as 'things' to be crated and moved around and fed, but as life-forms people were too stupid to understand or help."

"Henry Beston said something like that," Valerie told him. "He said, 'For the animal shall not be measured by man. In a world older and more complete than ours, they move finished and complete, gifted with extensions of the senses we have lost or never attained, living by voices we shall never hear. They are not brethren; they are not underlings; they are other nations, caught with ourselves in the net of life and time.' "

"Other nations," Josh said. "That's exactly how I've felt since I was fourteen."

Josh had stopped eating animals when his mother died. He said he simply looked at the meat on his plate and saw it, for the first time, as a corpse. Later, in military training, he had gone on a survival course where the men were to set snare traps and kill wild-life. Josh refused to do it. He ate roots, wild onions, bark, and berries.

"I knew I'd make it, and I had to put up with a lot of flack because I wasn't about to kill a rabbit or some other happy-go-lucky animal who happened to come our way through the woods. Before we left I read every wilderness survival book I could get. I xeroxed pictures of edible plants and taped them inside my shorts. A lot of the men got sick, but I came out in good shape. Hungry, but in good shape!"

When the stars came out over the beach, they sat wrapped in a blanket from Josh's car, while Valerie told him about the ALF and Ronnie's letter. He listened quietly to all she had to say. When Valerie asked him if he would be interested in coming back from Florida to help out once in a while, he said more than that. He'd come with her to California.

"Val," he said, "I have all the free time in the world now, and I've reached a point in my life where I want to do something worthwhile. For myself. I've come to realize that gut-level satisfaction is what I crave. Florida can wait."

They went back to Josh's temporary home, an old summer cottage with huge bay windows facing the sea. It was a comfortable place, warm and practical and full of the evidence of his interest in boating: boating books, boating magazines, even a grease-coated engine on blocks in the kitchen, surrounded by oily tools laid out on newspaper on the floor. There was no evidence of female influence in the place, but everything was clean.

Josh made a fresh spinach salad, threw a couple of frozen enchilada dinners in the oven, and opened a bottle of good red wine. He showed Valerie pictures of his boat, his obvious pride and joy.

"I hate to confess, Josh," Valerie said. "But I'm a terrible sailor. The romance of it all sounds marvelous, and I love the sea, but from the shore—with both feet planted on the ground."

"When we have time I'll break you in," Josh said. "Gently. Help you get your sea legs."

"I don't think so," Valerie shook her head at him. "I'm a land-lubber, and anyway we have too much work to do!"

Josh drove her back to Annapolis after dinner. The lights along the harbor walls danced in the breeze, and except for the cheerful faces of people drinking in the bar windows, the town was deserted.

"Tomorrow at lunchtime, then?" Josh said, bending over to bring his head down to the top of the window as Valerie started the car.

"Yes, Josh. Good night."

Valerie drove home feeling exhilarated and hopeful. She had instantly felt comfortable with Josh. There was no mistaking the kind of personal draw they were both feeling toward each other. She knew she didn't want that. She wanted to make her relationship with Sean work, and she regretted that she had taken her frustrations out on him. She would have to make up for that somehow. What she did want, though, was Josh's sensitivity and strength and willingness to be her professional partner—not her lover.

Valerie had longed to find someone like Josh ever since she was in England, but never believed she would: someone mature, intelligent, mechanically inclined, strong, committed, adventurous, and willing. She couldn't have custom-ordered a better partner to help her get the ALF going. That night Valerie slept soundly for the first time in a month.

She spent all of the next week with Josh. They found a ship-to-shore radio shop that could get the kind of reliable portable radios she had wanted from the beginning. They drove to North Carolina to register the Pennsylvania van and prepare it for the trip west. Josh installed a state-of-the-art police scanner in it, and rigged the backup and brake lights so they wouldn't come on unless you flipped a switch. He bought a 'Fix-A-Flat' repair kit to go under the seat, a hydraulic jack, and a new spare tire. Then he set to work fine-tuning the engine. Valerie felt like a pioneer woman watching her man dig the wagon out of the mud.

Josh needed the next week off to get his affairs in order, do some boat work, and close his Annapolis house. Then he and Valerie were off to California, Arizona, and Oregon to follow up on Ronnie's leads. Sean suggested that Valerie join him and

Mandy for a few days on the Appalachian Trail, and Valerie agreed. She had been telling Sean how things were going, and had seen him bristle at how enthusiastic she was about Josh. Although she told him not to be foolish, Valerie knew that he had good reason to be jealous. It was important, she knew, to spend some time alone with him.

The Appalachian Trail isn't crowded until summer, when city workers abandon their jobs and try to "get close to nature" for a week or two. Sean rented a cabin above Frederick and struck camp beside a stream flanked by dense forest. The days were restful and pleasant. Valerie was in a great mood, confident that soon the ALF would be active again. Sean had just signed a contract to landscape a golf course, taking it away from "a chemo giant," and Mandy was in her element. The woods were much more fun than a boring old yard. Her coat shone, and her feet seemed to have springs in them. She spent every second jumping—into the stream (shaking water all over everything), onto the logs, through the cabin, and at squirrels.

On their last night they had an old-fashioned barbecue on the tin grill outside the cabin. Valerie had marinated tofu in dill, garlic, and soy sauce and brought big baking potatoes to cook in foil. Sean made shish kebabs with onions and green peppers, basting them with peach sauce.

"There is no wine that goes with this, my love" Sean announced. "Too many flavors. We'll have to break out the strong stuff and start baying at the moon." They made bourbon cocktails and stirred them with a stick, "for that earthy flavor." Mandy came over to supervise, wrinkled her nose into a ball, and sneezed right into Valerie's drink.

"Yech! Mandy!" Pinching Mandy under her ribs in play, Valerie tossed the bourbon into the woods to make the ants happy. The glow of the barbecue coals provided the perfect backdrop to a howling contest. Sean and Valerie started it, then Mandy joined in, doing her best fire engine imitation. All the campers and animals within five miles must have wondered what on earth was going on at Campsite 47.

The Heart

Valerie and Josh spent the next six weeks on the road, Valerie filling him in on everything she had learned as they went. They tracked down all but two of Ronnie's contacts, people who had heard about the British ALF and put out a feeler. For the most part they weren't serious candidates, just people with good hearts who ached to think of what was being done to animals. A few, however, were stable people willing to take substantial risks under the right circumstances. Valerie met with each "possible" over a period of days, while Josh ran their car tags through the local Department of Motor Vehicles' computer (which is sometimes as simple as presenting a dollar processing fee and the tag number to the clerk at the DMV window), and otherwise they both made as sure as they could that these people were "real." Then they gave them assignments. "We'll see how they do," Valerie mused.

Valerie found herself constantly amazed at Josh. There seemed to be nothing he couldn't do. He looked at a problem practically and logically and then set out to solve it. Thanks to him the ALF developed headsets for their walkie-talkies, which allowed members to keep their hands free. He also outfitted them with mining lights that they could turn off without reaching up to the tops of their headbands. He kept up with every gadget and every catalog. What they couldn't get in the United States, he mail-ordered from Canada or West Germany.

For Valerie, the most promising part of the trip was their stop in Los Angeles. There she found Sitch. He was a young, ambitious, firebrand script consultant, a man consumed with anger about laboratory cruelty, but sensible enough to keep his anger to himself. There were three other potential ALF mainstays in or near the city, too: Vin, a Korean war veteran who ran a sports car garage, and his wife, Penny, who were both stable, controlled, willing, and capable people; and Eric, an electrician who barely said a word, but whose sincerity and reliability were impressive. He had made friends with a secretary at the University of California-Harbor. This woman was upset about the use of dogs in heart experiments. She had seen inside the lab and she wanted the dogs out.

It was clear that here was the making of a major ALF cell and a potential target. While Valerie flew back to Washington to begin serious work on their next East Coast target, Josh stayed in California to carry out her plans for forming the second cell. She found herself missing him immediately.

They had set up an emergency system before she left whereby they could call each other safely from phone booths. They arranged set times and set numbers. They would never have to make specific arrangements, other than to say "I'll call you at Sal's," the code name for one booth. "This evening" meant seven o'clock, "tonight" meant nine o'clock, and so on. They used Cleveland Amory's *The Trouble with Nowadays* as their code book. If Valerie said, "seventeen, three, four," Josh would know to look on page seventeen, third line down from the top, fourth word over from the left. That way they could easily construct sentences. It was inconceivable that anyone listening could figure out what they were saying.

Taking these precautions would come in handy later. Valerie was in the habit of being careful by the time the FBI took on the ALF. As she had learned in England, she shared a different book with everyone involved. All she had to keep track of was which book she shared with which person, and they had to do the same. No one ever knew or asked what books others shared.

On the road, trying to communicate long distance, Valerie found it best to have two contacts, and to choose something like Erica Jong's *Fear of Flying*, available then in every corner bookstore. In later years, she and Josh would use a laptop and a modem with a scrambler.

On that first trip, they also found activists with good potential to take on university researchers in Oregon and Arizona. She began to arrange safe houses where ALF operatives could rest when they brought animals out of labs, and she started piecing together temporary and permanent placement possibilities through Miki and her veterinarian friend in New York.

From the very beginning Valerie had kept a list of everyone she knew and how many animals they had. She counted friends, workmates, relatives, friends' relatives, anyone decent. Whenever Kay, Miki, or others traveled to animal welfare or vegetarian and health food conferences, which was not infrequently, or even to demonstrations, they asked people whether they were looking for dogs or cats, and wrote down their names and telephone numbers, putting asterisks by the names of those they felt were excellent prospects.

The Underground Railroad had begun laying its tracks. Valerie hoped she would be able to look back one day, the way Harriet Tubman had after leading over three hundred slaves to freedom, and know that the liberation train had never once fallen from its rails or lost a single passenger.

While Josh was at work in Los Angeles, there were two new developments. The ALF had made headlines in Canada with a break-in at the University of Toronto. The group had snatched five cats from a surgery unit. Valerie had no idea who these people were, but she was elated. The more action the better, she thought.

There were quieter developments in Bethesda. In the Navy's panic to increase security, Kit's command had been asked to handle sensitive information on the research institute's newest and most sensitive project, a secret underground laboratory.

"It's a wound lab," Kit told Valerie. "There's one at Fort Bragg in North Carolina and one at Camp Bullis in Texas, but they're old and only used once in a while to train medics and military doctors. The finishing touches are being put on ours in Bethesda. It's state-of-the-art. A full-fledged shooting gallery of goats, pigs, dogs, you-name-'em. They'll shoot the animals with different kinds of high-powered weapons fired by a mechanical device, and then study the effects of each weapon on bones and tissue."

"You mean this is offensive, not defensive weaponry testing?" Valerie queried Kit.

"Yes, some of it. Most of it is the usual nonsense, though. 'Basic research,' meaning basically meaningless research!" Kit gave Valerie the specs. This military animal shooting gallery was scheduled to open in September in the Uniformed Services University of the Health Sciences complex, a few buildings over from Vanguard's old kennel.

"The acronym is USUHS," Kit told her, "but everyone on base calls it 'Useless,' because it's failed every blue ribbon panel and outside review you can name. Some members of Congress have been angling to close the place down for years. Not because of cruelty, but because it costs too much to run and never produces anything worth a bean."

Kit had a list of the major players. Dr. Norman Rich was the chief surgeon in charge, and overall supervision fell to Dr. Richard Simmons. Valerie recognized Simmons' name from the Silver Spring monkeys trial—he had testified for the state. That was an odd turn of events. Valerie asked Kit if he'd met him.

"No, but if he's like most of them, he won't rock any boats. The Taub thing was a state prosecution, and he's a local research big-wig. Maybe he thought a purge of the likes of Taub would provide a nice screen for his own nasty business. Who knows?"

Kit was certain the underground bunker was impossible to penetrate. "You can't get to it except through a special internal entranceway that's equipped with a key card system and has military police on it around the clock. The military is so worried about security nowadays, they've worked themselves into the idea that someone might blow it up!"

"Well, they might be close. Maybe we can get one of the animal groups to blow the lid off it." Valerie couldn't wait to get this into Alex Pacheco's hands. "Kit," she asked, "would you meet with the head of People for the Ethical Treatment of Animals about this? They offer complete confidentiality."

"That's where I came in, remember?" Kit laughed. "Yes, I'll call him. I suppose there is a legal way to do this. I was beginning to forget!"

Kit was true to his word. For a timid-seeming careerist, he was willing to do a lot.

On July 26, 1983, while Valerie was back in Arizona, the wound lab story broke on the front page of *The Washington Post*. Other papers picked up the story. "Navy to Shoot Dogs," screamed one headline. Valerie read in the *PETA News* bulletin:

. . . [before breaking the case] we pored through ballistics jour-
nals and medical directories, contacting physicians who had
served in Vietnam and Korea. Unanimous in their opinion that
treating artificially induced firearm injuries in animals does not
prepare surgeons for successful treatment of missile injuries in humans, 700 doctors from across the country signed a statement join-
ing PETA in denouncing the DOD's proposal.

PETA has warned the Secretary of Defense that we will take
direct action, civil disobedience included, to stop the shootings.
Ballistics research utilizing non-animal techniques, such as x-ray
scanners, high-speed photography, human skeletons and cadavers,
video taping, and gelatin and soap block trials, are not only more
humane, but more reliable and applicable to the human situation.
The approximately 300,000 people treated for firearm wounds annually in this country alone already provide a wealth of important
information about the nature of wounding. Clinical data collected
over the past ten wars, combined with the information obtained
from M.A.S.H. units in Vietnam and Korea, as well as data from
the dozens of armed conflicts that have and are taking place
around the world, provide us with, indisputably, the most useful
research information of all.

The day after the *Post* story broke, Secretary of Defense Caspar
Weinberger suspended all military shooting of animals. Kit's tip
had paid off.

A few weeks later Josh returned to Washington. Had Valerie
confided in him about it—and she had made up her mind not to,
at least not yet—Josh might have been surprised to learn that she
was changing.

What Josh had seen in the Navy had toughened, embittered,
and angered him. Until he met Valerie he had felt alone, imagining himself the only person who understood how harsh reality
could be. Reading Kit's files and entering the labs had the reverse
effect on Valerie. She was softening.

As a police officer it had been expedient, a matter of her own
peace of mind, perhaps even a matter of preserving her own life
and limb, to see things in black and white and make snap judg-
ments about people and situations. Out on the street, the card-

board figures (of a masked robber, a mother with her child) that sprung up in front of her at rookie school (Friend or foe? To shoot or not to shoot?) had become flesh and blood. Cops can't afford to see too much gray or they end up in wheelchairs or graves.

Relieved of her uniform, she found herself contemplating the gray quite often. She had been a cop, now she was a "robber." She had been a hawk, but now was becoming a dove, albeit an unconventional one. Didn't *she* sometimes strike out and hurt others? If she had changed so much, perhaps people weren't "good" or "evil" after all, but complexities of emotions and experiences that might draw her anger or her sympathy, but not her hatred.

She *had* hated Taub and Morrison and the anonymous people who had mutilated the cats at Howard University. Somewhere along the line, though, her hatred had disappeared. She wanted only to stop them from causing harm, not do harm to them.

For Valerie, seeing Josh again was like getting a shot of adrenalin. Although her relationship with Sean was going well, she realized that being in Josh's presence provided more than a professional thrill, and she resolved to watch her step. There had been times on the road together when it would have been easy to surrender to her attraction to him, but she always had stepped back from that.

In the weeks he had been gone, Josh had assembled a team of committed activists. They were gearing up for action at the University of California-Harbor medical facility. Josh was excited about the prospect of the raid and thought the West Coast team was very strong.

"They have Last Chance for Animals, a live-wire group led by an actor called Chris DeRose," Josh told Valerie. "Last Chance and Chris will do whatever's needed to support the ALF, as long as they don't know enough to be named criminal coconspirators. They're vigorous, and they're really stirring that city up."

Two days before the raid, Kathy, one of Josh's crew, went to the back door of the animal laboratory at the UC-Harbor medical facility with a story that her daughter, soon to graduate from a veterinary technicians school, wanted a job there. She looked honest, so the caretaker believed her and let her in. Drilled by Josh and Eric on what to look for, her hawk eyes scanned every inch of the place as she walked about, chatting.

In contrast to the sunny campus filled with students strolling in the fresh air, eating their lunches, and studying under trees, the animal kennels stank of urine that had seeped into cracks in the cement floor. There were no resting boards to allow the dogs to get off the cold damp cement.

She counted sixteen dogs, most large, all mixed breeds, and most of them shaved over much of their chests. At least two seemed unable to stand. Several had wires sticking out of their throats. One young brown mixed boxer had only the hair left unshaven on his legs and neck. Out of his bare stomach and chest poked three large metal implants. Another had a metal box protruding from below her ribs.

One old dog had particularly upset her. "That dog looked just like an old man," she told Josh. "As much as I kept looking for alarm boxes and wires on the window, my eyes kept coming back to his eyes. That old man needs to get out of there."

Two nights later, Josh and Vin lay in the nearby bushes in a steady rain, watching the guardhouse. The rain was a godsend; security wouldn't be expecting even a lone prowler on a night like this. Just before midnight, the guard shift changed. Josh gave a radio signal to the two men and three women of the newly formed unit to move forward. WD-40 solvent had been poured in the hinges of the laboratory doors the night before.

The two men used a sledgehammer to bash off the bolts holding up the steel exterior doors. After no sign of movement from the guardhouse, they lifted the door clear off its hinges, and the women disappeared through the opening into the kennel. Valerie had advised them not to tranquilize the dogs, because stressed animals can sometimes collapse if tranquilized. Also, sedated dogs sometimes become confused, and howl or even bite out of fear. These dogs were going to walk out.

Two team members, Vicki and Sal, had smeared canned cat food on their arms and into the fabric of their cotton gloves. As soon as they reached the cages the barking died down, as the dogs began to smell something enticing. Those who could started licking their rescuers' arms and hands. Only a few dogs huddled motionless in the backs of their cages, heads down, watching fearfully out of the corners of their eyes. One of these was a female black mixed setter. Another was a collie with an adrenalin pump sticking out of his body. Sal felt the hard steel of the pump when she ran her hand over the shaved area on the dog's side.

The women moved rapidly from cage to cage, placing slip ropes around the dogs' necks and, a leash in each hand, running out to the truck. The dogs leapt in the air and strained at the leashes, joyous to be able to stretch and run and race.

Sitch had put up the money, $14,000, to buy the "West Coast" transport, a two-year-old luxury van registered to a California family that didn't exist. Josh and Vin had gutted it; all the pretty parts ended up in a pile outside the side door. With a soldering iron, hammer, and nails, they constructed two tiers of interior cage banks, a solid compartment between the cab of the truck and the back, and little storage cabinets for trashbags, water jug, jumper cables, Fix-A-Flat, and animal food and medications. They anchored everything firmly so it wouldn't shift. They took out the radio and put in a police scanner. Under the seats they fitted tools, road maps, flashlights, flares, a first-aid kit, rolls of quarters for telephone calls, and a niche for cash, bowls, and bandages.

Vin and Josh had put solid pieces of plywood between the cages to stop aggressive males from barking at or trying to bite each other through the mesh. This kept the noise and excitement level down. One of the crew had made curtains, a pattern incorporated with small black mesh flowers, which enabled the surveillance crew to see out undetected.

Within eight minutes of the women's entry into the kennel, a dozen dogs occupied the first custom-built ALF cages in the United States. Ironically, the cages had exactly the amount of space required by the U.S. Department of Agriculture for the lifetime of a dog in a laboratory: just enough room to stand, sit, and turn around.

Vicki and Sal were trying to coax the last two dogs out of the kennel when the men in the bushes sent them a radio signal. A guard had gotten into his car and was headed toward them. Paul was the leader of the loading crew; everyone kept going, waiting for his instruction. They had four minutes before the guard would wind into their quadrangle. If his lights touched the van, they'd be caught.

Each approach to the two dogs was met with raised lips, bared teeth, and deep growls. These dogs were not about to move willingly. It would take more than four minutes to get them to stop being threatened—and threatening. Paul made the decision: "We can't do it. Let's go!"

The team members raced to the van. Everyone's heart was pounding. Paul felt the two smokebombs in his pocket. Should he throw them and blanket their getaways in a yellow cloud? For a split second he hesitated, then thought better of it. If they made it around the corner, the building would shield their escape. The officer couldn't miss the two heavy steel doors off their hinges and leaning against the wall. Would he stop to check things out or speed up to catch the burglars? Would it be better to freeze in place and hope he wouldn't be curious about a van parked there, or make a run for it? Paul suddenly felt what he later described as "almost a premonition that we were going to be shot." The strength of this vision made up his mind: "Driver, start! No lights!" said Paul.

In seconds the guard's car would swing around the corner and catch the van in its headlights. Just as they made the corner, they saw his lights. Had he seen them? It was only a matter of seconds now before he would radio the security station. Behind the bushes, Josh and Vin had seen the guard drive toward the lab. They backed away on their elbows, praying there was no broken glass on the ground, and kept their eyes on the lighted window of the guardhouse, where two guards sat inside with their backs to the door, smoking cigarettes and talking.

"Damn," said Josh. "There should be only one there. The other's staying to chat. Now we'll have three to contend with after the alert."

In the shadows, he and Vin arose, turned, and ran silently

along the grassy stretch beside the main road. A car was coming from the other direction. Just before its headlights hit them, they threw themselves face down on the wet ground. Dressed head to toe in black, they had only to hide their faces and palms to blend into oblivion. As the car passed, Josh heard two students laughing and a radio playing. Then it was gone.

He and Vin ran through the main gate as fast as they could and across the street to the car parked in the shopping center lot. As they ran, they turned their jackets inside out; one became beige, the other, gray and yellow.

They saw the ALF truck come out of the entrance on their left and turn onto the main street at the same time they heard the alarm go off in the guard house.

Inside the ALF van the tail-thumpers were having a high time. They didn't know where they were going, but they seemed to know that the people here were a lot nicer than the people they had left. Anyway, going for a ride beat staying in the lab. The tail-thumping continued as the truck turned onto the freeway and headed for the desert.

"No more 'sorry,' no more 'please,' no more damned apologies," sang the raiders. "If you try to knock us down, we'll bounce back and stand our ground."

Earlier that evening Kathy and Valerie had driven to a house in the middle of nowhere. Its owner had gone to visit her sister in Omaha and had been delighted when Kathy had offered to housesit. Unfortunately, their police scanner was too far out of range for Valerie to pick up what was happening in town. So, too nervous to eat dinner, the two had the kitchen radio on an all-news station and were playing backgammon on a homemade board, using pieces of cut potato and cubes of sugar.

Just after 2:00 A.M. they heard the van come up the driveway and ran out to meet it. There were twelve dogs. Kathy raced out to search the van for the two sickest dogs she had seen on her reconnaissance. They were not there. Had anyone seen them? No one had. "Old Man" recognized her and wagged his tail. Kathy popped the lock on his door and down he jumped, spirits high, immediately lifting his leg on every bush. Free at last.

The dogs were unloaded and divided into different rooms in the house. It was important to check out who was compatible with whom, and to give a harsh word to anyone who growled at anyone else. ("Prison camp rivalries," Vin called these squabbles.)

Then Kathy went to wake up the veterinarian who had flown in to examine them. Earlier she and Valerie had prepared an examination area in the kitchen and unpacked the bag of veterinary supplies. They'd shaken down the thermometers and put out ice water and a stack of towels that Kathy would later be left to wash.

All but three of the dogs were males, and all of them had been operated on. The veterinarian ran his fingers slowly down Old Man's neck and over his shoulders. There was a three-quarter-inch chunk of scar tissue running parallel to Old Man's jugular vein and several deep scars on his shoulders. His right foreleg was a mass of scar tissue, as if he'd been stuck again and again with needles.

"This big knot," said the vet, feeling the dog's left foreleg, "probably came from a catheter inserted into his heart. Whatever they did to this dog, they did it over and over again without giving the skin a chance to heal. His neck is infected—look here, where the skin's sloughed off. See those two protruding wire ends? If they weren't under his chin, where he can't get at them with his mouth, he'd probably have pulled them out himself." An x-ray would later show that Old Man wore a crude metal and plastic pacemaker. The old fellow had been through the war and back. He was underweight, and a big chunk was missing from his ear.

"Looks like flies ate that ear off," the vet said. "When dogs can't get away from their own waste in summer, flies will be attracted to the urine and keep nibbling on the dog's ears until they're eaten raw. He's also got an irregular heartbeat. It could be a natural defect, but more likely they deliberately inflicted an injury on him to make him part of this experiment."

"Aunt Sally," the black mixed setter, turned out to be spayed (where had she come from?), perfectly housetrained, terribly timid, and hopelessly in love with Old Man. She would hover around him and wag her tail. She was also petrified of people. If anyone raised an arm innocently, she thought they were about to cuff her and dropped to the floor. People learned to move very quietly and slowly around her, so as not to frighten her.

All the dogs were heavily parasitized. Their fecal samples showed positive for hookworms, whipworms, and almost every other parasite that shouldn't exist in a clean kennel. In poorly run places caretakers just hose down the runs, so that feces from one run splatter into the next. If there is no veterinarian to keep the animals parasite-free, they all pick up parasites from each other.

After the examinations, the dogs were given a meal of boiled rice (to calm their excited stomachs) mixed with a little nutritious broth. After eating, they were allowed into the backyard. This must have been the first time they'd stretched their legs in months, or years. Out in the desert night they barked, howled, and rolled in the dirt, sometimes kicking their feet up in the air and *smiling*, lips back.

"It's a 'coming out' party," Josh said. He and Valerie sat shivering in the night air, their backs against the wall of the house, watching the dogs play.

"Bounce," the youngest dog, was so full of energy people could hardly get anything done. No matter what they were doing, he wanted to be there, have his head under their heads, his nose under their noses, and generally just be in the way. Everything interested him. Valerie thought how much like a child in a playground he was.

Only Aunt Sally did not enjoy herself. She crept into a corner and sat there surveying the scene, looking as if the end of the world was at hand. Old Man walked about stiffly, marking the fenced boundary, while the young ones romped, put their feet on each other's shoulders, and had mock battles.

Five of the dogs were to be placed in California and seven back east, so a fairly compatible group had to be selected for the journey. That done, the ALF members dismantled the cages and stacked them into a neat heap, except for a couple they left intact as a way to separate the dogs in transit if trouble broke out. On top of these Vin laid a board, to provide a sleeping shelf for two dogs. Bounce immediately commandeered the space for himself. He wouldn't let anyone else up there, using it as his vantage point, poking his nose out from between the curtains and, later, surveying the tumbleweed clumps blowing across the desert.

Chad, a lanky, redheaded geology student on his way to a midwestern university, was to be Valerie's codriver for the trip east. In Kansas an East Coast ALF unit member would replace him.

"I wish I were going back with you," Josh said, squeezing Valerie's hands in his as they said their goodbyes.

"You're getting too sentimental to be a real commando," she told him. She climbed into the van, angry at herself for wanting him to come along. Chad started the engine and they drove out of the gate.

"Wait!"

Josh was running after the van, waving his arms. Chad saw him out of the side mirror and punched the brakes. The van skidded to a stop, sending a cloud of dust into the desert night.

"Hey, remember we've got dogs back there, please," Valerie said sharply. "I need a conscientious driver at the wheel, not a rodeo cowboy." Chad didn't answer.

Josh caught up. Valerie was impressed to notice he wasn't even breathing hard. "I forgot to tell you," he said. "This van sometimes doesn't start in the cold, especially if it's been sitting. Let me show you what to do."

They got out again and Josh opened the hood. He unscrewed the wing nut that holds the air filter in place and stuck a pencil into the carburetor. "All you have to do is push this down here and turn the ignition. It'll start right up. If I hadn't thought of that, you might have been stranded in the desert or the corn fields of Kansas."

"Gee, thanks," Valerie teased him. "Any other household hints we should be taught?"

"Don't think so. You're OK for the agricultural inspection station, right?" he asked.

Valerie told him they were. At California's border with Arizona and Nevada, there were inspection stations where all vehicles passing to and from the state had to stop. Drivers were questioned about the transport of plants and live animals. The ALF had originally planned to use a horse trailer to transport the dogs, until one of the vets pointed out that there was an Equine Infectious Anemia scare. A horse trailer would have brought inspectors swarming. The dogs shouldn't pose a problem, but just in case, Miki had given Valerie blank rabies certificates. She assured her that rabies would be the only disease officials might be anxious about. Valerie had already filled out the certificates with descriptions of her canine passengers.

They said goodbye to Josh again and started their journey.

"Stay at least two miles under the speed limit at all times," Valerie warned Chad.

"You got it," he replied. There was something a bit too flippant about his attitude for Valerie's taste.

"Honestly, Chad, no speeding. There's probably an all-points bulletin out for an odd collection of large dogs, so we're 'hot.' "

"No sweat," he assured her, blowing dust off his sunglasses.

Chad had slept like a baby that night while Valerie and Kathy had strategized and worried, so as soon as Valerie had mapped out their route, she lay down in the back of the van with the dogs and tried to sleep.

With tumbleweeds blowing across the road, Bounce squashed up against her right side, and Old Man's head on her stomach, they moved toward Nevada. An hour later, Old Man let her know he had to get out. He had a case of the runs, so they stopped the van at a little drugstore beside a gas station and picked up some Kaopectate for him. Long-term antibiotics had messed up his intestinal tract; Old Man could no longer digest food normally.

Traveling with so many dogs made Valerie glad it was winter. In warmer weather she and Chad wouldn't have been able to breathe. Even with the side windows ajar and the chill wind blowing through the curtains, it was stifling inside the van.

"Keep your eye on the speedometer. Don't forget!" were Valerie's last words as she drifted off to sleep. It couldn't have been more than forty minutes before she woke up. The van had come to a stop.

Valerie knew, even before her eyes could focus, that something was wrong. "What is it?" she asked.

"We've been stopped by the police."

"What!" Valerie was laying, then sitting, and finally kneeling, trying to stand up in the mass of dogs. She couldn't see out the back door, but part of the side curtain had parted, and as the officer walked alongside she drew it closed.

"Try to relax. Try to look calm," she hissed at Chad. All she could think was, *please* don't start barking.

The Nevada state trooper stuck his head in the window—all the way in. Valerie had decided to lend her support to Chad by occupying the passenger's seat at this point. She had to keep her knees firmly between the two seats, because a lot of curious, hot noses were now trying to poke through the gap to determine where she had disappeared to. The curtains were jiggling wildly. Valerie tried to smile at the officer.

"Were we speeding, officer?" she asked.

"Yep." He wasn't smiling.

Valerie gave an apologetic grimace.

"Driver's license and registration. Where you going?"

They had rehearsed this, but before Valerie could give their pat answer, Chad blurted out, "Kansas."

Great, Valerie thought. Now the police had their route and could catch up with them later even if they got out of this problem. She could have killed Chad. He was handing over his real driver's license and the cop was reading his real name aloud.

"Where are you coming from?"

There were California plates on the van. Valerie let Chad take it. At this point, it didn't seem to matter.

"L.A.," he said.

"Whatcha got back there?" The second the cop said those words, Valerie realized they were probably on a drug-run route. With some confidence, she realized that neither she nor Chad fit the classic drug-runner stereotypes she had studied in rookie school. And drugs don't smell like wet, urine-coated dogs.

Behind Valerie there was no barking, but there was a lot of movement, and then somebody let out a big growl. "It's our mother dog and her puppies," Valerie said quickly. "The puppies are grown and we're trying to find homes for them. Can we interest you in a couple? They're real nice." If he was interested, Valerie'd find some reason not to give him one. Please don't ask to see them, she thought. Some of the dogs had huge patches shaved out of their backs and legs. They looked exactly like dogs stolen from an experimentation facility, or else dogs belonging to some kind of cult worshipers who took chunks out of animals for fun.

Valerie reached back and tried to get her hands on Sam. He didn't have any scar tissue and he hadn't been shaved. He was a bit old to be a puppy, but . . .

"No thanks. Got two of my own. Stay right there."

The officer retreated to call in their tag number. Valerie told herself they had nothing to worry about; the computer had no way of knowing the registered owner was fictitious.

"How fast were you going?" she raised her voice at Chad as they sat there, waiting to be arrested or released.

"It couldn't have been five miles over the speed limit," he said defensively.

"Well, there's nothing we can do about it now." The officer returned to Chad's window.

"I hope it's not too expensive," Valerie said humbly.

"Nope. Twenty dollars, but don't think of not paying it or you'll go to jail next time you come through Nevada." Next time sounded good to Valerie, but she would be sure to pay the ticket.

As soon as the officer stepped away from the van, Chad tried to brush it off. "Listen, we survived," he said.

Valerie wanted to hit him. "We're not out of it yet," she told him through gritted teeth. "We've got a straight road for the next three hours and nowhere to go in this desert but down it. If that cop stops for coffee soon—and he will—we could be in for big trouble."

"What do you mean?" Chad looked at her with no understanding of the seriousness of their dilemma. Valerie's eyes were ablaze with fury.

"If he meets a fellow officer or if the waitress behind the

counter asks him if he's busted anyone this morning, what'll he say? He'll probably say, 'Naw, nothing much. Just gave a speeding ticket to two people with a vanload of dogs.' And the other person may say, 'That reminds me, did you hear on the radio some people went in and took a whole bunch of dogs out of some L.A. lab?' And over his coffee, the officer will remember that, 'Hell, they were coming from L.A.' He'll radio ahead. And here we are, stuck on this road with hours ahead of us and no place to turn off. We're dead, Chad. And so are the dogs."

Chad drove on, not daring to say a word. Valerie got out the map and looked for other possibilities. If they slipped down into Arizona it probably would take them just as long, and she was sure the Nevada police had a reciprocal arrangement with their brethren in that state. To catch the crossroad, they would have to turn around and pass the point where they'd been stopped. There was nothing to do but press on. Valerie would have given her right arm for teleportation. Or a small ALF helicopter landing in the middle of the desert.

The trip to the state border seemed to last a lifetime. Valerie kept her eyes glued to the road behind the van. Hours later, the "Welcome to Utah" sign finally appeared in the distance ahead of them, along with two blobs next to a larger blob that, as they neared, became two Nevada state troopers leaning against their car. They were staring straight at the van. The troopers watched it come toward them, gave a little nod, and the van's occupants left them behind.

Valerie felt relieved, but Chad suddenly seemed exhausted and needed to rest. She borrowed his Walkman and they switched places.

Valerie drove through Utah all day, stopping only occasionally for coffee and to let Old Man out. Toward early afternoon she was very tired. She turned the Walkman to an ear-shattering pitch to keep from nodding off, and stuck her arm out the window to allow the cold breeze to make her uncomfortable. She had been well rested, but the monotony of driving and the hours of worry were taking their toll.

The dogs slept. They were no longer keen to get up, even when the van stopped. They seemed to want peace and rest more than anything. The floor of the van must have seemed like a luxurious mattress after their lives on cement. They kept pushing Chad with their legs as he slept on the floor in the back.

When they reached Colorado, the dogs smelled the crisp air through the cracks in the windows and got so excited they had to be let out. At the roadside turn-off they lapped the dew off the grass and bushes. They put their noses in the air—all of them, that is, except timid Sally—and sniffed noisily, taking in a multitude of signals and analyzing them. "Reading the newspaper," Miki called it.

The road was very curvy now. Valerie took her turn in back, but found it hard to sleep with all those lively feet walking on her. The van wound around and around. Lying on the bottom of the truck bed, Valerie felt queasy. She was half asleep and half awake when she felt a warm sensation on her chest and neck. A dog they'd christened "Christmas" had thrown up all over her jacket! Valerie leapt up, revolted. Then she saw Christmas's face. He looked really upset. Without a word, she wiped up the mess and then gave him a reassuring pat. "You old, sick thing," she said, "I was close to doing the same myself." The smell of vomit filled the van, making the atmosphere even less tolerable.

On day three they entered Kansas. The strong, unmistakable smell of the feed lots filled the van. Looking out, Valerie could see thousands of steers being fattened for slaughter. They were sitting down, mostly, their world an enormous, flat, brown, dust bowl. People sped by, not noticing, in their air-conditioned cars.

Valerie no longer had to remind Chad to keep his eye on the speedometer, and at every stop he got out and dutifully checked the turn indicators and brake lights, as she had asked. Valerie didn't want them to be pulled over for a mechanical failure. They reached Kansas City ahead of schedule and in good spirits.

Two of the dogs now had some sort of exudate coming out of their wounds, and Valerie called her friend, Lily, an animal technician she had met in New York, who was coming by plane to relieve Chad. Because Lily took in so many strays, she had a wealth of friends in the veterinary profession and humane community who knew her well. She picked up some medicines on her way to the airport. Meanwhile, Valerie and Chad tried to keep the dogs' wounds clean, despite the dust that had blown through every available crack in the van framework.

With free time on their hands, they drove to a state park. Valerie trusted Old Man enough—and he trusted her enough—that she decided to let him off the leash to relieve himself more comfortably, away from prying eyes. He stuck to Valerie like glue. She and Chad took turns walking the others in the wheat field, sitting with them at the picnic table, scratching their stomachs and ears, and generally working on their psychological well-being.

Valerie had seen enough rescued animals by now to learn that their eyes held the history of what they'd been through. She wondered if, in their dreams, they still heard cage doors slamming and felt rough hands on their flanks. Were their dreams as vivid as a human's coming home after the war? Perhaps some never recovered completely.

There was a tiny stream in the park. The dogs drank from it, the icy water dribbling off their faces and clinging to their whiskers. Valerie couldn't cope with seven wet bodies, even though it would have been nice to wash the filth of the lab from them. They did, indeed, smell. In fact, by now, so did Valerie and Chad. Something a critic said in a review of Fred Wiseman's documentary film, *Primate*, came into Valerie's head. "The smell is not of urine," she told Chad. "It's of greed."

Aunt Sally wouldn't go near the water. Chad brought her some in a little plastic cup and Sally drank timidly. It would be two years before she began to let her guard down. Until then, she would leap under the furniture if there was a knock at the door. Sometimes she'd scream during the night, and the woman who took her in would have to reach out and reassure her.

They found a motel with a room in the back at ground level, so they could push the dogs quietly through the door. They were the sort of people motel owners never rent to knowingly. As if to prove it, Christmas lifted his leg and marked every stick of furniture, while Valerie said, "No, no." She gave up and brought out wads of paper towels from the van. Although he'd been in the park just an hour ago, another one of the dogs immediately relieved himself in the middle of the rug. "Oh, no," Valerie groaned. "It's shag. We'll never get it clean."

The beds looked wonderful to Chad, Valerie, and all the dogs. There was much shuffling and reshuffling as they all tried to get some space to lie down and sleep. Valerie set the alarm for midnight and called the desk clerk to confirm a wake-up call.

It seemed only a minute before the bell went off. By now used to sleeping in her shoes and clothes, she was on her feet, out the door, and headed for the airport in minutes, pushing her way through a sea of deliriously happy dogs who wanted to go anywhere she went.

Lily's plane had arrived early and Valerie found her waiting at the gate. She couldn't wait to see the dogs. Back at the motel, as if she were handling fine china, she ran her hands over each dog's face. Then she and Valerie walked out behind the motel, each of them with two dogs at a time straining at leashes. When the dogs finished with every bush, they loaded them into the van for the second stretch of the journey. Full of energy, Lily would drive the first lap while Valerie went back to sleep.

A long haul lay ahead. The plan was to drive to Pennsylvania, drop off four dogs, and then proceed to upstate New York, with Lily making the last drop in Connecticut. On Josh's next trip he'd pick the van up from Lily and return it to the West Coast.

By the time Lily and Valerie finished their deliveries thousands of miles away from the lab, the story of the missing dogs was all over the newspapers and television. According to Carol Schmidt, information director at UC-Harbor, the dogs were valued at $100,000. She said this figure included research that would have to be duplicated and all the veterinary care the dogs had received. This figure seemed ridiculous, since Harbor had admitted buying the dogs from a local pound for $160 each, and since many had open sores attesting to a lack of veterinary care (two of the dogs had infected necks from implants that weren't "taking").

UC-Harbor officials fumed and sputtered. Five of the dogs,

they said, were being used to test pacemakers, while another was testing an infusion pump delivering norepinephrine, an adrenalin-type drug. Michael Criley, chief of cardiology, announced that he was receiving hate calls. Frank DeSantis, executive vice president at Harbor, told a magazine interviewer, "As far as I'm concerned, we're pursuing prosecution to the fullest if we're able to catch these people. We're not letting up; we're going to pursue them both criminally and civilly."

The police did not share his enthusiasm. "I have no idea," Sheriff Lenny Chow announced, "if the dogs are still in California. As for information on who did this, we haven't any."

Two weeks after the trip, Valerie received a UPS package from Lily. After reading the letter, she reluctantly tore it into small pieces and flushed it down the toilet. But she couldn't throw away the pictures Lily had enclosed: four of the dogs lounging around a picnic table in someone's backyard in Pennsylvania; Old Man and Aunt Sally sitting side by side, looking out from the porch at the antics of the younger dogs on the lawn below; Bounce, all his scars showing as he rolled in the grass with his legs straight up in the air.

On the back of one of the photos was an unfamiliar hand: "They are grateful for even the smallest kindness." On another, the same hand wrote, "Christmas loves his food bowl. He carries it with him in his mouth now. Inside the house and out." A third photo inscription read, simply: "We love them very much."

Valerie thought of the dogs she had come to know. She imagined them on the operating slab at UC-Harbor, lined up like so many instruments on a rack—"preparations," the experimenters would have called them. The ALF had made them whole again, but would twelve other dogs simply take their places? The facility, she was sure, would be made spotless for inspections. A regime of veterinary care would start as soon as the ALF released its report showing a failure to provide the dogs with even basic medical needs. All this would cost money. Animal experimentation would become more expensive. Eventually, she hoped, it would become cost-prohibitive, and one day it would dry up forever.

6

The Head

When the dogs had been taken care of, Valerie said goodbye to Lily and caught a Metroliner back from upstate New York. Reflecting on the ALF's progress so far, she remembered something she had read in an Australian newspaper account of British liberations. "As raids go," Glennys Bell, the reporter, had written, "they sound more like the imaginings of a Disney film script writer than the operations of a commando war machine, but they have one thing in common. They are performed with daring skill and surprise, and executed with such finesse they still have the police guessing."

Although she'd been sitting for days, she found being on the train soothing. She pushed the recline button on her plush coach seat, popped up the footrest, and watched the rooftops and fields go by for at least an hour. Then she broke open her pocket chess set and tried out some new theories she'd been developing to occupy her mind on the long ride home. When she looked out of the window again, the train was swaying gently over the smooth waters of Chesapeake Bay. It was past Baltimore, headed for Washington's Union Station.

Sean was waiting for her in the coffee shop by the ticket office. The station was being renovated and janitors moved about fighting a losing battle with the dust that settled on everything. Only the tired-sounding man announcing arrivals and departures on the loudspeaker could be heard over the jarring whine of electric saws and drills.

They walked down the makeshift plyboard tunnels that kept travelers out of the hard-hat areas, and out into the Washington sunshine. Flocks of pigeons took off, as if on cue, as they exited the station and made their way past the huge, gray-smudged statues to the parking lot.

"Any news of Carmelita?" Valerie asked. With El Salvador's civil war in the newspapers almost every day, she was concerned for the safety of her foster child. Villages were being ransacked, women and even little girls raped, people murdered. No one was allowed to be apolitical any more. Everyone had to take sides. Valerie's last two letters had gone unanswered by this little girl who loved to write and send drawings. She wondered if the fighting had interrupted the mail service, or if something worse had happened.

"Actually, there is," Sean said. Before Valerie left, Sean had promised to try to send a telegram to Carmelita's cousin, Maria, who was looking after her since the death of her uncle. "But let me tell you about that later. OK, Val? It's nothing conclusive and it can wait. I don't want you brooding. Right now there are people waiting at the house to meet you."

Valerie agreed to put her worries about Carmelita aside for the moment, but they weighed heavily on her mind. As for what else was going on and who the visitors were, she couldn't cajole or bully Sean into telling her.

"As long as it's not Clayton Prather armed with a gun or federal agents with a warrant."

"Far nicer, you'll see," he said. Valerie was disappointed and annoyed that they wouldn't have any privacy. She felt the need to tell him everything that had happened.

Mandy had been waiting in the station wagon and gave Valerie an enthusiastic face cleaning. She considered Valerie and Sean a family unit and always got excited when they were together. She jumped back and forth between the seats while Valerie leaned up against Sean, feeling, as she always did at these times, glad and lucky to be home again and in one piece.

Brooks, one of the Silver Spring monkeys. He spent his entire life in a small cage before dying in 1986, under suspicious circumstances at the Delta Regional Primate Center in Louisiana.

Activists protesting the treatment of the Silver Spring monkeys block the doorway of the Health and Human Services building in Washington, D. C., August 6, 1986.

Vanguard (covered with mange and bite wounds) after his rescue from the U. S. Navy's diving experiments at the Bethesda Naval Research Institute.

Old Man, rescued from a lab at the University of California-Harbor, showing some of the scarring he sustained at the hands of researchers.

Helen (later rechristened Goofy), infected and guarding her dying puppies on the filthy cement floor of their cage at City of Hope Medical Center.

Prince (right) and one of the many cancer-infected beagles liberated from City of Hope, pictured here with Valerie.

Geraldine, one of the cats rescued from the University of Pennsylvania. The implant in her skull held wires that ran through her head, down her throat, and into her stomach.

Alex Pacheco (left) of PETA with Cleveland Amory after the National Institutes of Health sit–in, 1985.

Britches, his eyes still sewn shut, shortly after his rescue
from a lab at the University of California–Riverside.

Britches,
wearing baby
clothes for
warmth, eyes
open and
taking in his
new world.

Kyle (left) and Eric, two of the baby chimps rescued from SEMA, with a masked ALF member.

Kittens rescued from the Beltsville Agricultural Research Center, with liberator.

$2,000
★REWARD★

**For information leading to the arrest and conviction
of person or persons involved in the July 4, 1989
break-in of the Texas Tech University
Health Sciences Center Lab, Lubbock, Texas.**

Individuals having information may contact the Texas Tech University
Health Sciences Center Police Department at (806) 743-2000. **STUDENT
SERVICES**
Persons wanting to remain anonymous may do so.

AUG 1 1 1990

APPROVED

Handbill posted at Texas Tech University following ALF action there.

Ingrid Newkirk (right) with her longtime companion, Conchita.

They drove straight to Sean's. The two cherry trees at the front of the house had just shed their blossoms, and the ground was awash with their pretty, pinkish-white petals. The flower beds shone with color, and a new wave of tall prairie grasses, taupe and beige and flaxen, told Valerie that Sean had been doing some serious work in her absence.

Whoever the visitors were, they didn't have a car here. The driveway was empty and only Sean's Jeep was in the open garage. Valerie walked into the living room and two strangers rose to greet her; a delicate woman of about twenty, with straight black hair cut in a page-boy, had been sitting on the floor doing a jigsaw puzzle with a pretty little girl of about nine or ten. All she could register was that they were Hispanic. She smiled at them and looked, questioningly, at Sean.

"Valerie," Sean said as the young woman shyly took the little girl's hand and brought her forward. "Meet Carmelita, and her cousin, Maria."

Valerie's first thought was, "How on earth?" Then, recovering, she said, "Welcome, welcome to the United States." She reached out to accept Maria's hand. "My God, this is wonderful. How did you get here?"

"Buenos Dias," said Maria politely. Valerie realized that she didn't speak English. Carmelita took Valerie's hand and shook it. She was smiling uncertainly.

"Good morning," she said with great pride.

"Good morning," Valerie answered her. "I am so happy to see you. Welcome."

Carmelita looked down at the floor and moved her feet shyly.

Sean said something in Spanish. They both smiled warmly at him and sat down again. Sean began to explain what had happened. He had contacted Maria by telegram, asking her to call him collect. Maria had done so, telling him that the crops the families depended on had been burned by government troops and that many people had fled.

Sean had made inquiries, and, through the sanctuary movement, made the arrangements necessary to bring Maria and Carmelita to the United States. Officially, they were tourists, but the sanctuary movement would make sure they found somewhere to live by the time the Immigration and Naturalization authorities realized that their visas had expired and came looking for them.

Sean had arranged Carmelita and Maria's journey as much for Valerie as for them. It had cost a lot of money to bring them here, but Sean could afford it. Valerie's pride had always made her uncomfortable about accepting expensive gifts from him, but this was one he knew she could not refuse.

After a while, as Carmelita adjusted to Valerie's presence, she let her help with the puzzle of Monet's lilies—clearly a Sean purchase. Valerie watched the little girl as she searched for the pieces. She and her cousin had left behind the only life they had ever known only to hide now from new enemies: the U.S. government. For the first few weeks they would stay in Sean's home, where Val could help ease their transition into American life.

That night, Valerie thought through her relationship with Sean. It wasn't as if she could put him in one column and Josh in another and add up their attributes and choose her favorite. She respected Josh; she had been overjoyed to find him, and they got on well together. But her feelings for him were not as deep as her feelings for Sean. The attraction Valerie felt when she was with Josh came from a shared thrill. She had seen the same thing happen when a happily married man or woman joined the police force and ended up in a patrol car with a member of the opposite sex. Thrust together in dangerous situations, they begin to believe that their shared feelings of risk, power, and sexual presence are worth more than they really are. She'd seen too many solid relationships wrecked because of false expectations beyond the line of duty.

Valerie chided herself for failing to detect this pattern in her relationship with Josh. She had allowed herself to tease and be teased by Josh: to want him, and to let him want her.

"Sean," she whispered to him.

"What, Val?" he said, sleepily.

"You don't have to worry about us, you know. I love you."

"Glad to hear it," Sean reached his arm behind her back and

drew her to him. "Now get some sleep. You've got to play mother tomorrow."

Valerie sank into sleep, feeling very happy—about the UC-Harbor dogs, about Carmelita and Maria, about Sean. By the next evening she had made a landmark decision. She would try living with Sean. He had long ago given up asking her to move in with him.

"Is it because of Prather?" he asked when she told him that, if his offer still stood, she was ready.

"No, it's because I want to see if we can make this work, and I think we can."

"We can, angel. We can," he said.

While Valerie had been on the road, there had been an important development. On one of her volunteer days, Kay had intercepted a letter sent to PETA from a University of Pennsylvania mail carrier. He had delivered a package to an unmarked laboratory in the basement of the Anatomy-Chemistry building, a lab that was not on the carrier's list or listed anywhere in the campus directory. Officially, it didn't exist. The carrier was a peace movement activist, and the mystery surrounding the lab piqued his curiosity. Suspicious that the university might have signed a contract with the Defense Department, he decided to make it his business to find out what went on in there.

The carrier's quiet snooping had finally paid off. It wasn't war research, but equally nasty. The lab belonged to the infamous head injury experimenter Thomas Gennarelli and his partner, Thomas Langfitt.

Gennarelli had first come to the attention of the animal protection community in the mid-seventies, when students at Penn had tried to blow the whistle on his experiments. They had been afraid to come forward with their names, but three of them had called the local humane society and begged for a visit from its law enforcement officer—Miki's Pennsylvania equivalent. When the uniformed officer arrived on the campus and asked to see the lab, the school denied him entry. The university went so far as to go to court to obtain an order barring humane officers from the Ivy League campus. Such a move was unheard of.

As far as Penn was concerned, Gennarelli's experiments were off-limits to the outside world. All attempts to discuss the complaints with university administrators were met with rejection or silence. The humane community reached a dead end.

Ten years had passed since the whistleblowing students had graduated and the old lab had vanished from the campus map. In 1983, The Fund for Animals received an anonymous tip that Gennarelli was not only still in business, but videotaping the infliction of head injuries on monkeys. The caller failed to say where the lab was and never called again. Thanks to the carrier, Gennarelli's hiding place was now known. Valerie decided to pay him a visit.

She asked one of her new ALF colleagues, "the Hacker," to case the university during the three weeks she was occupied with Carmelita and Maria. Now in his sixties, Hacker had grown up in Nazi Germany. The cruelty he had seen and experienced there as a little boy was still as real to him as the tattoo that marked his stay in a concentration camp. He had come to the United States in his early teens and been apprenticed into the meat trade. He had been adopted by the owner of a New York neighborhood butcher shop and had ended up running it himself, until an escalating revulsion toward slaughterhouse horrors finally drove him out of the business. A widower with two grown sons, Hacker was now a health food advocate. Bear had introduced Valerie to him after making his acquaintance at a vegetarian Thanksgiving dinner in Queens.

"I believe what Isaac Bashevis Singer wrote," Hacker had told Valerie. " 'In their behavior toward creatures, all men are Nazis.' Human beings see oppression vividly when *they're* the victims. Otherwise they victimize blindly and without a thought."

Hacker reported back that he had met with the mail carrier and checked out the location. They would need a driver, two people to accompany him inside the building, and a lookout. Could Valerie pull the team together for the next holiday weekend? He would do a briefing for the cell at a safehouse it had established in the Philadelphia suburbs.

It was time to get back to work. Valerie had enjoyed having Maria and Carmelita to look after and show the sights. They made the house come alive, and each day brought new delights and discoveries. During the weeks they had spent together under Sean's roof, she had shared in their worries and their exhilaration, and had learned a little Spanish to boot. She and Sean had seen them off at the train station, where they boarded a sleeper for Boston. From there, a church family would pick them up and help Maria find work. Staying in touch would not be wise, so Valerie's contributions from now on would have to be given to the sanctuary's general fund.

The weather forecasters had predicted temperatures in the seventies for an ideal Memorial Day weekend. Valerie got up early that Saturday morning after a restless night, breakfasted on soy sausages and rye toast, and dressed in her all-purpose blue janitor's slacks and shirt, a dark blue Sears worker's jacket, and dark shoes and socks. She pinned her hair up in a bun, slipped her heirloom ring from her finger, and, on her way out, grabbed a bagful of bagels she had bought the evening before.

When she got to Sara's building near the Connecticut Avenue entrance to Rock Creek Parkway, she found Sara waiting at the curb as planned, dressed in her own brand-new janitor outfit. Valerie noticed she was shivering. The sun had not yet vanquished the cold on the northerly side of the building.

"Did you sleep?" she asked.

Ginger, the young cell member who had befriended the guard at Howard University, had met Sara at a community clean-up and introduced her to Valerie a few months afterward. Valerie could tell that Sara's shivering was only partly because of the chill. She looked nervous; this was her first raid.

She gave a wan smile and said, "I dreamed we got caught. I hope that's not a bad omen."

"Just nerves," Valerie said. "Scary dreams come with the territory. Here, have a bagel." She didn't mention her own nightmares.

The highway was fairly deserted for a holiday weekend. When they reached the outskirts of Philadelphia, Valerie wound through a subdivision and, at its edge, down a long driveway to an isolated country home. It was turning into a gorgeous day.

Sonia greeted them at the front door.

"Sonia, this is Sara," Valerie made the introduction as they entered. Sonia shook Sara's hand warmly. At the same time, Valerie felt herself being enveloped from behind in a bear hug she would have recognized anywhere. "Let me go, Josh." She turned to look up into Josh's eyes.

"Sara, meet Josh," Valerie said. They smiled and shook hands, and everyone moved into the living room. As they went through the door, Valerie held Josh back.

"What are you doing here?" she asked him. "You're supposed to be three thousand miles away."

"When you left with the UC-Harbor dogs, I could see that you felt the same way I did," Josh said, his eyes holding hers with an unmistakable intimacy. "I think it's time to do something about that. Right after this job."

"Josh, don't be silly," Valerie didn't know how to put this. "You're reading too much into my fondness for you. You have to consider me married to Sean, as good as married. That's how it is."

Hacker coughed in the doorway, then came over and patted Valerie on the shoulder. "You two coming or not?" he said, good-naturedly.

Josh and Valerie followed him into the room. "Are you serious?" Josh whispered.

"Sorry, yes. Dead serious." She whispered back.

Ginger was already there and her presence seemed to calm Sara's nerves. Valerie and Josh joined them, Sonia, and Hacker around the table.

Hacker shared his briefing, describing their target. He passed around a very old photograph from the lab. It was of a chimpanzee restrained in a water-filled tank, breathing through a tube, her head being slammed around inside by a machine. He distributed an article from the *Toronto Globe*. No reporter in the U.S. had been able to get Gennarelli or Langfitt to talk about the experiments, but Gennarelli had granted one interview to the Canadian press in 1983. In the article, he denied accusations of cruelty to animals and touted his experiments as vital to the development of better football helmets.

Hacker went over what The Fund for Animals and PETA already knew: Dr. Gennarelli and his research crew used dental cement to seal monkeys' heads into metal helmets. A pneumatic device violently "accelerated" the head at varying angles and degrees of force up to 3,000 g's (3,000 times the force of gravity). According to NASA, a force of only 15 g's can kill a human being.

Although the experiments were conducted in the subbasement laboratory of the Anatomy-Chemistry building, the primates were housed on the fifth floor. But the ALF would not be taking animals this trip; the spoils they sought were the videotapes that they hoped were stored in the laboratory office.

"We feel we'll have only one shot, so we had to choose between the tapes and the baboons," said Hacker. "It was a hard call, because on one of my reconnaissance missions I saw the baboons. Their cages are standard-sized, but obviously the tapes are the evidence we need to stop animals from being tortured here in the future. And this campus is crawling with security inside and real cops outside. We have little to no chance of springing the baboons."

Hacker had set up a model of the building, with detailed drawings of its layout, the grounds around it, and the buildings nearby. The mail carrier was to leave a second-story window open so they could avoid the guarded entrances and the electronic security system. Hacker, Valerie, and Sonia would enter the facility while Sara and Ginger waited with the van. Because guards were "more plentiful than flies on a cake," as Hacker put it, Josh would remain in the bushes. If it became necessary, he would tackle and restrain any outside guard who gave them trouble when they came out.

Each member of the team would carry bail money, and Hacker and Josh would each have $1,000 cash, to pay off someone bothersome but bribable. This money kept "recycling" because it was never needed. If anyone took it, Valerie's resources would be drained. It would be time to push ALF members for more money. As it was, some already "tithed," giving ten percent of their income. Others, like Hacker, had been consistently generous. The first awkward time Valerie asked, he responded, "What does a retired widower like me need with money?"

The briefing and deliberations ended around 7:45 P.M. Sonia laid a Monopoly game out on the dining room table, and everyone seated themselves around it, eating potato chips and trying to take their minds off what lay ahead. In the middle of the game, Josh looked at Valerie and said, "Seriously?" She knew what he was talking about. "Seriously," she said back. It was not easy to say, but she was trying to mean it.

At 11:30 P.M., they put the game away, got their gear, and headed for the van. Otto had painted it with flat black undercoat, and it faded almost totally into the night.

Ginger drove them out of the suburbs and onto the campus. Traffic was very light and they were within the university boundaries in less than fifteen minutes. They cruised once around the target building, an ancient red-brick monster, following Hacker's instructions so they could confirm the placement of its doors, windows, and shrubbery. It was brightly lit and had far too many windows facing the van. It wouldn't be prudent to let anyone out there. The team would have to come in on foot, as Hacker had said. Ginger turned the van away from the building, back past the Nurses' Hall, out onto the little roadway, and stopped by the front gate.

"You're gone!" she said, hitting the brake pedal a bit too hard. They lurched forward, righted themselves, pulled open the side door, and threw themselves and their flat black aluminum ladder into the bushes. Ginger pulled away.

Valerie, Josh, Sonia, and Hacker squatted in the bushes, listening to the hum of the van engine fade away down the street. Valerie stuck her head out cautiously and gave the all clear.

"Remember, foot patrols," Hacker said as they followed him quietly up the driveway, hugging the line of shrubbery with their bodies, the ladder at their sides. They crossed the lane before the entrance to the Nurses' Hall, and flattened themselves against the wall of the enormous southwesterly wing of the Anatomy-Chemistry building.

Hacker leaned against the wall, counting windows, then double-checking his count. Everything depended on finding the right window. Having an exposed ladder was risky business in this heavily guarded complex. Silently, Hacker moved with the ladder along the side of the building and set it against the wall. Up he went, like a man of thirty, not sixty, while Josh held the bottom of the ladder steady.

Valerie held her breath, hoping that Hacker had not miscalculated, and that the mail carrier's information would prove reliable. A few seconds later, Hacker disappeared inside the building and Valerie was on her way up the ladder, Sonia following close behind.

They stood in the little office into which they had climbed and got their breath back. Hacker listened at the door. All seemed quiet. By his calculations, the guard for that block would be at his desk. Hacker opened the door and slipped noiselessly into the hall, Valerie and Sonia keeping about four doors behind him.

A man's voice rang out as soon as Hacker turned the first corner. Sonia and Valerie looked at each other, eyes wide. For a split second the two were paralyzed. Then, realizing their feet were only inches away from the corner around which Hacker had disappeared and made his encounter, they turned and fled softly back the way they had come.

Around the next corner, they stopped and tried to listen to what was going on, but the voices were too muffled to understand. All Valerie could determine was that Hacker had been seen. She trusted him implicitly to do everything in his power to deflect attention away from them. They waited. No Hacker.

"Oh, God," Valerie whispered to Sonia. "He has the walkie-talkie and the pick gun."

"And the bribe money!"

"We can't stop now, right?"

Sonia nodded in agreement. "Let's go before we meet up with one of the guards."

Hacker's floor diagrams were engraved on Valerie's brain. She had to make her way down from the second floor to the sub-basement and find the lab. The elevators would be too risky, and being in the open corridors wasn't so hot either. She and Sonia raced through the halls, found the stairs, and bounded down them three at a time. The stairs ended at the basement. They needed the sub-basement.

Out in the hallway, it took only moments for Valerie to spot the sign she wanted. A metal door with a red lightning bolt painted over the words: ELECTRICAL HAZARD. DO NOT ENTER! That was where the mail carrier had delivered his parcel.

The door was locked, but a quick kick at the frame sent it flying open. Sonia pushed it closed behind them and they went down the filthy, seldom-used stairs. They knew they were seconds away from the target. Valerie pulled open the metal door at the base of the stairs and they entered a cramped little hallway, a dead end filled with metal drums. Only one door opened off the hallway, directly to the right of the sub-basement door. That had to be Gennarelli's lab.

The noise from the machinery in the adjoining boiler room was deafening. A battalion of guards could have walked up behind the women and they wouldn't have heard them. There was nothing they could do about that problem except forget about it. The carrier had said there was a slim chance he could get a key to the lab. If he did, he'd tape it behind the duct work hanging exposed from the ceiling next to the lab door. Valerie ran her hand through the cobwebs along the dusty metal. Nothing. She tried the door. Locked tight. She pushed against the metal framework. Solid as a rock. This was a door that couldn't be kicked in.

They crouched behind the drums farthest away from the stair-way to collect their thoughts.

"We don't have a crow bar or a pick gun, and there's no key. That's great!" Sonia almost had to shout to be heard above the din of the boiler. "What next?"

"We'll try to pick the lock," Valerie told her, pulling two bobby pins out of her hair and straightening them out. "It can be done, depending on the lock, but it's usually hard and it's seldom fast.

While I start with these, you look around on the floor and see if you can find a thin, straight piece of metal that we can hook at the end like this."

Valerie drew what she wanted in the dirt. She had bought different locks, as she had been instructed to do at camp, and clamped them to a table in Sean's basement workshop. When she was in town she spent an hour or two a week, more when she first started to learn, feeling her way into the locks with a pick. She had become proficient enough to feel confident with the proper tools. The question was, could she make bobby pins work?

Valerie stuck the straight pin in at the bottom of the lock to keep the lock pin down, then began fiddling with a curved pin, running it back and forth like a mini-saw, working at the top pins, then trying to turn the mechanism to see if she had found the right combination of strokes.

Sonia found a metal shard on the bottom of a barrel and worked it loose. She gave it to Valerie to bend into the right shape. It was an improvement, but Valerie still couldn't trigger the lock. After half an hour or so, her wrists were aching and she showed Sonia how to take her place. Sonia worked on the lock, and when she tired as well, Valerie took over again.

They looked at their watches. It had been almost two hours since they found the lab. It was time to take a breather behind the barrels and talk.

"You know," Sonia said. "It's funny. I'm not nervous any more. I'm damned irritated!"

"I know. I feel the same way. We can go out now, if we're not caught like Hacker, and try the whole thing again another day—if they haven't realized what's going on yet. Or, we can make it work now. Damn our luck!"

"Think there's any chance?" Sonia looked at Valerie hopefully.

"Sure. Let's keep at it. See if you can find any access through the ceilings, through the boiler room, or through the vents, and I'll have another go at the lock."

Sonia disappeared, only to report back that she could find no other access to the lab. Valerie wondered if frustration could give a person the strength necessary to kick down a metal door, when suddenly she felt the locking mechanism turn in her hand.

"Jesus! Sonia, we're in."

Afraid the knob would turn back and lock again forever, Valerie gave the door a shove and it bumped back against the wall. The women both sucked in their breath. Every light in the lab was on.

We've walked right into a trap, Valerie thought.

But the room was a tiny office, empty except for a baby crib. Could it belong to a caretaker? They walked, almost on tiptoe, through the next door and into the laboratory. Perhaps the caretaker was asleep. They had lost so much time, they didn't really care any more.

A huge, black, hydraulic jack, the size of a small crane, dominated the main room, its thick wires ascending into the ceiling, its solid tree-trunk-like base anchoring it into the floor. The center of the jack opened up to a table covered with plaster of Paris, bloody instruments, and unraveled bandages. More dirty instruments—surgical pliers and a hacksaw among them—filled a tray jutting out from the table, and dirty bandages were strewn on the floor.

There were two tiny offices and a sink room adjoining the central room. No caretaker, no animals.

"I'll do the smaller rooms if you do the lab," Sonia said.

"Deal," Valerie replied.

For forty-five minutes they ransacked the place with surgical-gloved hands. There weren't just a few videotapes, but dozens. More than they could carry in the pockets they had sewn into their jackets, designed to hold six standard-sized tapes each. There were reams of files, too, some of obvious value but most undecipherable statistical tables and such.

They bound the extra tapes into four cardboard boxes and sealed them with duct tape. Then they taped a Penn letterhead envelope onto each one and addressed them to the PETA address, without using the organization's name. It was ridiculous, but worth a shot, Valerie thought. Perhaps there was a chance they could put them in another department's mail drop and they'd get mailed out. At least it was a chance they could take if they couldn't escape the building without being caught.

The pair worked quickly. They had spent almost four hours trying to get into the place, and whether Josh, Sara, and Ginger knew Hacker had been caught or not, they would be frantic by now.

Sonia was systematically destroying everything in sight that contributed to the monkeys' torture, from test tubes to video equipment. She found a bottle of iodine and poured its contents into the computers' disk drives.

"You should go into professional wrecking," Valerie said, watching Sonia smash the front of the computer and pocket the key. There was something almost frightening about her intensity and concentration. Valerie had never seen this side of Sonia.

"I'm not finished yet," Sonia called back. She dashed back into the small office and started pulling all the computer hard copy files out of the cabinets and dousing them with chemicals.

"Let 'er rip, Sonia," Valerie yelled.

She looked at her watch. It was dawn. Oh, God. In daylight, they could not get out of the building the way they had come in, and it was far too early to be found walking down the hallways. The guards knew no one was meant to be inside. Yet, if they waited until later, they would probably be caught. Valerie and Sonia discussed their options. There was one thing they could try.

In the basement hallway they had noticed construction going on. Perhaps they could find a way out through that area, Valerie thought. They divided up the boxes of tapes between them, securing the two smaller boxes and some files in their jackets, and carrying the two larger boxes in their arms.

One floor up, but still one floor underground, the area under construction led into a room with a cracked cement floor. The floor was covered with about half an inch of water from rain that had come in between the scaffolding. Valerie looked up through the boards and saw a pinhole of daylight.

"Maybe there's a way out through this mess," she told Sonia. Sonia gave her a leg up onto the first metal pole and she climbed toward the light, dismantling the woodwork as she went. At the top, ground level, she found a sheet of plywood covering the opening, with fragments of light coming through.

Balancing herself with both legs pressed against the poles lining the shaft into the basement, Valerie slowly lifted the plywood sheet and found herself looking into a corner of the quad.

She called down to Sonia. "Quick, come on up."

Using her belt to tie the two loose packages of tapes to her coat, Sonia hauled herself up between the rickety boards. She was older and not as agile as Valerie, and found the climb tough going. When she reached the top, Valerie pushed back the plywood sheet and the two of them scrambled out of the hole and onto the ground beneath the exterior scaffolding. It afforded some cover, but not much.

No sooner had they flattened themselves against the muddy earth-covered cement than Sonia pointed to the bottom of a doorway, just visible from where she lay. Two sets of shiny black men's shoes were coming out of it. They stopped, facing each other, about twenty-five feet away. A man's voice said something about coffee, then the first pair of shoes turned and walked out of the compound. The second pair went back inside the building. Valerie looked at her watch. It was 5:40 A.M.

Valerie told Sonia to pass her the two loose packages of tapes. There was a pile of two-by-fours within arm's reach of where Valerie lay and she worked the boxes under the wood, out of sight. She didn't feel they could risk walking out with them.

"Shall we?" Sonia asked.

"Let's do it," Valerie answered. They stood up and stepped out from behind the scaffolding. All cover was gone, and they were still trapped in the quad. They started walking.

"So far so good," Valerie exhaled. They moved briskly through the gate and onto the lane. As they turned right, toward the street, Valerie turned her head instinctively in the opposite direction. Out of the corner of her eye she could see a uniformed man walking toward the quad.

"Follow my lead," she said sharply to Sonia, picking up her pace and starting to jog. Sonia looked over at her and started to jog, too. "Hands over your head and wiggle your fingers," Valerie called out, demonstrating, her feet moving rhythmically. "Now, hands on your hips and bend." They kept moving forward, putting on their jogging act and trying to increase the distance between themselves and the man.

Valerie heard the guard call out. It was a half-hearted call. She didn't turn and neither did Sonia. "You have to feel it in your hips," Valerie yelled, swaying her arms from side to side as they ran. "Up with your knees, high," she continued, bouncing energetically, then bending and waggling her fingers to the ground. She could sense Sonia's nervousness.

"Ladies!" yelled a man's voice, way behind them now.

Not stopping, Valerie turned, looked at the guard, waved, and cheerfully yelled back, "Morning!" She turned face-forward again before he could gesture. They were almost out of earshot. If he wanted to catch them, he'd have to decide they were worth it and give chase. Valerie figured that she and Sonia looked weird, but don't most joggers? She bet the guard wouldn't exert himself for such a tiny possibility that they had done something wrong.

It wasn't until they were at the gate that Valerie looked at her hands and realized she was still wearing her white plastic surgical gloves. So was Sonia. Lord knows what the guard had thought. Worse, two of the fingertips on Valerie's gloves were worn through and Sonia had lost about a half-inch piece of plastic from the end of her left thumb. Their prints were somewhere on that campus, possibly on machinery in the lab.[1] Valerie looked at Sonia and knew that nothing could be done about it now. The two of them balled up the gloves and tossed them into the bushes.

All Valerie cared about at that moment was that they had escaped. Under the two-by-fours they had hidden two boxes of videotapes, and inside their jackets they carried twelve more tapes, which she hoped would damn Gennarelli, Langfitt, and those who funded them.

---

[1] Whether the police obtained ALF members' fingerprints from the University of Pennsylvania is unknown. The investigation was taken over by the FBI and the case file is not available under the Freedom of Information Act because it is still open.

The van was parked about a block further down the street, visible from the exit gate. Josh, Hacker, Ginger, and Sara were waiting inside it almost catatonic with worry. When they saw Valerie and Sonia emerge from the campus unharmed, Josh yelled, "Hot damn!"

The van pulled away and everyone started speaking at once.

"The guy I ran into assumed I was a custodian, so I let him," Hacker explained. "He figured I was on my way home, and I was afraid that if I didn't leave the building with him he'd get suspicious."

Valerie told the group that the majority of the tapes were still stashed in the construction site. "Someone has to go back and get them," she said. "Hacker, want to do it?"

"Is that age before beauty or are you helping salvage my pride?" Hacker asked.

"Neither," Valerie assured him. "You just look the least suspicious."

It was Sunday morning. The streets were empty as Ginger maneuvered the van through the back streets of downtown Philadelphia, looking for an early morning coffee shop where they could wait.

It took Hacker less than fifteen minutes to get back to the quad, poke through the construction site, toss the tapes nonchalantly into the van, and drive out again.

The ALF now had seventy hours of videotape in its possession and many hours of work ahead copying the tapes. Four borrowed VCRs sat waiting at the safe house, ready to go, but this much tape would require far more than four machines. Valerie called Kay, who looked up the Philadelphia group's list. What could be done except to call activists and ask to use their VCRs for a vital animal rights project, no questions asked? On Sunday morning, early, it was easy to catch people at home. The first six people she reached agreed without hesitation. Ginger took the van to the Walnut Street shopping center and waited to collect the equipment.

The cell members watched the tapes as they were being copied, and all thoughts of sleep vanished. Sonia popped open a six-pack of beer and started to drink her way through it. Hacker and Josh joined her. Valerie put on a pot of coffee.

Nothing could have prepared them for what they were to see on the screen. The primates' heads were cemented into helmets attached to wires, just as they had been told. The experimenters—students mainly—listened to rock music, smoked, laughed, and mocked the baboons as they attached the wires to the "Penn 2," the hydraulic device that slammed the animals' heads. Not a word of kindness passed their lips as they pushed a switch that thrust the primates' heads at a sixty-degree angle at a force of up to 1,000 g's.

Two vivisectors laughed as a small, helmeted baboon, strapped to an operating table and probably under the influence of an administered dose of phencyclidine (also known as PCP or "angel dust") struggled with the canvas straps that held him down.

"One, two, three . . . ," there was a bang as the Penn 2 jack did its work.

"We should have blown the place up," Sonia told Hacker, downing her beer. She watched two students attempting to cut some tubing and handle a struggling baboon at the same time. In the melee, a bottle of liquid overturned and spilled over the monkey.

"This makes my day," said the first student.

"Why don't you put him in the fucking goddamn cage?" yelled the second.

"I'm working on it, I'm working on it, I'm working on it. I'm trying to get . . . would you cut this? I'm trying to cut this damned thing. What was in there?"

"Acid. It's gonna eat your balls off."

Hacker was waxing philosophical. "The human animal is capable of great kindness and great callousness," he said. "Anyone who'd do something like that isn't quite normal, you know. Don't get like them, Sonia."

"I guess you've seen more callousness than any of us," Sonia said. "But I don't see how you can *not* hate them. ALF actions have to be more than symbolic. They have to be sabotage. We should offer a reward for the skin of a vivisector and see if there are any takers!"

"You're buying into *their* violence that way, Sonia," Hacker told her.

Josh had stepped into the room.

"I agree with Sonia," he said. "Nonviolence is a middle class obsession. Bullies are cowards, and we need to get these bastards' attention. You *support* violence if you don't *stop* violence; by not taking strong enough action, you support violence. In a way, we're pussy-footing around the problem. A really good scare might do more to stop these folks than all our raids."

Josh's attitude made Valerie uncomfortable. Sonia was Josh's age. They were not young punks. Somehow that made their remarks seem even more offensive to her. She could hear him from the next room where she was trying to watch the screens on two VCRs at the same time. She turned up the volume on both and tried to concentrate.

On one screen, two vivisectors were performing electrocautery, an extremely painful procedure for an unanesthetized animal. The baboon kept lifting his head, yet the men continued to cut. On the other screen, the experimenters were preparing to press the switch when the baboon managed to turn his body around on the table.

"As you can see, he, uh, is very active, with normal motor functioning. He is quite agitated, also," the experimenter talked into the microphone as he repositioned the monkey.

No sooner had he stepped away from the table than, somehow, the baboon managed to turn over onto his side again, though his legs and arms were now bound more tightly. The baboon was so agitated that he rolled over a total of five times before the researcher taped him to the table.

In the next scene, Valerie could make out only the legs of a restrained baboon as a vivisector bent over him.

The man was saying, "He was banged once at a 680 g force and quickly recovered. Cheerleading over in the corner, we have B-10," the camera panned to a disabled monkey strapped into a chair in the corner, brain damaged and drooling. The experimenters laughed.

"B-10 wishes his counterpart well," more laughter. "As you can see, B-10 is alive." There followed scenes of experimenters banging at the monkeys' helmets with a hammer, trying to remove them. "Look! He's moving, he's moving. See! He moves. We have this little string on his tail that we just pull," one said. Valerie watched as the men tried to force the helmet off a monkey's head. "Push . . . hhhh! . . . it's a boy," the helmet came off in their hands and the monkey's head hit the table. The experimenter with the hammer made a face. "Looks like I left a little ear behind. Eeeeh!"

Valerie took a break. When she returned, the students were still going about their work.

"Why's it so dusty down here?" one student asked the other, rhetorically. "Why? Because they're basically incompetent down here. It's, well, I mean just in general our procedures are [unintelligible]. They're not . . . they're not regular in their cleaning at all, and I've called them three times. Ah, when they do clean they're half-assed. Lately the ventilation system's been spewing out some sort of . . . dust. It's the type of thing that I, you know, I complain about, but, you know."

The student agreed. "I mean, you come down here and it smells like urine. I mean . . . we have three months of urine down in the bottom of that thing . . . uh, urine asphyxiation. We had to get her out of there. She was just filling it up with buckets of urine."

The surgery scenes showed clear violations of the NIH *Guide*, which Valerie knew backward and forward. Experimenters failed to perform sterile surgery, and, although some wore gloves, no masks, gowns, caps, or surgical drapes were used. Valerie watched one researcher rest his surgical instrument on the baboon's unshaven chest, then, after dropping the instrument to the floor, pick it up and place it back in the baboon's head without even wiping it off.

Also in violation of the *Guide*, the experimenters smoked at the operating table, despite open surgical incisions and close proximity to bottled oxygen and nitrous oxide, both highly dangerous gases.

As time went on, the ALF members barely spoke. Each of them was glued to a VCR. Occasionally, someone got up to get fresh tapes or take a brief break, but otherwise there was silence, even from Sonia.

The last two scenes on the last tape to be copied, which everyone gathered to watch, involved an experimenter tying an injured, conscious baboon to the operating table as he prepared to leave.

"Oh, have some axonal brain damage there, monkey, or else we'll have wasted five hundred dollars' worth of HRP on you, you sucker!"

There was a break in the tape, then a dazed baboon appeared on the screen, held up by a young, female experimenter. The baboon's head had been shaved, and was covered with stitches.

"Get him closer," this from a male voice off-camera. "Don't be shy now, sir [to the monkey], nothing to be afraid of [laughter]. Oh, what's going on here, tsk, tsk, tsk, tsk. Look, there she goes; she's on TV [laughter], holding her monkey. Look! Yeah! Go! Go! Ta da! Just like a cat! Here kitty, kitty, kitty—look at the cat commercial. Say, over here, say 'cheese.' Looks like he's gonna fall over. You better hope the, uh, the, uh, antivivisection people don't get ahold of this film."

"The who?" asked the female student, her grin fading.

"The antivivisection people. They got a nice shot of you. They got Larry's name . . . in the picture. And Karen." Then, referring to the massive stitched wound extending the entire length of the monkey's cranium, "There, look at that part on his head [laughter]. Hmmm, that's some part you've got there. He has the, uh, the punk look."

"The punk look, is that what you said? [laughter]"

"Friends! Romans! Countrymen! [laughter]. Look, he wants to shake hands. Come on. Oh, not again. Put your head down [more laughter]. He says, 'you're gonna rescue me from this, aren't you? Aren't you? You're gonna rescue me, aren't you?' "

If the ALF had written the script, it couldn't have topped this. Hacker and Josh slapped their hands together.

"Just watch us try!" Valerie promised.

It had taken the whole day, and into the early hours of the next morning, to copy all the tapes. Now that the job was done, fatigue hit fast. Valerie and Sara, bone-weary and minds spinning from all they had seen, prepared to leave. Josh said he was heading for Florida to help a friend fix a boat. Valerie said goodbye and left quickly. Ginger would return the VCRs and drop Hacker off at the station to catch the train to New York.

After dropping Sara off at her apartment, Valerie made a planned detour on her way to Sean's. She had almost forgotten they were living under one roof now.

The sun had already risen again when she ran up to the doorstep of the PETA headquarters—now installed in a house in Takoma Park, Maryland—to leave the copied tapes there. On the way home, she stopped at a phone booth and made a call to PETA's answering machine to report the delivery. She kept the message short, speaking in deliberately stilted tones, purposely disrupting the natural dips and rises in her inflections. She knew PETA would erase the tape, but she didn't want to take any chances. Then she went home. Sean was out and Mandy was nowhere to be seen. She showered and collapsed into the delightfully soft bed.

Because they had to familiarize themselves with the tapes, PETA delayed sending out a press release until the next afternoon.[2] Among other things, the release noted that "the ALF found no painkillers or euthanizing agents in the laboratory. This is consistent with papers in which Gennarelli describes killing primates by injecting formaldehyde into their brains. Bottles of curare-type drugs, which render the animal helpless but heighten awareness and fear, were found and destroyed."

---

[2]Due to the delay in copying the tapes, and miscommunication, PETA mistakenly believed the ALF raid had occurred that Monday, rather than the day before.

From the stolen tapes, Alex Pacheco started to piece together a powerful twenty-four-minute documentary. Referring to the March 6, 1983, interview in the Toronto *Globe*, in which Gennarelli had said, "I'm not willing to go on the record to discuss the studies . . . it has the potential to stir up all sorts of unnecessary fuss . . . I would like to lie low . . . we're trying to keep ourselves out of the newspapers," PETA named the documentary *Unnecessary Fuss*.

On October 2, 1984, Alex Pacheco held a news conference at the Hilton Hotel in Philadelphia. Every television and radio station in town was there, along with both the Philadelphia *Inquirer* and the *Daily News*. Attacking the Commonwealth's Ivy League university is not a small matter in Philadelphia.

The video was devastating. Several observers sobbed unabashedly, some people covered their faces with their hands, and others walked out of the room. Philadelphia activist Gloria Cohen asked an *Inquirer* reporter, "If you can't be emotional about pain and death, what *can* you be emotional about?"

Daily News columnist Jill Porter summed it all up this way: "The tapes told you one thing for sure. It takes a definite kind of person to indulge in animal experimentation, the kind who has a high tolerance for sadism or the kind who is alarmingly insensitive to animals."

As the tape played, Alex looked out from under the glare of the television station lights to see uniformed and plainclothes officers filing into the room. They lined the walls and waited. There must have been two dozen of them: in the back of the room, big men in raincoats over their suits; along the sides of the room, big men in blue uniforms.

No sooner had the press left than "the law" swooped down on Alex, and on anyone else they could collar. It was chaos. Activists who had stayed behind to help load pamphlets and videos into the cars were stopped and their identification was demanded of them.

"You are to appear before the grand jury . . ." the officers recited, as activists found themselves holding a piece of notarized paper.

"Am I under arrest?" people asked. "Not yet," they were told. The subpoenas, most in the names of John and Jane Doe, commanded the bearers' presence before a Grand Jury. Instead of the prosecution of Gennarelli and Langfitt, there was to be a witch-hunt through the animal rights community for the raiders. The Commonwealth planned to seek out and destroy the ALF, and PETA was about to face some hefty legal bills.

The university had started preparing to defend itself the morning after the ALF break-in, when students discovered the shambles that was left of the baboon lab.

Dr. Robert Marshak, dean of Penn's veterinary school, had prepared a statement denying all charges of wrongdoing. "It is absolutely false that we are inhumane or cruel in our research," he told the Associated Press. "We treat these animals better than most people treat their pets."

Dr. Thomas Langfitt, who was not only Gennarelli's partner, but also chairman of the University of Pennsylvania Hospital's department of neurosurgery and a chief investigator at Gennarelli's laboratory, told the press that the animals had not been treated inhumanely. "Researchers would never laugh at the apes," he told the *Daily News*, "We treat the baboons the way we treat human beings." In the Pittsburgh *Post-Gazette* he insisted, contrary to the evidence, that "The animals are anesthetized and feel no pain."

Without looking at the tapes or batting an eye, Dr. James Wyngaarden, director of NIH, the single largest funder of experiments in the world and Gennarelli's "deep pocket," supported the experiments and the university. "That laboratory," he said, failing to mention that he had conducted research himself at Penn, "is among the best in the world." An NIH site visit determined that the head injury research "was being conducted in accordance with protocol and [NIH] found no evidence of mistreatment of animals." The university's own "review" of the clinic found "no evidence of wrongdoing," and university officials refused to allow the tapes to be shown to its "investigators," many of whom were former head injury clinic personnel.

Meanwhile, PETA was having the tapes reviewed by experts in anesthesiology, neurology, and veterinary medicine. The experts began to battle it out. For each crony who would defend Gennarelli and Langfitt's work, there were two who would sharply criticize the experimenters' abusive actions and attitudes.

Dr. Jay D. Glass, a neurobiologist at the Center for Brain Research, stated that " . . . the animals were subjected to unnecessary pain, the experimental protocols followed in the work invalidate the results . . . ." Patrick D. Wall, world-renowned expert in pain, wrote from University College, London, that "these animals were not anaesthetized at the time of head injury. . . . " to counter comments from Penn's Dr. Lawrence Thibault that "the monkeys experience no pain. They are unconscious."

PETA's next move was to submit copies of the tapes to the U.S. Department of Agriculture, which promised to investigate the lab. It made good its word. A June 5, 1984, USDA inspection report cited seventy-four violations of animal-care-and-use regulations in Penn's baboon facility. Two or three violations are considered average for such an inspection, the inspectors observed. The report concluded that "all animals should be moved out of there immediately."

Before the fight was over, there would be rallies on the Penn campus, national news stories, and a petition from twenty-eight members of the United States Congress to stop the baboon experiments. In May 1985, over 1,500 people descended on the campus, holding signs accusing the university of being an "animal Auschwitz" and chanting, "Close down the lab, close down the lab."

The university and NIH were getting buried with mail on the issue. However, they would not budge. Defiantly, NIH upped Gennarelli and Langfitt's grant by another $500,000: a decision that angered even the most conservative "reformists," and caused PETA to organize an invasion of NIH.

Activists all over the country responded to the call to take part in "an unspecified act of civil disobedience." One hundred and one people were to descend on the NIH campus and gain access to Dr. Murray Goldstein's funding office on the eighth floor of NIH's Building 31-B, then sit down and be arrested. The action required a plan of almost military precision.

"NIH has gone too far," Alex Pacheco told the activists who gathered in Bethesda the evening before the sit-in. "Together we're going to make them do what is right and just."

The next morning, 101 people, dressed in the "business-type clothes" they had been asked to bring, prepared for what—for most—would be their first arrest.

Sharon Lawson sat nervously at the steering wheel of the bus in which she was to chauffeur fifty activists through NIH's main gates and deposit them in the driveway outside Building 31-B.

"Sharon, calm down," Susan Rich told her, stepping onto the bus and adjusting her blazer. "I hope this clipboard convinces them I'm a tour guide." Like everyone else she kept looking at her carefully synchronized watch.

At exactly 9:00 A.M., in an action that went like clockwork, the elevator and stairwell doors opened on the eighth floor as if pulled by a single string, and out streamed 101 people who didn't belong there. There was no stopping them, and no one tried to. NIH's director of public relations happened to step out of his office on his way to who-knows-where and, finding the hall inexplicably crowded, stepped back into it. A few other NIH staff, unsure what was going on, stood still and let the "biomass" pour past them down the hall.

"We're here to sing 'Happy Birthday' to Dr. Goldstein," explained Sue Wiedman over her shoulder, as the orderly column made its way briskly to the office with its oversized oak desk, conference table, and plush chairs.

"We're going to make it," Ann Pacheco, Alex's mother, whispered to Ilene Cohn. Those at the head of the column pushed open the double doors and kept moving, past the secretaries outer sanctum and into Goldstein's inner one. Then they sat down and waited to be arrested. The sit-in was a reality! When all the activists' bottoms touched the carpeting, they had taken up the entire suite of rooms.

"What are you doing? Get out of here!" the woman occupying the desk outside Goldstein's door fumed.

"We are occupying these offices," Bobbie Wright said, loving the sound of the words. She had flown in from Arizona to be part of this historic occasion. Howard Edelstein started a chant and everyone joined in.

"Goldstein, Goldstein hear our cry. Baboons don't deserve to die."

"There he goes!" called out Alan Bullington from ARIS, the animal rights cable television company in New York. Goldstein had arrived late, caught a glimpse of what lay ahead of him and executed a sharp about-face. Seeing Goldstein in flight, the secretaries picked their way toward the door through a sea of legs, their departure followed almost immediately by the arrival of NIH security.

"You will have to leave," the chief officer announced uncertainly.

"Gennarelli needs to fry, baboons don't deserve to die," answered the activists.

The officers milled about, but made no move to effect arrests. It was too big a task. People started reading Goldstein's files and answering the phones, telling callers that the offices were "under siege until the baboon experiments are terminated." Alex got out his address book and began dialing reporters' numbers. The demonstrators unfurled banners from the windows, and Nancy Hey, a student from the midwest, addressed people eight floors below through a bullhorn.

By lunchtime the police still didn't seem to know what to do. Alex typed up a list of demands that began, "Cut the funding to Gennarelli's lab," and ended "Release the Silver Spring monkeys," and handed it to the officer in charge.

"Those women'll leave when they have to go to the bathroom badly enough," the officer said.

"Afraid not," Alex told him. "We've set up a latrine of plastic bags in wastepaper baskets in Dr. Goldstein's office." Within fifteen minutes, the police were allowing activists access to restrooms.

"They'll probably make their arrests after dark when the television cameras have gone," Alex predicted.

The activists were determined not to go quietly. They split up into watch shifts, taking turns lying in the corridor leading to Goldstein's suite. To make a path, the police would have to drag people away one at a time, giving time for the others, all the way in the back, to call the press and get them to the scene.

By morning, the occupation was the top news story in Washington and activists from other states were giving "live, on the spot" interviews over the phones to their local reporters. Sympathizers gathered on the grass below the site.

The demonstrators were jubilant but famished. Enough string and cord and other materials were scavenged to allow a wastepaper basket to be lowered to the ground. It was quickly filled with food and raised, but the second attempt was thwarted by a guard with a knife who cut not only the string but the hand of the person filling the basket.

By the end of day two, NIH escalated its attempts to oust the invaders by cutting off the phones and turning on the cold air. That night the activists were not only starving, but freezing. A sweater had been found in a desk drawer, the only two curtains had been pulled down for use as blankets, and three people lay on the floor wrapped in an American flag they had removed from its stand. Those who felt comfortable doing so huddled together for warmth.

Worn down by stress, having to sleep in shifts on the floor, feeling the effects of lack of food, and now freezing, some people faced an additional burden: angry messages from home. Not all husbands, wives, employers and friends on the "outside" were coping well, and those on the "inside" had no way to communicate back to them. Tom Regan, the philosophy professor and author, set up counseling sessions for those torn between continuing the occupation and saving their relationships or jobs.

Alex demanded to speak with his lawyers, Roger Galvin and Gary Francione. They had to get help from sympathetic members of Congress and pressure NIH into listening to the demands. Congressman Tom Lantos' wife, Annette, was already on the phone to NIH. "Fair's fair," she said. "Arrest them or don't, but don't torture them."

There was constant singing in the hall. The lyrics of the Battle Hymn of the Republic became "Our eyes have seen the glory of the closing of the labs/We will pester Gennarelli 'til he ends up driving cabs." As she sang, Betsy Swart, who had traveled from San Francisco for the sit-in, discovered that by opening the stairwell door and allowing the singing to travel to the floors below, the group attracted visitors. The police thought they had effectively sealed off the floor by commandeering the elevator, but now whistleblowers, sympathizers, and reporters began sneaking up the back stairs to relay messages, get updates, and tell tales on their bosses.

People who had to go home disappeared quietly down the stairs, so as not to alert the police to their departure. By day three, the 101 had become eighty-six. Alex had a set of walkie-talkies delivered via the back-stair route, and also bags of food, clean T-shirts, and underwear. Even razors, toothpaste, and soap began arriving and were very quietly distributed. Unaware that the food blockade had been breached, Alex Hershaft, the leader of the Farm Animal Reform Movement, started a hunger strike eight floors below the protestors.

That afternoon, a surprise visitor arrived. Word traveled down the hall, and soon Alex crept quietly into position behind the activists who blocked the guard's view of the door.

"I'm Don Rheem, Margaret Heckler's assistant," the young man in the stairwell said. Alex couldn't believe it. Was this really an aide to Reagan's cabinet member, the secretary of Health and Human Services, NIH's overseer? Why would *he* have to creep up the stairwell?

"Ms. Heckler wants to see the Gennarelli tape. I know it sounds crazy, but sometimes channels don't work the way you may think they do."

Alex slipped out onto the concrete stairs and the two men talked for over an hour. Then Rheem left.

Alex wondered how long he could hold the group together. Some squabbles had broken out; there had been tears, two people were sick (one with terrible back pain), and one activist had broken into Goldstein's liquor cabinet.

At nine o'clock on the morning of day four, Francione and Galvin returned and asked Alex to accompany them to a meeting with the head of NIH, Dr. James Wyngaarden. Alex wondered if it was because the sit-in had been covered on the "Today" show that morning or if he was to receive an ultimatum. When he returned, the people in the hall knew that whatever the news, something good had happened.

"Last night, Margaret Heckler, the secretary of Health and Human Services, watched the tape," Alex told them. "She was sickened and appalled. First thing this morning she called James Wyngaarden. She has ordered him to immediately cut all funds from the lab."

It took a moment for the news to sink into the tired minds around him. Then the cry went up: "We've won!" Pandemonium broke out. People hugged and jumped about and cried openly. It was over!

Plans were laid for an orderly departure and the press was notified. People dusted, reinstalled the drapes, wrote thank-you notes to the secretaries, tied up the trash bags, scrubbed the sinks, and said goodbye to the officers they had talked to about vegetarianism and animal testing over the four days and nights. They combed their hair and tried to look their best, then they stepped out into the sunlight of a gorgeous day, home-made signs held aloft, and held a news conference on the grass.

It was a total victory: Gennarelli and Langfitt were never to scramble baboons' brains again. NIH had no choice but to do what Secretary Heckler demanded. Behind the scenes, however, they would fight her every step of the way. Years later, when Secretary Heckler had been replaced by a new administrator, Dr. Louis Sullivan, a staunch supporter of all animal experiments, NIH quietly returned funding to Gennarelli to revive his laboratory. This time he worked on miniature pigs and rats—species he hoped would be less appealing to the public should word get out.

By that time, NIH had come up with a plan to fight the growing animal rights movement. Part of it involved turning back the hands of time: NIH set out to reverse any gains the movement had made since it burst onto the experimentation scene with the Silver Spring monkeys case.

In 1991, as part of its campaign to stop General Motors from using pigs, dogs, and ferrets in impact and skin-shredding tests, PETA relaunched *Unnecessary Fuss*. General Motors, the only automaker still using animals in lieu of more sophisticated alternatives, had installed Thomas Langfitt as chairperson of its committee on crash tests, and PETA used the tape to remind the public exactly how grotesque Gennarelli and Langfitt's experiments at the University of Pennsylvania were. *Unnecessary Fuss* did its job, motivating activists to disrupt General Motors' exhibits at auto shows, to chain themselves to the steering wheels of new General Motors models, and to petition dealers to join the campaign to bring General Motors "out of the Dark Ages of animal tests." The tapes the ALF removed from the University of Pennsylvania continue to serve the animal rights movement well.

7

The Vet School Revolt

I must interpret the life about me as I interpret the life that is my own. My life is full of meaning to me. The life around me must be full of significance to itself. If I am to expect others to respect my life, then I must respect the other life I see, however strange it may be to mine. . . . We need a boundless ethics which will include the animals also.

— Dr. Albert Schweitzer, *Civilization and Ethics*

W hen the ALF drove away that morning from the University of Pennsylvania campus, Valerie didn't expect to be back at all, let alone within a matter of weeks. She had other projects in the works and "scouts" doing surveillance on both coasts. She expected to be able to concentrate on the administrative side of things, and to formalize the ALF's loose structure. Casual and spur-of-the-moment meetings needed to be replaced with orderly, scheduled meetings, she felt. However, as Hacker told her, life is a maze you are guided through but will never understand.

When the story of the stolen tapes appeared in the *Daily Pennsylvanian*, the campus newspaper, there was already discontent brewing among students at the university's School of Veterinary Medicine. Dean Robert Marshak's attitudes toward animals and his belligerence toward students who dared espouse animal rights philosophy was, for some, more than annoying. It was intolerable. Some students, like Eddie, were wrestling with tangible examples of the school's tolerance for animal suffering.

For ten months, Eddie and the other students had listened to the cries of a dog confined inside the school. The dog's howls echoed through the cinderblock walls day and night, but particularly after dark, when the animals in the veterinary school were left alone. People listened to the sad wailing sound and some couldn't help but feel uneasy about what went on in the building.

The vet school lies across the road and a few blocks east of Gennarelli's laboratory. It is the university's biggest moneymaker, attracting donations from all over the country, and not only from alumni. People bring animals through its doors when their particular problems have exhausted the talents of local veterinarians and other institutions—dogs with brain tumors and inner ear infections, horses with game legs (whose problems may be alleviated in a horse "swimming track" at the university's New Bolton Center), and a host of animals with exotic infections.

The front of the school has been modernized and painted white. A large, circular driveway leads to its front door, through which visitors enter a reception area filled with potted plants. But that's as far as they get. No outsiders are allowed to set foot in the back of the school, the older part. There, dirt fills the cracks in the cinderblock walls, the pipes are old, and the lighting poor.

Adrian Morrison and Peter Hand, who traveled to Maryland to testify for Dr. Taub in the Silver Spring monkeys case, conduct their animal experiments in the old part of the building. On occasion, Hand's car, with its vanity plate, "PAIN," is parked in one of the spots marked "Faculty Only."

The morning Eddie read about the Gennarelli tapes in the *Daily Pennsylvanian*, he could barely contain himself. He wanted to link up with the ALF. To Valerie's annoyance, her source couldn't remember if Eddie had "come in" through the American Anti-Vivisection Society, PETA, or the local Pennsylvania group, the Pennsylvania Animal Rights Connection. Eddie had called them all.

Not knowing if his intentions were honorable or if he might be a university security plant seeking information, the ALF's Philadelphia contact told Eddie that, although Valerie knew nothing about illegal activities, she had expressed an interest in doing something about his complaint.

Valerie and Eddie met for coffee in a restaurant called "The White Dog," across from the university law school. Eddie was all-American looking, tall and clean-cut, like the students pictured in college promotionals. He took off his sunglasses to reveal a pleasant, intelligent face and dark brown eyes that contrasted with his trendy, bleach-streaked hair.

Eddie was a second-year student in the vet school. He, like Kit, had been particularly affected by the plight of one animal. The soft, strangled sounds of the unseen dog students called "The Phantom" had been bothering him for two terms, but it wasn't until just a couple of weeks back that Eddie had seen inside the laboratories.

The opportunity presented itself when Eddie saw a research assistant struggling through the door into the old section, carrying a load of syringe packs. Eddie's offer of assistance was accepted, and it gave him a ticket into the labs.

There were no clean, stainless steel cages or antiseptic smells here, as in the client's section of the school. This was like a dungeon. Eddie's parents were having a hard time paying Penn's massive tuition bills, and their son was smart enough not to show his disgust at what he saw. He went back to his room and brooded. His ten minutes inside the lab made him determined to do something to help the animals he had seen.

"It's a total dump," he told Valerie. "Granted, I'm a pretty clean person, but even someone with low standards of hygiene would be nauseated. Animal hair is stuck to the bars of the cages. The place is so old and dark it's a wonder anyone can see to clean it at all. But the worst part is the animals. There were two dogs in there. One's a very thin mixed German shepherd. He's the one who howls, the one the students joke about. They say the sound comes from the soul of a research dog who haunts the place. The lab assistant called him a 'pain in the butt,' because he makes so much noise.

"Then there's a golden retriever, or at least half golden retriever. They've taken out one of her eyes, I think. It's stitched up and a real mess. She keeps her head to one side, as if she's in pain, but she didn't make a peep.

"I could hear cats, too, calling from one of the other rooms. And birds, either doves or pigeons. The assistant said the cats belong to a sleep-deprivation experimenter called Morrison, and that they have a mass of electrical hardware in their heads. Supposedly the pigeons are there for us to practice surgery on, although I looked in the curriculum and there's no mention of it. It may be for special projects. The assistant said he breaks their wings so students can fix them and then wring their necks."

"Was he kidding?" Valerie asked.

"No," said Eddie. "If you'd ever been in vet school, you'd believe it. Some things they make you do here are just sick. I mean, even as far as the birds go, there's a wildlife sanctuary just outside of town. My girlfriend and I took them a pigeon we found poisoned in the square, and we were really impressed. They run on a shoestring. They'd be thrilled to death if veterinary students set wings for them."

A delivery truck had pulled up across from the restaurant and Valerie watched the driver unloading boxes of lettuce. She had been listening to everything Eddie said with a growing sense of commitment to getting the animals out. Now she was thinking of the mechanics.

"Listen, if you don't know how to get in touch with the ALF . . . " Eddie said with some annoyance. He had mistaken Valerie's concentration for indifference. "I'll keep calling until I find someone who can help. My parents have busted a gut to pay tuition here, but I can't stick it out if I don't do what's right. I'm going to risk getting expelled if that's what it takes."

Valerie didn't doubt Eddie's sincerity. It shone out of him. "Listen, Eddie" she said. "Perhaps I can help you, but you'll need to play a role and be smart about it. That means not telling anyone else anything, no matter what. That's the only way we stand a chance of getting the animals out and not letting anyone get nailed for it, OK?"

Eddie nodded. Valerie hoped he'd graduate and become the sort of veterinarian animals need so badly. Meanwhile, they needed a plan that wouldn't get him thrown out. She had him walk her over to the vet school so she could take a look at it, while she asked him more questions. She felt odd to be back on the campus, in broad daylight, watching the police cars cruise by. Hacker had been right—the campus was crawling with security.

"Eddie," Valerie asked, as they crossed at the light. "The student who works in the lab. Is he a vet student?"

"No. He's just someone strapped for cash like the rest of us. There are quite a few rich kids, but most of us do what we can to make ends meet."

They made their way directly to the back of the school. Things were quiet away from the main street. Valerie looked at the building carefully. It was like an old European prison—heavy stone, old construction, windows high up, and thick steps leading to a big metal door. Impenetrable, she thought. No hinges on the outside, but—oddly enough—no visible burglar alarm wiring either. Regardless, a break-in was out of the question without an extension ladder to get to the windows, and that would leave the interested party fully exposed on the street.

Valerie told Eddie to find out anything he could about the research assistant and report back. Who were his friends? Where did he live? Where did he hang out, and, most particularly, what was his financial situation? There was one other student who worked in that lab, and Eddie needed to get a profile on him, too.

They shook hands, having made arrangements to meet again in a few days. Eddie promised he would work fast. Before Valerie left, he pressed something into her hand.

"It's sixty bucks," he said. "My mother just sent me some money for my birthday and said to buy what I want. I know what I want—those two dogs and the rest of the animals. It's all I can put in, but please accept it."

Valerie could see Eddie was absolutely committed to being part of a rescue effort. "That," he said, "is what a veterinarian is supposed to do, isn't it? That's what I came here to learn to do. Save animals' lives."

The black van was in the shop getting an oil leak fixed, so Valerie decided to use the gaudy blue and green van that had run into trouble at Howard University. Unfortunately, it had District of Columbia tags. In the wake of the Gennarelli raid, it would be unwise to have the campus police notice a van with out-of-state plates, particularly plates from PETA's neck of the woods.

Bear's wife, Bobbie, was an artist. She agreed to draw an exact replica of the university campus parking sticker Eddie had xeroxed and color it in. Now Valerie needed Pennsylvania plates.

Maxine, the waitress, accompanied Valerie to Philadelphia the night before the action. Valerie had thought of taking Sonia, but was becoming uneasy with Sonia's attitude. Sonia had met with her twice since the first University of Pennsylvania raid and was agitating for more militancy from the group.

"Is it a war on vivisection or isn't it?" she had challenged Valerie. "It wasn't Martin Luther King who ignited the civil rights movement. It was Malcolm X. Anyone can talk—it's *doing* that counts."

Valerie had disagreed, vehemently. Like Sonia, she held no illusions that Congress was the animals' "Great White Hope," but "doing" was not synonymous with "doing violence." The two had parted on bad terms. Valerie planned to try to smooth things out after the vet school job.

As soon as it got dark, Valerie and Maxine drove through the city looking for parked vans of the same make. Valerie knew that when police run a license check, colors don't matter, but manufacturers do. Only car-smart cops notice the model year, unless there's a huge difference between the tag or registration and the vehicle they're looking at.

It didn't take long to find what they were looking for. Maxine dropped Valerie off and turned the van around to face downhill, leaving the door ajar so Valerie could jump in if they were chased. In Valerie's pocket she had a can of rust-eater to move the bolts, just in case, and two screwdrivers.

After a quick look around, Valerie walked over to the van, sat on the curb beside it, waited about half a minute, then moved up and began to undo the tag. Her "pocketpanion" hammer did the trick, and she needed only to tap the unscrewed bolts with it to move them out of the sockets. A young boy appeared out of nowhere, as young boys sometimes do, and watched her work.

"Whatcha doing?" he asked.

"Just changing the tag," Valerie told him.

"Ain't that Mr. Shupe's van?" he said, matter-of-factly.

"Uh-huh, sure is." He sat and watched Valerie. She only needed two minutes. The tag came off in her hand, and she stood with her back to the kid so he wouldn't "make" her.

"Take it easy," Valerie said to the kid, without looking back.

She could hear him moving back down the street behind her, the show over. Valerie put on her best purposeful stride and made it to the van. Maxine pulled away.

Their next stop was an all-night drugstore. Just in case the kid said something to Mr. Shupe, or Mr. Shupe himself noticed his front plate missing and reported it, Valerie had decided to change the "F" to an "E." Then it wouldn't come up as stolen in the computer. All she needed was adhesive mounting tape and the job was done.

Valerie met Eddie for breakfast the next morning. She wasn't hungry, but Eddie was definitely a growing boy who appreciated an invitation to eat. Over hash browns, buckwheat pancakes, two orders of rye toast, and two large glasses of orange juice, he recounted what he'd learned about the work-study students at the lab. The one he hadn't met was what he called a "research worshipper," a foreign exchange student who thought American scientists were gods. He was a volunteer, grateful for the experience. The one who had let Eddie into the lab was the best bet.

"He's definitely broke," said Eddie. "He said he can make a jar of peanut butter last a month. He doesn't open the jar, just rubs it over the bread. I've been thinking about this bribe thing. If he's a creep, he's not going to care why we want access. And if he cares about the animals, all we have to do is persuade him that we won't hurt them."

Eddie couldn't have anything to do with the animals' removal beyond contact with the research assistant. But he needed an alibi, and to stick to his guns about knowing nothing when questioned. Val gave him his story. He was to tell the research assistant that he had been trying to date an attractive girl by stringing her along with a story of how he was doing important research in the lab. He'd tell him that now the girl wanted to look around.

Then he'd wave a nice, juicy, hundred-dollar carrot at the assistant in return for his help.

"I'll give you eighty bucks . . . make it a hundred bucks," Eddie would tell him, "if you leave the place open tonight. Just give me an hour. You can come back at nine or ten and lock everything up. I just need to show her around. We've got a date at eight. I guarantee we won't touch anything. All I need to do is walk her through and impress her, OK?"

Eddie was to leave immediately and stay with friends, highly visible and in a public place, until ten o'clock. He would tell them he was waiting for a girl. At about ten, Eddie would get his friends to walk with him to the lab assistant's dorm so he could tell the caretaker that he hadn't been to the lab because he had been stood up.

"You can keep the hundred," he would say, if all went according to plan. "I don't have anyone to spend it on anyway."

What would happen when the liberation was discovered was anyone's guess. Perhaps the research assistant would be smart enough not to implicate himself in taking money to leave the lab open. Perhaps he'd say he'd locked up as usual. Perhaps he'd point the finger at Eddie. Valerie told Eddie to expect to be put in the hot seat, and to prepare for it. His alibis were genuine and honest, and would come across that way. Eddie had only to stick to his story. Suspicion, Valerie kept repeating to him, is not enough. Remember, *you* are the only person who can give them the proof, so don't do it.

That way the risk all belonged to Valerie and her team. If they walked down that long corridor and found the door closed, the animals were out of luck. They were out of luck, too, if they found campus security waiting to nab them.

That evening, Hacker, Maxine, and Doug, the science teacher who had been part of the Howard raid, joined Valerie. The group cruised up and down the road behind the veterinary school until the right parking space opened up. Valerie had picked up Hacker that afternoon. It seemed only fair, after being denied the opportunity to go in on the last Penn raid, that he should be one of those going inside to get these animals out. Hacker had no doubt the mission would succeed. "It is fate," he said.

It was still quite light when they pulled into a good parking spot. From the driver's seat, Maxine could almost see the entrance to the Schuylkill Expressway—their passage out of this place. The time passed slowly. Cruisers flitted by in the fading light. Students walked past chatting and laughing, headed for home. After a while the traffic, pedestrian and street, trickled to almost nothing.

A little before eight, they spotted the assistant emerging from the back door of the old building and heading for the Burger King, a stop Eddie had said the assistant made every night on his way to his dorm. Hacker opened the van door and stepped out, carrying an empty cat carrier in each hand. He made his way to the front of the building. Eddie had said it was not unusual for people picking up animals to walk into the building, even at that hour.

A few minutes later Hacker had wound his way through the labyrinth that comprised the vet school and followed Eddie's directions to the back of the building and the door to the street. Doug saw the door open and motioned to Valerie. They leapt from the back of the van onto the pavement and made for the opening. Making sure no one was watching, they passed through into the veterinary school. Valerie wondered if, the next time Maxine saw them, they would be in the back of a police car or coming out the back door with the animals in tow.

The door closed behind them. Not waiting for their eyes to adjust to the gloom, Valerie and Doug started down the dark corridor. Their footsteps echoed through the walls of the old building. Hacker had vanished. For a moment, Valerie felt as if she was in a horror film. Then she heard a pathetic wail, and the spell was broken. It must have been "The Phantom."

Hacker reappeared as they turned the next corner. He had propped open the next door, the one that led into the main laboratory complex, and was already at work. He had the howling German shepherd on one leash and the mixed golden retriever on the other. The golden was moving along, her head cocked sideways, but the shepherd seemed not to be able to walk. Hacker was coaxing him, but something was wrong with the dog's feet.

As the golden shook her head, fluid flew from her ear. Valerie could smell it a few steps away, and wondered if she would ever truly adjust to the assault on her senses that came with every raid.

"Come on, boy," Hacker was saying to the shepherd, stroking the dog and trying to persuade him to put one painful foot in front of the other. At this rate it would take hours to get back to the street, but Hacker was patient.

Valerie whipped out bags for the cats. There were only three, each housed in a wooden cage in the room behind the dog runs. There was no time to examine them, but Valerie could see wires sticking out of their heads. As they pushed forward to rub their heads against her hands, she could feel hard knobs of some sort where fur and flesh should have been. Valerie stuck ketamine-filled syringes into the cats' thighs and waited for the animals to space out.

Across the room, Doug was loading pigeons into a big cardboard box. The pigeons had greasy, ruffled feathers. They were like ones Valerie saw in Chinatown, miserable birds waiting to have their necks wrung for meat, while healthier street pigeons pecked for scraps on the sidewalk beside them.

There was a tremendous thud from outside the door in the main part of the lab. Then another thud. Hacker was talking to himself in Yiddish and ramming boxes up against the lab door. If anyone tried to get in, they'd find an obstacle course that would give everyone on the inside time to make it to the back door.

Hacker had given up on the dogs for the moment while he made his fortification. He saw Valerie look at them, raise her eyebrows, and then look at him. As she opened her mouth to speak, he raised his hand.

"No nagging, Val" he said. "I'm right behind you." With the strength that came from years of lifting carcasses on and off trucks, he scooped a dog under each arm and headed for the door.

Valerie radioed Maxine for the all-clear. To her relief, it came back right away. She opened the door, took a deep breath and stepped out onto the street. There was no foot traffic, but the tail end of a cruiser was disappearing around the corner. "Brilliant, Maxine," she said under her breath.

Doug stepped out onto the sidewalk with his box of pigeons, their feet skidding across the cardboard. Maxine had moved the van five paces from the door, and as soon as she heard the radio signal, she leaped into the back and swung open the rear doors. Hacker handed her the dogs, one at a time, while Valerie climbed in the side door with the cats. As Maxine returned to the driver's seat, Valerie was carefully laying the first cat on her side in one of the carriers.

Hacker climbed into the back after the dogs, closed the door behind him, and started making them comfortable on the thick quilt that covered the floor. That's when he saw what was wrong with the shepherd's feet: his nails had grown so long that they curled back under his pads. Each step for him was like walking on scissor points. Apparently the experimenters had never looked at his feet, because it was clear that all they needed to do was cut his nails. Now the quick of the nail was so long that cutting them back far enough would be painful. He would have to be anesthetized.

Doug took the passenger seat, the box full of scuttling pigeons on his lap. Maxine threw the van in gear and headed off toward the freeway. From entrance to exit, the operation had taken twenty-one minutes. Pretty good going, Valerie thought. Almost as much time later, the van turned onto the street that led to the ALF's Philadelphia safehouse.

The owner of the house would deliver the pigeons to a wildlife rehabilitation center that specialized in birds. The pigeons would be quarantined together in a big flight cage, so as not to risk spreading any diseases to other birds. Later on, when they were healthy enough to leave, the cage door would be left open so they could come and go as they chose.

Doug photographed the animals, naming them as he went. The cats were now Geraldine, Ethel, and Alice. The dogs were Jasmine and, because of his condition, Toes. Valerie and Doug talked about plastering the Penn campus with photos of the animals and waiting to see how the vet school would justify their condition. They also needed photos PETA could use to send to the press.

The woman who had opened her house to the ALF insisted that the dogs be allowed to rest on the bed in her guest room, although Jasmine's undercoat and stomach, coated with urine, would leave a lot of washing to do. Jasmine had suffered multiple injuries, and a closer inspection revealed that it was pus that was draining from her ear. Her inner ear had been surgically removed. She was extremely weak, depressed, and dehydrated. Her right eye had been sewn shut and was draining, too. All the cats had electrical implants sunk into their skulls, and Ethel, a shorthaired tortoise shell, was pregnant and had earmites.

"Don't be revolting," Maxine told Doug as he put his finger on the plastic plug in Geraldine's head and wiggled it about. "It looks like a faulty electrical socket," he said. "See this, it's a place to insert other wires." The wound floated in a sea of infection and to stop the run-off from getting into her eyes, Geraldine kept her eyes half closed and looked as if she was dozing. Geraldine's wounds were cleansed, Jasmine's eyes and ears were swabbed, and each of the animals was given food before being allowed to sleep.

The next day, the New York veterinarian would arrive to put Geraldine and Jasmine on antibiotics. When the cats were back at normal weight and their infections were gone, they were to be scheduled for surgery to remove the hardware from their skulls. Even though the electrodes had been implanted haphazardly, it would take a delicate operation to remove them. If a wire were cut in the wrong place the cats could become epileptic.

Valerie looked at the cats stretched out, the dogs snoring on the beds, and the pigeons feeding and flapping their wings in the outdoor aviary. The enormity of her cause made her feel cheated. How many animals *hadn't* they rescued? She longed for a vacation. To get away to Maho Bay, perhaps, and feel the cool turquoise water on her skin.

"Not much to show for our work, is there?" she sighed.

Maxine's face dropped. "You can't be serious, Val," she said. "Even one animal, one sparrow . . . "

"Don't mind me," Valerie cut her off and put her arm around Maxine's shoulders. "I'm just tired, that's all."

For now, the animals would stay in Philadelphia, just a few

miles from the university, while the police scoured Maryland, Virginia, and Delaware for them, convinced that they had been moved out of state.

The campus erupted in controversy. Veterinary students began to hold meetings questioning the university's use of animals. Even the staff of the university's own campus paper, the *Daily Pennsylvanian*, was split on the issue.

Dr. Gloria Binkowski, then a veterinary student at Penn, would later write of how profoundly she was affected by the administration's speciesist attitude. She and another veterinarian, Dr. Eric Dunayer, would end up suing the university to demand the right not to hurt and kill animals in their veterinary training. They would prevail as "conscientious objectors." Their first, much-publicized efforts lent strength to students all over the country who were beginning to stop apologizing for broaching the issue of animal use and abuse.

The Philadelphia *Inquirer* and other papers ran the photographs of Geraldine and Jasmine in their stories on the second University of Pennsylvania raid. Local television stations were begging for interviews. By prearranged agreement, PETA posted coded messages on its bulletin board to let the ALF know someone needed to call in for specifics. A hooded ALF member met with the *Inquirer*, a sympathetic local television reporter, and *Omni* magazine.

PETA's university sources reported that donations to the veterinary school were plummeting. Clerks in the administration offices leaked copies of some of the nasty letters sent in from across the country. The second raid spurred renewed interest in Gennarelli's experiments, and *Unnecessary Fuss* was seen by more and more of the public.

Dr. Robert Marshak, dean of the School of Veterinary Medicine, found himself trying to answer some tough questions. He was responsible for overseeing the use of 60,000 animals used in experiments every year on campus. People the university cared about had read the reports and wanted to know how, with so many people on fixed incomes forced to give up their dearly loved animal companions because of the high cost of veterinary care, the university could justify buying animals from dealers and operating on them. Surely the university would better serve the community if it opened a low-cost clinic and saved animals' lives.

Marshak rigidly stood his ground. "I have no apology to make for the experiments," he said. He alone spoke for the school: Morrison and Hand, despite calls from the press, had made themselves unavailable for comment.

Professor Gary Francione from the law school appeared front and center in the animal rights battle against the university administrators, assisting Gloria Binkowski and Eric Dunayer in bringing suit against Penn for the right to make sick animals better, rather than well animals sick. At the same time, a high school student named Jenifer Graham made news by refusing to dissect in her California biology class. In medical colleges all across the country, students started picking up their books and walking out the door rather than cut open that dog, frog, or cat. A classroom revolution had begun, and in many cases instructors were backing the students.

Valerie rejoiced. She knew the ALF's actions had provided some of the impetus for the revolution in attitudes on the Pennsylvania campus and elsewhere. Compassionate veterinarians and compassionate physicians could continue the fight in their own way, becoming people who applied the Hippocratic oath from their first day of training and set out to heal, not harm. She took pride in knowing that she and her organization were responsible (in part) for encouraging the humane education of the sorts of physicians and veterinarians who would never refer to a patient as "the kidney in room 101."

8

The City of Hope

Valerie was receiving regular communications from her contacts in Britain, as well as newsclippings of ALF activities there. She knew that on a rainy November night in 1984, shopkeepers all over Britain had been forced to remove Mars candy bars from their store shelves. Warning notes had been found in seven bars from stores scattered across the nation: if Mars did not stop using restrained monkeys in tooth decay studies, the notes said, the ALF would adulterate the chocolate bars with rat poison.

Ten million Mars bars came "off sale" in the little island that was the world's highest per capita consumer of sweets. Days later, Mars gave in: the animal tests would end. The £1,000 reward offered by the London *Sun-Mirror* for information leading to the arrest and conviction of the Mars bars hoax perpetrator went unclaimed.

Valerie was impressed with the simplicity of the action and the instant results it garnered, but she hated this new tactic. She and Josh argued about it over the phone. She thought it was "dirty." He believed it was justified as long as no one had been hurt. "So the ends justify the means?" she had asked him. "Sometimes," he said, "as you well know."

"Val, I need you in California tomorrow," he said, the next time they spoke, about a month later. The invitation came at a good time. Sean was moody because he was absorbed in the annual task he hated most—carving out Wildnear's company budget in preparation for the next fiscal year. Every available piece of flat, elevated space in the house was covered with balance sheets, pieces of paper with scribbled figures all over them, and the other mess that meant at least two more weeks of misery for him. Valerie's disappearance would mean a quieter house in which Sean could get his work done faster and yell "damn!" to his heart's content.

He was so distracted that when Valerie said she was going away, she wouldn't have been surprised if he had reacted like the old stereotype of the husband who, failing to absorb the news, grunts, "That's nice, dear," from behind his newspaper.

As it was, he looked up. "You know I always worry, Val," Sean said. He put his papers down. "I've been lost in my work lately, I know. But I have a present for you."

"Not an expensive present, I hope?" she said. Sean gave money to the ALF and looked after her expenses, and she had to come to terms with that; but she didn't want to be "kept."

Sean handed her an envelope. "It's just a poem," he said. She opened the envelope and read from the notepaper inside.

Orbits of the planets all lie in a plane,
As neat as a moth in a cocoon:
Obedient, orderly, easy to find—
Save Pluto, the runaway moon.
The planets all stay in their spaced-out domains;
To trespass is not opportune!
So orbital limits they always observe—
Save Pluto, the runaway moon.

Valerie read through the verses. Sean's love for her was spelled out at the bottom of the page.

"So," she rubbed his hand, "I'm your runaway moon?"

"Yes, you are. And as soon as you leave, I get Mandy with that 'What have you done to Val?' expression on her face. She thinks you're playing hide-and-go-seek and I'm too dumb to find you."

Valerie knew he was right about Mandy. Having found a family unit that suited her, she wanted a full roll call every night. Valerie couldn't blame her, considering Mandy must have had who-knows-what unsettling experiences before ending up at the pound. How could she be sure Valerie or Sean wouldn't disappear? "Mandy, I'll be back. I promise," Val said, rubbing Mandy's ears.

The next morning, Valerie drove down I-95 to make a call reserving a seat on the evening plane to Los Angeles. She went four exits out of her way because she knew that FBI investigators, re-creating a trail, will check all calls made from phone booths within three miles of their suspect's home and office.

It was a dinner flight. Valerie didn't special order a vegetarian meal for fear of "flagging" her ticket, but she wasn't going to arrive on an empty stomach, especially with no idea of how long it might be before she would have a chance to eat. On the way to the airport she and Sean had one of their "last suppers" at Cafe Italiano near the National Zoo. They both loved the place, and ate there whenever they could.

They sat at a window table, watching people hurry up and down the Metro escalator or stop to pull a *City Paper* out of the machine. She knew she and Sean were both thinking the same thing. If something went wrong they might not be together for a long time. Neither of them wanted to dwell on it.

Valerie had booked her ticket under a no-frills, no-fuss man's name: David Litton, after Litton Bionetics, a company that kills monkeys and mice by the thousands. If the FBI decided she was someone to look for, they'd check the female passengers to see if she'd traveled under an alias, and they'd bat zero. Luckily, the flight had been wide open. If she had to travel standby, the gate agents would have noticed she was no 'mister.' With a regular ticket, Valerie had learned, they assume a woman is checking in for her husband or boss. The few clothing and toiletry items Valerie had packed fit under her seat with room to spare. Checked luggage can get lost or stolen, and she didn't want any complications or delays.

It was thirty minutes to flight time when Sean pulled the station wagon up outside the terminal. Valerie got out, kissed Mandy on the nose, and told her not to let her spaghetti leftovers get cold. Sean came around to the curb and Valerie gave him a gentle kiss.

"Give me a proper kiss, Mr. Litton," he complained.

"What'll you give me?"

"Actually, I've already decided. Canter's going. You'll never see his 'God, Guts, and Guns Made America Great' bumper sticker in the Wildnear lot again!"

Canter was a hunter who had tried to rile Valerie about his "sport" in Sean's office parking lot a few weeks ago, just as deer season opened. He had purposely pulled his truck up to block her car as she tried to leave after dropping something off for Sean. He leered out of his truck window and called, "Wanna come hunting Saturday? I'll show you how to gut a deer. Being a real gentleman, I'll even let you keep the heart. How about it? Scared you'll like it?"

Valerie had seen two of his coworkers walking in their direction, so she called out loudly to him, "What's the matter, Canter? Still dreaming your rifle belongs in your pants? You know that's why they say hunters do it in the woods. Because they can't 'do it' anywhere else."

Canter was out of the truck in a flash, his face almost touching hers. "Your face is so red—you should loosen your tie," she said. Canter's coworkers started hooting.

Valerie was embarrassed to be so crass, but not much, because if anyone had asked for it, Canter had. A year earlier, at Sean's office Christmas party of all places, Canter had told a gory story about shooting a deer over and over again and how "that stupid son of a bitch wouldn't die." He had called the suffering creature every swear word in his limited vocabulary and was enjoying his own adventure story so much that Valerie thought he might burst with pleasure. He had never forgiven her for telling him publicly exactly how disgusting she found his habits.

Whenever birds unlucky enough to be called a "game species" flew overhead, Valerie's thoughts went to Canter and all the other hunters. Geese and lots of other birds choose a mate for life, so a "kill" means not only pain and death for those blown out of the sky by hunters, but also grief and loneliness for their partners who survive.

She smiled. Canter might have less money to buy all his fancy weaponry and less time to be out in the woods if he had to look for a new job. Valerie gave her lover a kiss right out of the movies.

Thirty-five minutes later, the United Boeing 727 took off for Los Angeles. As it lifted though the curtain of clouds over Dulles airfield, Valerie knew she was about to get her "fix"; it felt good to be useful again.

She pulled a pillow and blanket out of the overhead bin and, helped by the generous snifter of Amaretto she'd finished at Cafe Italiano, dozed off. There are benefits to arriving well rested when you don't know precisely what life is about to offer.

When the plane landed in Los Angeles, Valerie found Josh waiting near the gate, trying to be inconspicuous. Big as he was, that was like trying not to look like a grapefruit in a bowl of cherries. She had learned to look above the crowd for him, and there he was, propping up a pillar near the exit.

As Valerie came level with him, he stepped out and lifted her clear off the ground, gently but with enormous and unmistakable strength. "How's the family?" he asked as her feet returned to a solid surface.

"Great. *You've* obviously been eating your Wheaties. Are you doing all right?"

"I'm just beat. I had to keep my head out of the window to keep from falling asleep on the way here. We've been working around the clock. Now that you're here I can catch some Z's."

Josh handed her a bunch of keys that had a bit too much motor oil on them, and led her to where the ALF's "new" ex-government van was parked. Although it was a "stretch," it looked impressively undistinguished, the sort of vehicle that you probably wouldn't remember seeing if asked. As they got in, Valerie noticed some of its old government green paint on the inside door frame, bits that had been missed during the new, dark-blue paint job.

Josh wasn't kidding about being tired. Valerie noticed that his eyes weren't fully open and his face sagged, the way people's faces do when they aren't alert enough to keep their muscles at attention.

"Josh, lie down in the back. As much as I'm dying to hear the scoop, I can wait. Go on, don't try to be brave for me. We know each other better than that."

Josh didn't need a second push. He was on his way to the back. "All right. Just wake me if you're about to career off a bridge abutment or something, OK?"

He went out like a light as soon as his body touched the moving company quilts littering the van floor. Response time erodes quickly when you're sleep-deprived, and Valerie wanted him in top form.

It turned out they were going to Vin and Penny's house in Burbank. From the solid feel of the van and its smooth acceleration as it slipped down the highway, Valerie could guess that Vin had already been working on it. Making getaway vehicles reliable and equipping them with important little extras, like heavy-duty suspension, detachable police scanner radios, and under-the-seat storage compartments, was Vin's job. He took pride in doing it well.

Vin and Penny's house was one of those dull, prefab boxes plopped down in an undistinguished subdivision. Among its redeeming features, from an ALF perspective, were a garage, alongside which thick bamboo grew next to a tall privacy fence, and no neighbors with windows that overlooked the driveway or front door.

Vin had been waiting for them. He raised the garage door the moment Valerie pulled into the driveway and closed it again the second she cleared the entrance.

Josh didn't need waking. He was on his feet in an instant, and met Vin as he entered the garage from the kitchen. He and Vin were so close, politically and in personality, that in ALF circles they were called "the twins."

"Still breathing, old man?" Josh teased Vin.

"Now you're here, I'll get my exercise counting your gray hairs. I see God's getting you back for teasing me about my age. Look at those distinguished temples."

Vin made a grab for Josh's hair and Josh side-stepped him.
"At least I've got hairs to count."

Vin and Josh had their fists up in a mock fight. Penny came
through the kitchen door to rescue Valerie. "Vin, there won't be
anyone left standing if you hit everyone who notices you're bald-
ing. Bring that man into the house. Val, it's good to see you."

"Penny, you look terrific."

"In working order. Vin spent the last two weeks working on
that van and the equipment, and rounding people up for the
party. He's tired, but I'm fighting fit."

Valerie was genuinely pleased to see Penny looking so well.
Penny was on painkillers for a degenerative spinal disorder. She
had an obsession about hiding her physical problems and was always careful to mask her pain. Sometimes she crashed, and Vin
had told Josh that, at those times, she simply couldn't function.
Rather than be seen in that state, she locks herself away and will
only let Vin, her cats, and their part-time housekeeper near her.
Tonight, she looked fine.

"Come on in. The cat gang will want to see who's invading,"
Penny said, holding the door open for them. The cat gang is composed of seven "legal rescues" from the local shelter where Penny
does volunteer fundraising. As Valerie came in from the garage,
Roxy, the oldest, loped up to rub against her jeans. She scratched
his back with her nails.

Six years earlier, a terrified Roxy had been found by a man
walking his dog by the reservoir. Roxy's leg had been cut down
to the bone by a steel-jaw leghold trap that still held him in its
grip. If the man hadn't come along, Roxy would have been discarded by the trapper as a "trash animal," one of the estimated
two-thirds of all animals caught by this undiscriminating device,
which is still the trap of choice for people out for raccoon, fox,
and beaver pelts. Roxy had been in the trap long enough to lose
his leg—it was amputated later that day—but not his life.

"Pepper, my man. What a great guy," Josh said. Pepper, the
youngest and least aloof of the cat gang, had joined Roxy for the
inspection. He found himself scooped up, turned upside down,
and stroked by Josh. The rest stayed put, stretching and yawning.

It was late, and intrusions aren't appreciated by most self-respecting, middle-aged cats.

"Let's not wait for the sun to come up to get started," Vin warned. A stocky man of sixty or so, Vin looked and sounded ornery, and people were easily intimidated by him. He was in a Japanese prisoner-of-war camp in Burma during World War II, and could jury-rig anything electrical or mechanical. His grown sons have become successful business people, not because of what they learned in school, but because of what they picked up at Vin's elbow.

As everyone settled into the living room furniture, Josh started his briefing. "Our target," said Josh, looking at Val and pausing for effect, "is the City of Hope."

Valerie had waited thirty hours for his first words, but she didn't like what she heard. Conflicting feelings fought it out inside her. How in the name of God, she thought, could we ever convince anyone that a raid on the City of Hope, a facility held in the highest public regard, was justified?

"Josh, this is scary," she said. "Hope is the darling of the Hollywood benefit set. It's seen as the Holy Grail for every parent with a child who has a rare cancer. No one will believe anything is wrong in its labs.

"On the other hand," Valerie then found herself saying to Josh's broadening smile, "if we could prove that conditions are wretched in that bastion of glitz, people would have to accept that things are probably even worse in the less touted, less well-funded labs."

"Bingo. Let me tell you why I don't think we need to worry," Josh continued, giving a brief rundown on how the City of Hope was named to inspire people with a vision of medical miracles, and how it receives a multitude of benefit-show dollars and private bequests, in addition to more than $5 million a year in federal grants earmarked specifically for animal experiments.

"Those lovely gleaming buildings you see on television out here may reflect its prestige," he said, "but they don't reflect what we've seen inside."

"You've already been in!" Valerie gasped. "Then we're not starting from scratch." This was the news she needed to quell her uneasiness. This was no trash heap they would be rummaging through, but a revered research institution. She concentrated on what he was saying and stopped worrying, at least for the moment, about the pros and cons of the target.

"The labs lie about a quarter-mile behind the main medical center," Josh continued. "They only show the main building—that's the showcase on the news and in their glossy brochure. The animal labs are off-limits. Out of sight, out of mind. We've done a quick inside recon thanks to a hand.[1]

"The hand says animals routinely die before experiments on them are even begun, and that once the 'great science' starts, they go like flies," Josh continued, his tone reflecting his rage. "Apparently, the bastards don't even have the decency to give the animals painkillers after major surgery. Many of their "subjects" just lie down and die in their own filth."

"What kind of animals, Josh?" Valerie asked. Josh was a little too angry for her liking. Perhaps he was just tired, she thought.

"If things go well, we can probably get out all the dogs and some of the cats. We haven't seen the dogs, but the papers indicate they're all beagles—purpose-bred, so there'll be problems.

"Beagles are the most common purpose-bred dogs," Josh went on. "Born on cement in a commercial supply kennel, they go from the frying pan into the fire. They are 'created' specifically to be used in experiments, a fact researchers think somehow justifies their use and abuse. They are doomed to die on a laboratory floor or an operating table. They've never been socialized. They've never known kindness or felt a friendly touch, so they cower when you go up to them, their legs start to tremble, and they may even urinate on themselves. For them, handling at its most benign means being thrown onto weighing scales, getting an injection, or being cuffed out of the way by an impatient whitecoat in clumsy rubber boots armed with a hose. When once-owned dogs end up in the labs, they still hold hope in their thumping tails and

---

[1]A "hand" or "helping hand" is the ALF term for a past or present insider, and for the tips or material assistance, such as keys, that person furnishes.

in their faces. Purpose-bred dogs have never had hope. They don't know what it is.

"We've uncovered some pretty nasty stuff we can't touch, too. There's a whole colony of cats infected with a highly contagious respiratory virus. They're in a specially marked containment shed. We can't get near them for fear of carrying the infection on our clothes, let alone get them out. We probably can get out rabbits and rats, though. If we could borrow a UPS fleet we could get all of them, but how many we'll end up taking we'll have to decide after tonight, when we do the count."

They were out of the house by 1:20 A.M. City of Hope was in Duarte, about twenty-five minutes away, and they needed to rendezvous with Sitch. As he drove, Josh filled in the blanks while Vin tested the radios and checked frequencies. They rehearsed their roles and code signals. Radio silence is the general rule, but when a warning must be given, it can't sound like one to any nosy hobbyists listening in on their own equipment. Tonight, the signals were designed to seem like dispatches from a tow truck company.

Before long they were driving past the main entrance of the Hope complex. Peering out, Valerie wondered if it was foolish to contemplate a raid on such an imposing place. A scene from an old movie, *Topkapi*, starring Peter Ustinov and Melina Mercouri, popped into her head: jewel thieves with an elaborate and improbable plan to raid a Turkish palace were lowering a man by his legs through a skylight. She wondered if the ALF had bitten off more than it could chew.

They seemed to glide down the little-traveled dirt road, which led to a housing development. Off to their left, they could make out the shapes of a dilapidated cinderblock building and several trailers placed helter-skelter around it. A high chain-link fence enclosed the compound. Josh pulled to a stop. Below the van was an enormous storm culvert. Directly across the road, behind a fence, some houses marked the end of civilization; from here the road trailed off into scrub brush, open desert, coyote land.

Vin took over the wheel. Receiving his all-clear, Valerie and

Josh bailed out the side door. The van interior had been painted flat black. Vin had rigged the brake and interior lights so that a switch had to be thrown to turn them on. Val and Josh were nearly invisible in their dark blue nylon masks, which were pulled down and tucked into their dark jumpsuits.

Vin was to remain with the vehicle, driving it away from the drop-off point, where he would be vulnerable, and keeping in radio contact with Josh from an inconspicuous distance. He would pick them up at the appointed time or come for them if they had to get out unexpectedly.

Josh and Val scrambled into the culvert to find Sitch and his people already in place, as expected. Sitch led the West Coast ground crews. His job was to hand-pick and train the ALFers who scout for regional targets and do the local work. Most of them would never know each other's identities or see each other's faces. Discipline is tighter on the West Coast than on the East. Interstate crossovers happen on an "as needed" basis, arranged by Sitch in his area and other ALF unit leaders in their states. In theory, the system allows for whole units to be "busted," say, by infiltration of a ground crew by a federal plant, without links being made to other units. In practice, it has never been tested.

"Glad to see ya," came Sitch's deep and unmistakable voice. Sitch had moved west to pursue a career in movies eight years earlier. Out of his ALF "uniform," everything about him—from his sun-streaked hair to the way he had his shirt collars pressed up James Dean-style—seemed so "California." His Brooklyn accent, however, had refused to integrate into Hollywood society.

He grasped Josh's arm, then Valerie's. "We'll give you a minute for your eyes to adjust to the darkness," he said.

That done, without another word, a dozen people vanished behind him into the blackness of the storm culvert. Seconds later, they climbed out to stand by the mesh fence next to one of the trailers inside the City of Hope's unmarked compound. Sitch was first over the fence, showing them exactly where to put their feet so as not to leave prints in the soft ground. It had been drizzling all day.

One man lay down on the wet culvert edge, taking his place

as the relay guard they would call "R." If a guard or errant experimenter happened through the compound gates, R would see him before he suspected anything. R would decide whether to warn the group to keep down, keep quiet, or get out.

Crouching, out of habit, they padded behind Sitch to the old trailer. Its wheels had been removed and it sat up on chocks. A few bits of wood nailed together made steps into it from the ground. By prearrangement the door had been left unlocked by the hand. Sitch reached into the middle drawer of a small desk, pulled out a ringful of keys, and pressed them into the hand of C, one of the women in the group.

"These will get us through any door in the compound," he explained. "The photo crew will start here. Everyone else, follow C here and split as you go." Valerie looked around in the lighted room. She could stand up and move around freely. The only uncovered windows faced the culvert where R lay, listening and watching for trouble. Two people had already pulled out their camera equipment and were moving systematically from one filth-encrusted cage to another. The faces of mice and rabbits, many with red, infected eyes and sores on their skin, looked out at them through the bars. Next to Valerie lay a mother rabbit, nine baby bunnies asleep by her side, their noses buried in her white fur. As Valerie moved past her out the door, she wondered how the rabbit had lost almost all of her left ear.

C led them past the second trailer without stopping. "Supplies," she explained. The third and fourth trailers were much like the first, smelling of soiled mouse bedding. Valerie thought of what Alex Pacheco had once said: that if only God had made the animals so they all cried out at the top of their lungs when they were suffering, it might be a different world.

C, who knew her way around, was picking up the pace. Not wanting to lag behind, Valerie moved too quickly down the trailer steps. Unable to clearly see where the bottom step met the ground, her foot hit the earth at an angle and twisted badly. "Damn," she muttered to herself.

For a moment, the pain was almost blinding, then it eased. Valerie hurried to catch up.

Sitch had disappeared, four people were counting, and two were photographing their way through the trailers. Now just Valerie and four others were left. Valerie could make out a large mesh pen filled with cats on her left as she walked to the cinderblock building. The cats hunched on the bare ground, watching the visitors move through the night.

"Wild as March hares," said C. "We'd scare them to death if we tried to move them, and it would be cruel to let them go out here. Tumbleweed does not a meal make. We're going to have to leave them behind. They must have been box-trapped from someone's barn and brought here by dealers."

C stopped at a tin shed. The group was shielded well enough for her to pull out her flashlight (the lens had been coated with green nail polish), cup the beam with her hands, and, holding it up close to the shed, show them the sign before snapping it off. It read, "KEEP OUT. BIO-HAZARD, HIGH RISK OF INFECTION. FULL PROTECTION MUST BE WORN TO ENTER."

Valerie felt frustrated. First there had been the hundreds of rats and mice, the "invisible" animals almost no one cared about. Too many to carry. Then the doomed wild cats. Now these.

"Listen." Josh had his ear up to the shed door.

They put their ears to the door.

It was perhaps the eeriest sound Valerie had ever heard. Made by who-knows-how-many tiny throats. A rasping, wheezing, almost but not quite synchronized, rattling sound of difficult breaths inhaled and expelled. The sound of thirty, fifty, or more cats trying to breathe, their respiratory passages deliberately infected with a strange virus.

The man beside her spoke up.

"Jesus, I hate these people," he said, his voice thick with emotion. Valerie understood his anger although she didn't share it. When she looked over he was shaking his head, so she squeezed his arm.

"I've got two cats at home," he said.

"Come on," nudged C. They moved on to the main building. Even though Josh had prepared her for it, the stench made her gag. At the same time, her frustration began to evaporate. Finally, they were going to see the animals they could liberate.

C led the group through a small anteroom into a dingy, windowless area. The barking, faint before, now filled the room. They were surrounded by caged, baying beagles—two, three, even four to a cage. There was something very strange about these dogs. Every one of them had big round lumps growing out of their backs.

"They've made them look like miniature deformed camels," the cat man shouted over the din of the barking dogs.

"The lumps you see are raised pouches of fluid injected under their skins," C answered him.

"They're definitely purpose bred, damn it," Valerie shouted to Josh. The beagles, who had been raising a ruckus, pulled back sharply when the ALF team entered the room, yowling and cowering when anyone moved within a few feet of their pens or laid eyes on them.

The beagles needing immediate veterinary care after their liberation had to be identified. For these beagles, a hands-on exam would be too traumatic. Valerie walked the pens, trying not to seem threatening, making soothing sounds while assessing the dogs' physical condition and being careful to keep her eyes on their bodies, not their faces.

She wrote what she needed to remember on the palm of her hand, using a personal shorthand that, in case of arrest, could be erased with a quick lick of the tongue. Some of the dogs had cuts on their legs; several looked pregnant. The ALF would need to determine what could be done to get rid of those raised fluid pouches, if that was possible.

"Val, come here, catch this," shouted Josh.

He was crouching by a cage door. An old beagle, her eyes clouded with cataracts, was pressed up against the wire, wagging her tail as fast as it would go, howling at him with sheer delight. He was tickling her through the wire.

"She's hardly purpose bred. What on earth?"

"She's old as the hills. And she's been somebody's baby. Who knows?" Through the haze of what remained of her sight, the old beagle had instinctively recognized Josh as a potential friend. She wanted out.

"She's singing," Valerie told Josh, and she was—a high, joyous sound came out of her mouth as she tipped her head to the ceiling.

"Chessie, old girl, we're going to put you back in a real home," Josh told her, calling a photographer over to take pictures.

"Chessie, is it?" Valerie asked him.

"Yup. I found her; I get to name her."

The timer on Valerie's watch went off. They were only twenty minutes from departure time. They needed to get a move on.

The next find wasn't so pleasant. A bloodhound lay on the wet cement. Beside her were nine wet blobs—her newborn puppies. They were scattered about, rather than clinging to her as normal newborns would. Some were moving, some weren't. Valerie opened the pen and knelt beside the mother. The dog looked up, but her eyes held no welcome, just pain and exhaustion. She seemed barely able to hold her head up.

The little bodies beside her were soaked with the bloody mess that covered the cold cement. Five were dead, and four were alive but hardly moving. When Valerie touched them, the puppies moaned. She patted the mother's head, but the bloodhound didn't seem to have the energy to respond.

"Her nose is burning," Valerie said. "Something's very wrong with her." She felt down the dog's chin to her chest. As she made her inspection, Valerie could see that the bloodhound was lying in a greenish pool of muck that was not just afterbirth or waste. Gently, Valerie lifted the dog's tail. The dog growled, but didn't move. To be on the safe side, Valerie withdrew her hand and told the others, "She's severely infected. There's a nasty discharge from her uterus and her nipples have clogged up. The puppies can't nurse. They're dying."

In the very last pen, waiting for his turn, was the mixed black Labrador Valerie had seen out of the corner of her eye, standing patiently, watching her make her way up the runs. Now that they were face-to-face, Valerie found him a peculiarly out-of-place picture of dignity in this hellish sewer. He was so reserved and noble.

"You are a prince," she told him, opening the door and hugging him across his shoulders. The bond between them was instant, and she felt right away that it could never, ever be broken.

Using her belt as a leash, she walked Prince out to be photographed. He stood patiently, allowing the masked ALF agent to turn him this way and that for the camera, looking at Valerie with affection. When it came time for him to go back into the pen, he wouldn't budge.

Valerie knelt, took his big head in her hands, and told him with as much confidence as she could muster, "Please, Prince. Go in. We'll get you tomorrow, I promise."

Reluctantly, he surrendered himself to his cell again. Valerie prayed that nothing would happen to make her betray his trust.

"Twelve minutes to go," said C, "let's move it."

"There are more cats down the hall," yelled Josh.

"Ones we can help this time, I hope," Valerie called back.

The next room held banks of cages, many red with rust, in which cats, those cleanest of animals, perched awkwardly on the cage bars. Their own fecal matter, which had caught on the slats, was caked to the fur on their feet.

"Not even the decency to give them a litter tray." It was the cat man again. He moved forward to give some attention to the cats who had come to the fronts of their cages looking for a rub. Others, probably those who had been there the longest, kept their backs to him. Valerie wondered how many of them had once been people's companions.

The cat man had finished his count and was petting a big, black and white shorthair whose head never moved from the black paws on which it rested. "You'd better wash your hands well and strip out of those clothes before you touch your cats at home," Valerie warned him. "That cat's fur is clammy and her third eyelids are up. She's not well."

"Thanks, I've got some disinfectant in my car. I'll use it."

There was just time for the photographers to finish taking shots of the insulation and wires that were falling from the ceiling, the various trash strewn on cage tops, the animal hair littering the cages, and the broken and stained tiles on the floor. Valerie's watch alarm gave the "one-minute break away" signal a second before R came over the portables.

"Mobile One to base. I'm 10-10 at the Greasy Spoon."

"Roger One, bring me back a cup of coffee," came Sitch's prearranged reply. It was 4:00 A.M. as the shadowy figures climbed back out of the drainage ditch and headed for their beds. In less than twenty-four hours, if all went according to plan, they would liberate Prince, Chessie, the bloodhound mother (if she lived that long), and many of the other victims left behind in the vivisectors' domain.

Valerie knew it would be hard to sleep, but she was determined to rest for the job ahead. When she got back to Vin and Penny's house, she found Josh had put his sleeping bag beside the couch that served as her bed. He came out of the shower, bare-chested and in a good mood, just as she had propped her swollen ankle up with a cushion and settled down for the night.

"Don't you snore, Val. I need my beauty sleep," he grinned, swatting her with his clean shirt.

"I'd give up if I were you, Josh. You'll never get enough to undo the damage."

Valerie wondered if he knew how incredibly attractive he looked, standing there putting on his shirt. "For God's sake," she chided herself silently. "That's all I need, given everything else there is to worry about. Just go to sleep," she told her brain, trying to ignore Josh's closeness and concentrate on the cat who lay across her chest, purring into her left ear. Valerie dissolved into a sleep punctuated by confused dreams of what she had seen, and what she and the others were about to do.

Penny woke them in the early afternoon, with news that PETA's research team had studied the Hope files and written a synopsis that they sent to Last Chance For Animals by Federal Express. The ALF contact there had been alerted, and had intercepted and copied the document. Penny poured coffee and fresh orange juice. The assembly dug into the scrambled tofu and toast Penny had prepared before sounding reveille. As Penny read aloud from the report, Valerie started to believe that no one could successfully defend Hope now.

237

"Of the dogs used in Hope's cancer experiments from 1975 to 1981, over half died before the experiments even began. Seven dogs died of 'unknown causes,' eleven from poisoning by overdoses of introduced substances, ten of bronchial bleeding associated with sloppy insertions and broken catheters, and thirteen of pulmonary infection."

"Don't forget how much money Hope's getting from the feds," Josh interjected. "They're not supposed to be playing 'learn as you go' over there, it's a medical facility."

"I wonder if they're this sloppy with the kids they treat?" Valerie mused.

Penny continued, "Of twelve dogs used in an experiment on esophageal cancer, four died of 'complications,' two of anesthetic overdose, and one of 'unknown causes.' One simply 'disappeared,' and one died after bronchial pneumonia had been noted for three months. Only three dogs were left alive in the experiment." Penny paused. She didn't look particularly well. Vin caught her eye, leaned over, and took the papers from her.

"You go rest," he said. "Let me read awhile."

"Maybe I will, if you guys don't need anything?"

"We'll wake you if we do, we promise, Pen."

Vin began reading, "The substance forced down the animals' throats is Croton oil, a poison described in Harrison's Principles of Internal Medicine as causing 'burning pain in the mouth, esophagus, and stomach, and hemorrhage, shock, coma, death.' Harrison's classic medical textbook described Croton oil administration as 'usually the work of ignorant pranksters' and of 'no therapeutic use.'

"In 1978, fifty-four dogs were killed in another set of experiments. This time only twenty-three survived long enough to develop cancer—the beginning point of the experiment. Eighteen died of 'infection complications and/or generalized debilitation,' i.e., weakness—not hard to imagine in stressed pound animals. One was so 'severely debilitated' that he was killed and found infested with 'massive intestinal and pulmonary ascariasis' [worms] although he had been under Hope's 'care' for over one year."

One after the other, the dogs had died, often slowly, because the experimenters were slobs. "These findings are dynamite," Valerie exclaimed. Dynamite whose fuse the ALF would light in just a few more hours.

Vin continued. "Five dogs belonging to an experimenter called DeBonis were used in 1982. Of these only one survived. The others suffered miserable deaths due to poor procedures or overload of carcinogenic substances, and one was killed due to 'labored breathing.' An autopsy showed he was wall-to-wall roundworms and tapeworms, even though he had been at Hope over two years."

They looked at each other. The information in the report would devastate Hope. PETA had booked a conference room at the downtown Holiday Inn and was planning to go public with it in two days. Whatever else was being planned for Hope, PETA didn't want to know and the ALF didn't need to tell them.

Josh absentmindedly tapped his foot against Valerie's under the table. She screamed as if he'd struck a knife into her ankle.

"Val, what's wrong?" he said, startled.

"You just don't know your own strength, Josh," she said, trying not to show how much pain she was in. "You could cripple a woman just by playing footsie."

"You sure nothing's wrong?"

"I'm sure. I'll take a quick shower and be right out. We can load the van, alright?"

In the bathroom, Valerie stripped her socks off and looked at the swollen mass that had once been her ankle. Standing on it was now very painful, and although she could walk, she would be in trouble if she had to run. She found an elastic bandage and some gauze in the cabinet and bound her foot. There was a prescription bottle of Tylenol 3 in the cabinet, and she took one and popped more into her shirt pocket, just in case.

After Valerie dried off and dressed, she hobbled to the garage and found Josh on his back bolting the cage frame to the body of the van. She moved to the side door without Josh noticing her limp. The cages they needed to strap into the stretch van were stacked against the garage wall. A diagram of how they could be positioned so as not to waste an inch of space was posted on the wall near the doors.

"With this set-up we can front- and back-load. There are two main tiers of cages attached, and then room for newspapers, trash bags, leashes, water containers, and food up front. We can also stack and strap portable cat carriers in the area by the side door, floor to ceiling," Josh told her.

They worked the whole afternoon, side by side, discussing details of the job ahead. By dinner time, they knew they could load over thirty small dogs in twenty-two small cages in the stretch van. Valerie was to be the exit driver. Josh's job was to remove the stereotaxic animal restraint device, in which animals' heads are pinned with rods to stop them from moving during brain surgery. He would also help break up the cage bars with bolt cutters so that Hope couldn't simply buy another batch of animals and resume their "work."

Vin went into town to meet with Sitch. When he got back he led a final briefing, finishing up at about eleven o'clock. Then every minute dragged by. They tried playing poker but couldn't concentrate. Everyone was driving everyone else mad, looking at their watches. They wanted to go.

At 2:00 A.M., Josh lowered Val into the storm culvert, where they greeted Sitch's crew. She had been forced to confess about her ankle because she could no longer move on it very well; it had to be sprained. Despite her discomfort, Valerie was in such high spirits that she could imagine broad grins under all those masks, even though she knew there were bound to be some people here who were scared to death. There was a pale moon, just right for the ALF's purposes but not so bright that figures moving around in its light could be seen from a distance.

Climbing the fence with a swollen foot was out of the question, but so had been staying behind. Valerie felt Josh's muscular arms around her waist as he lifted her up and gently set her on the other side. She and Sitch were to take the path to the main gate. The others set off to box the rabbits and rodents. Every step hurt like hell.

"What's up with the leg?" Sitch asked.

"Nothing. I'm practicing for a play. I'm Festus in 'Gunsmoke.' "

"Here, climb aboard. We've got time."

Sitch bent down and offered Valerie his back.

"Thanks. This will look great if the police show up. The ALF giving piggyback rides during a raid. Shoot our image to bits."

"I wonder what the relay guard's thinking."

At a signal, Valerie and Sitch were to let the truck through the gate. They sat down in the dirt to wait. Somewhere, a dog started to bark persistently.

"Damn. Could be one of our drivers chose a bad place to pull over and wait." A silly, unpredictable thing like that could upset the entire plan, and Sitch was rightly worried.

The barking got louder.

"It'll be a bit too ironic for my taste if we're turned in by a dog," Valerie said.

"I know you're not religious, but pray. Hard."

The barking stopped.

Sitch laughed. He had been religious since he was old enough to hold a Bible. Valerie knew more than she was supposed to about Sitch. They were "family" in animal liberation matters, but they were worlds apart in almost everything else. Sitch loved living in the make-believe world of Hollywood, spent his social life in the company of the sort of starlets who make feminists lose their breakfast, got excited negotiating big-money deals that rarely materialized, kept his body in shape, had his own tailor, and was never seen with so much as a hair out of place. As they sat on the hard ground, passing time, Valerie just had to ask him how things were going in his life.

Everything was quiet. They sat in the semi-darkness, Sitch filling Valerie in on the latest industry gossip, telling her how his little sister had come to Hollywood, having saved up her money to go to stunt school, and now couldn't get a job because she wasn't in the union. They could have been two people sitting and waiting to go into a show.

"Unit two to base. Tell the lady with the flat that I'm almost there. I can see her car from the ramp."

"Ten four, unit two."

The message was for Sitch. He jumped to his feet. Valerie tried to do the same, but her foot wasn't behaving. She held the chain taut while Sitch cut the padlock. As the chain fell, Sitch tossed the broken lock behind him into the scrub brush. On the way out, he would put a new padlock on, making everything look in place if a guard cruised by and shone a light at the gate. Seconds later, the van swung past, leaving pale red dust clouds in its wake. Valerie pulled the gates closed behind it as Sitch started running ahead. Her ankle felt as if it would explode as she hobbled as fast as she could back up the path.

Tonight the trailer door had been locked. The hand had called in sick. Jimmying it cost only a minute or two. Everyone was working swiftly, deliberately, and in silence so as to hear any alert over the radio. Valerie had barely got inside the cinderblock building when it came. Her heart stopped and she avoided looking in Prince's direction.

Josh was listening to his radio. "Trouble," he said. "A patrol car has pulled off the road near the gate."

"What's it doing?"

"We don't know. Let's keep working." Then, an instant later, he hissed, "Wait. He's out of his car."

Everyone stopped and waited. Strangely, even the dogs were quiet.

"All clear. He's gone."

They resumed working, carrying the beagles out and loading them into the truck. With the exception of Chessie, the "singing" beagle, they had never been trained to walk on a leash. The feel of something pulling their necks made them freeze. Whenever a cage door was opened, the beagles huddled together at the back of the pen, pressing their bodies tightly against the concrete wall.

Valerie leaned over a young female. The dog's stomach was grossly distended. Valerie lifted her gently and felt her go rigid with terror. She felt like a sack of cement. The other beagles were also paralyzed, except for Chessie, whose joy seemed to calm her two cagemates. Although this pair trembled when touched and their eyes never left Chessie, they didn't freeze. The others were sure they were going to be tortured.

Prince, his eyes glued to Valerie's every move, stood motionless except for his tail. When she finally reached his pen he came straight out. She kissed his face and hobbled with him to the truck. As she opened the cage door, he leapt inside without a word said. Valerie looked at him over her shoulder as she scrambled back inside and saw him sitting there, statue-like, waiting.

Although weak and still bleeding, the mother bloodhound lumbered to her feet as L and Valerie coaxed her out on a leash. The poor dog stank to high heaven. Tonight only one puppy remained in the cage with her. C found the others in the freezer. They placed the living pup, a tiny female clinging precariously to life, in the makeshift bed they'd prepared on the truck. As the bloodhound mother sniffed the tiny body, Prince—who Valerie suddenly realized must be the pup's father—gave an affectionate bark. Her doubts dispelled, the mother summoned up what remained of her energy and hauled herself into the cage.

The cats were frightened. Perhaps they remembered that the last time someone had moved them, it was to this place. They sank their nails into the wire of their cages or flattened themselves under the wooden ledges. They were lifted out, quickly deposited into collapsible boxes, and carried to the truck, past the wild cats who were to be left behind in their outdoor pen.

By now Valerie's ankle was on fire. Every move brought shooting pain. She had taken another painkiller, but it didn't seem to be having much effect. It was almost time to move out. The ALF had loaded thirty-two beagles, Prince, Helen (the bloodhound) and her pup, fourteen shoebox containers of rodents, eighteen rabbits and their families, and ten cats. Every square inch of space had been filled, and yet somehow room had to be made for the stereotaxic device. L helped Valerie shove and pull cages this way and that. "How did Noah do it?" L asked.

The night was mild, but Valerie was boiling hot under her mask. She wondered if she had a fever. "The hell with caution," she thought, "I need to breathe." She pulled the mask off, exposing her face.

Suddenly, a man came up behind her, a cardboard cat container in each hand, and another under his arm. Valerie recognized the cat man's voice. It was shaking. "We can't leave these behind."

He left the carriers at Valerie's feet and turned to run back inside.

"I'm bringing you three more," he called out.

They had less than four minutes to hit the road. There was simply no space to put the carriers he had left with her, let alone three more. She opened her mouth to argue, then caught herself. The cat man was right. How could Valerie give him or the cats "no" for an answer, even if there were already 100 animals carefully packed in the truck?

The cages will have to go beside me, Valerie thought, in the space between the two front seats, an area already taken up by the newspapers she needed to change the cages and keep the animals clean. Valerie threw the piles of papers out onto the ground.

The cat man was back. Together, he and Valerie raced to load the cages, balancing them precariously against the dashboard, displacing two cartons of mice—one containing a mother and her ten babies—which Valerie would have to put on her lap. If the police stopped her for any reason, the game would be up.

The cat man put his arms around Valerie.

"Godspeed," he said. "Drive carefully."

Valerie eased herself into the cab and started the engine as Sitch came up to the window. "You'll have to take the stereotaxic device out on foot. Sorry," Valerie said, "We only had a mousehole left, and we filled it with six cats."

"We've got a bigger problem. There's a garbage truck coming down the road," he said.

"Oh, God. Not now."

The sky was getting light. Valerie tried not to think about how little time there was before it would be too late to move unseen.

"Everything finished up inside?" she asked.

"Almost. We broke into the cabinets and found some real interesting documents. Also something weird: the surgery room was covered with blood and feathers; someone slaughtered a chicken in there."

"We knew these people were weird, but voodoo experimenters? Is Josh nearly finished?"

"He's fine. He and L are leaving their calling cards. They've added tar to the mix this time. It's a nice touch. They've covered the operating tables and the floors with it and used red paint to symbolize the blood of Hope's victims. They're doing the walls with slogans, then they're gone."

Josh had told Valerie what he would write. "CITY OF HYPE," "SCIENTIFIC FRAUD," "CITY OF HELL," and "ANIMAL LIBERATION FRONT." She felt an increased sense of urgency. Sitch's hand froze on her shoulder. He was listening to the radio.

"We're all clear. Drive carefully."

"Like a driving test instructor, don't worry."

The truck pulled forward. Seconds passed. Valerie was through the gate. Seconds more. She was past the medical center. No sirens, no cruisers. Minutes passed. She could see the freeway entrance sign. "Oh God, let us get away," she said out loud, two pictures in her head: one of the road, the other of her precious cargo. Up the ramp went the van, and out of Duarte.

With few exceptions, cars on the road just before dawn belong to the police or to drunk drivers. Valerie practiced plausible explanations should the police stop her, knowing all the same that the cages beside her and the mice on her lap would give her away.

About an hour later Valerie spotted the neon sign she had been longing to see: the "Chicken Inn," an all-night fast food restaurant. In this unlikely spot, she was to rendezvous with contacts from the Underground Railroad.

Valerie turned the van into the parking lot and drove to the back of the building. A man she recognized, and a woman she didn't, were sitting in their vehicles, drinking coffee and trying to look casual. The tension that had gripped Valerie from the time the truck glided out of Hope's compound finally dissolved. The first stage of the rescue was successful. One hundred and six animals had been liberated! And in front of her were the people who would take them to safehouses, where they could at last let go of the trembling fear that must have gripped them every day in the laboratory.

A mixture of joy, relief, and perhaps also the increasing pain in her ankle (which Valerie now suspected—rightly, as it turned out—was broken) started the tears streaming down her face.

The worst was over for these animals, and the scales had been tipped in their favor.

9

Run, Rabbit, Run

Do you think then that revolutions are made with rose water?
— Chamfort

Penny had been sitting in a window booth inside the restaurant, trying to look casual but watching anxiously for anyone who might take an interest in what was going on in the rear lot. Wearing tinted glasses and a cheap nylon scarf on her head, she blended in well with the few long-distance drivers trying to keep awake and the nightshift workers catching a cup of coffee before heading home.

When she saw the Underground Railroad vehicles move out, Penny paid her check and walked out through the grimy double doors. No one so much as looked up. She walked casually to the van, pulled open the driver's door, and slipped behind the wheel.

When she saw Valerie's foot, she gasped. "What the hell happened to you? Did you have to kick the doors in?"

She stared at the black, swollen piece of flesh Valerie had excavated from its sock and shoe. Once liberated, it had refused to go back in. Valerie found a towel under the passenger seat and was constructing a wrap out of it.

"I thought I had an award-winning sprain, but this ankle's broken. Pen, the pain's pretty bad, so forgive me if I groan as you drive."

"Vin *always* groans when I drive. Here, take a couple of these."

Penny dug around in her jeans pocket, and found her cache of Tylenol 3. The effects of the other two Valerie had taken had worn off, so she accepted two more gratefully.

"What a pair we are," Pen said, pushing a folded sweater between the seat and the small of her back. "Look at us. We should be in the Special Olympics, not the ALF."

"You know," she mused as they slipped out of the parking lot and onto the still-quiet freeway, "I've had to take stuff for my back for years. I complain to my doc that I'm addicted to prescription drugs. I pop painkillers like Lifesavers, and that's exactly what they are for me. He can't offer a solution. He just pushes more pills, different kinds. But what bothers me most is knowing I'm buying a product that's still tested on animals. I feel like a hypocrite."

"Penny, you shouldn't get guilt trips over things you can't control." Valerie could see that Penny was serious, and she felt sorry for her. "In Virginia, the roads were built by slaves, and we can't undo that. If we lived back then, we'd have been working to abolish human slavery, but we would have had to use those roads to get places. All you can do is keep trying to change the way things are. You can't control everything."

The sun was coming up, and its first beautiful, orange and pink rays tinted the highway. Despite the smoldering pain in her foot, Valerie felt very satisfied with life. She filled Penny in as they drove to the airport, both of them wincing whenever the van hit a bump. By the time the morning rush-hour traffic hit, Valerie was in the airport and Penny was back downtown at a car wash, vacuuming the van, soaping the floors, and flushing all the animal hair irretrievably into the Los Angeles sewer system. "Dog groomer," she told the quizzical attendant.

Once inside the airport, Valerie gave up trying to walk, and summoned a wheelchair to get her to the ticket desk and, from there, to the gate. She sat "parked" in the chair, uncomfortably conspicuous, wondering if the bloodhound would live and if she would ever see Prince again.[1]

Meanwhile, somewhere out on the highway, a recreational ve-

---

[1] While Valerie waited to flee east, I was at Dulles International Airport waiting for a flight west. PETA had been asked to reserve rooms, including one suitable for a news conference, at the downtown Holiday Inn, "no questions asked."

hicle filled with rabbits and mice was cruising uneventfully toward San Francisco. And, in a little town just outside Pasadena, two veterinarians were risking their licenses to check temperatures and run their stethoscopes over the dogs and cats who had recently been Hope research fodder.

The flight to D.C. was smooth enough to allow Valerie to catch up on her sleep. She hadn't risked calling Sean from Los Angeles, but once on the ground in D.C., she rang his office.

"Sweetheart. Your errant moon needs a ride."

"Be right there. Meet you out front."

Sean was at the airport within twenty minutes. He had made a bouquet of pink gardenias, which Valerie suspected were snatched from his reception room vase, and wrapped them in a newspaper. He wasn't cheap, just creative. When he saw that Valerie was sitting in a wheelchair, he almost dropped the flowers.

"It's only a small war wound. I fell and twisted it," she said. As he bent down to inspect, Valerie added quickly, "Oh, God, don't touch it. I'm sure it's broken."

Sean crouched and hugged Valerie to him, burying her face in his neck. "I've always wanted a woman with well-turned ankles. One's a good start," he told her. It was good to be back with her predictably unshakable man. Valerie suspected that even if she were near death, Sean could cheer her up.

Valerie didn't want to go to the emergency room, but she knew she had no choice. The x-rays showed not one, but two broken bones in her foot, and a lot of blood amassed under the swelling. Serious hardware discussions began at her bedside, and by that evening she had been wheeled into the operating room and out again, and was staring down at a dull metal pin sticking out of her ankle.

A few days later, when the swelling subsided, she was allowed to go home, "under certain conditions."

"Now, we don't want an infection. You have to promise me you won't get out of bed, young lady," said Dr. Morley, the attending physician, a round, ruddy-faced man with a fatherly approach to what he called "doctoring." Sean had landscaped his private office and the two had hit it off. "Not even if that man of yours leaves his gardening boots in the living room and covers the kitchen in fertilizer."

"Sounds like every woman's dream," Sean winked at Dr. Morley. "Lie in bed, eat chocolates, read magazines, be waited on hand and foot."

"Men! Able-bodied women are too much of a match for you, aren't they?" Valerie retorted.

Relieved as she was to be home, Valerie found it almost unbearably irritating to be confined to bed. After a day, she wanted to tear the cast off her ankle and get back to work. Instead, she remained in bed, calling her ex-sergeant to see if Prather had been caught (he hadn't), her parents ("no, Mother, there is no need for you to come"), and her sister. She caught up on recent changes in the way the Supreme Court viewed police searches—bad for the ALF, but a long-awaited conservative turn-around for the police. She napped a lot, played chess over the phone with her father, and watched the birds drawn to the berry bushes Sean had planted outside the bedroom.

When he first moved in, Sean visited his neighbors and told them how chemical pesticides can poison the birds who eat the insect victims of "perfect lawn syndrome." His immediate neighbors respected him enough to consider the information, ask questions, and cancel their ChemLawn contracts. People farther down the street, too, were mostly receptive once they realized he wasn't trying to sell them on his own services. As a consequence, the neighborhood had become a sanctuary for wildlife marooned in a sea of pesticides.

In the mornings, while Valerie perused the *Post* and saturated her rice cereal with ice-cold soymilk, the birds breakfasted on the viburnum bushes edging the porch. At first light, they would sit in the branches of the oleander tree and fluff up their feathers against the morning chill. Sean had installed a small fountain in the garden pond, and at its shallow end the water spilled over adjacent flagstones. Here, as the temperature rose, the robins, finches, doves, and others took turns bathing, shaking water all over themselves and preening their feathers.

Two weeks dragged by. Sean knew Valerie's incapacity was driving her nuts, and he did everything he could to keep her resting. He installed a dog door and spent hours on his hands and knees going back and forth through it with Mandy, until she was convinced it really wasn't a guillotine. He also banned her from the bed, afraid she might bump Valerie's cast. Mandy reluctantly accepted the ban with her "Did I do something wrong?" look, until Sean left the room. Then, up she went.

Mandy took to lying on the bed all day, stretched out on her back with her legs pointing to the ceiling, delighted to have Valerie captive around the clock. Once in a while she would sniff the medicine smell coming from Valerie's cast, wrinkle her nose in disgust, and sneeze.

It was a mild winter. In the evenings, Sean set Valerie up in a chaise longue on the insulated patio where they ate their dinners al fresco.

His business budget behind him, Sean had begun to wade through his investment portfolio, weeding it of "non-green" stocks and exploring new, more ethical investments. He was exploring the soy companies, and while Valerie was away he had been taste-testing veggie burgers.

"Try this one," Sean said, handing Valerie a fake steak sandwich. Mandy nuzzled her head under Sean's elbow, making a low "broof" sound that meant "What about me?"

Sean rubbed Mandy's ears while she cocked her head and furrowed her brow. She was trying her best to understand English. He used a pair of tongs to break off part of a fake steak, blowing on it before offering it to her. This was one of those times when Valerie felt awed by his patience, his steady mood, and how controlled he always seemed.

Just then, a squirrel interrupted Valerie's thoughts by jumping from the oleander onto the porch rail outside the window. Insulted by the intrusion onto her turf, Mandy leaped up, toppling the side table with the salad and the plates on it. Sean reached to catch the dishes, missed, and lost his balance. He sat down with a thump amid chunks of onion and green pepper.

"I was just thinking how in control you always are," Valerie grinned at him. "A woman can only dream."

"A woman is going to get covered in barbecue sauce if she doesn't stop laughing," he said, brushing himself off and advancing with a big spoonful of peachy-brown glop.

That night, as they sat in bed, Sean suddenly took Valerie's head in his hands and brushed her hair away from her face. He looked far too serious. "Val," he said, "You'd tell me if you were in trouble, wouldn't you?"

"What a funny thing to say. Everything's fine. Why?"

"I don't honestly know why. I just can't shake a nagging feeling that something's brewing. That you're not out of this Hope thing scot-free."

"Sweetheart, nothing went wrong. Nothing."

Sean flicked the TV off, and they sank under the warm blankets. His arms enveloped Valerie protectively. She put her head on his chest and snuggled up to him. His body was warm and reassuring. She felt his kiss on her forehead and hoped he was wrong.

A week after Valerie's return, she received a package. It bore a St. Paul postmark, which meant Vin had chosen a Minnesota mail-forwarding service, probably from an ad in *Popular Mechanics* magazine. Inside were two videotapes. The first was of PETA's news conference, the one I had flown west to lead at the Holiday Inn.

The room we had reserved was jammed with people. Valerie tried to pick out plainclothes police officers on the video as the camera panned through a sea of reporters and others. There were several candidates.

"Before I answer your questions," she heard me tell the assembly, "I would like to address issues raised by City of Hope officials. Hope has issued a statement that it is concerned for the liberated animals' health and safety if they are not returned. This concern must be a new one. A reading of the autopsy and other City of Hope reports shows that officials there have a long history of negligence, sloppy surgical and other procedures, and failure to provide appropriate post-surgical care to the sick and dying animals they abandon in their laboratories. Dogs are routinely found dead in their runs after being left unattended overnight or over the weekend. Animals bleed to death alone in their cages, their implants puncture their lungs, they suffocate in their own fecal matter."

People were scribbling, and microphones seemed to be sprouting from the crowd like so many black tulips.

Watching the tape, Valerie noticed a tall young man with dark, greased-back hair leap up from his chair at the first break. "But what kind of care will the animals get from the vandals in the ALF?" he asked. "Presumably *they* don't have any medical training?"

A second question was lobbed from a deep-voiced, sturdily built man in his thirties. Unlike the first inquisitor, this man looked businesslike and spoke matter-of-factly.

"Yes, how do you know the animals aren't already dead? Have you spoken directly with the ALF?" Valerie saw now that the second man was part of a pair. His partner looked as if he never missed a day at the gym. His standard-issue dark glasses peeked out of his breast pocket, and he was holding a camera. As he leaned towards the podium for close-ups, Valerie could see that his camera bore no station identification, only the word "News."

"The ALF rescues animals to save their lives from certain death, not to kill them. The ALF has consistently shown its ability to provide emergency medical care for the animals it rescues. After many raids, photos have been made available showing the same animals, months after their rescues, glossy-coated, revived, and healthy. In fact, I have some here to show you."

The FBI cameraman bumped against the bona fide reporters as he jostled for shots of the photos of bright-eyed, healthy dogs, some still showing scars from experiments they had undergone.

His partner still wasn't satisfied. He drowned out the others.

"You haven't answered as to how you communicate with the ALF. How can you contact them?"

"They communicate with us. How, I am not willing to say. PETA has no interest in knowing who the ALF members are or in assisting others in identifying them. We are here to discuss what the ALF found and what needs to be done to shut Hope down."

There were lots more questions, the usual stuff about why the raiders didn't go to the authorities instead of taking the law into their own hands and whether PETA condoned this kind of action. They were dealt with, and the news conference ended with an appeal to the press to demand accountability from Hope for operating out of compliance with the federal Animal Welfare Act.

The second tape Valerie received was of the City of Hope's own news conference. Its administrators must have been scrambling to repair damage to their donor base. Dr. Joseph Holden, the assistant director of research at Hope, stepped up to the podium. He was carefully dressed and accompanied by a researcher in a white coat. Valerie was pleased to see that he talked down to the press, which they didn't like one bit. He introduced another administrator in a dark suit who read, in an absolute monotone, a prepared statement in praise of Hope's "life-saving work." Then Holden returned to the podium for questions.

A chic-looking woman stood up and challenged him to allow PETA to tour Hope's animal labs. The room fell silent. Holden began to sweat under the camera lights. What could he say? Another reporter joined in: "If you have nothing to hide, and everything is in good order as you say, what would be your objection to a tour?"

Holden looked as if he'd explode. Different expressions, from confusion to fury, played themselves out in rapid succession on his furrowed face. Then he answered the only way he felt he could. Yes, he told the cameras, Hope would allow a tour. No, there was nothing to hide, they would see.

"What a coup," Valerie thought. "No amount of elbow grease could make that dump presentable, even if he delayed by a week."

Valerie switched off the VCR and tried to doze. She remembered a pain-relieving exercise Penny had taught her. "Imagine a bright, white light. Start with it at your forehead and move it down to the place where your pain seems most concentrated. All the while, say to yourself, 'I'm healing.' The positive force you create will help you heal," she said.

"Only in California," Valerie thought, "but it can't make it any worse."

The next day, Mandy found a dead thrush outside the bedroom window. Valerie saw her put the bird in her mouth, and called to her to "drop it." She did. Valerie limped out and retrieved the body. Not a mark on it. There hadn't been a frost the night before, food was plentiful, and there were no cats around. As she contemplated the little body, the doorbell rang. It was the delivery man from the local florist, a sky blue rhododendron in his hand.

The note on the pot read simply, "Soon, please." There was no sender's name included, but Valerie knew "Phil A. Dendron" was how Josh had his phone listed. "If you ever leave Sean and marry me," Josh had said, "you'll have to call yourself Rhoda Dendron if you want to get calls." This message meant something was up. Valerie wondered if Sean's "funny feeling" was right after all.

As soon as Valerie could get around well enough to travel, she took a plane down to Tampa to meet Josh. She was anxious to hear all that had happened since she left California.

Josh had sailed down from Pensacola. He looked in great shape for a worried man. His white crew shirt made his tan glow a deep mocha brown. Through the thin cotton Valerie could see he had been working his muscles, winching sails and working out. They sat in a Mexican restaurant with a bar overlooking the bay where his boat was moored and ordered margaritas. The sunlight sparkled on the water and the warm air felt refreshing, even therapeutic, after Washington's chill.

"You can just see it near the entrance to the bay, by that sea wall," Josh said, passing Valerie a tiny, folding pair of racing glasses. A small, elegant sloop with its sail tied to the boom bobbed gently in the water, turning ever so slightly in the wind.

Valerie wanted to get to the purpose of her visit. The small talk made her uncomfortable, but she didn't want to seem overly anxious, either. "Josh, I don't mean to disappoint you, but remember, I'm the woman who gets seasick sitting still in a rowboat."

"A few days at sea and you'd be fine. It sleeps two human beings and a couple of large, messy dogs comfortably. There's a well-stocked galley and room to sunbathe on deck. One day, you'll come out on my boat and we'll sail around the Caribbean and rescue 'soup turtles' from the hotel kitchens.

"Don't forget we'll need some space for Sean and Mandy, too," Valerie said. She wasn't about to let him go on pretending, even though it would have been easier to let his remarks slide by rather than say something and see the anguish that brushed his face.

Then, as if her comment had never been made, Josh straightened up, all seriousness. "Time for work," he said.

"OK, Josh. Tell me things. Did anyone get inside Hope on that promised tour?"

Josh rubbed the salt from his lips and squeezed more lime into his glass. "No go. Once the camera lights were turned off, PETA's activist contact in L.A., Lucy Shelton, kept calling Hope but Holden wouldn't take her calls. Finally, she got him on the phone under some pretext. He denied ever having made the offer."

"What a predictable sleazebag. Remember George Bernard Shaw's wonderful line about experimenters?"

"Yes, 'He who won't hesitate to vivisect, won't hesitate to lie about it.' What happened next bears that out even more."

"So there's real trouble?" Valerie asked.

"Afraid so. Right after the raid, Hope came up with a plan. Their spokesperson told the press that some of the liberated rabbits were infected with oral herpes."

Valerie listened to Josh, stunned. "But we knew who was sick and who wasn't. They weren't," she said.

"That's right. It was a total lie. The rabbits were fine, but no one knew that. Hope said the rabbits posed a 'serious health threat,' particularly to children. Of course, everyone went crazy. The same night, California news stations broadcast an all-points bulletin for the 'infected' rabbits."

Hope's cheap ruse had worked. The morning after the all-points bulletin, a woman in Calistoga had called the police to say that a man had given her daughter a doe rabbit and nine baby bunnies. The little girl had kissed the rabbit, and the woman was in a panic. She was afraid her daughter was going to die.

"Oh no, the mother rabbit with only half of one ear?" Even if you know them well, albino rabbits are pretty hard to tell apart. Since Valerie knew Hope had not tattooed or stained the rabbits, she realized the mother was the only one they had a prayer of positively identifying.

"Bingo." Josh waited for the waitress to set down colorful, pottery dishes full of bean tacos, Spanish rice, guacamole, and salsa. The smell of fresh, warm tortillas mingled with the salty air.

"The man the police were looking for was named Bruce Jodar. It turned out that he and his wife, Carol, were the people you passed the animals to behind the Chicken King, or whatever it was."

After the call from the panicked mother, the police did a smart thing. They rounded up the Jodar's babysitter. Threatened with jail, she told them she had overheard Carol Jodar say that she and Bruce were going to pick up animals from a Southern California research laboratory. When the Jodars returned home from the trip, she said their Toyota wagon was almost overflowing with animals.

The babysitter told police that Carol had phoned her and asked her not to tell anyone about the animals. Carol insisted that she and Bruce didn't break into the place, but had only accepted the animals to keep them safe.

The police had what they needed. By 3:00 A.M. the next morning, Sgt. Mike Dick of the Calistoga police department, accompanied by eight other officers, had his feet firmly planted on the Jodars' porch. Using the butt of his police-issue flashlight, he banged on the wooden door.

The Jodars' young children, wakened from a sound sleep, were scared. Uniformed officers moved from room to room, opening drawers, looking under beds. They rounded the family up and made them sit in the dining room, an officer holding a gun on them, while they searched the house for three hours. They didn't find anything except a biscuit a friend had made for the children, which they thought was a dog biscuit.

Valerie grimaced. "So, Bruce Jodar wins the dubious honor of being the first person taken into custody for suspected ALF activities?"

"Yup. And boy, is he being given a rough time. Which makes me very nervous for you. I suppose he and Carol saw your face?"

"She didn't, but he did. He looked familiar to me, but I couldn't place him at the time. Now I remember. It was at the Mobilization for Animals conference in Ohio."

"Well, he's trouble for you now. The feds may be at your door any time. Passing on stolen goods over the value of a thousand dollars can get you ten years. Crossing state lines in the commission of a crime, breaking and entering, conspiracy to commit . . . you know the laws better than I do."

"When I saw him at the Mobe, he had just come back from the Aleutian Islands. He gave a talk about the seal kill. His sincerity and his compassion moved everyone. I believe he's far too decent to turn anyone in."

"Val, you're too trusting to ever have been a cop! Think back. Did he seem to recognize you?"

"I don't think so. At the Mobe, he was on the podium and I was in the audience. Wait, I did go up and talk to him briefly in the hall afterward, but so did lots of people. But before you go on, tell me first: did the police get any more animals?"

"No, luckily. But they're doing well in the people department."

Josh told her more about the Jodars. They were young, ethical, and had family money. When they first heard about the Aleutian Island seal kill, they had gone there to document it firsthand. They hoped their video footage would shock people into action, and it did. When they returned, they moved closer to the marine mammal protection organizations in the San Francisco Bay area. They bought a mountainside ranch in Calistoga, complete with a little vineyard, where their two adopted Asian children could grow up in peace.

Shortly afterward, Carol started to experience intermittent loss of sensation in her legs. She was diagnosed with multiple sclerosis. Not complacent enough to sit and wait for the day she would be confined to a wheelchair, she and Bruce searched for ways to fight off the disease. They even traveled to a hospital in Mexico to try an experimental treatment outlawed in the U.S. Since she and Bruce were already strict vegetarians, her immune system had more than an average chance of at least slowing down the progress of her MS.

Bruce volunteered for Greenpeace, helped out at the California Marine Mammal Center, and financed a newsletter called *Consequences*, which covered stories about seals and whales, and also what domestic animals go through to become burgers and sandwich fillings. People who saw him speak or read about his work sensed he could be trusted. One of those people had put him on the Underground Railroad list.

"Did the police haul him away in the middle of the night?"

"Yes. And without a lawyer on call, he also spent the next day in jail. He was pretty numb from going without sleep, and, obviously, being a strict vegetarian, he wouldn't eat the food put before him. Afterward, he said that the most amazing thing was that the police never asked him a single question."

While they waited for another order of margaritas, Josh told Valerie the rest of the story. The police already had seized the mother rabbit and her babies and taken them to a "quarantine cage" at the Napa County Animal Control shelter kennel, where they sat huddled together listening to the barking dogs. The tag on the cage read, "police evidence," and people were allowed to peer at them through a window in the kennel door.

Within hours, City of Hope officials had flown to Napa, pulled the mother rabbit out of the cage by her good ear, and confirmed her as "stolen property." Bonnie Rogers, Hope's spokesperson, then admitted that none of the missing rabbits had ever been inoculated with herpes. By that time, however, the excitement of having landed an ALF suspect in jail had grabbed the press' interest.

Bruce was charged with the December 9 burglary of the City of Hope National Medical Research Center, as well as one count of receiving stolen property. Bail was set at $15,000. Score one for Hope, thought Valerie.

"The police are determined to bring in a 'big fish,' " Josh continued. "They've really gone to work on the only people they have been able to link to the action. They got themselves some more search warrants and made a helicopter search of the Jodars' five-acre ranch. They've also combed their home twice more since Bruce's arrest."

"But that's illegal."

"Probably so. They've confiscated a whole bunch of things that have nothing to do with the case. A copy of *Animal Liberation* [the book by Peter Singer], a rubber stamp reading, "1984—Still Eating and Wearing Dead Animals?," animal rights bumper stickers, assorted magazine articles, all sorts of stuff."

It got worse. On the morning of January 3, police arrested Carol and charged her, too, with the Hope burglary and one count of receiving stolen goods.

"I suppose women's rights mean women's obligations, so that's fair," Valerie spoke up, "but I'll bet that's not why the police did it. During the Silver Spring monkey arrests, Sergeant Swain spoke about always trying to find the weak link in the chain. They know about Carol's condition. That's why the prosecutor nabbed her. He's hoping she'll cave in, or else Bruce will to help her out."

The net was being thrown wide. A "Deep Throat" in the Napa Valley police department had found out that a Philadelphia Grand Jury prosecutor had flown to California to search for evidence of a link to East Coast raids. The FBI had entered the investigation and was in competition with the local police department. Their agents had gone to the City of Hope research compound and searched it with a fine-tooth comb. Among some newspapers blown against the fence, they found a business card. The name printed on it was that of PETA's Los Angeles contact. Score one for the FBI.

"Oh God," Valerie grabbed Josh's arm. Being in jeopardy herself hadn't felt that bad somehow. Putting someone else on the firing line made her sick. "I left those newspapers on the ground when I made room for more cats. If they go after that activist, it's my fault."

"Val, calm down. No one in L.A. seems to think it's a problem for her. Detectives have already been out to her home and left cards in her door. They've also left messages on her answering machine, and they're hanging around outside her house as if it's a doughnut shop. From what I hear, she's 100 percent ALF-supportive and, perhaps even better, clean as a whistle. She knows the rules *and* her rights. She isn't answering the door or the phone, she looks outside before she makes a move, and if they drag her into the police station, the L.A. people believe she not only knows nothing, but won't answer questions on principle. With her, the police's only live lead will go dead, and with luck they'll waste a hell of a lot of time pursuing it."

"Pretty impressive. Why hasn't she been recruited?"

"Apparently it's been tried. She's got about seven dogs and her husband's something ultra-respectable in the construction business. They're both great volunteers and devoted to animal rights, but ALF action isn't their style."

"Any guesses how her card got into the papers?"

"No one knows for sure. She maintains that she always takes her newspapers to the recycling center or to the animal shelter, so it could well be that the newspapers came from either of those places. Of course, the fact that her card was found at the scene of the crime doesn't look very good, but it proves nothing."

It was dusk. The temperature had dropped a few degrees, but it wasn't cold. The gulls circled above the dock, watching people load their boats back onto their trailers after a day on the water. Valerie could still make out Josh's sloop in the distance. She felt strange sitting in such a peaceful place, eating, drinking, and chatting with Josh, yet knowing that across the continent the Jodars were fighting a jail sentence for offering sanctuary to animals whom other people wanted to reduce to slivers under a microscope.

"What became of the poor mother rabbit and the babies?"

"Well, that's another story. When Sitch heard what had happened, it really bugged him. You know how personally neat and particular he is. He doesn't like straggly unfinished business."

"So what did he do?"

"He was in the middle of some screenplay deal, and he just walked out. He told me no one was going to make rabbit fricassee out of our bunnies! He got into his car and drove nonstop to Calistoga. He found the place where they were being kept, and as soon as it got dark, he got them all out again and drove them back to L.A.!"

"How did he do it?"

"Well, the place wasn't exactly Fort Knox. Apparently all he had to do was break out a pane of glass on the back door, reach in, undo the lock, and snatch them. Although, we're not to know that. It would ruin Sitch's carefully cultivated mystique! He even left ten dollars to replace the broken pane of glass, and a 'no hard feelings' note. He said that, after all, it wasn't animal control's fault."

"Well, at least there's some good news. So, that leaves only the Jodars in the soup."

"And you. Luckily, the Jodars have enough 'negotiable lettuce' to fight hard. Val, you're the one I'm worried about. The Jodars are Railroad people, not ALFers. They've never even heard of the 'I am you, you are me' pledge. Married people talk. If he recognized you, he must have told her. What if he's decent, but *she* can't take the pressure? Or if he feels he can't let her take the pressure and gives in? The D.A. out there is playing hardball. They want to win one."

"Josh," Valerie hit him playfully in the shoulder. Maybe it was the margaritas, but she didn't feel worried at all. "Lighten up. You're getting soft. Pledge or no pledge, I trust Bruce."

"It's no joke, Val. The Jodars are followed everywhere they go. Bruce has told his friends that their life has been turned upside down. They're under a lot of pressure from their family to find a way out. They may sing."

His words suddenly reminded Valerie of the dead bird Mandy had found that morning. Valerie's mother had always believed that a dead bird is an omen of impending doom. Stop it, she told herself, that's stupid.

"Time will tell, Josh. There's nothing we can do, is there? The biggest problem I see is whether the Jodars' high-priced attorneys will screw them worse than the courts do. I've seen it happen too many times. Sometimes I think you can get a law degree at the 7-Eleven, free with every purchase of a large Coke."

"You might be right about their lawyers. All I know is that they're big-time civil lawyers, not criminal defense types at all. No one has managed to see the Jodars once since Bruce's arrest. Their lawyers have sealed them off. They don't take calls."

They had been talking for hours, and now it was getting dark. Valerie had a return flight to catch. Ignoring her earlier reference to Sean, Josh pleaded with her to stay over.

Valerie reached across the table for his big square hands. For the first time ever, she saw fear in his eyes.

"Josh, I care for you and I always will. You've shared the most exciting and inspiring times of my life with me. You've come to know my strengths and my vulnerabilities, as I've learned yours, and when I'm with you I feel like there's nothing we can't accomplish."

He stared at the glimmering patterns the candle between them was sending across the glass-topped table.

"Besides that," Valerie went on, "you're incredibly attractive to me . . . as I know you realize. And, I've noticed, to scores of other women. But I'm lucky enough to have another incredible guy in my life."

Josh gave her a half-hearted smile. "Yeah, I see that, but I keep thinking there's still a chance you and I will end up together." Valerie stopped him.

"Josh, you and I are too much alike. Two hurricanes can move side by side, but can you imagine what would happen if they tried to merge? Sean is my mooring post. He's not flamboyant, but he's steady. He's the fire waiting to warm my soul, he's tender and giving, and . . . "

"OK, OK, Val!" Josh's voice had a sudden harsh edge. "I hear you. My God, Sean isn't the only sensitive son-of-a-bitch in the world!"

"Josh . . . " Valerie began.

"No, now you listen. I don't want to feel like the man who sent his photo into a Lonely Hearts Club and got it returned, marked 'We're not that lonely.' I hear you, and I promise to work at not making it difficult for you. Just bear with me, Val." He moved his chair back. "And if I get out of line, just give me a good punch. Now let's get a move on for that airport."

At the airport, Valerie propped herself against a wall while Josh went off to hijack a stray wheelchair. Then he chauffeured her to the gate, just in time.

"Tell those quacks to give you a bionic leg in exchange for that loser," he said as she left him. "If our friends call, you may need your feet in working order."

Valerie took her seat on the plane. She could see the waiting area through the window. Josh was still in the lounge, his huge frame plunked down on one of the little modular plastic chairs. He was just sitting there, looking very alone. For a moment she thought of going back to him, but that wouldn't help him adjust to the facts of their relationship. They were buddies. That was how it was going to be. As the plane taxied out of the gate, Valerie watched him stand and walk slowly back toward the exit.

When the seat belt signs were turned off, Valerie dug into her bag and unraveled the package of papers Josh had handed her. They were medical reports from PETA's chief veterinary advisor, known affectionately as "Dr. Ned." Charismatic and sincere, Nedim Buyukmihci had fought hard to overcome the long tradition of hurting and killing healthy animals in practice surgery classes at the University of California at Davis, where he taught. He was well respected by both animal rights advocates and his students for instituting alternatives in his classes. He was less popular with his colleagues in science and veterinary medicine, who he let know that if they did something they shouldn't do to an animal, he wouldn't behave like a good "company man," but would try to stop them. That was too much for them to take. At his own university, the administrators plotted how to deny him tenure and throw him out. To them, the bounds of academic freedom stopped short at animal rights.

Dr. Ned reviewed Hope's history of animal "care," and the critique Valerie held in her hands was no doubt circulating among many others. It must have had Hope's administrators choking and spluttering.

"It seems clear," he wrote, " . . . that the dogs used did not receive adequate veterinary care in situations not a part of the research itself. . . . Because of this lack of care, many of the dogs probably endured considerable unalleviated pain and suffering before dying. The autopsy findings corroborate the hypothesis that careful examination of the dogs prior to death would have revealed the cause of their illness and perhaps prevented their untimely deaths."

Attached to the report was a chart that Hope would have a hard time explaining away. It listed the cause of death for each of the dogs in a series of experiments.

"Dog #56: suffocated in his own fecal matter; Dogs #34, 37, and 193: died of exsanguination [bled to death]; Dog #173: plug inserted too far—perforated his lung; Dog #188: plastic mass found in intestine; Dog #103: anesthesia overdose; Dog #101: died after a 'routine injection'; Dog #70: died after a bronchial washing; Dogs #97 and 176: no known cause or noticed symptoms; Dogs #171 and 189: died of overcrowding/bite wounds."

According to the records, the ALF's informant was right: it had been routine for Hope to abandon the morbidly ill dogs overnight, without care, and to dispose of their bodies with the morning trash. The deaths were casually recorded in a logbook no outsiders were meant to see.

Dr. Ned's report continued, "The surgical technique for lobectomy [removal of part of the lungs] must have been poor, since the autopsy reports frequently cited infection of the thoracic [lung] cavity and tissues. From a scientific standpoint, the 'technical' failure would seem to have rendered the study useless: the researchers lost a considerable number of their subjects long before onset of tumor formation. From an animal welfare standpoint, the suffering endured by these dogs was unconscionable. . . . there appeared to be gross neglect and perhaps incompetence in that these deaths . . . occurred frequently and over a long period of time."

Valerie thought of Prince. How would he have died in that stinking place? Bled to death? A dirty tube piercing his lung?

"There really is no excuse for the researchers not to have

learned from their mistakes or sought assistance to improve their techniques. As a biomedical researcher and a veterinarian, I was appalled by what I read in the autopsy reports."

Valerie pressed the call button and ordered a tomato juice. Dr. Ned's indignation warmed her own pride in what the ALF had accomplished. She knew their efforts would make a difference. She wasn't inclined to take Josh's worries seriously, and she couldn't wait for the next call to action.

Months later, the *Los Angeles Times* reported that, on August 7, 1985, the National Institutes of Health had frozen "several million dollars" of the approximately $5 million the City of Hope receives in U.S. Public Health Service funds annually, while they investigated conditions unearthed during the ALF raid. A preliminary investigation had confirmed at least ten "major deficiencies" and thirteen "minor" ones.

"Three areas of serious non-compliance with Public Health Service Policy were found: veterinary care, physical environment for animals, and administrative oversight," NIH spokeswoman Ann Thomas had announced.

The experiments had been shut down! For a few animals at least, the torture would end.

On Friday, November 8, 1985, the *Times* would also report that the City of Hope National Medical Center had been fined $11,000 for violating the federal Animal Welfare Act. Dr. William Stewart, senior veterinarian at the U.S. Department of Agriculture's Animal and Plant Health Inspection Service, cited the facility for failure to establish adequate veterinary care, failure to consult a veterinarian regarding the use of anesthetic and analgesic drugs, failure to maintain adequate sanitary conditions in surgery areas, use of an inadequately sterilized bronchoscope to examine dogs' lungs, and failure to properly monitor and shelter dogs following surgery. He found that shelter for some cats and dogs was inadequate, and proper records of the number of cats used for research were not kept. Concurrently, the National Institutes of Health announced it had suspended more than $1 million of federal grant funds for animal research at Hope. Many experiments would never resume.

What happened to the Jodars is another story. Their lawyers convinced them to refuse all offers of support from the animal protection community, fearing that such associations, although already well established, might turn the judge against them. Stress aggravated Carol's condition and she worsened steadily. When she could no longer walk, and attorney's fees had topped $50,000, Bruce took his lawyers' advice and accepted a plea of *nolo contendere*, or "no contest." He trusted the judge would allow him to remain free to care for Carol and the children.

Judge Scott Snowden did just that, fining Bruce and Carol $10,000 each and giving them probation for three years, during which time they could not be involved in animal rights. A link in the Underground Railroad had been severed.

As news of what had been uncovered at Hope spread, newspapers were flooded with letters to editors from an outraged public. Society's comfortable belief that all animal research was conducted humanely began to collapse. There was a crack in the laboratory door and people were glimpsing something shocking.

In response to an article in the Syracuse *Post Standard* criticizing all this new attention being paid to research on animals, a PETA member wrote, "Perhaps you don't know that more than 70 million animals are ground up annually in U.S. laboratories. Perhaps you haven't heard there is only one federal law that gives any protection to animals in research, that it covers only 20 percent of these animals and excludes pigs, cows, rats, mice, birds, and horses,[2] and that it does not require painkillers or anesthesia and prohibits no experiment whatsoever, no matter how much suffering it entails.

"Could it be that you don't know any of these things because you are one of the people who has never lifted a finger—or a pen to paper—to stop even the most blatantly worthless and cruel ex-

---

[2]In 1992, the Animal Legal Defense Fund and the Humane Society of the United States won their suit against the USDA to compel the inclusion of rats and mice under the Animal Welfare Act.

periments but will not hesitate to write of his or her sense of humanity and fair play?"

The furor was growing. That same year, 1985, the City of Hope case and other instances of animal abuse at major research facilities prompted Congress to amend the Animal Welfare Act and require minor improvements in housing and care standards. The amendments, sponsored by Representative George Brown and Senator Robert Dole, required proper exercise for dogs, psychological stimulation for caged primates to prevent them from going insane, improved housing, and expanded institutional animal care and use committees that include members not affiliated with the experimental facility. But the research community's backlash movement to keep animals in the laboratories, and the public out of them, was growing too. In 1990 the amendments were scuttled by backstage machinations at the Office of Management and Budget.

The tiny bloodhound puppy died in an incubator at the veterinary hospital less than twenty-four hours after she was rescued. But the other 105 dogs, cats, mice, rats, and rabbits liberated from the City of Hope lived and went on to spend their lives safely and in good hands.

There is little doubt that Prince was the father of the bloodhound's puppies. They were all black—and he was the only candidate. The bloodhound, whom the ALF had first christened "Helen," was later renamed "Goofy," and she and Prince once had a reunion in Denver during the filming of a television segment on the ALF. Both of them slept on the same motel bed while Prince's new guardian, her face in shadow, described what it was like to rehabilitate a dog scarred by lab experience. The dogs later roamed through a field full of prairie dog dens, playing and "talking," but giving a wide berth to the camera crew. Prince barked without let-up at the men with black boxes on their shoulders.

In 1988 Valerie had a chance to see Prince again. The bond between them remains incredible and magical. She believes that he understands absolutely everything that happened, and that he knows she was one of those responsible for his rescue.

Goofy died peacefully in 1990. Valerie asked her people to write down something about their experiences with her, and shortly afterward this letter was published in *PETA News*:

To Whom It May Concern:

A few days ago a bloodhound died a quiet death at the country home she shared for five years with her human and animal companions. We are writing to notify and thank those responsible for bringing her to us and to tell you a little about her and her last years, because our dog was rescued from a laboratory by the ALF.

When she first arrived she was emaciated and covered with large tumors, and had just delivered a litter of puppies who had died. She would huddle in the corner and shake and was described by the vet as being in a state of extreme depression. There was concern as to whether she would live, but they had named her anyway . . . Helen, for Helen of Troy. Although she improved physically and emotionally, she remained terrified of certain gestures. For example, if someone raised a broom or rake too quickly, she would fall to the ground and cringe and even howl in fear. She was a little territorial about food. If someone brought out a hose she would run away and hide.

But she would also run three quarters of a mile down our country lane each afternoon to wait at the gate for her friend coming home from work.

She touched the hearts of everyone who ever met her and grew to be a trusting, gentle, and protective member of our family. Gradually the clown in her personality surfaced and the nickname Goofy began to stick.

Her death was peaceful, and many people old and young will miss her and hold happy memories of Goofy.

We learned much from her courage, loyalty, and loving ways. Thank you so much; our lives are much enriched for having known this exceptional and endearing creature.

Sincerely,
The family and friends of Goofy

10

The Baby Monkey Who Couldn't See

In March of 1985—three months after the City of Hope raid—Josh flew to Washington to break the news to Valerie in person.

"I'm moving to California," he said.

"Josh, when?" she asked, feeling vaguely panicked. The expression on Valerie's face must have let him know his words upset her.

"I've really already gone," he answered.

It made absolute sense, Valerie realized. He could have his boat there. The West Coast ALF units were crackling with activity and could use his skills. By now everyone in animal protection circles knew that the Philadelphia Grand Jury was heating up and subpoenas were flying around like June bugs. Already thirteen people had been snatched up since the University of Pennsylvania raid and whisked away for questioning behind closed doors. East Coast actions were temporarily chilled. Then again, perhaps he'd met someone.

She would miss him, she knew. Florida was only two hours away, just down the coast. Now they were to be a continent apart. Josh was her ALF anchor, the person to whom she could express her innermost feelings. They felt the same way: that the world is basically cruel, a place where good has to struggle for a hearing, where evil is accepted as long as it keeps its work quiet, and where many people wear "civilization" as a thin coat over their cold hearts. She and Josh weren't morbid about it; they simply accepted life as being that way.

Josh was angrier than Valerie, and they had their differences, but they had agonized together over the most embarrassing traits of the human species, and identified the depths of human greed even in themselves. They were, in Josh's words, "realistic idealists." Through their actions, they could hope to show some of the planet's citizens some of the abuses they could recognize and stop. They could shake up the status quo a bit, stop some individual suffering, even frighten some of the perpetrators into modifying their own behaviors, but they knew they couldn't change the whole mess. Having each other had eased that realization.

"Josh, don't make the move sound so final," Valerie said, her voice sounding very small. "Promise me you won't disappear, will you?"

"No, I won't disappear. As soon as I get there, we're doing a big job in Riverside at the university. It's the biggest party anyone has ever planned. We'll need you."

"How many animals?" Valerie asked, glad they'd be working together again right away.

"Seven hundred," Josh said.

"You've got to be joking! What are they, mosquitoes?"

"Mice, rabbits, pigeons, opossums, rats, cats, and one very sad little baby monkey."

"Fill me in."

"Riverside has a huge psych lab. Over the years, it's grown like a bamboo forest," Josh told her. "Instead of doing away with the old animal exercises for the students, the university has sucked in tons of federal and state funding and kept expanding. There's almost nothing they don't do to animals."

"It's funny how people think of psychology research as benign, isn't it?" Valerie said. "Then you read what they do—Harlow scaring infant monkeys with metal 'monster mothers' that blow cold air at them, 'mothers' with spikes coming out of their chests, and Skinner putting his own child in a box!"

"Riverside still uses Skinner boxes for pigeons," Josh told her.

"The birds have to press the right switches in the dark or they get an electric shock. All repetitious stuff, pure show and tell. Luckily, one of the students has quietly pressed the switch on his professor."

"Turnabout's fair play! What else do they do?" Valerie asked.

"You name it. They sew cats' eyes shut, mutilate opossums' eyes as soon as they leave their mother's pouch, starve pigeons and rats, feed nutritionally deficient diets to mice just to see their bellies swell or their bones break. It's a regular house of horror, although the buildings look very nice from the outside."

"One day someone should do a paper on the psychology of animal experimenters. What kind of people can do this to animals and then go home to a nice dinner with the wife and kids?" Valerie said.

"No argument there. This student's professor is a woman. Hard as nails, he says. The kind of woman you despise: one who thinks that feminism means the right to do every atrocious thing men do."

The cell had been having a hard time convincing the student to act. They had been nurturing him since his initial call to Last Chance for Animals, where he'd been picked up by an ALF contact volunteering at the group, who was returning messages left on the answering machine. The student needed his courage built up. In his naivete, the student at first thought he could meet with the dean and talk alternatives. The cell persuaded him to get a friend to do that, to show him what would happen. The friend was patronized for a little while, then thrown out of the dean's office on his ear. It was business as usual, and money in the bank, for the university.

"There's a baby monkey there he, and we, want to get out," Josh said. "They call him Britches. He's a stumptail macaque monkey who was born into Riverside's breeding colony, where babies were taken away from their mothers right after birth. Psych professors are so eager to supply 'subjects' for their own absurdly artificial classroom experiments that they never let the psychological suffering of the mother monkeys or their infants enter their rigid, overeducated minds.

"Right now, Britches is three weeks old. Sitch is worried that he may not live until we get inside. Lots of the infants don't make it, but we have no choice but to wait for winter break. Otherwise, the campus is too busy. Students work in the labs at all hours. Penetration is a nightmare."

The little monkey was being used in what was to be a three-year sight-deprivation experiment. Exactly what was being done to him Josh didn't yet know, other than that he was not allowed to see and was being kept all alone in a cage. All the papers concerning the experiment were kept under lock and key in the researcher's office. The ALF's student contact had tried once to get into that office when the janitors were cleaning, but had lost his nerve. It would be up to Sitch and his team to break the lock and retrieve the papers.

"My leg's not so bad nowadays," Valerie fibbed. "I'll come with you."

"Frankly, I think you should get the damned thing x-rayed again. I watched you walk in here, and you're still not right. We're going to have to crawl into the first floor by removing the air conditioning units, break down a lot of doors, charge up and down stairs, and hike to vehicles parked way off campus to avoid roving security guards. You know you're not up to it right now. Anyway, Britches will be too hot to keep in California. If we get him out, he'll need a mother. How about taking care of that?"

"You got it." Valerie was already leafing through back issues of the Simian Society newsletters in her mind, remembering articles about sympathetic primate handlers. A subtle call to one of the refuges, or to Sam, Miki's zookeeper friend, might net helpful information, too. She would have to pick Miki's brain and call the ALF vets.

"Get that foot x-rayed," Josh told her when she dropped him off at the airport. "I'm serious," he shouted as he pushed the revolving door. Then he was gone. Sean had been threatening to hoist Valerie over his shoulder and carry her to the emergency room if she didn't do just that. When I come back from L.A., she promised herself, I will.

Two weeks later, Valerie was aboard a U.S. Air flight, nonstop to California, her luggage stuffed with diapers, baby skin cream, a baby bottle, and formula. She had made over $200 worth of phone calls, trying to nail down the right advice about infant primates and find the right foster mother for Britches. All the reliable primate people had said more or less the same thing, basically this: we're all primates, a baby monkey is just like a human baby, the people who know most about their problems are pediatricians.

More than once Valerie had been advised to call Dr. Bettina Flavioli, a retired pediatrician living in Utah. "She saved our orphaned baby woolly when he had pneumonia. Carried him around in a papoose, stayed up all night with him. She'll do anything to help," said Dorothy from the Simian Society.

It had taken Valerie the full two weeks to track Dr. Flavioli down because the doctor had been on vacation in Venezuela with her sister. The morning before she left for California, Valerie had dialed Dr. Flavioli's number again, quite scared that she would end up trying to look after Britches herself, a childless woman armed only with baby books. Luckily, Dr. Flavioli had stepped through the door at that moment, put down her luggage, and answered the phone.

"Yes," she said, "I understand. You are Dorothy's friend. Yes, you can tell me anything in confidence. Yes, whatever you want. You bring him here, dear. Don't you worry."

At Los Angeles International Airport, Valerie found Josh outside the terminal, waiting for her beside a gray, late-model Mercedes.

"What is this?" she asked him.

"I haven't gone nuts," Josh countered. "This is L.A. You can rent things like this here. It's my idea. A necessary expense." The West Coast ALF had come up with a useful fundraising idea. Sympathizers collected money at animal rights tables in the malls and sold raffle tickets in the name of registered animal protection and other charities. The money they collected was channeled into the ALF's L.A.-based cell.

"How is *this* necessary?" Valerie asked Josh.

"If we get Britches and an all-points bulletin goes out for him, which it will, I want you to be driving him out of the state in the least suspicious vehicle on the road. Tell the truth, now, don't the police go easier on rich people?"

"Actually, I hate to admit this about my uniformed brothers and sisters, but the police are as influenced by money as anyone, unless you're talking something that looks like a pimp-mobile."

Josh outlined where and when Valerie was to make the rendez-vous. She decided not to check into a hotel because there was so little time. She didn't want to go to someone's house either: having such a limited role, she didn't fancy being underfoot while others were preparing for the most ambitious job the ALF had ever undertaken. Josh had Valerie drop him off a block from Sitch's apartment in West Hollywood. The job would require several trucks, and Josh was in charge of coordinating their drivers and equipment.

Valerie parked the Mercedes on a lot and took a taxi to the ren-dezvous spot. She wanted to avoid having such an opulent and ob-vious car seen going back and forth, yet she wanted to be sure of her bearings before it got dark. After that, she picked up a can of chickpeas and two Burger King Whoppers without the meat and went to the park to eat an early dinner and kill time.

As usual, the pigeons ended up with most of the food. City birds, scavenging for the tiniest crumb of discarded food, had al-ways been able to take her appetite away. To her they are like hobos, but without soup kitchens or warm shelters or social ser-vices. She knew they had been brought into cities hundreds of years ago, and she admired how they eked out an existence in the crevices of old buildings or on the cold metal under bridges, rais-ing their squabs while exhaust fumes billow up into their nests.

When I get old, Valerie thought as she watched the birds feed, if I'm not rotting in jail somewhere, I'll be in a Washington park, one of those old women people make fun of, sharing their meager resources with the birds and breaking the ice in the fountain to let them drink.

A blue-gray male puffed up his chest and proudly circled in front of his intended romantic interest. She pecked at the ground and moved coquettishly away. He followed, making a deep "currr, currr" sound in his throat, turning circles to impress her, and trying, at the same time, to keep up as she drifted away. Valerie remembered the pigeons the ALF had rescued from the University of Pennsylvania. She remembered, too, the poisoned pigeons Miki had told her that she found writhing under the metro bridges. She thought of the birds trapped inside Skinner boxes at Riverside, waiting to be shocked. What on earth was our society thinking about?

Driving around, Valerie noticed several Spanish bookstores. She doubled back and went inside the biggest, finding some cute children's magazines for Carmelita. Maria had recently sent her their address in Cambridge, Massachusetts, and let Valerie know she and Carmelita were doing well. Valerie and Sean had talked about going to Boston to see them at Christmas.

Now all that was left to do was wait. Valerie popped a pain killer and tried to meditate.

At 11:00 P.M. she filled the gas tank, checked the tires and oil, and drove to the Beverly Hills Hilton. She tipped the valet parking attendant and had the car put among the other expensive autos on the lot, then found a secluded corner of the hotel where she could sit undisturbed. The luminous hands on her watch seemed to crawl around the dial. She started thinking about the grand jury in Philadelphia.

Alex Pacheco and thirteen other PETA members had been subpoenaed during a swoop raid on a news conference. Sue Brebner, PETA's director of education, had almost escaped, but an agent had written down her license plate number as she drove away. The D. A. tracked her to the hospital in Delaware where she worked. Summoned to the Head Nurses Station as she hurried out of a Code Blue early one morning, she was handed a "must appear" summons, commanding her to appear before the grand jury.

Sue fought extradition to Pennsylvania and eventually won the court battle not to return her to Philadelphia for more fingerprinting, photographing, questioning, and other nonsense. She was in the middle of a campaign to ban the decompression chamber and didn't need the harassment.

As a cop, Valerie had been exposed to a grand jury only once. From the law enforcement side of the fence it had looked pretty good. The state's attorney had employed one to hear the evidence against two old-time Montgomery County land developers, men well connected to the governor's office. The state's attorney, protecting his own career and anxious to avoid any political fallout, convened a grand jury, which met in secret and dutifully indicted the two men.

From the ALF side of the fence the grand jury looked pretty rotten. Valerie knew it was considered unconstitutional by many attorneys, and for good reason. First, because grand juries hear only one side of a case, they are often used as rubber stamps or to legitimize a case that wouldn't be strong enough to warrant prosecution under normal circumstances. Second, unlike other controlled proceedings, prosecutors can introduce rumor, gossip, hearsay, and the most personal, possibly irrelevant, and certainly otherwise inadmissible details of a person's private life. Third, witnesses before the grand jury are not usually allowed to have their attorneys present during their interrogation by the prosecutor, who can say anything at all without fear of being caught out of line. And, if witnesses invoke their Fifth Amendment right not to answer a question, they may be forced to answer or plunked into jail.

The Pennsylvania commonwealth attorney was rounding up perfectly law-abiding volunteers who had done nothing more radical than lick an envelope. These witnesses were being asked to name anyone they had ever seen at animal rights meetings or rallies, to offer up anyone they might have heard utter a sympathetic word about the ALF. Surely, the commonwealth attorney must have reasoned, if enough people were brought in, someone could be forced to implicate someone. Pretty soon, grandmothers of friends of anyone who had ever said "yech!" during a high school dissection would be on the stand.

However, the state prosecutor had made a critical mistake. At the end of each day, all remaining witnesses needed to be resworn. Somehow, on the night before Pacheco was to be interrogated, no one had resworn him. Without that little formality, the power of the original subpoena expired, and Pacheco caught the error right away. He held his breath, waiting for someone else to catch it. No one did. Needless to say, Alex Pacheco was on the 5:30 P.M. train out of Philadelphia on a one-way ticket, looking over his shoulder all the way.

"Why hasn't Ingrid Newkirk been brought in?" the Philadelphia prosecutor fumed. "She's the one who shows up after the ALF raids, armed with documents from inside the labs. Why can't you get her in here?"

"The process server thinks she's been tipped off by friends in the sheriff's office," he was told. "She hasn't been seen."

Agents and process servers were sent back to PETA's "animal house," where they watched the comings and goings with mounting frustration. They couldn't tell who was who. With the exception of the mail carriers and delivery people, everyone wore a monkey mask.

At 11:40 Valerie pulled out of the Beverly Hills Hilton parking lot and drove carefully to the rendezvous spot, a side street in a residential area on the outskirts of Santa Monica. The street was quiet and tidy, with cars parked here and there along it. The other side of the road was a no-parking zone. Less than a block away, Valerie could see the signs for a dry cleaner, a bank, and an antique shop in a little neighborhood mall.

She looked at her watch. Fifteen minutes to go. She tried to guess in which direction Riverside lay and sent positive vibes toward it. A police cruiser drifted by without noticing her.

Midnight. Time to keep her eyes peeled for Josh. He could be along at any moment.

No Josh—12:15, 12:30, 12:45, 1:00 A.M. Valerie tried not to think of how ambitious the job was. Seven hundred animals. A campus with thousands of students. University security. She knew that all it took for something to go wrong was one false move, one fluke, one person out of place.

Just after one o'clock, the police cruiser came by again. The shift had changed and a younger officer had come on duty. Valerie kept the top of her head level with the headrest and closed her eyes to a squint. She was sure he hadn't seen her.

By two, Valerie was agitated. What if Josh and the others were in jail? Worse, a failure meant seven hundred animals left to rot. She couldn't drive to Riverside. That would be pointless. There was nothing to do but wait and hope the cruising neighborhood police didn't come over. Valerie forced her mind to concentrate on other things: what to buy Sean for Christmas, whether to try hydrotherapy for her leg. After this many hours without being able to stretch out, she had to prop her ankle up against the passenger door to keep comfortable. It was swollen again.

The luminous small hand on her watch dragged its way toward three. Valerie had visions of Josh, Sitch, Vin, and the cat man lined up outside the lab at Riverside. Other people she didn't know were with them, dressed in ALF "uniform." She could almost hear someone barking at them, "Turn around, hands against the wall, feet back, and spread 'em." Valerie could see Josh's face as he was frisked for weapons. He would be shaking with frustration and rage at his failure.

Would the animals be stacked up outside? They would be scared, confused, wondering what was going on. The cops wouldn't notice the animals, other than to say, "Hey, look at these ugly 'possums" or something, and maybe nudge a few cages with their polished shoes. "Get some evidence tags," they'd yell, shining their bright flashlights into the animals' eyes.

What is the point of thinking about this, Valerie disciplined herself. It either is or isn't happening that way. Just wait and see. The cruiser was coming back. Valerie could see the outline of his top lights as he slid down the street behind her. Then she saw the lights of a second car, not a block behind the cruiser. Was it Josh?

Valerie scrunched down in the seat and let the cruiser pass, being careful not to let her foot touch the brake pedal. Seconds later, Josh pulled up level with the back door of the Mercedes, jumped out and opened the door.

"Time to get going," Josh said, placing a cardboard box on the front passenger seat and thrusting a sheath of papers under it. He reached back into his car and drew out a duffle bag. Valerie noticed that he was dripping with sweat as he placed it on the floor behind the passenger seat. "Tools," he said. "Ditch them when you cross the state line, OK?" Val nodded.

"And take this, for self-defense. I meant to give it to you at the University of Pennsylvania."

"What is it?" she asked.

"A stun gun. The directions are inside."

"Josh, I couldn't . . . I don't want it." But Josh wasn't listening.

"Take care, Val. Now, vamoose," he said and shut the car door.

Josh pulled away, and Valerie followed him up to the light, then they turned in opposite directions onto the freeway. Every two minutes or so, like clockwork, a frenzied, scraping sound came from the box.

Several miles down the road Valerie pulled into a rest stop and took a look at her passenger.

Britches was so small that if she had picked him up, he would have fit in her two hands cupped together. His head didn't look like a head anymore. A green plastic box, almost as big as he was, was attached to his scalp somehow. It weighed so much that Britches' underdeveloped neck couldn't support it. He clung to a filthy, toweling-covered post, his "surrogate mother," Valerie guessed, and his little head fell constantly to the side. A plastic lead that once fed from the box to who-knows-where dangled down by his ear. Sitch's people had cut this baby monkey loose from some other device.

Below the green box, with its odd indentations, were bandages where Britches' eyes should have been. Only his tiny nostrils and wrinkled baby chin were visible from beneath the tight strips of cloth bound about his head and face. Then there was his chest: a snow-white, soft-haired monkey body visible beneath a strange bodice with a harness.

"What on earth?" Valerie said softly to Britches. Instantly, Britches grabbed his penis and kicked out his foot. The action of his flesh moving quickly along the cardboard created the sound she had heard coming from inside the box. She didn't have to be

281

a primatologist or pediatrician to know that this was his neurotic response to stress.

"Don't worry, little guy," she told him. "We're going to get you some help."

It was quiet in the rest stop and she felt safe enough to try to bottle-feed him. She opened a can of soy baby formula and poured it into the bottle. The sound made him try to raise his head. Gently holding his chin up, Valerie made the nipple wet with milk, then eased it into his mouth. Britches shot both arms up and started to suckle, almost tearing the bottle from her hands. The formula was a huge success. This little man was hungry!

When Valerie had convinced Britches there was no more milk to be had, she wiped his mouth with a towel and tried to make a little bed for him. The device on his head made it impossible for him to lie down; he could only lean against the edges of the box to sleep. His bottom was caked with feces, and his skin was chafed and raw. As Valerie moved him, she noticed he smelled sour, like milk gone bad.

Valerie had taken the precaution of filling a thermos with hot coffee before leaving. As the morning wore on, she needed it. Stopping for gas, she covered Britches' box with towels, then pulled over a little way away from the station, as if reading the map. Propped up in his box, Britches would doze, then start, clutching at himself and kicking, again and again. When Valerie offered him the bottle, he was as anxious to be fed as he had been the last time. As soon as she pulled the bottle away, he immediately defecated a soft, messy, and smelly stool into the box. Valerie picked him up and exchanged the ruined towel underneath him for a fresh, clean one, then set him down and on they went.

The scenery was breathtaking. Valerie wished Britches were well and she could pull over and enjoy the views she was missing. The scrub brush had given way to mountains, and there was still snow on the road in places. Here and there, tiny little blossoms of spring flowers (she recognized crocuses) were peeking through the bushes, and the grass was rich and green. To help keep herself awake, she looked for different kinds of flora she could tell Sean about. Thoreau wrote that "what we call wildness is a civilization other than our own," and here, Valerie thought, it seems far superior to the one we have built in its stead.

Valerie turned off Highway 15, west of Provo, and headed for the Great Salt Lake. It seemed a satisfactory final resting place for the UC-Riverside tools. At the lake's edge, she threw each heavy piece into the water. Then, without hesitation, she pitched the stun gun in, too. "Sorry, Josh," she thought.

The only time a police officer is supposed to draw a weapon is when she or he means to shoot it. She had been taught to shoot to kill, to aim for the "K-5 area": the chest, the head, the heart. She had lived with the awareness that she might have to fire at someone in the line of duty for three years. Lately, however, she had begun to feel uncomfortable with keeping a weapon at home. It wasn't that she believed that violence begets violence; it was simply a matter of no longer feeling good about violence per se—any kind of violence.

While Valerie drove, the press wires were buzzing in California. A student who had stayed late to study in the Science Hall had seen a man in a white lab coat directing others down a stairwell. According to the student, the man was white, of medium build, between twenty to thirty years old, with close-cropped hair and a brown beard. The intruder had yelled, "Let's get the hell out of here," and beckoned to someone out of the student's line of sight.

The student told police that he assumed the noises he heard from the floor below him meant an experiment was in progress, so he had not called campus security. Four hours later, a cage filled with mice was discovered in the hall, indicating that the raiders had been interrupted. By noon, an Identi-kit drawing of Sitch was running on the wires and would be printed in the next day's papers. Luckily, the student had been too tired to register Sitch's appearance accurately. It would require a leap of imagination to believe that the computer drawing was of the ALF's debonair West Coast leader.

Valerie pulled into Salt Lake just before 1:00 P.M. the next afternoon and found Dr. Flavioli's house without any trouble. Val was rumpled and smelled of monkey feces and coffee. She left Britches in the car while she made sure everything was going to work out.

"I have a bed for you," Dr. Flavioli said, hugging Valerie to her huge frame. She looked exactly the way mothers look in Italian films—nurturing, round, and happy. "We'll see the patient and then you collapse."

As Valerie carried the box into the office annex and lifted Britches onto the table, Dr. Flavioli watched with her chubby hands on her face, shaking her head. She had put a thick towel on the table in anticipation of his arrival.

"My dear!" she said. "What have they done to you?"

Dr. Flavioli gently ran her fingers around the surgical tape binding the box to Britches' head. Then she wrapped Britches' fingers around her own index finger. He grabbed on and kicked.

"He's like all babies, he likes contact with other living beings. If I'm the first one he sees when we take this contraption off him, he'll think I'm his mama! Now, you let him hold your finger please while I cut the tape away."

"Dee, can you get in here please," she called through the doorway, causing an equally rotund woman to enter the room on tip-toe. "This is my assistant, Dee," Dr. Flavioli explained. "She'll videotape the exam. Dee knows all my secrets, so don't be worried."

"Will do, Betty," Dee replied.

"And let's get the tape recorder on so I can dictate what we're seeing here," Betty said, slipping a tape into the boom box on the counter by the examining table and pressing the "on" lever. She began to speak in a loud voice:

"On this day, April 20, 1985, I have been called upon to administer an examination and follow-up care to an infant stumptail macaque, male, my guess approximately five weeks of age. Said infant allegedly liberated by the Animal Liberation Front from the UC-Riverside laboratory.

"Attached to infant's head by means of bandage and tape is an apparatus of some sort with what appears to be some sort of electrical cord extending from it. It has been cut. Bilaterally are short lengths of tubing emerging from the bandage. Tape is in direct contact with the face and neck. Bandage lifted rostrally from right eye due to excessive moisture and right eye partially visible."

Betty snipped at the bandages and tape around Britches' head, working some soothing cream onto his skin as she exposed his crusty scalp. Soon, the device was detached and set down on the table.

Betty moved down to Britches' eyes, gently pulling the bandage wrap away inch by inch. A string of damning Italian words fell from her lips as we saw what was beneath the tape. Britches' eyes were sewn shut with thick, black thread. The researchers had taken a massive sewing needle and stitched his upper lids to his lower lids on both eyes.

"Beneath the bandage are two cotton pads," Bettina continued, "one for each eye. The cotton pad for the right eye has slipped laterally beneath the tape. Both pads are filthy and soaked through with moisture. Bilaterally upper eyelids are sutured to lower eyelids. The sutures are grossly oversized for the purpose intended. Many of these sutures have torn through lid tissue resulting in multiple lacerations of the lids. There is an open space between upper and lower lids of both eyes of about one quarter inch, and sutures are contacting corneal tissue resulting in excessive tearing, which explains the soaked cotton pads. There are multiple bandage lesions on head, face, and neck of infant."

"Surgical scissors," barked Betty.

Dee pulled the smallest scissors with curved ends from the tray on the shelf beside the table and handed them to her, then went back to filming. Britches was making quiet sounds, murmurs and peeps, not normal monkey screeches and clicks.

"We must be absolutely sure he doesn't move. Can you hold his head very, very still please?"

Valerie did as she was told. Betty worked the ends of the scissors under the stitching material, keeping the pointed ends curved away from Britches' eyes as much as possible. She made a sharp cut, then delicately pulled the first long thread out through Britches' upper eyelid and laid it on the table. It was nerve-wracking work. Britches' twitching could be violent, and a sudden jog might send the scissors into his eye. If a minute passed without a twitch, Betty would withdraw the scissors and wait for the spasm to pass before resuming work on his eyelids.

Slowly, the stitches were extracted. Betty called for a warm, wet cloth and carefully began wiping the crust from Britches' eyes, trying not to touch the sensitive holes left by the oversized stitching material she had pulled out. Occasionally Britches would flinch and squirm, but was very quiet.

Betty carried on dictating: "One can only conclude that the suture placement must have been performed by an unqualified or incompetent person and that the infant was not receiving proper ongoing medical care. Such care would also clearly be subject of malpractice given a veterinary or infant practice situation.

"Infant demonstrates photophobia. Penis of infant is edematous and inflamed. There are smegma accumulations. Generalized muscle development poor. Skin dry. Body odor foul."

At last, Betty was finished. Britches seemed not to know that he could finally open his eyes. Then, realization dawned. His fingers shot up to his eyes. Betty grabbed them and held them at bay, afraid he would hurt himself by rubbing. At first in one eye, then in the other, cracks appeared between Britches' upper and lower lids. His eyes began peering out. He was squinting into the light, looking at the world for the first time since his eyes were sewn shut. Fascinated by the experience, two now-twinkling eyes opened fully. His head turned to the right and then the left, then back again: it was as if he was saying, "I can see! Look at that! I can see!" He popped his thumb into his mouth and started sucking.

Betty took Britches' tiny fingers and wrapped them around her own. She carried him over to the medicine chest and chose an ophthalmic ointment. As she squeezed the moist gel into his eyes, Britches wiggled vigorously, objecting to the loss of his newfound sight. She worked the ointment into his eyes gently, allowing Britches to see again. He calmed down right away, and put his thumb back into his mouth. Betty took a second salve and rubbed that on his face and scalp to soften his skin.

"That's nothing more than dry skin," she said. "We'll let him rest."

Betty peeled off the stinking jacket Britches had been wearing, cleaned his skin, applied salve, and dressed him in a clean, cotton baby smock. It fit perfectly. Then she wrapped him loosely in a towel and held him in her arms like any human baby, rocking him back and forth. He clung to her finger and watched her, fascinated by his new mom.

Dee brought in cups, some oatmeal cookies, and coffee. It smelled exquisite. "Hawaiian kona," Dee told Valerie. "Betty used to practice in Hawaii. Now we only have memories of the palm trees, but we still treat ourselves to the coffee!"

"What do you think this device is?" Valerie asked Betty. Britches watched them examine it, his eyes glued to Betty's face one minute, then switching to look at Valerie as she turned the box over in her hands. There were thick, square plastic pouches in the device, and electrical wires.

"No idea, unless they were planning on sending him to a fancy dress ball. Do you have any electronic experts you can ask?"

"Yes," Valerie told Betty. "When I get home, I'll see what we can find out."

Dee handed Valerie the video cassette from the camera and she put it safely in her jacket pocket.

Britches was peeking out of the towel in Betty's arms. It was the first time since he had left his mother's arms that he had been able to lay his head back comfortably, or feel a soft surface against his skin. His eyes were closing reluctantly, as if he was scared they might never open again if he let go. His little pink tongue stuck out of his mouth as he drifted off to sleep.

"Off to the land of Winkin', Blinkin', and Nod," Valerie said, watching Britches' eyelids come together and stay that way, and sensing that she was not far behind him.

"Filthy, soiled, foul-smelling jacket removed from infant's body, and infant wrapped in soft, warm towel," Betty finished the tape. "Infant bottle-fed and rocked to sleep. Prior to falling asleep, digit-sucking behavior replaced self-clutching. Infant placed in towel-lined cage (still wrapped) next to surrogate mother with which he had been reared."

The research papers the L.A. cell removed from Riverside showed exactly how lucky Britches was. He would not have lived that long in the lab, if the fate of the other infants was any indication.

"Infant kept in dark and died," read the terse commentary on the monkey who had gone before him. The infants in the colony cages attached to the university, born to neurotic mothers driven crazy by confinement, suffered earlier but no less nasty deaths: "Outside temperatures very cold and windy—infant died." "Baby torn apart. Picked up part of the skull, bones from arm. Parts missing, head, neck, forearm, hand, half of back and chest, most of inside organs."

The device that had been strapped to Britches' head turned out to be a variation on something called a Tri-Sensory Aid, or TSA, that emits auditory signals from sonar input. The protocol submitted by the Riverside researchers to justify the abuses Britches suffered was priceless. It looked as if they might have been hoping to reap the benefits of a commercial deal for their homemade tracking device. The taxpayers were certainly to foot the bill for experiments, scheduled over the next three years, on twenty-four monkey infants.

According to the researchers, studying an artificially blinded primate was "necessary" because "sufficient numbers of blind human infants [to study] were not within driving distance" of Riverside, and because the experimenters did not wish to be "inconvenienced" by the "normal household routine" if forced to work with blind children living at home.

PETA sent the Britches research work and the examining veterinarian's (anonymous) report to leaders of organizations for the blind, asking for their input. Dr. Grant Mack, president of the American Council of the Blind, was among the first to respond. He was appalled at both the cruelty to Britches and the waste of federal funds needed by the blind for worthwhile projects that didn't involve animals. He agreed to appear on film to condemn the experiment as "one of the most repugnant and ill-conceived boondoggles that I've heard about for a long time."

The Riverside experimenters had to cover up fast. Instead of trying to justify what they had done to Britches' eyes, they decided to try some real bravado and deny it altogether. The thickness of the stitching material shown on video, they announced, was caused by black mascara or paint applied onto normal-sized sutures by the liberationists. The damage to Britches' eyes was not caused by their handiwork, but by a sloppy ALF veterinarian removing the stitches. The device was not secured onto Britches' head as shown on the tape, it had been removed and improperly reaffixed.

NIH decided that these explanations were more palatable than admitting they had failed in every way to apply critical review or oversight to Riverside's monkey experiments although the researchers' own protocols—obtained by PETA under the Freedom of Information Act—showed the lie. "The first attempt at suturing the eyelids," the experimenters had written, never imagining anyone on the "outside" would read their words, "came loose after several days, and subsequent attempts caused the eyelids to tear, producing infections and making further suturing impossible."

Ignored, too, were the statements flowing in from experts, some animal experimenters themselves, who had viewed the tape. Wrote one neurophysiologist, "During my fifteen years of vision research activity, I used this method (suture closing) in several hundred experimental animals. Any competent researchers would have known to use the appropriate type of suture material, drainage methods, and antibiotic delivery well known within the field of vision research."

"One need only imagine," wrote one ophthalmologist, "how painful and irritating a speck of dust in any eye is in order to understand the extreme discomfort these large, inappropriately placed sutures caused this infant."

Others were less charitable. "Unlike blind human infants," wrote one scientist, "Britches was also deprived of all social interaction, including contact with his mother, and kept unstimulated in a wire cage since birth. He could not have developed as a normal blind child would. It is rubbish research."

Their words fell on deaf ears. Although it was clear that the experimental procedures had violated both the *NIH Guide for the*

Care and Use of Laboratory Animals and the Public Health Service policy directing experimenters to "avoid all unnecessary suffering and injury to animals," NIH ruled that the Riverside "scientists" had done no wrong. Officially, Riverside was off the hook.

While Britches discovered the pleasures of being alive and loved, PETA was filing formal complaints with the government and asking its members to write to their members of Congress. Under scrutiny now from the public and federal agencies, Riverside's image was changing. Humane students and humane teachers, people who had never known what took place in the animal labs, were unhappy at the revelations and, behind the scenes, demanded explanations and changes in policy. Perhaps for the first time in their careers, experimenters had to stand in their shattered labs and think. Sadly, their conclusions were not always sane. Sometimes they were downright bizarre.

Sally Sperling, one of the professors whose Riverside lab had been raided, wrote in the American Psychological Association *Monitor*:

> I can describe in detail how [the lab] looked when I first saw it after the crime—the images are etched into my memory with acid, and I never will be free of them. But I can't describe the emotional impact of what I saw in any meaningful way. Words are isolated, and it all hit me at once—horror: feelings of violation; anger; concern for my pigeons, for the other animal researchers and their animals; sadness; depression; frustration; physical symptoms of shock, and a sickening sense of loss.
>
> My lab was my haven and refuge for eighteen years. Even when an experiment wasn't going well or the equipment was acting up, I wanted to be in my lab and missed it badly when I wasn't there. Now, I barely can make myself open the door, and I can't stand to be in there for more than a few minutes at a time. Unfortunately, these reactions aren't restricted to my lab. I'm almost as depressed anywhere else in the building or even anywhere on campus.
>
> The reactions of other researchers to the break-in, however, are most disturbing of all. I just assumed that everyone committed to research would be outraged by this senseless, tragic crime, that

they'd offer sympathy and help to us victims. I couldn't have been more wrong.

Frighteningly few colleagues, inside or outside the psychological community, including the members of my department, even seem to care. The students haven't been any better.

"Yes, you've been violated," Valerie thought. "But not as hideously as you have violated others." She wondered if Sperling's experience would burrow through this defensiveness one day and turn her against her training. It didn't seem likely.

No sooner had Valerie gotten home from Salt Lake than Sitch asked her to come back to L.A. to meet with a reporter named Gordon Dillow. Dillow wanted to do a long piece on the ALF, and he wanted to meet its American founder. Mr. Dillow was known to be a man of integrity, the kind of reporter who would go to jail before revealing his source. Valerie hopped a standby and met him in a cocktail lounge at Los Angeles International Airport.

Dillow warmed to Valerie. He wrote later that he expected a "typical, wild-eyed, true-believer fanatic, cold, humorless, maybe even psychotic, a person motivated more by hate than conviction." He found, instead, a "soft-spoken, articulate, obviously well-educated woman in her thirties with a straight day job who just happened to spend her weekends flying from coast to coast committing burglaries." It was a bit off-base, but Valerie had not been prepared to say then that she was a former cop who now devoted every day to trying to find targets and form a functioning ALF organization from a rag-tag bunch of diverse people.

The interview was well worth the extra travel and expense. Dillow's piece took up two pages in the Los Angeles *Herald Tribune* and was picked up by the Associated Press wire. He spoke to his readers from the heart, asking them a question he must have asked himself. What if you had a dog at home and you loved that dog a lot and, one day, the experimenters came a-knocking?

'Listen, we're going to take your dog, Fido. We're going to sew his eyelids shut, shave his head, and attach a sonar device to his skull. Then, we're going to keep him in a cage in a laboratory for months or even years, assuming he survives, so that we can study whether this device might someday be used to help blind people detect objects. Of course, this is going to hurt like hell, and we're not promising anything: maybe using Fido will help, maybe it won't. So how about it?'

Sure, you probably would like to help blind people. But chances are you're going to send the guy packing because you aren't going to let anybody do that to Fido. This isn't some anonymous pound mutt we're talking about, or a rat, or a frog. This is Fido, a member of your family! And if you thought Fido had been snatched up and was locked in a lab somewhere, being subjected to painful experiments, there's a good chance that you might go to any lengths— including, as a last resort, breaking and entering—to get him out.

The point is this: Animal liberationists feel about all animals the same way you feel about Fido. And if you can put yourself into that frame of mind, if you can imagine that each of the estimated 80 million animals used in research every year is actually a Fido, with an individual personality, and individual feelings, then it's easier to understand what the animal liberationists are doing.

Betty and Dee became Britches' foster parents. Their love could never restore him to his mother or give him back the trees where his grandparents lived, but for a few vital months it gave him safety and warmth and an anchor from the storm that had raged at Riverside.

Betty had been in touch with a primatologist who worked on rehabilitations. He told her that if she didn't give Britches over to a monkey mother, disaster would hit when Britches reached puberty. He would be strong, aggressive, unmanageable, and hopelessly confused about his identity. He needed to be allowed to live as a monkey among monkeys.

So, when Britches was five months old, Dr. Flavioli paid Valerie to fly him to Mexico to meet his new foster mother, an old macaque who had raised several orphans in her long life. By that time, Britches almost had stopped his spasms, although they still happened occasionally when he was tired or upset.

He had grown quite spunky, and his hair had turned from snow white to honey beige. Betty drove Valerie to the airport in Las

Vegas, where it is a common sight to see show animals come and go. They listed Britches as "surplus entertainment stock" and had acquired the export permit for him without trouble.

They sat in Betty's car, waiting for the last minute before going into the terminal. Betty handed Valerie the daily log she had kept on Britches' care, and Valerie leafed through it, reading bits and pieces. What a difference each day had made to this little fellow.

"Day #1," Betty's notes read, "In cage with surrogate rigged with bottle. Spends most of time clinging to surrogate. Photophobic, so towel over cage to darken interior. Spasms and intermittent shrieking elicited by majority of environmental noises. Tolerates handling if towel-cuddled and rocked, but after short period begins to spasm and shriek if not put near surrogate. Spasms and shrieking continue intermittently for thirty to sixty seconds when returned to cage. Also rear-up posture and clutching."

Valerie looked at the entry for Day #11: "Essentially no more spasms. 6:45 A.M. Ampicillin. 7:15 A.M. Formula and bath. 7:30-8:25 A.M. Socialization in pen, formula, banana, vocalization continues to increase. Varied patterns of sound. Facial expressions markedly varied last three days. VERY affectionate. Gentle stroking of my face. Much face to face contact. Lots of springing and swinging on bars and on me. 9 A.M. Formula. Normal feces. Cleaned bottom and rocked to sleep. 12:40 P.M. Woke up. Formula, banana, cleaned bottom. Self play with ball and rings. 2:00 P.M. Ampicillin. 2:15 P.M. Formula, self play, fed and socialized all afternoon and evening. Carried around. 8 P.M. Bed."

The final entry read, "Today we transport to permanent home. Very traumatic separation for me. It will be easier for infant, since he was carefully socialized to three other handlers, by design." When she looked up, she saw the tears running down Betty's face.

"He's like my kid," Betty said, wiping her eyes. "It's hard to let him go, you know, but I realize it's for the best. I wanted him to be free, but it's impossible. Tell me we're doing the right thing. I need to hear you say it again."

Valerie told her. Britches would have almost a quarter of an acre of habitat.[1] In winter he would have heated indoor quarters, and the people who ran the habitat had done all they could to make it livable and to minimize boredom. He would have friends and a small monkey family. He could wrestle and play, and perhaps, one day, even fall in love.

"I look back on my training," Betty said, "and I see all the muck that was hidden behind scientific jargon. We are so desensitized to suffering as a profession that we can't usually see it. This baby was put in a cold cage and 'objectively' watched. It's crap! Experimenters should be required to rock these infants to sleep, bathe them, take them for walks, carry them, and exchange long, reciprocal eye contact with them. Watch them with their pacifiers, watch them play. It would teach them a stunning lesson in connectedness and bring them back to where they should be. How can normal human beings with feelings become robots?"

Betty had given Britches a tranquilizer. He was drowsy and falling asleep as they watched him loaded into the cart to be taken out to the plane. By the time the billboard lights lit up the Las Vegas strip, she and Britches would be on foreign soil. It was very, very hard for Betty to let him go, but she and Valerie both knew that now, against all odds, he had been given the chance to live to a ripe old age.

It wasn't until a year later, when the dust had cleared, that the long-term success of the raid was ascertainable from reports Riverside filed with the government. Eight of the seventeen research projects "interrupted" that night by Sitch and his group were never begun again. The Britches study was not ended, but monkey babies' eyes are no longer permitted to be stitched shut. Heat was installed in the outdoor monkey colony, and the whistleblowing student's teacher quit animal research.

---

[1] A PETA video made about this case shows Britches in a huge outdoor enclosure with his new mother. She hugs and caresses him, and he hugs her back, romps about, and looks out at the world through inquisitive eyes that UC-Riverside would have kept shut forever.

11

Breaking the Species Barrier

June 23, 1986. A quiet night in Poolesville, Maryland, forty minutes outside Washington, D.C. The opossums and raccoons and foxes still living wild there crept through what was left of the hedgerows surrounding the Primate Center Complex. Under the lights of the loading bay at Building 11, a few men worked stealthily, loading monkeys into an air-conditioned truck. Two security guards, a veterinarian, and two administrators stood at the back of the truck watching anxiously as four caretakers and the driver helped load each cage and secure it in place.

The driver and veterinarian climbed into the truck and the vehicle moved away, headed for the main gates. The guard in his little plastic booth was expecting them and pressed the button that raised the red and white entry barrier. The truck pulled out onto Elmer School Road and faded into the night.

The Silver Spring monkeys were on their way to the Delta Regional Primate Research Center in Louisiana. The promises NIH had made to members of Congress, promises that the monkeys would stay "safely" in Poolesville pending the outcome of litigation, weren't worth the paper they were written on. The next day, when news of their secret transfer reached PETA, there would be an uproar, and new promises would be made. At Tulane, NIH would assure Congress, the monkeys would be socialized, their damaged limbs would be properly amputated, and all would be well.

Would NIH attempt to reinstate the experiments on them? Absolutely not! As Alex Pacheco said, red with anger at the news, "They'd lie to their own mothers if they thought they could benefit from it."

The first signs of liberationist activity from France were forwarded to Valerie in 1985 via the British ALF Supporters' Group.

"Les chiens maltraités delivrés de leur enfer par un commando," or "Mistreated dogs delivered from their hell by a commando," sang the headline in *France-Soir*. The article described 'Opération Délivrance,' an ALF action in Montpellier in which 120 dogs were liberated. Incredibly, a mother dog had given birth to four puppies during an action that involved an estimated thirty raiders.

To Valerie's delight, the Canadian ALF, with which she still had no contact, also had carried out two more raids in 1984 and 1985: the first, a daylight raid on a burn laboratory at a children's hospital from which cats were taken; the second, a raid on a university to rescue a rhesus monkey. They called the rhesus "Grandma," and her photograph, in which she appeared wearing a hideous electrical box that descended into a hole cut into her cranium, appeared everywhere in the Canadian press. The Royal Canadian Mounted Police were reported as having "no suspects."

In the U.S. Valerie had recruited ALF operatives in seven states with Josh's help, and now had a sizable network of foster homes. The Underground Railroad was up and working, ready to facilitate the disappearance of any number of rescued animals coast-to-coast.

The Californians had struck off on their own, and now there were separate groups working out of that state, two in Los Angeles and one in Sacramento. With the exception of some minor territorial squabbles among the two Los Angeles units, everyone got along well and shared information as needed.

From early 1984 through the summer of 1986, there had been small raids at the University of California at Berkeley (three cats), at California State University in Sacramento (twenty-three rats), at two University of Florida campuses, (totaling more than 100 gerbils, rats, and rabbits), at the University of Maryland (forty-two rabbits), and at Johns Hopkins University in Baltimore (six rats).

Despite the activity of her recruits, Valerie herself was out of commission again in the spring of 1986. She lay in Suburban Hospital in Bethesda, recovering from osteomyelitis, a chronic infection of the bone. X-rays had shown that the site around the pin in her ankle had festered. The cause of all the pain she had experienced was now being dealt with: she was hooked to an IV dispensing antibiotics around the clock. Her stay ended up lasting over two months.

While Valerie cursed the problems incapacitating her, she was thankful for finding Edna, the nurse who kept her company for part of every day. Valerie awakened after her second surgery to find Edna at her bedside. Several afternoons a week after that, whenever things on the ward were slow, Edna was back: knitting an afghan, and telling Valerie the latest scandals involving Hollywood stars, the horrible things her "ex" used to do, and all the things that went wrong in the hospital.

Edna was Valerie's age, very tall and thin as a rail. She wore her dark hair pinned back, which made her look like Olive Oyl. Edna had opinions on everything, and shared them without needing an invitation to do so. Valerie quickly learned everything Edna thought was wrong and right about nursing and nurses' training. More interesting to Valerie than how doctors view nurses ("they treat them like know-nothings"), how nurses react to night shifts ("their diurnal rhythms are upset, they go nuts after six months"), and the inequities of the pay scale ("a national scandal"), was the fact that in nursing school Edna had persuaded several students to join her in refusing to participate in an animal lab.

"They would take these kittens and shove tubes down their throats as if they were no more than plastic dolls," Edna said. "I told them, if you want to poke and prod with these tubes, get a model. These kittens have feelings. Let's act as if we've got some brains around here."

Edna had been too tough to be intimidated by a threat of a failing grade. "I told them," she continued, "here's the catalog, here's a dummy you can mess around with, you buy it. We paid good money to go to this school, don't tell me you can't get training tools. I didn't come here to kill animals."

Edna's first job had been at the Veteran's Administration Hospital near the Washington Reservoir.

"That's a place that should be shut down," Edna told her. "Understaffed and sloppy. Plus, they've got dogs on the roof. You can hear them if you stand in the nurses' station behind the emergency room. They howl and carry on. I raised hell, told them it wasn't right. They said, 'Edna, wear earplugs if you don't like it.' I told them, 'You've just lost yourselves a nurse,' and I quit."

"Edna," Valerie said to her, after about a month, "What do you think of the Animal Liberation Front, the people who break into labs and get the animals out?"

"If I knew how to join 'em, I would," Edna said. Valerie didn't discuss the subject with her any further then, but the more Valerie heard from Edna—which was a lot—the more she realized Edna was fearless, and the more Valerie believed she was telling the truth. They became friends.

Edna was interested in the food Sean brought in to supplement the hospital's diet of vegetable bouillon, mashed potatoes, and steamed broccoli. "About all I ever eat is chocolate bars and potato chips," Edna joked. "Does that make me a vegetarian?

"You love your cat, right, Edna?" Valerie asked her.

"Certainly," Edna answered.

"Well, you probably wouldn't eat him, even if you were desperate, right?" Valerie said. "There's a bumper sticker that says, 'Why call some animals pets, and some dinner?' People seldom get to know cows or chickens the way they get to know cats and dogs. I remember at the 4-H auction barns, when I was in school, I'd see kids of fifteen and sixteen, kids I knew who'd raised a lamb or a calf all summer, just cry their eyes out when auction time came. They didn't see those animals as a sandwich filling, they were their friends."

Edna never fought Valerie on the ethical issue. She asked a lot of questions about health. Where do vegetarians get their protein? Does fish count? What about eggs? What about calcium? Valerie had Sean bring her a copy of Keith Akers' *A Vegetarian Source Book*. She knew Edna was going to make the switch.

Confined to her hospital bed, Valerie decided to put her time to better use than watching soap operas. She learned all she could about the fur trade. Valerie was opposed to fur wearing, of course, and she knew about leghold traps, but she didn't know anything about fur ranching. Until then she had supposed it was probably much more humane than trapping. The specifics of the ranch-bred animals' deaths disgusted her: minks suffocated by having their heads stuffed into chloroform bottles; coyotes injected in the stomach with weedkillers, animals choked to death on hot, unfiltered carbon monoxide from a lawnmower engine.

Taking a leaf out of the British ALF book, she decided to coordinate a "Night of Action" against the fur trade. Being immobile was driving her nuts. The idea of hitting fur stores across the country seemed one way to be active again.

Valerie could hardly leave a record of calls to every ALF contact on her hospital bill, so Kay volunteered to do the work. She reported back, very pleased, that almost every point person, from Palm Beach to Palm Springs, Seattle to New York City, had agreed to get people involved. If things went well, the ALF could educate—or scare off—potential buyers at exactly the right time.

An Oregon group, which was casing the University of Oregon in Eugene, decided to go a step further. Pelting season was coming up. Just north of Portland, they located a silver fox farm. The forest lands surrounding the farm spread for many square miles, an area that would provide the foxes with ample space, cover, and food, if the foxes were wild enough to keep going once the cages were cut open.

The Oregon ALF's preliminary visit to the farm told them what they needed to know: the foxes were turning circles in their small wire cages, showing the same sort of behavior you see in tigers or leopards at the zoo. These animals were far from domesticated. To release them would mean the loss of a year's "work" to the farm.

The "Night of Action" went off without any arrests. That July, stores in all seven states and throughout California were left spray-painted and damaged, and in Oregon sixty-six silver foxes watched in the moonlight as strangers crept under their cages, cut holes in the wires, and sent them running for their lives

Spurred by the coverage of these events, activists started escalating their objections to the fur trade: smearing hair remover or concentrated ammonia on coats hanging on department store racks, leaving cards describing the torture of the leghold trap in fur parka pockets, and talking loudly to browsers about how mother raccoons lose their legs in traps, and how, on farms, foxes are anally electrocuted with an electric prod pushed into their rectums.

The end of the summer of 1986 marked an escalation in the "Fur Wars." Recognizing the strength of public opinion gathering against them, the furriers put their heads and their purses together and hired a public relations firm. Soon, newspaper ads appeared: a Woody Allen look-alike in a black ski mask, above the caption "Some people want to deprive you of your rights." Then the absurd slogan, "Fur is for *Life*." It was hard to believe the fur industry had paid so dearly for a slogan that would strike the average person as so obviously off-the-mark.

By fall, Valerie's ankle had finally healed completely and she had strength back in her foot. She felt whole again, and ready to start work in earnest. Two potential targets, a university in New England and one in Michigan, had been scrutinized while she was out of commission, but neither had panned out. A call for help from Oregon resulted in several people from Maryland and California heading to Eugene for another raid, this time on the university itself.

In October of 1986 the University of Oregon was hit hard. A hand had supplied the ALF with keys to the campus breeding facility, a place in which few students and only select faculty ever set foot. Described by a witness as "looking like Ninjas," the new ALF unit rushed into the buildings at night, and managed to load 264 animals into vans and station wagons and destroy over $120,000 worth of experimentation equipment before making a clean getaway.

On the night of the raid, a fifty-five-year-old retired school teacher named Roger Troen got a call. Roger was known in humane society circles as a dedicated worker, always willing to go the extra mile for an animal in need of a home. Apparently, ALF-Oregon was short a few.

"Will you take some rabbits, no questions asked?" the caller had said. Without hesitation, he agreed. Months later, when Troen was handcuffed and brought to jail, there were questions. Did he know the animals were stolen, and that to receive them was to commit a crime, the prosecutor would ask. "If I had lived in Germany in World War II," the gray-haired teacher replied, "and someone had knocked on my door and asked me to take people in and hide them, my conscience would have told me to do it. That night, my conscience said the same thing."

Before his trial that fall, Mr. Troen learned how he'd been caught. A veterinarian who was asked to make sure the rabbits were not in need of special care had noticed tattoos in the rabbits' ears and called the police.

Along with the pigeons, rabbits, cats, rats, and hamsters, the ALF had removed the files of two then-unknown experimenters, Barbara Gordon-Lickey and Richard Marrocco. Neither had any veterinary or medical training. Marrocco had been a student of Russell DeValois, the notorious "Butcher of Berkeley," a man who had allowed a monkey to develop such severe gangrene of the testicles that the monkey had to be destroyed. What the ALF found put both psychology professors on the animal rights map.

Gordon-Lickey had killed hundreds of kittens over a seventeen-year period at a cost to the taxpayers of over $1.2 million. Her experiments involved cutting into kittens' eyes, rotating their eyeballs up to 110 degrees in their sockets, and then forcing them to jump from a wooden tower onto a ten-inch wooden platform in a pan of water.

Ten percent of the rhesus monkeys used in Marrocco's experiments died from the sheer stress of having to endure as many as seven twelve- to fourteen-hour surgeries. These were invasive procedures in which the monkeys' heads were riveted into stereo-taxic devices, their skulls opened up, and electrodes sunk into their brains. Marrocco even allowed his students to conduct the surgeries alone when other business kept him out of the lab.

Troen insisted on telling the truth about his involvement, even if it meant jail, and PETA helped by hiring a well-known and vigorous defense attorney, Steven Houze, to defend him. Animal rights attorney Lucy Kaplan[1] agreed to volunteer her time to carry out the legal research necessary to bring a rare defense: Houze would argue that Roger Troen had committed a criminal offense in order to "prevent a greater evil," the mutilation and slaughter of the animals.

Meanwhile, back in Maryland, unexpected information came Valerie's way. As interesting as it seemed, it was difficult to figure what to do with it.

Miki and a group of friends had been drinking at a Jamaican bar called Hideaways in the District. They had ended up playing a friendly game of pool with a couple of men in their fifties. Soon enough, everyone was talking about what they did to earn a living. One of the men, whose nickname was "Simba," told Miki he worked for a laboratory where chimpanzees were being infected with AIDS.

"Chimpanzees?" Valerie queried Miki. No one in the animal protection community had heard of any chimpanzees in the area, outside of the few at NIH. "Are you sure he doesn't mean monkeys? Most people don't have any idea there's a difference."

"No, I checked it out with him. They're definitely chimps. That's why his nickname's Simba, the 'king of the jungle.' He's a chimpanzee caretaker."

"How many chimps?" Valerie asked.

"Forty some!" Miki told her.

"You've got to be joking." It was very hard to believe. Chim-

---

[1] Lucy Kaplan became PETA's staff attorney for its research and investigative department in 1990.

panzees are an endangered species, and here there were forty in the ALF's own backyard.

"No, he's a straight-shooting sort of man," Miki insisted. She played pool with Simba twice more. She was doing her best to cultivate him.

"Why didn't you tell me before?" Valerie wanted to know.

"I wanted to be sure before you got your hopes up," Miki explained. "I knew you'd be jumping up and down as soon as I opened my mouth!"

"You're right! Tell me everything."

"The chimpanzees are kept in isolation chambers called 'isolettes,' " Miki started. "Simba says they're about the size of refrigerators for the really big ones. He says they bang their heads against the bars all the time, they just go nuts being kept alone like that. It's a private company that does government contract work for NIH. They infect the apes with diseases; it used to be hepatitis mainly, but now they get lots of money to give them AIDS."

The lab was called SEMA. Simba didn't think the name was short for anything. He'd worked there for ten years.

"He doesn't like his work for a lot of reasons," Miki said. "He's worried sick about getting AIDS or something from the apes. The incinerator where they're supposed to burn the animals' waste is always broken, and they're always getting scratched or stuck with needles when they're taking blood. He doesn't trust his bosses. They tell him there's nothing to worry about, but the workers are required to get blood samples taken and checked all the time. He says that doesn't make sense if you can't catch anything from the apes, like they say. Thirdly, although he's scared to death of these apes, since some of them are almost as big as he is, still he doesn't like what's being done to them. Doesn't think it's right."

"Don't keep me in suspense," Valerie urged her. "Does he dislike it enough to help us?"

"No, I can't imagine it," Miki shook her head. "He's a decent man, but he's never been exposed to animals much. Guard dogs in his neighborhood, that sort of thing. It's too big a leap."

"What if we just paid him $500 to let us go through their files and $500 more if there's any chance of removing a chimpanzee? What do you think?"

"Hard to say. He's been at Hideaways on three Wednesdays now, so let me try him next week, if it seems OK at the time."

That Wednesday, Simba didn't show up at the bar. The next seven days seemed an eternity. The following week Miki came straight to Sean's from the bar. She had seen Simba.

"Not a prayer," she said, "He's too scared."

"What did he say?"

"That he's a Christian. He thinks taking money to do the dirty on his employer isn't right, even if they are crooks and creeps."

"Christianity has a lot to answer for," Valerie said, angrily. "Miki, what if we load him up with things to read about our moral obligations to be kind and just, some of Dr. Stephen Clark's stuff about responsibility to all creation? It couldn't hurt."

"Val, he won't read stuff like that."

"Well, let's not throw in the towel yet. Will you keep seeing him, and at least try to get him thinking?"

"Yes. Fat lot of good it'll do, but I will."

The next day Valerie sent Kay over to the PETA library with instructions to grab anything they had on chimpanzees. She came back with two books and two thick files. She learned that chimpanzees share 99 percent of human DNA and that humans are biologically closer to them than chimpanzees are to gorillas. Chimpanzee blood plasma can even be exchanged for our own. Scientists all over the world were beginning to challenge the use of any of the great apes in labs, calling them too close, phylogenetically, to experiment on.

That Saturday, Valerie and Sean were getting ready to eat dinner when the doorbell rang. Coming out into the hall, Valerie could see two police hats through the glass above the door.

Her first thought was, "Oh God! The grand jury." She stepped quickly back into the living room. Sean saw the look on her face and stopped in mid-stride.

"It's the police," Valerie whispered to him. "You get it. They know someone's here. Tell them I'm away. Don't get specific."

Sean went to the door. Valerie could see he was nervous. He

wasn't a good liar. He looked like a child about to go on stage in his first school play.

"Oh, Greg, Mike," Valerie heard him say, "Nice to see you." It was Greenwald and Fitch from the Silver Spring station.

"Hi, Sean," Greenwald's voice boomed. "May we come in?"

Valerie had known Greenwald since her first day on the force. It would look more than suspicious not to let him through the door. What would Sean do? Valerie tried opening the porch door, but it started to squeak. There was nowhere to hide in the kitchen. Unless she was outside Mandy would come right over and give her away.

"Sure," Sean said. He was leading them into the living room. "Down, Mandy. It's OK, girl." Valerie heard Sean close the door.

Just don't ask them to have coffee, Sean, she thought.

Three or four minutes passed. Valerie could hear voices, but not what they were saying. Then, the door opened and they were back in the hall. Sean was wishing them goodnight.

"What is it?" she said, as soon as he came through the kitchen door.

"They've caught your stalker, Clay Prather. They wanted you to know."

"Good grief! Is that all?" Despite her nonchalant words, Valerie could feel relief flooding through her veins.

"Is that all?" Sean was laughing at her. "This calls for a celebration, my love."

"Darned right!" They hugged and Valerie let the good news envelop her. She danced around the room. "Finally! I'd better call and thank them for stopping by."

"Not too quickly. I said you were out of town."

"Thanks, Sean. That was good practice for next time!"

The news about Prather meant more to Valerie than she had been willing to admit. Knowing there was a madman out there somewhere, bent on killing her, had magnified the stress of her underground activities. Now that he was locked up again, she felt she could cope better. Prather had entered her dreams many times since 1981. Now, at last, he was taken care of.

They were almost ready to give up on SEMA when Simba came through, at least in part. In late November of 1986 he decided to let Miki's friends go into the lab at night and look at the records. They weren't to remove anything and Miki had to promise to tell him if they found any evidence that the experiments were dangerous. That is, if Simba and the other caretakers were likely to be exposed to a virus, fatal or otherwise. Simba wouldn't touch the ALF's money.

Valerie couldn't believe it. "We've got to get video. Will he allow that?" she asked Miki.

"I didn't ask. We can see how it goes. He's cautious, to say the least."

Bear was Valerie's best video operator. "Next Saturday night," she told him, "Simba will let us in the front door. They've just hired a new weekend caretaker. He started learning the job last weekend. This Saturday's the first time he'll be on his own. We can go through the files in the offices while the new man's cleaning cages in the back."

"Won't it look odd, Simba showing up late at night on a weekend?" Bear queried.

"Apparently not. Miki asked him the same thing. He's been there for ten years. He can drop in without anyone thinking anything of it. Anyway, the new man won't know what's weird and what's not."

Bear would get the smallest video camera he could, in case they had to hide it from Simba. Just he and Val would go inside.

Come Saturday, Valerie's nerves were jangling. She and Bear drove out I-270 to Gaithersburg. Miki and Simba were waiting for them in the pitch dark, in a Buick parked at Harvey's Lobster and Steak Restaurant. SEMA was supposed to be right next door. Bear and Val got out and leaned in the car window. They introduced themselves. They had invented names to satisfy the moment.

Here they were, in the parking lot of an ordinary restaurant, smack behind a very ordinary hotel, looking at an ordinary, single story office building, not a lab. The building in front of them was modern. It was small, and it had plate glass windows, from ground to roof level, all the way around. It couldn't look less like a laboratory if it tried. How could there be forty diseased chimpanzees in cages in there?

"*That's* it?" Valerie asked, pointing at the structure next door.

"Sure is," said Simba.

"Are you sure this isn't a joke?"

Simba shook his head.

They got into Simba's car and drove the few yards into the next parking lot, pulling up outside SEMA's front door. Simba refused to let the "visitors" out of sight. If the new man happened to be in the wrong place, he wanted to say they were acquaintances. Valerie noted he didn't use the word "friends."

Simba used his key to go through the door, Valerie and Bear hot on his heels. The alarm sounded as soon as the door opened, filling the foyer with noise, then stopped as Simba turned the key again in the lock.

"Is that heard all the way in the back?" Bear asked.

"Yup. Gives caretakers a chance to look smart, knowing their supervisor's probably coming," Simba responded. Valerie exchanged an unhappy look with Bear. "Y'all can wait here. I'll go tell the new kid it's just me."

Simba left them in the foyer and made his way into the bowels of the building. Valerie looked around. Everything was shiny and bright. No odor, no cages, no telltale animal noises. Just a reception desk, a calendar from a pharmaceutical company, two chairs for visitors, a telephone, and a potted plant. "Weird," Bear said.

A few minutes later, Simba was back. He led them into the hallway and opened the office doors with his master key.

"This is the secretary's office," Simba pointed at each office. "This is Max Shapiro's office; he's a researcher. This is the boss's office, this one is where the veterinarian stays if he's in town, and this is where the government man sits when he comes 'round. You look at what you want. I'll go on back and make sure Chuck, the new man, stays put," he said.

As soon as he was gone, they pulled their two pairs of talcum-dusted gloves from their pockets[2] and pulled them over their fingers. "See if you can find a Xerox machine," Valerie told Bear.

She had brought a document camera, in case Bear was unlucky. They might not be allowed to take any of the papers out of the building, she figured, but Simba hadn't said anything about replicas.

Bear was back in a few seconds. "I've found it," he said. "It's warming up."

They wasted no time. If Simba found them using the copier, they knew their "visit" might be over. First, a cursory look through all the offices, noting which files and binders seemed the most promising—notes from the Institutional Animal Care and Use Committee, autopsy reports, grant applications, daily logs, and internal memoranda. Certain there would never be enough time to copy even a fraction of them, Valerie wanted to be sure they were going for the best chance of pay dirt. "Select now, read later, hope for the best," she thought.

Valerie had Dr. William London's desk drawer open, looking for some post-its, when she found a set of keys. They were marked, "Front," and "Back," and "Do Not Copy." She picked them up and ran to the Xerox room.

"Bear," Valerie ripped the papers he was copying out of the machine. "Quick. Xerox these keys, front and back." Bear looked at her as if she was out of her mind but did as she asked. As soon as the papers came out of the machine Valerie bunched them into her pocket, snatched the keys off the plate, and ran back into Dr. London's office, restoring them to their place.

As soon as Bear finished one lot of copying, he stashed the copies away in his knapsack and came racing in to pick up another set. They worked undisturbed for over two hours before Simba returned.

Valerie heard Simba coming down the hall and raced into the copying room. Bear had switched the copier off in time.

"We'd best go now," Simba said.

---

[2] Fingerprints can now be traced from marks left by the outside of a latex glove, so this extra precaution has become necessary.

"Simba," Valerie said, "please let us see the chimps. It means everything to us."

"Lady," Simba said, "I can't do that. You people are going to get me in a mess of trouble if I'm not careful."

"Simba," she begged. "Please. Just for a minute. It won't hurt anything. Please."

"We won't disturb anything. No one will ever know," Bear added.

Simba looked at them, and gave up.

"OK," he said, shaking his head. "For one minute. That's all, then we've got to go."

He led them down the hallway to the door that separated the lab from the offices. Valerie could feel her pulse racing as Simba opened the huge dividing door. What would they see on the other side? Half of her wanted to know; the other half wished she had never known about this place. Already, she could hear what she would soon see: chimpanzees hitting their heads against the solid metal doors of their isolation chambers.

Simba led them past two huge stainless steel cage washers and into a corridor. The banging was getting louder and louder.

"You go on down this way," he said, pointing to the corridor on the left, away from the lighted hallway on the building exterior. "I'll go keep the boy company. You just take a look and turn around and come straight back here. Don't dawdle now."

The hallway stretched out for what seemed half a city block, with doors at about ten-foot intervals all the way down it. As soon as Simba turned away, Bear pulled out the video camera. He raced with Valerie for the first door and pulled it open. Then Bear stopped dead in his tracks.

Valerie was a split second behind him. Bear's eyes were glued to the sight before him. Neither he nor Valerie had ever seen a chimpanzee in real life before. The sight was awesome. The apes in front of them must have weighed sixty to one hundred pounds. But it was not so much their size that had Valerie and Bear riveted. It was how the apes were kept.

In the first room there were eight steel chambers, cages with solid steel bars that must have been an inch thick. The cages were encased in solid metal sheaths, except for the doors, which were covered in some sort of extra-heavy-duty plastic, like the bullet-proof plastic on a drive-up bank window. A cage within a cage. Exactly as Miki had related, they were the size of stand-up refrigerators, and inside each one—barely visible through the foggy, scratched plastic—was a full-grown chimpanzee, able only to stand and sit. That, and nothing more.

Valerie's attention shifted to the noise from the third cage. A huge male who seemed to occupy every square inch of his chamber was hitting his head over and over again into the sides of his tomb. From elsewhere Valerie could hear other chimpanzees doing the same thing. The cacophony mixed with the strange, wheezing noise and incessant roar of the pumps, which sucked air in and out of the sealed chambers through long, black tubes.

A numbered tag, like the tag a store would put on a dress for sale, hung from each cage. Number 1164, read the first tag, "Infected with viral hepatitis." Inside the chamber sat Number 1164 himself, rocking back and forth and mumbling to himself as though demented.

Next to him, but unable to see the other inmates through the solid metal doors, stood Number 87, staring into the nothingness that his or her world had been reduced to, forever. Next, Number 41, a smaller chimpanzee, who turned on his heels, around and around, performing a macabre circular dance that expressed his insanity at having nothing to touch but the metal bars, no other living being with whom to communicate. Not one of the inmates in the room acknowledged Valerie's or Bear's presence. They were too far gone.

"It's primate hell," Valerie whispered.

Valerie and Bear forced themselves from that white-walled room and into the next. It was the same. And beyond it was another, and another. How many chimpanzees they saw, Valerie does not remember. Bear kept shooting as they went, trying to capture in a matter of seconds the crazed chimpanzee faces and the perpetual motion of their bodies. At the end of the corridor, they turned and raced to the boiler room they had passed on their way in.

Valerie knew from the case sheets that some of the immense apes she had seen had been locked inside their chambers for seven years. Even as she ran she realized, so acutely that she could feel her heart ache in her chest, that they would never be able to release them. The chimpanzees were simply too large. They were ten times as strong as an adult human male, and obviously insane and unmanageable. They would live there—if you could call it living—for the rest of their lives.

That night, even before Valerie put her head on the pillow, she knew that of all the grotesque things she had seen done to animals in laboratories, the psychological suffering and confinement of the chimpanzees at SEMA had the profoundest effect on her. If she heard on the news that nuclear war had been declared, she might actually have cheered for the end of a world that puts no brakes on cruelty. It had been all she could do not to break down in front of Simba, but she wanted him to have confidence in her. She wanted to expose that lab, and Simba was her only sure ticket through its doors.

The sight of Number 41 was ingrained into Valerie's memory. Whether her eyes were opened or closed, she could see him rocking, and she could see his jowls waggling as he blew out his cheeks to coincide with each grotesque movement. She had an absolute camera-clear vision of the deep melancholy in his glazed eyes. He was a zombie, a shadow, who resembled only in physical form the wonderful, life-filled, social chimpanzees of the Gombe forest whose stories filled Jane Goodall's books.

Sean held Valerie to his chest and her tears soaked his pajama top. "Why can't they die?" she sobbed to him. "Why is life so cruel that they stay alive through this?"

She didn't want to recognize why their suffering affected her so deeply. Was it because these were our closest animal relatives on the face of the earth? Somehow, as much as she wanted to see the suffering of a mouse or a dog in the same way, Valerie had to admit that at some subconscious level, the chimpanzees' undeniable similarity to human beings was making what she had seen even harder to bear.

Simba's fears for his own health and well-being were grounded in fact. Valerie arranged to meet him as soon as Kay got the report back from PETA. Valerie showed him an inspection report from a laboratory-accrediting agency that had conducted an inspection of SEMA's parent company, Diagnon, just a month earlier. The report railed at the lack of safety standards and revealed that, among other things, a technician had already been infected with Strongyloides, a parasite that had been given experimentally to certain of the animals. It pointed out that personnel were being exposed to the "volatile toxic effects" of acetone, and criticized accidental death rates of animals from plumbing failures and other, often unidentified causes.

The report went on, " . . . experiments involving the use of hazardous materials, including infectious agents as well as chemical carcinogens [cancer-causing agents], are not reviewed, approved, or monitored by a safety committee."

Simba listened intently to what Valerie had to say. He wasn't happy, but now he had something tangible to work from in trying to improve working conditions at the lab.

"I'm sorry I can't help you any more," he said.

"I understand how you feel, Simba," Valerie said, "but, please, keep thinking about it. The whole world should see what they're doing in there. You know the animals have it worse than the employees."

Simba conceded that this was so. He had found animals scalded to death during a steam pipe accident and knew of an old male chimpanzee who suffocated in his chamber when the air valve failed. He had watched them rock, and spit, throw their feces, and bang their heads, but he wasn't budging.

Valerie knew she had to find a way to help the chimpanzees. She just didn't know how.

In the days that followed, Valerie watched the videotape and read more about the goings-on inside SEMA. She learned that there were two other corridors filled with rooms of primates: patas monkeys, rhesus monkeys, endangered marmosets, tiny squirrel and owl monkeys, even rare green vervet monkeys. Many, according to the USDA inspection reports, were kept doubled up in their cages, in violation of the Animal Welfare Act.

The autopsy reports were particularly nasty reading. Accidental deaths among the entire monkey population were the norm, not the exception: some died quickly, others were unlucky enough to have their conditions go undetected for days or weeks before death claimed them.

Chimpanzees had not escaped "accidental deaths" either. Justifying the expense of their loss had taxed the SEMA management's imaginations. Number A51 had "vomited, inhaled ingesta, and expired in a very short time," while being "prepared to be shipped to New Mexico." The death was attributed to "a breakdown in normal procedures."

Number A117 "suffocated to death" due to the use of "a cage that was too small." Number 904's death was listed as "bloat," which was described as a possible consequence of "an inadequate number of caretakers." Number A11 apparently had not been able to breathe following an injection of a sedative and died of "acute respiratory arrest." The report stated that "in response to the increasing workloads and more intensive studies we have adopted the practice . . . of having a technician anesthetize more than one chimp at a time."

Number 56's autopsy report described "death due to postsurgical complications." SEMA's veterinarian had apologized to the government that he had not been aware that it was "necessary to forcibly bag the animal at intervals . . . so that the lungs remained fully inflated."

If she could have pressed a button and erased SEMA from the face of the earth, Valerie would have done so. She had no idea how to proceed. In the labs, cruelty is legal—give or take a few discrepancies, like failure to clean cages. The Taub case had shown that. Could SEMA weather a public exposé? Valerie knew that NIH wouldn't help. As their contract holder, NIH would back SEMA all the way rather than admit its own complicity. Helping the chimpanzees seemed as unlikely as climbing Mount Everest backward.

At Valerie's insistence, Miki continued to meet with Simba.

His heart was giving him trouble and he was getting ready to re-tire. He was grateful for the information they had found out about the lab. Already, at a staff meeting, he had raised questions about safety that had irritated his bosses. The nerve he had struck in them had been noticed by other staff. A general panic was on. People wanted safety clothing, standard operating procedures, as-surances in writing. A request for hazardous duty pay had been raised by another caretaker.

"My friends need more records," Miki had told him. "They want you to let them inside again. Nothing more than last time. Will you do it?"

Simba had hemmed and hawed, then agreed.

Bear couldn't make the second visit, so Valerie chose Edna. She worked weekdays at Suburban, but subbed on some weekends at a nursing home. She could get someone to cover for her.

"It's legal, so far, Edna," Valerie told her. "We're there by invi-tation, not trespassing. We're not stealing anything, just copying records."

"Val, do I look like such a drip to you?" Edna had taken offense. "I'm thrilled you asked me, and I'm going to help out and not worry about it."

Valerie had sent the Xerox copies of the keys to Hacker, whose nephew was a locksmith. The nephew had cut out the paper forms and made real keys that fit the indentations. There was about a 30 or 40 percent chance they would work, he told Hacker. All Valerie could do was try.

Driving into the SEMA parking lot, Valerie found herself star-ing again, in disbelief, at the innocent tidiness of its office build-ing facade. It was as phony as a Hollywood set.

As soon as Simba walked into the back, Valerie ran to the door and tried the key. It was stiff, but it turned! To open the door would risk setting off the alarm, so she kept turning the key back and forth in the lock, satisfying herself that it seemed to work.

There was one filing cabinet that had been locked during the first visit. Valerie contemplated picking the lock but had decided against it in case she left scratch marks on the soft, black metal.

Tonight, luck was with her. It was unlocked. She pulled open the top drawer and looked at the contents. "Inventory," read the label on the first set of files.

"Xerox room, first on the left, turn on the machine," Valerie indicated to Edna. "Turn it on, and I'll pick out what to copy."

Edna had barely left the room than she was back to break the bad news.

"Out of order," she said.

"Can you find another one in this sector?" Valerie asked her. If not, they would have to use the document camera, which took more time.

Edna hurried out, but returned with bad news. "No luck," she said. "That's the only one."

Valerie didn't even look up. She didn't care any more. Her initial annoyance had been trumped by what she was reading. She had found the possible answer to what to do about SEMA.

"Edna, quick. Photograph all the pages in this book."

Edna did as she was asked while Valerie moved on to the next file drawer. Symposia minutes, sick leave requests, personnel policy manuals, vendor requisitions. Nothing of use.

Simba returned and announced it was time to hit the road. This time, no amount of pleading would persuade him to let them go beyond the dividing doors. As they drove away, Valerie had to share the news with Edna.

"I found their shipping receipts," she said. "They've got five baby chimpanzees in there. Babies worth over $40,000. Babies we can handle, who'll hold your hand and walk out with you. Babies who haven't been infected yet!" Valerie could hardly contain herself. "We can save those five."

It was all systems go. Edna and Bear were in. All Valerie needed now were lookouts, a surveillance crew to start immediately, a key that really worked, and a boatload of luck.

They could park at the lobster restaurant until it closed, then move to the hotel lot behind SEMA and achieve fairly good surveillance angles of the back and side of the building. Lucky for the ALF, a new building was under construction directly across the street in front of the lab. It made for an excellent vantage point from which to observe SEMA.

The morning after the second visit, Valerie drove through the area to see what there was to see in daylight. Two blocks from SEMA's front door, she got a nasty surprise: a new police station. If a burglar alarm went off at SEMA and was hooked directly into the station, response time could be as little as two minutes.

The surveillance team quickly learned the work pattern at SEMA. Clerical staff out between 5:00 and 5:30 P.M. Researcher types out between 5:00 and 6:00 P.M. Trash taken out to the dumpster behind the building at about 8:30 P.M.: caretaker goes into the fenced trash area, sorts things out, and packs the trash down. Caretaker shift change at 11:30 P.M. No guards. Departing caretaker usually hangs around for twenty minutes or so, then hits the road. Lots of police cruisers traveling the road in front of the building.

Valerie was forming a plan. If they waited, as they usually did, until the early hours of the morning, they would stick out like sore thumbs on this block where the only traffic after midnight seemed to be the police. Why not go in before the restaurant closed, during normal hotel comings and goings times, when there were people all around SEMA? They could wait for the caretaker to leave the building to dump trash, then open the door, if the key worked. The alarm would sound inside the building until the door was closed, but the caretaker wouldn't hear it because he would be fifty feet away.

The plan seemed solid. Besides, it was all she had. Kay began to prepare news releases while Valerie chose her team and rehearsed the plan in her head. "It's a relief to see you without your head in your hands," Sean told her.

The ALF had two weeks of surveillance under its belt before D-Day. The red fox who had been evicted from the now-bulldozed woods across from SEMA, and who, they discovered, still came back to hunt there, had recovered from his initial shock at finding Leonard, a new ALF recruit from Maine, sitting half-frozen beside the stacks of concrete blocks. A pair of lovers—Bear and his wife, Bobbie—were becoming a permanent fixture outside

Harvey's restaurant. If any diners noticed them, they noticed only two heads of hair: whenever another car approached, Bear and Bobbie kissed, melding their faces together into happy anonymity. Valerie and Kay took the hotel parking lot, glad to have the little heater in their van. Occasionally, a researcher stayed late, or someone dropped in for no reason Valerie could discern. Other than those interruptions to the schedule, there were no surprises.

On Saturday afternoon, Valerie called a meeting in a room at the Holiday Inn on Rockville Pike to go over the plan. She, Bear, and Edna would go inside SEMA as soon as the caretaker left to dump the trash. Edna's assignment was to keep track of the caretaker once he reentered the building.

Valerie and Bear would go immediately to the room numbers listed on the inventory sheet for the baby chimps. Once inside, they would reassure the babies by offering them fruit. Hopefully, they would not start screaming. If the chimps were very quiet, Valerie and Bear would try removing them, cages and all, without tranquilizing them. If they seemed noisy, they would be injected with ketamine hydrochloride. The chambers couldn't be detached from the walls, but Simba had explained how the units were cleaned. The interior cages were removed. Valerie was banking on infant chimpanzees, not yet infected, being housed in cages about the size of the standard cages for adult rhesus monkeys. If that were true, they could double the chimpanzees up and fit three of the cages sideways into the van. All she had to go on was guesswork.

The lookouts would warn the inside team if a police car was on the street or if anyone pulled into the SEMA lot. If there was an "all-clear," depending on what the caretaker was doing, Valerie and Bear would try to line the chimps up, in their cages, at the side exit door, the one away from the restaurant. Kay and her partner would wait for the signal, then drive around and help hoist the cages into the van. Then they'd be gone. That was the plan. Whether it would work or if they'd end up in the slammer was anyone's guess.

They were in place, waiting, as soon as the sun went down.

The waits never got any easier. Edna whispered to Valerie all she had learned about AIDS and chimpanzee experiments. "It's indefensible, medically," she said. "Chimpanzees never die of AIDS. *We're* the only animal who does, so no one is going to feel comfortable taking a vaccine made for adult chimpanzees, when AIDS never even kills them. Using baby chimps is even sillier. They aren't sexually mature, let alone sexually active. If these folks inject the virus taken from human rectal swabs into chimpanzee brains, how can that mimic AIDS in human patients? It doesn't."

Edna had done her homework well, but Valerie couldn't absorb what she was saying. She wanted to concentrate on SEMA, the building, the parking lot, the front door. The last caretaker had left at 4:30 P.M. and all was quiet. There was nothing to watch, but Valerie felt better watching the nothingness of the target, making sure nothing happened.

At eight o'clock Edna, Valerie, and Bear crouched by the van door, like parachutists ready to jump. Bear had the video camera in his backpack; Valerie had the key in her right hand.

"He's out!" Leonard gave the call from the back of the building as soon as he saw the back door crack open and the caretaker start out, dragging his trash bags behind him. Edna said later that her hand seemed to freeze on the door latch, but Valerie didn't notice any hesitation. The door opened, and the three ALF members walked as briskly as they dared to the front door.

Valerie plunged the key into the lock. Please, please, work, she prayed to any god who might be listening. The key turned, she swung the door open, and they were inside. The alarm sounded loudly, then shut off as Valerie pulled the door closed again, making the contacts touch. It would be about five minutes before the caretaker would reenter the building. Valerie set the timer on her watch for four minutes, thirty seconds.

Their feet flew down the corridor, then they were through the dividing door and into the laboratory. Bear began to shoot video, while Valerie searched for the right rooms. The place was a maze of corridors. Valerie could only hope Edna had found a useful hiding place.

The numbers on the doors did not correlate to the numbers from the inventory sheets. They were all wrong. Then it dawned on Valerie that she might be in the wrong corridor. She moved over one and suddenly the numbers made sense.

"Bear, here," she yelled. Rooms 35A and 35B were about half-way down the central corridor, only about sixty feet from the dividing door. Valerie's watch alarm went off as she approached them. Thirty seconds more and the caretaker would be back in the building. Valerie and Bear pulled on the white rubber face masks Valerie had brought along. If they had to run for it, at least the caretaker wouldn't be able to identify who he had seen.

Room 35A was empty. Nothing in it at all except the smell of insecticide. Valerie's heart skipped a beat or two. She stepped back quickly and gritted her teeth for a look in the next room, 35B.

There they were: five precious chimpanzee infants. The room was much the same as the others they had been in, and filled with chambers, not standard cages. These chambers were of the same sort of construction as the enormous ones they had seen before, but far smaller, about the size of washing machines with glass fronts.

Three of the youngsters had already been isolated. The other two sat bottom to bottom on the metal, hugging each other, their eyes wide with excitement at the commotion. The infant closest to the door started jumping up and down, banging her feet onto the floor, and screaming. She tried to reach through the metal bars, but her hands hit into the glass front door of her chamber. Her pale face was dotted with little freckles, as if she'd been out in the sun. Valerie looked at her tag. There was a red 'X' on her cage. Valerie knew from the records what that meant. This baby chimp had already been infected. Valerie's fingers "touched" her tiny fingers through the glass. Pull yourself together, Valerie told herself.

Thankfully, the other tags bore only the names of the chimpanzees, names Valerie had already gleaned from the records of their shipment from the Texas breeding laboratory where they were born. They had all been removed from their mothers eighteen months to two years earlier. Kyle, Eric, DeeDee, Bertha, and Barbie—the infected chimp.

"They're all squeeze cages," Valerie said to Bear, over the din of the air pumps and the infected chimp's screams. "If you pull the bar at the back it will press them up against the front of the cage. Let's do it. These guys are like jumping jacks."

Squeeze cages are designed to make giving injections and taking blood easy on the handlers. Valerie pulled out four of the five prepared syringes full of ketamine and laid them on the tiled floor. All around her chimpanzee babies were hooting and trying to bang on their chamber doors. They were lonely and they wanted attention.

Bear clicked the latches on Kyle's chamber door and leaned forward. Kyle had his lips puckered and was trying to smell or kiss Bear, his hands grabbing for Bear's mask. Valerie passed grapes over to him and Kyle's tiny, human-like fingers clutched the fruit. He wanted to eat, but he wanted attention, too. His other hand plucked at Bear's shoulder, his fingers pushing into Bear's hair.

While Bear moved Kyle's squeeze mechanism forward, Valerie snapped open the other chamber doors and started handing out grapes and holding hands for reassurance. First Kyle, then Eric, then Bertha, then DeeDee, felt the sharp, momentary prick as the smooth needles nipped at their thighs. It would be about eight minutes before the drug took effect.

Valerie had already decided to risk feeding Barbie. It was hardly compensation for having to be left behind, but it was all Valerie could think to do. Barbie was at least five months older than the other chimpanzee infants. As Valerie opened the chamber door and handed Barbie the grapes, she realized that Barbie had begun to show the stereotypical behavior that is the first sign of dementia: she was already rocking back and forth. Valerie clasped Barbie's free hand in hers and talked to her. "Barbie, my love," she said, "You'll be all right. Don't even think about it, my sweet girl. Everything will pass."

Barbie looked at Valerie as she swayed back and forth, holding Valerie's hand for dear life and making hooting sounds. If she lived through it all, into chimpanzee old age, she had fifty years of incarceration ahead of her. Valerie let her chew her grapes and dream for a moment that someone loved her.

Outside, Kay was trying not to panic. A late-model Ford four-door had pulled up outside the front door. She had radioed into the lab as the car entered the lot, again when it stopped, and now again as the driver, a middle-aged man, came up to the front door and turned his key. There had been no acknowledgment. Kay hoped that Valerie had heard her but was unable to respond. In fact, Valerie's radio wasn't working.

Valerie and Bear jumped as the alarm rang through the building. They looked at each other for a split second. Someone had come through the front door. There was nowhere to hide in the room. They had to get out. The dividing door opened directly onto their corridor. There was no time to close the cage doors, Valerie realized, or do more than push the syringes back into her pocket.

They were on their feet and out the door, running down the corridor to who-knows-where. As they reached the corner, Valerie prayed they would not run into the caretaker. She had no idea where he was.

Two corridors up, Bear was slightly ahead of Valerie when he saw the sign on the door. "Storage," it read. He turned to grab Valerie and together they slipped on the wet tile. As Valerie fell, she realized it had just been mopped. They were leaving footprints and the caretaker must be close by. Scrambling to his feet, Bear pulled the door open and they slipped inside.

The mop bucket was directly in front of them. So was the caretaker. He was loading a cart with bags of cedar chips. His back was to the door and he hadn't heard the masked intruders enter. The sound of the pumps was almost as loud in this room as in the others. Valerie and Bear crept behind the paper goods stacked on dollies immediately to their left and froze.

The caretaker was moving about through the stacks of paper towels. When he turned, Valerie saw that he was young, about twenty, pleasant-looking, and maybe twenty pounds overweight. She could see perspiration beaded up on his forehead. Simba had said the caretakers were overworked. It also felt about 80 degrees inside SEMA.

A man was yelling outside in the corridor, trying to be heard above the din. "Chuck, where are you?" he called.

"Damn!" said the caretaker out loud to himself. He walked past the towel stacks and opened the door into the hall, where alien footprints, Valerie had no doubt, had messed up his nice, clean mop job.

Bear pointed to a ladder going up to a platform to their right. It looked like a good hiding place. Valerie nodded and followed him quickly and quietly up toward the ceiling. They had to bend their heads as they moved to the back of the platform, and they were careful not to bump into the collection of empty drums and cages that had been tossed there.

Valerie was sure they would be caught. Whoever this man was, he had a key, which meant authority. He had walked down the corridor and past Room 35B. If he had glanced in as he walked, a natural thing to do, he would have seen cages open. If he had stepped into the room, he would have found four chimpanzees who, by now, would be showing noticeable effects of the drug. Was that why he was yelling for Chuck?

As Valerie bent her knees to crouch into place, she felt a sharp pinch on her thigh, then another. She knew exactly what had happened. There hadn't been time to put the protective caps back on the syringe needles. She had scooped them into her pocket uncapped and now at least one of them had pierced her skin. The infants she had injected with ketamine were not infected, so there was no risk of contamination from them. Barbie, on the other hand, had been given hepatitis B, which can be fatal to human beings. Some of the smears of blood, urine, and fecal matter on the floor from which Valerie had retrieved the syringes were very likely from her.

Edna had warned Valerie to be careful. Two nurses in her hospital had come down with hepatitis B after stabbing themselves accidentally with a patient's used needle.

There isn't much point in worrying about that now, Valerie thought. There are more immediate problems to resolve.

She and Bear settled in to wait. If the police were coming, she'd better try to stash the syringes. She pried the lid off one of the barrels, releasing a sharp chemical smell into the air. There was still something in the barrel. She dropped the syringes into it and heard them splash into the liquid.

Valerie and Bear weren't scared for themselves. If the police came, they would likely be found and booked, that was all there was to it. They both felt rotten about the chimpanzees, who were now so close to freedom. Would they fail them?

Chuck banged back into the room, collected his cart, and wheeled it out into the hall. He looked tired and bored, not like someone who has just been told that intruders are somewhere in the building.

The other man could be anywhere, possibly making his way back up the hall to leave, giving him one more shot at looking into Room 35B. The alarm went off again. Did that mean the visitor had left? Or had he been joined by others?

"Battery check, Victor" came Edna's voice, as Valerie's walkie came back to life. It was an all-clear. Thank you, thank you, Edna, Valerie thought, for having common sense. She must have seen the visitor leave. She had deduced that Valerie and Bear were flying blind and had decided to break radio silence for them. Valerie's radio had recovered just in time.

They climbed down the ladder and into the hall. No sign of the caretaker. Surely, Edna would not have given an all-clear unless it included him, but they couldn't know for sure.

Except for Barbie, who leapt to the front of the cage and started jumping and screaming when she saw them reenter the room, the scene in Room 35B was tranquil. DeeDee and Bertha were asleep in each other's arms. Kyle had propped himself up against his cage bars. When he saw Valerie, he tried hard to get excited, but was too tired. He yawned instead. Eric was awake, but calm and spacey.

Bear lifted Kyle out of his cage and gently put him into Eric's. Eric and Kyle got wide-eyed for a moment, then Eric rubbed his chin into Kyle's neck and the two sat quietly together watching what was happening, as if not sure whether they were part of the action or dreaming.

One at a time, they pulled the cage interiors out of the chamber shells and into the aisle between the two cage banks. Valerie took all the fruit out of her pockets and handed it to Barbie. Then they took their leave of her.

"Victor, test, test, test," Valerie spoke into the walkie.

"Roger, Victor," came Edna's voice. There were limitations to this communication. It meant either that Edna knew exactly where the caretaker was at the moment and that he was safely occupied, or that all she knew was that he wasn't close by right now. It was the best they were going to get.

"Take care, my love," Valerie bent over Barbie. The chimpanzee reached up to touch the cheek of Valerie's white mask as Valerie bent over her. There was no time to linger. Four other lives hung in the balance.

The cages were heavy. The metal bottoms scraped the plastic tiles, carving long ruts through the floor as Bear and Valerie dragged and carried and pushed them through the door, along the next corridor, and toward the side door. The pair were working as fast as they could and sweat was pouring down their necks and backs.

About halfway down the corridor Valerie heard fast footsteps. She turned and there was Edna, running down the hall, calling into her walkie-talkie for Kay.

"He's just finished the far corridor. He's heading this way," she panted.

"Bear, you pull that cage behind you," Valerie said. "Edna, help me with this one. We can carry it." Summoning all their strength, they reached the door within seconds. Kay wasn't there. Hurry up and wait, hurry up and wait. The words stuck like an unwanted jingle in Valerie's head.

"Come on, Kay, come on," Bear was saying aloud what Valerie and Edna were repeating to themselves. Getting out was the immediate problem.

Suddenly, Kay's headlights reflected in the glass. Bear swung the door open. The alarm filled the building. Doesn't mean a thing, Valerie told herself, he'll think his annoying boss has just come back in.

Kay stayed in the driver seat while the man with her helped lift from inside the van. Valerie, Bear, and Edna clambered in behind the last cage. Kyle and Eric's eyes were like those of little boys watching a Christmas tree light up. They were having an adventure!

Kay drove cautiously out of the lot. All the lookouts' eyes were on her truck. As Kay came past, Leonard, who was stationed at the restaurant exit immediately next door, pulled out behind her. If there was a chase, Leonard would do his best to tie things up.

The next thing they knew, they were on the beltway, heading toward southern Virginia and Bear's farm. Personnel from the CBS news show "West 57th" were waiting there to interview them. The chimpanzee babies could sleep for a couple of hours before Meredith Vieira would appear on camera with them. Vieira said later that she had felt no sympathy for the infants, only fear that she might contract AIDS from them.

The video Bear had made was left in a drop box for PETA that night. It was made into a touching tape called *Breaking Barriers*, which was sent to every primatologist and concerned scientist PETA could find. Affidavits and letters of concern over what the U.S. government was doing to "our closest living relatives" began to pour in from around the world.

Most influential of all was Dr. Jane Goodall, Bear's hero. The tape disturbed her so much that she decided she would visit SEMA for herself. This caused a tremendous stir. Goodall was refused at first, but then the realization sank in that it was impossible to exclude the world's foremost chimpanzee expert from your lab. A tour was arranged for Dr. Goodall and Senator John Melcher of Montana.

When they emerged into the sunshine outside SEMA, they were both visibly shaken. What Dr. Goodall wrote in the *New York Times Magazine* bears that out:

> Just after Christmas [1986] I watched, with shock, anger and anguish, a videotape called *Breaking Barriers*—made by an animal

rights group during a raid—revealing the conditions in a large bio-medical research laboratory, under contract to the National Institutes of Health, in which various primates, including chimpanzees, are maintained. In late March, I was given permission to visit the facility.

It was a visit I shall never forget.

I shall be haunted forever by . . . the eyes of the infant chimpanzees I saw that day. Have you ever looked into the eyes of a person who, stressed beyond endurance, has given up, succumbed utterly to the crippling helplessness of despair? I once saw a little African boy, whose whole family had been killed during the fighting in Burundi. He too looked out at the world, unseeing, from dull, blank eyes.

Though this particular laboratory may be one of the worst, from what I have learned, most of the other biomedical animal-research facilities are not much better. Yet only when one has some understanding of the true nature of the chimpanzee can the cruelty of these captive conditions be fully understood.

Chimpanzees are very social by nature. Bonds between family members and close friends, can be affectionate, supportive, and can endure through their lives. . . . Indeed, the death of a mother may be such a psychological blow to her child that even if the child is five years old and no longer dependent on its mother's milk, it may pine away and die.

It is impossible to overemphasize the importance of friendly physical contact for the well-being of the chimpanzee.

Chimps enjoy comfort. They construct sleeping platforms each night, using a multitude of leafy twigs to make their beds soft. Often, too, they make little "pillows" on which to rest during a mid-day siesta.

In most labs, the chimpanzees cannot even lie with their arms and legs outstretched. They are not let out to exercise. There is seldom anything for them to do other than eat, and then only when food is brought. The cages are bleak and sterile, with bars above, bars below, bars on every side. There is no comfort in them, no bedding. The chimps, infected with human diseases, will often feel sick and miserable.

I have had the privilege of working among wild, free chimpanzees for more than 26 years. I have gained a deep understanding of chimpanzee nature. Chimpanzees have given me so much in my life. The least I can do is speak out for the hundreds of chimpanzees who, right now, sit hunched, miserable and without hope, staring out with dead eyes from their metal prisons. They cannot speak for themselves.

Valerie and other ALF members found themselves having to take turns helping Bear and Bobbie look after the chimpanzee babies in their first year of life outside the laboratory. It took almost fourteen months' work to find the right permanent place for them and the right people for them to spend the rest of their lives with.

The babies were very dependent at first. They looked out for one another, cooing and touching and gently grooming, always sleeping curled up in a big, black chimpanzee knot of feet and hands. They chased and tumbled and rolled themselves up in rugs, played hide and seek, and did all the things SEMA had prevented them from experiencing.

Eric didn't survive. At three, he became lethargic and suffered a marked drop in weight. His blood work revealed an impaired immune system, and despite heroic efforts to save him he died quietly at his new home in 1988.

Valerie spent some anxious weeks examining the whites of her eyes for any sign of jaundice and looking out for all the other symptoms that Edna had told her could mark the onset of hepatitis B. To her relief, the incubation period passed, and she remained fit and unaffected by her close encounter with the soiled needles that had pricked her thighs in the attic at SEMA.

To make life in captivity easy and relaxed for Kyle, the decision was made to neuter him. Human beings are ill-equipped to deal with a male chimpanzee, up to ten times as strong as a man and with incisors three inches long, when he reaches puberty. Some ALF members criticized or contested the decision initially, and Valerie realized that Kyle was so human-like that the men were relating to what was to be done to him in a very personal way. The fact that Kyle was also a member of an endangered species (whose population in Africa has been decimated by international trade) made the decision even more uncomfortable. However, consensus was reached after a minimum of hair pulling.

It was agreed: they had saved *Kyle*, not his imaginary unborn progeny. It was all they could do to make his life and the lives of the other two chimpanzees full and enjoyable, and that was an enormous task indeed. If the chimpanzees remained sexually intact and were "allowed" to have young, what would become of their offspring? The ALF could hardly charter a plane and deposit them all in their African homelands or send them to a zoo.

"It's not as if we're operating in a perfect world, is it?" Valerie reminded Bear, whose objections were the strongest. "We have to do this to Kyle for the same reason we advocate spaying and neutering of dogs and cats, for the same reason we can't let animals free to roam the streets. The world in which they once lived so perfectly has been destroyed. There is almost no place for them. Our job is to save individuals and to try to change the machine that started this whole mess."

As it turned out, Kyle's lack of sexual aggression made for peace within the group.

Following a front-page article in the Boston *Globe* by reporter Diane Dumanowski, Dr. Goodall's intervention, and a BBC special program aired throughout Europe, which asked the question, "Aren't chimps God's children, too?" some changes were made at SEMA. New babies are now kept together in an open room, and some adults are given "toys" to hold and tear apart. It is some compensation, but not much. Toys do not make a life. The chimpanzees need room to move and to be with others of their own kind.

SEMA changed its name to Bioqual and still gets lucrative government contracts to infect primates of many species with hepatitis, AIDS, and influenza. Dr. Goodall still speaks out against the horrors of treating chimpanzees like disposable objects and has opened many eyes to the obscenities our government endorses in the name of science.

Dr. Alfred Prince, who himself once did research that required him to chain chimpanzees by the neck and infect them with deadly viruses, has demanded that NIH adopt a "Chimpanzee Bill of Rights." Professor R.A. Gardner of the University of Nevada at Reno has called on NIH to "break down the species barrier." Dr. Roger Fouts, whose noninvasive work with a rescued family of chimpanzees provided a breakthrough in American Sign Language training, has challenged NIH to recognize that chimpanzees are "a sibling species." So far, NIH has ignored them all.

One day, perhaps, as Leonardo da Vinci predicted, the murder of beasts will be looked on as the murder of men. Meanwhile, Barbie and others like her remain locked in their chambers.

12

Fire Starters and Farm Freedom Fighters

At about the same time the American ALF was breaking into SEMA, Scotland Yard was putting the final touches on its case against Ronnie Lee. By February of 1987, Lee had been brought before Her Majesty's Crown Court in Sheffield and sentenced to ten years. Unable to tie him to any specific crime, the police had charged him with that convenient, blanket offense: conspiracy. Or, as it is known in police circles, "failure to do right."

While Lee sewed mailbags and refused to use the prison blanket because it was made from animal hair, PETA was given the news that Brooks, one of the Silver Spring monkeys, had died. Since the monkeys' transfer the previous year to Metairie County in Louisiana (where Tulane University had built a sprawling laboratory complex, called the Delta Regional Primate Research Center, on the edges of a swamp), the monkeys had been caged individually. Valerie and Bear had checked the place out, but Delta was hard to reach, and not only were the Silver Spring monkeys monitored by closed-circuit television, but there were glare lights in the hallways and armed sheriff's deputies on site.

According to review committees, Delta had failed to produce anything of scientific merit since coming into existence, and its mortality rate was extremely high. Agreeing to take the political heat associated with accepting the Silver Spring monkeys was part of a secret deal, most speculated, that would change its NIH funding status from bottom of the barrel to top of the heap. With AIDS research funds now flowing as if out of a tap, NIH could afford to pay Delta off.

Brooks had died in his cage not many months after the transfer. Delta was less than forthright about the cause of his death. As details emerged, it seemed he had choked and suffocated on his own vomit while being force-fed after a debilitating, undiagnosed "illness." Delta refused to hand over the body for an autopsy, burning it instead.

PETA's case to free the monkeys was still being bounced from jurisdiction to jurisdiction. Angry members of Congress discovered that NIH was up to its old tricks. A memo leaked from NIH by sympathizers outlined the government's plans to kill the Silver Spring monkeys, despite written assurances to the contrary.

One hundred thirty-seven members of Congress signed on to the Silver Spring monkeys bill (legislation that would free the remaining monkeys) and humane groups formed a coalition to lobby for the bill's passage. The furor netted concessions from the government: five of the monkeys—Chester, Hayden, Adidas, Sisyphus, and Montaigne—were transferred under heavy congressional pressure to the San Diego Zoo. Alex went to see them there, in their private indoor/outdoor enclosure, and pronounced them well cared for and as happy as captive monkeys can be.

By March of 1987, Valerie was still spending a lot of time helping with the SEMA chimps and had not seen Josh in almost a year, although they had spoken by phone. When he called, she was delighted to hear his voice and the words, "Let's meet."

"I can't wait to see you, Josh" she said.

"You don't have to wait," he answered. "I'm at the airport right now, so come get me and let's have dinner."

Valerie ran into the potting shed, where Sean was working on his hybrid azaleas, and told him where she was going. He raised his eyebrows at her. "Who loves you, baby?" he asked.

"Mr. Insecurity does," she retorted, heading for the driveway.

Josh looked tanned and well. California agreed with him. They drove to Crystal City and chose a Mexican restaurant where

Valerie knew the beans weren't cooked in lard. They ordered a couple of Dos Equis beers and looked each other over.

"Tell me how things are going," Valerie asked him.

"Pretty well," he said, leaning his tall frame back in the chair. "All the groups out there are going through some changes, though."

"What sort of changes?" Valerie tried to read his face, but he seemed genuinely untroubled. "Rifts?"

"Oh, there's always some of that. Sometimes I think that if we were working with gorillas instead of human beings, life would be easier. No, I mean philosophy. Some of the kids are totally anti-euthanasia, which I don't go along with. I'd rather die quietly in the arms of someone caring than be tortured to death slowly by ghouls. We've got some folks who want our focus to shift to meat production sabotage, and some young people who are hot to get into remodeling."

Valerie knew what remodeling meant: bombs. They were talking about bombs. Above Josh's head, there was a painting of Pancho Villa, the revolutionary bandit. Appropriate, she thought.

"Doesn't that make you a little nervous?" Valerie asked. It certainly made her nervous talking about such things in public, even in code, despite the mariachi music drowning out their conversation. It was Friday night and the place was filling up.

"Not any more. It used to, but I agree with what they say. It's unrealistic to think we can continue to find homes for all the animals we get out of these places. We need to switch focus, go after the buildings and equipment. Economic damage not only slows these bastards down more than anything else, but money's something they understand. It makes 'em quake!"

The waiter took their order of bean enchilada dinners. When Josh bent his head over the menu, Valerie noticed that he had about twice as many silver hairs as when she had first met him.

"We've got blueprints for three places," Josh sipped his beer. "Two under construction and one about to be. We'll pick a site and see how it goes."

"I guess it'll go 'bang,' won't it?" Valerie didn't mean it to sound funny. She was sensing the end of an era. She and Josh had joked long ago about how the ALF was like Robin Hood for the animals, but explosives hadn't been part of the picture.

"I don't like it, Josh," she said. "It smacks of terrorism."

"If children were being held in the labs, would the people who brought *them* out and bombed the buildings be called terrorists?" Josh burst out.

"Easy," Valerie said. "You and I may believe that what is done to other-than-human beings equates to what is done to human beings, but most people don't buy that. It's a totally alien concept to them."

"I know," Josh said, "but it's our challenge to keep hammering away at that kind of elite mentality. People have got to face facts: we're *all* animals! What does Fouts say? We're all different members of a big symphony. We may each play a different instrument, but the man on the big bass drum doesn't count for more than the kid playing the triangle."

Josh was too wound up for Valerie to stop him.

"The big question is, will our own movement turn on us? Will the groups run scared?" he continued. "Most of them like the rescues, but they get the shakes over graffiti! The goal has to be to bring down the machinery and bring down the labs. Labs don't burn down themselves, they need our help!"

Valerie didn't smile.

"No one could possibly be hurt," he went on. "We'll be so careful, we should get a safety award, but even the most radical groups are going to have to answer some nasty new questions, like 'What if someone had been hurt?' It'll be so hot *they'll* think they're in those burning buildings."

"*Are* they careful, these kids?" Valerie asked.

"About other people and animals, yes. Absolutely. About themselves, no. They take crazy risks. When they showed me what they were putting together, I almost died. They'd found some recipe in an underground booklet from the sixties. The kind of dangerous, amateur stuff that makes you wake up in the hospital with a few less limbs than you started with. So now I'm doing the homework."

"Josh, that's big-time jail."

"Wait a minute, Val," Josh looked at her hard, "You've never stopped doing what you believed in because it would be 'big-time jail.' What's on your mind?"

"You're right. I guess I feel left behind," Valerie admitted. "Old-fashioned, maybe? I can't accept blowing things up. I'm not condemning it, I understand that if you could blow up Hitler's bunker, you should and all that. It's just, forgive me for saying this, but it's not my style."

"Think about it," Josh said, kindly. "I didn't accept this overnight either. But now I'm off the fence, and I'd like you with me. Give me a few months to get things worked out right, and then, if you want me to come east and train you or someone else, I will. I'm feeling my mortality, and you're still too young to understand that. When I look back on my life, I want to have done everything I'm capable of: not just to rock the vivisector's boat but to capsize and sink 'er. Please, don't write it off yet."

"OK, but I can't see it happening," Valerie said, wondering who or what had influenced Josh.

They finished dinner and took a ride to Maine Avenue, where they could sit on a bench at the wharf and look out over the water. Josh told Valerie about sailing off the Baja Peninsula: how the water was "white-tipped turquoise," and how the fish would take food from your hand. He told her how he loved to dive from the deck as his boat was drifting along, grab the tender, and let it pull him through the cool water. "Heaven," he said, smiling with the memory. He turned to face her and put his hands on her shoulders lightly.

"Sean still your true love?"

"Yes," she said.

"Just checking," he said.

Valerie took Josh to the Tabard Inn, a tiny old hotel off Connecticut Avenue. When he'd checked in, they saw the bar was still open. They had a nightcap together on the oversized, old sofa in the deserted lounge. Valerie had missed him and was glad to be able to spend time with him like this.

"I have a present for you," Josh said, after a while.

"Hmmm. What is it?" Valerie sipped her cherry brandy and

watched as Josh unzipped his duffle bag and pulled out a plain black box.

"It's a little something for you to wear at night," he said, handing her the box. His eyes were dancing from the brandy. Was it professional or personal? She opened the box, a vision of Sean on the potting shed floor squarely in her mind.

"Josh, this is wonderful!" she cried. Valerie felt ashamed for having doubted his motives. They had talked about getting night-vision glasses, but they cost many, many thousands of dollars. Now she had her own pair.

"They're 'on loan' from the Navy," he said. "I've got a pair now, too. All part of the government's secret plan to help undo some of the damage they've done to animals, by subsidizing the ALF."

"Secret plan?" Valerie asked.

"Yeah, secret to *them*," Josh winked at her.

The young radicals didn't wait for Josh to perfect a "remodeling device," although they did take his advice not to use the Weathermen-style homemade bomb they had originally set their hopes on.

On April 16, 1987, they entered the University of California's new diagnostic laboratory, still under construction. They crumpled styrofoam cups together, made a bed of rags and kindling around them, and soaked the whole thing through with a gallon of kerosene. Then they threw a box of lighted matches on it and fled.

The University of California at Davis laboratory, almost half-way finished at that time and designed to cater to the needs of the agribusiness industry, burned to the ground that night. Damages were estimated at $3.5 million.

Josh had been right about how such an action would affect the animal protection groups. Many of them were genuinely disgusted at the idea of arson. Others who used the term "animal rights," but had not incorporated the systematized abuse of "farm animals" into their agendas, couldn't "see" an attack on the farm industry at all; some may have secretly cheered, but recognized political suicide when they saw it. A few agreed to criticize the ALF only if the ALF's detractors would condemn what was being done to animals. One or two actually applauded the action.

Valerie followed the news with more than casual interest. She knew Josh was right. Although she wanted no part in such actions, they escalated the war on animal abusers. She recognized that there always had been room for different styles in any social struggle, from the mild to the vigorous and everything in between. Was she too soft to be a true revolutionary? She wondered. What held her back? She had no problems with breaking locks, smashing equipment used to pummel baboons' heads, trashing labs where animals had suffered and been killed. All she knew was that she could not, would not, be part of a bombing.

Valerie found a good use for Josh's present the following August. A horticulture student at the Beltsville Agricultural Research Center had discovered some nasty goings-on. Ginger heard about it from her roommate at school, who had been collecting spores for her class and made friends with a man who mucked out the barns. He showed her around, thinking he'd impress her. She ended up running from the place.

"What did she see?" Valerie asked.

"The place looks nice from the outside," Ginger said. "Don't they all? Green fields, grazing cows and sheep, a real fairy land. But, inside, it's standard factory farm stuff. They keep the mother pigs in 'iron maidens,' sets of bars sunk into a concrete floor. The pigs can't turn around, not even when they give birth. This girl didn't know that sort of thing existed. When she saw the pigs living in their own filth, unable to move, she freaked.

"There was a pig there who had been given the human growth gene in some kind of experiment. He was hopelessly crippled, couldn't even stand. The man who was showing her around was proud of the whole ugly place. He acknowledged that the pig was riddled with arthritis, but thought it was great science!"

"The old 'the patient died, but the experiment was a success' attitude," Valerie said. "What's the deal with using human genes?"

"It's called 'transgenics,'" Ginger explained. "It's all the rage. Ag researchers want to 'make' new, patentable animals. Farming in a test tube, biotechnology, or as someone at school aptly named it, 'animal agricide.'"

"You'd think the religious groups would object," Valerie wondered out loud. "Tampering with God's creation and all that. Can you hit the Ag library tomorrow and see if you can get a bead on what they're up to over there?"

Ginger agreed. She would come over to Sean's house afterward. Valerie had read Jim Mason's book, *Animal Factories*, and the "Down on the Factory Farm" chapter in Peter Singer's *Animal Liberation*. She hadn't heard of transgenics, but she knew that most of the 85 million pigs, 9 million sheep, 1.1 billion cows, and 3.3 billion chickens slaughtered each year in the U.S. were raised in "factory farms," a system of intensive confinement that caused numerous stress-related diseases. She knew that 50 percent of all the antibiotics used in the U.S. now went into livestock feed. To those who complained that without meat consumption, none of these animals ever would have had a life, Valerie's reply was, "Before they die, they'll wish they'd never been born."

The next night there was a torrential thunderstorm. It was late afternoon when Ginger arrived. As she ran up the driveway, her bag blew open and the papers she had so carefully acquired got soaked. Valerie dried them in the oven while she made coffee.

"I've found some wild stuff," Ginger said, "but not what we were expecting. They've got an Asian experimenter over there called Dr. J.P. Dubey. He does experiments on toxoplasmosis, whatever that is. He infects mice and then kills them and feeds their ground-up brains to cats. The cats get sick and Dubey writes down their symptoms—diarrhea, dehydration, lung and intestinal tract infections. He's been doing that for fifteen years!"

"Cats? At the Ag center?" It seemed ludicrous.

The Dubey papers were approaching crisp when Valerie removed them from the oven. The first one contained a sort of chart showing morbidity and mortality in Dubey's experimental subjects going back to 1971. It showed that some cats lived for years until Dr. Dubey was ready to help himself to cross sections of their brains. Others, particularly young kittens, died immediately or a few days or weeks after infection.

"Here's a truly charming one where he infected eighty kittens by stomach tube," Ginger read. "Catch this: 'Fifty-eight cats were newborns, one to five days of age. They were infected heavily by stomach tube with brains of no less than twenty to twenty-three heavily infected mice. It is not surprising to see kittens, fed this way, become extremely ill and die in a few days . . . ' " Ginger flipped through the papers, stopping here and there to read other parts out loud.

"He's fed infected brain cysts to one-day-old and one-week-old puppies and then killed them and examined their tissue. Oh, listen to this. Dubey reports getting pregnant cats from 'homes in Kansas City.' That doesn't sound very legal, does it?"

Ginger brought out a map of the center and pointed out which buildings housed the pigs. "The odd thing," Ginger said as she was leaving, "is that there's nothing about their pig experiments anywhere."

Valerie wondered if perhaps the center was too territorial to risk publishing anything about such a project-in-progress. If things worked out, the animals would be patentable, and patents mean money. Maybe they aimed to have the factory farm equivalent of a goose with golden eggs.

By the time Ginger left, Valerie knew that Jitender Prakash Dubey had put himself on the ALF visit list.

The Beltsville Agricultural Research Center is composed of several hundred acres, two large clumps of woods, several streams polluted with agricultural chemicals and waste runoff, and dozens of barns. The area the ALF was interested in was off a series of farm roads. At its most western tip, it backed onto a residential area where, unbeknownst to them at that time, Dr. Dubey and his wife lived.

The road between the center grounds and the residential area was barricaded by a large, wrought-iron gate that was fastened with a heavy chain and kept padlocked. Every few hours a security vehicle drove down the road, doubling back at the gate or parking there for a while for no apparent reason.

There were several places in the fence line near the target buildings where the wire mesh "gave" enough to allow someone to lie on his back or stomach and squeeze or crawl under it. The tufts of opossum and raccoon fur stuck in the mesh made it clear that these were well traveled entrances to "the Farm."

End-of-summer thunderstorms crashed down on Washington almost every night, lighting up the sky with sheet lightning and making reconnaissance hellishly difficult. In spite of the rains, the evenings were steaming hot, with temperatures still near 90 degrees after 8:00 P.M. most nights.

Before midnight, Valerie and her volunteers would go through the fence. Keeping their bodies bent over, especially when the moon bathed the compound in light, they made their way across the two huge fields between the fence and the closest barn, using any tree, furrow, or bush they could find as cover.

The grounds surrounding the center were extremely buggy due to accumulations of urine and dung from the large animal husbandry areas. To avoid detection at the perimeter, the cell members had to squash themselves into the few remaining hedges or prickly bushes along the fence line. On the first muggy night, they found that the mosquitoes and other biting insects had greeted them enthusiastically—all the way through their cotton trousers and shirts. After that miserable experience, they sweated it out in heavy jeans, long black socks pulled up over the jeans to the knee, long-sleeved sweaters, and acrylic gloves and face masks. Liberal applications of bug repellent helped, too.

When the first crack of thunder sounded, the lookouts would pull on their plastic, hooded ponchos to keep dry. It was like working in a steam bath.

Even when there wasn't much light, the stark whitewashed barns, sheds, and outbuildings seemed almost luminescent. A single lane of asphalt for trucks, tractors, and security vehicles linked them to each other. After sinking thigh deep one night into a wet, black, stinking mixture of mud and manure that had not announced its presence, they found themselves using the lane whenever they were in doubt about any patch of ground. It felt strange to walk out in the open, like parading down a pageant runway, exposed to a hundred spectators.

The night-vision glasses were cumbersome and took some getting used to, but they were a blessing. Josh had warned Valerie that, despite manufacturers' claims to the contrary, people can ruin their eyes using them. She paid attention to his advice and used them sparingly.

Sitting on the hill above the long series of goat and sheep barns, Valerie could look over at the free-ranging cattle. She wondered if cows have natural night vision: on really dark nights, without the glasses it was impossible to know they were there at all, but when she put the goggles on and looked at them, they were always looking right back at her, watching intently.

Sometimes she saw a fox moving along the fence line, and one night a mother raccoon and her three young "bandits" walked across the field, standing up on their hind legs and sniffing into the wind every few yards.

The best place to use the glasses was in the barns. They were meant for long-distance viewing, and adapting their use to close-ups took some adjustment, but it could be done. The goggles were much safer than using flashlights. The barns and sheds were pitch dark, but there were windows and cracks in the wooden boards. If a patrol car or someone cn foot had come over the ridge from the main gates and caught the most uncertain glimpse of a flicker of light coming from the barns, it would have been the kiss of death. On a farm, light inside the barn at night can mean kids with cigarettes and a burned-down building.

Watch #1 was the most tolerable lookout spot. When it was Valerie's turn to take that site, at the top of a knoll overlooking the entire complex, she felt peaceful. When it wasn't stormy, she sat on the grass in the night air, feeling part of the countryside, leaning up against one of the enormous old trees that had been allowed to remain intact when the ground was churned up for agriculture. If it hadn't been for her knowledge of what the animals were feeling in the buildings below, Valerie could have been exquisitely happy there.

Watch #2 was beside the cat barn, two fields away from Watch #1. Watch #3 was back at the main road behind the compound, near the iron gate. Comparing notes, they found there were two separate security patrols. The outside one was sporadic, unpredictable, a problem. The inside patrol usually operated like clockwork: patrolling every hour just past the top of the hour.

One night, a few days into surveillance, Valerie was sitting at Watch #2, passing time, using the goggles to watch the cows in the field to her right. She couldn't have been looking at them for more than five minutes, because she was careful about hurting her eyes. When she turned back, she almost had a heart attack. A security patrol car was parked in the dark, with its lights off, about forty yards away. It hadn't been there minutes earlier.

Valerie felt herself tense. The car door opened and a man got out. The goggles made everything seem green and slightly shimmery, but Valerie could see him as clearly as if it had been daylight. She had to remind herself that he could not see her unless he was Superman. He took several steps away from the car, lit a cigarette and smoked it slowly, blowing the columns of white smoke into the hazy night air. Then he got back into the car and continued his slow glide down the lane without headlights. Valerie could only think that he had good eyesight, or that he'd traveled the route a million times before. How he did it, she didn't know.

There is no question that without the glasses the "silent patrolman" easily could have surprised the ALF members. On the weekends, whoever used the police cars used their lights, too, but on week nights the ALFers got used to the silent patrolman's routine, waiting for him to creep over the hill in the darkness and coast eerily down to the barns.

Valerie and her cohorts inventoried the barns gradually, working their way through fields full of gopher holes from the barns at the bottom of the Farm, near the woods, up to the most exposed barns near the rise that leads to the main gate and the security post.

The lower barns contained a few veal calves kept in elevated wooden stalls, their heads chained to the wooden fronts of the stall and their legs bent under them because there was no room for them to stretch out. They stank of scours, a diarrheal disease common in intensive farming operations, and their knees were raw from falling and kneeling, falling and kneeling, on the hard metal gridwork. Valerie saw them only once and decided not to enter those buildings again. The presence of people petrified them, and they would scramble up, eyes big as saucers, bucking their chains against the stall, slipping in their own waste and scraping their shins on the slats. During her watch time, if Valerie found herself slipping into thoughts about them, she would deliberately blot them out.

The second set of buildings, longer than the first, held sows of various ages. Some were very young; others' charts (these were read using a cupped, nail polish-coated penlight covered with cloth) showed recent artificial insemination. Sows in the final stages of pregnancy or who had delivered recently were the worst off, although all the sows were uncomfortable on the bare concrete. These enormous sows were kept in metal racks—the "iron maidens" Ginger had mentioned—face-forward, unable to turn or scratch or stretch. If they had given birth, the piglets could suckle between the bars, but the sows couldn't turn to them, or reach to lick them, or nuzzle them. They couldn't even see them.

With the goggles, Valerie could make out thousands of cockroaches moving around the floor and climbing onto the pigs' bodies as they tried to sleep. Pigs are very noisy and difficult to move, but she considered trying to get at least some of the small ones out.

The building that formerly housed the human-gene pigs was empty, cleaned out, and bleached. The transgenic pigs had died. The experiment had been a failure from the start—which is not to say that it wouldn't be repeated all over the country.

The last barn on the lower level held the cats. Through the windows, an observer could see them sitting up, alert, or sleeping in their tiered cages. For some reason, this barn was kept bolted and the windows locked. It would be unwise to try an entry or do anything that might arouse suspicion. A rough count could be taken through the windows, and Dubey's research papers told the rest of the story.

Farther up the hill, the barns were used for intensive sheep production. Like the veal calves, mother sheep were kept individually in elevated, wooden slat-floored chutes, barely an inch or two longer or wider than their bodies. Any lambs who hadn't already been taken away to slaughter were huddled together in large pens behind them. Factory farmers never allow mothers to be with their young, and they make sure all natural movements are contained. To them, animals are meat machines meant to reproduce and grow fat, then be processed. Nothing else.

These buildings were dangerously near the rise in the lane and there was no cover of any sort. Not even a ditch or a bush. If someone came over that hill, they'd be on top of any ALF intruders before they could escape.

The cell's first visit into the sheep barns was a disaster. It was a very quiet night, windless and still, without a storm cloud in sight. As soon as Valerie opened the door and crept inside, about sixty sheep and lambs started to bleat. The noise carried through the open windows, and was so loud Valerie had no doubt it could be heard all the way to the guard station. She and the others bolted back down the hill. Halfway up the embankment on the other side, she turned around, goggles on, to see the silent patrol car gliding over the ridge. It stopped outside the barn they had just left and the officer got out. The group members flattened themselves into the hillside as he walked around the building, shining his powerful flashlight through the windows and sending a fresh wave of panic through the "flock." As he turned the corner of the barn Valerie and the others rose and ran, hoping he would figure that the sheep had been disturbed by a fox or raccoon.

They didn't go back to those barns until the next major storm, when the thunder and rain drowned out all sheep-to-guard communication.

Beltsville also kept hundreds of chickens, ducks, geese, and guinea fowl in a series of tiny, oddly shaped buildings that looked like gazebos. The birds were crammed together into wire cages in typical factory farming style: five to seven birds kept in a cage barely larger than a refrigerator vegetable bin, without enough room to spread a wing; birds sitting on top of each other trying to sleep, their feet no doubt hurting from weeks of balancing on the tilted wire-mesh flooring. After a cursory look, Valerie stayed clear of these buildings. The presence of human beings towering over the cramped cages frightened the birds far too much.

She went over the logistics of the raid in her head. They needed two vans, one for the pigs and one for the cats. Unless they planned on spending the night traipsing back and forth through the fields, they needed enough people to help carry out some pigs and the forty or so adult cats housed in Dubey's barn in only one or two trips. By Valerie's calculations, that meant a minimum of seventeen live bodies.

The local, unwritten roster of solid, available, and experienced ALF members had grown to twenty-two, not counting people willing to provide homes or help with other needed accessories to the actions. However, Valerie had been thinking, this job would be easy enough to use as an opportunity to bring in some new recruits. Miki had a few people in mind and so did Kay.

Miki was getting cardboard cat carriers wholesale from a pet supply business, and her cousin was helping outfit the vans, building layers of shelving all the way up to the roof for stacking cat carriers. Floor space alone wouldn't be anywhere near sufficient, especially with seventeen human beings to transport in addition to the animals.

Edna briefed Valerie on toxoplasmosis. It is a protozoan parasite, a single-celled organism sometimes contracted by eating raw or lightly cooked pork and other meats. Infections also occur in cats who eat mice, rabbits, and birds. But when contracted normally (as opposed to having mass quantities of the concentrated organism shot into their systems) the cats remain unaffected, shedding the larvae in their stools.

The Public Health Service had published an advisory in which pregnant women, for whom the disease can be more dangerous, were cautioned to wear gloves when cleaning litter boxes, parents told to keep children's sandboxes covered when not in use, and everyone warned to avoid uncooked or lightly cooked meats.

The real villain, Valerie learned, aside from Dubey and his funding agency and employer, was factory farming. Diseases like toxoplasmosis have become endemic in intensively raised animals. Nature never intended dozens, hundreds, or thousands of animals to be crowded together in a small space, unable to escape their own droppings, their immune systems weakened from the stress of confinement. The animals can't take it. Predictably, they get sick. The agribusiness response is always the same: fund more research and put more pharmaceuticals into the feed. Never more space, more hygienic conditions, or less stress for their "productivity units."

"Ding dong, the Philadelphia grand jury is dead—or at least disbanded," Valerie told Sean, elated, as soon as she heard the news from a police contact. Their investigations and interrogations into the ALF activity at the University of Pennsylvania had left them without suspects.

"Don't celebrate yet," Josh warned when she relayed the information by phone. The UC-Davis fire had ignited an intensive police investigation. "There's something worse: a *federal* grand jury has convened in Sacramento. It has subpoena power across state lines. Apparently, its primary charge is to investigate the UC-Davis fire and the University of Oregon raid. The feds have pulled a theory out of their hats that the same people were involved in both jobs. The D.A. in Sacramento has already filled three single-spaced pages with names of 'animal rights sympathizers' to be brought in and questioned."

There was more bad news. Roger Troen, the retired school teacher who had received rabbits taken during the University of Oregon raid, had been found guilty of accepting stolen property. Roger had been looking at twenty-five years in jail, but the judge in the case, Edwin Allen, had been moved by testimony from a string of primatologists and other experts brought in by PETA to blast the university's practices and record of cruelty to animals.

At Roger Troen's sentencing, the judge chastised the university for its treatment of animals in its laboratories, saying it was a case of the foxes guarding the chicken coop. "I've wondered what I would do," said Judge Allen, who had graduated from the University of Oregon thirty years earlier, "if, as a member of the state board of education or as a legislator, I heard and saw what I *have* heard and seen. Very frankly, it is disturbing to me as a citizen of this state and this city."

Among other things, Judge Allen listened to witnesses who testified that the university's 20,000 "laboratory animals" had been routinely deprived of veterinary care, left to die in their cages, and used in "joke photos." In one such photo, the university's director of animal care appeared, a lit cigarette dangling from his lips and a bottle of beer in one hand. In the other hand he held up a screaming, frightened primate infant—umbilical cord still attached—pretending to have just delivered him from a female student sprawled out on an operating table.

Judge Allen decided to spare Roger Troen any jail time, sentencing him instead to wear an electronic leg monitor for six months and to pay restitution. PETA filed an appeal.[1]

Valerie decided it was time to provide some relief to the West Coast ALF groups. She would turn the federal grand jury's attention to suburban Maryland.

Finally, the time came to act. Valerie crouched beside the fence line, peering through the night-vision goggles into the fields beyond. No sign of human life, just a herd of "dairy" cows, bodies facing west, but heads pointing at a forty-five degree angle, watching to see what the people in black body suits and masks were going to do next. The cows no longer moved away when they entered the fields. The nightly visitors were clearly harmless, possibly mildly amusing to them.

Tonight there was no need to hold the fence wire up and crawl under. The boltcutters made a "door" wide enough to drive a truck through. How Valerie wished the ground was firm enough to support one. There was a lot of walking to do.

It was a beautiful night, a little cooler than usual. The bugs weren't biting much and the sky was black, cloudless, and full of

---

[1] In December of 1990, the Oregon Supreme Court declined to accept further appeal.

dancing stars. Valerie looked for the North Star and remembered her days at camp in England. For the first time, she had a little nervous "rush," as if she'd swallowed a glass of good wine on an empty stomach. Perhaps it was having so many first-timers along; perhaps the presence of Mike Sager, a reporter from *Rolling Stone*, was worrying her. The reporter was a neighbor of an antivivisectionist who had vouched for him, and he'd covered, without betrayal, everyone from South American freedom fighters to drug lords. He wasn't terribly moved by animal suffering, but Valerie was counting on him only to be fair.

The group had assembled about a quarter-mile from the rise. They waited for the signal that the patrol car had gone back over the hill according to schedule. When they heard the radio clicks, they rose and walked through the fence. Valerie had warned the group to follow closely. Having found, by accident, every possible wallow from the fence line to the cat barn, she knew where to step and where not to. It was like having a mental map of a minefield.

Kitty, the youngest of the group, held onto Valerie's sleeve as they moved forward. From her grip, Valerie could tell that Kitty was much too nervous. Valerie could almost feel the electricity generated by her fear. She hoped it wouldn't spread.

After a few minutes' walk inside the perimeter fence, they passed the outdoor hog pens. The huge boars grunted in irritation, alerting each other that people were coming by and disturbing their peace. Fourteen pairs of black-gloved hands grasped the pigpen fencing and squished past on their way to the low white building directly behind.

The group was completely hidden from the patrol lane as they came up to the cat building and approached the side door. Valerie had reserved the job of punching out a pane of glass in the door for Joe, a young Giant Food stock clerk. He was spunky and anxious, and Valerie wanted to give him every opportunity to gain confidence quickly.

The glass pane hit the sheet of newspaper Joe slid under the door. He pulled it out, stuck his hand through the opening, and snapped open the door.

"Careful of the stray glass," Joe said, letting people file in.

Four teams of two headed for the windows facing the road. Sonia had made black-out curtains to tape over them so that their flashlights could be used. Everyone else began folding the cardboard carriers into usable form and securing their undersides with masking tape.

"Tight?" Valerie asked, as each window crew stopped work. When the last team said, "Yes," she told Joe to signal to Watch #1.

Joe hit the transmitter button on his walkie-talkie twice. Immediately, two contact taps answered. Watch #1 was ready and looking in their direction. Joe switched on the flashlight and shone it at the blacked-out windows, then signaled again.

Two more contact taps from Watch #1. The lights could not be seen. People could start work.

The cats were already making noises, little anxious sounds of uncertainty. "Friend or foe," they may have been asking. Valerie could hear human voices in each room answering them: "It's OK," "We're going to take you home," using the endearments people use at home with their own animals.

Valerie took Kitty with her into the first room. Kitty held the flashlight while Valerie showed her how to pick the cats up by the nape of the neck, support their hind legs, and lower them into the cardboard boxes without frightening them or letting them escape. There was a calico mama cat with three kittens in the second cage.

"Put her kittens in the box first, then she'll want to join them," Valerie said. Without warning, the flashlight started jumping around in Kitty's hand. Valerie reached out for it, and got Kitty's hand instead. Her skin was cool and clammy.

"Are you all right?" Valerie asked, knowing perfectly well she wasn't. "Kitty, tell me what's wrong."

"I think I'm going to pass out," she said. Her voice was shaky and weak.

"Sit down. Quickly." Valerie told her, wondering what the hell they would do if Kitty was having some sort of serious problem. "It's just nerves. Now, stick your head between your knees, and don't move."

Valerie raced into the next room and grabbed Edna. She didn't want the *Rolling Stone* reporter to know anything was wrong. Regardless of Kitty's condition, the emphasis of his story must remain on the animals.

Edna immediately snapped into nurse mode. "Don't suck air in like that or you'll hyperventilate," she said, addressing Kitty in her take-charge voice. "Breathe in and out evenly, normally." Edna put her hand on Kitty's shoulder and it seemed to help calm her. "You'll be fine. You just need to relax a minute."

Edna jerked her head at Valerie to leave it to her. Valerie acquiesced gratefully. Bear, Hacker, Doug, and two rookies—Tiger and his friend from school—were already at the pig barns, and Valerie was anxious to get over there right away. She left Edna with Kitty and the rest of the group busily boxing cats, and high-tailed it along the patrol road as fast as she could. She found them in the wrong barn having a pointless discussion about trying to move the sows. The sober reality was that each animal weighed over five hundred pounds. It was impossible. Valerie had to get the group moving.

They went on to the barn housing the small pigs and everyone cheered up. Miraculously, the pigs made very little noise as Hacker stood in their pen and lifted them up and over the cement walls, into the arms of their liberators. They gave a few muffled grunts and snorts as they adjusted their bodies into as comfortable a position as possible, then sank into silence except for the occasional contented snuffly sound.

With the exception of Tiger's friend, all the men could manage two of the pigs. They were African miniature pigs, not young ones. The men set off through the fields with their pig bundles to wait for transportation, a little pig snout and pink pig face poking out of each bag slung across their shoulders.

Valerie raced back to see how things were progressing in the cat barn. At the edge of the lane she looked around carefully through her goggles. Green cows, a couple of green bats fluttering about under the eaves, but no green people. It was all pretty eerie.

Valerie was back at the cat barn within about seven minutes, in time to count the last cat carrier being lined up inside the barn door. Thirty-six. Taking a carrier in each hand, they'd have them all out within two trips.

"Do we have them all?" Valerie asked. Joe said they had. Valerie noticed Kitty standing by Edna. It was impossible to tell how she was doing, but at least she was on her feet. The man from *Rolling Stone* was helping move the cats through the door for the first trip.

Valerie had picked a route that would take them behind Watch #1, through three fields, over a trickle of a stream, up a rise, and to an L-shaped line of trees. At the end of the trees was the exterior road. Only yards from that point was the main gate.

They set off in single file through the damp grass. The boxes of cats, which seemed so light at first, grew heavier with each step, and Valerie could feel the muscles in her arms pulling.

At the stream there was hardly a tap flow despite all the storms, but the embankment was steep and the boxes had to be handed over. This slowed everyone down; by the time they made it to the woods by the road Valerie knew they would be cutting it close if they wanted to get back to the cat barn and get another group of cats before the patrol.

Nine people were needed to go back and get the remaining cats. They left the others to catch their breath in the shadow of the woods, and made their way back along the tree line, moving briskly, although it was too dangerous to run on the patches of slick mud. An owl called, and for a split second Valerie thought it was Watch #1 trying something different. Then she saw the owl's great wings flap out of a tree as he moved to a less disturbed hunting ground.

Watch #1's voice suddenly hit Valerie in the ear and made her jump. She had the volume turned up so high that it almost put a hole in her ear drum.

"Dispatch to #3," he repeated. That was the signal. The team had ninety seconds or so to get out of there.

"Patrol's coming," Valerie relayed to the others, "Let's go. Quick!"

Their exit was shielded at first by the barn as they moved rapidly through the slick grass, trying to put as much distance as possible between themselves and the lane. At forty-five seconds or so, Valerie looked back through the goggles. There he was, gliding silently down the lane.

She motioned everyone to get down. Lying with their faces pressed to the earth they were invisible, but the cat carriers, although painted black, made noticeable little rectangles sticking up in the field. Valerie knew the spotlight could reach this far. She just hoped the guard wouldn't use it.

They squinted through the grass. He was in no hurry. One minute, two, three, four. The car looped around the poultry barns, paused at the front of the cat building, then turned and headed ever so slowly back up the lane. They were on their feet again and heading for the stream before he reached the bottom of the hill.

At the end of the L, hidden by the trees, Valerie radioed Watch #3. He had a clear view of the road and gave the all-clear. Valerie and Joe ran to the gate and cut off the padlock, then raced out of the compound and down the street into the development where the vans had been parked in an apartment lot. They moved silently and reclaimed the vehicles, careful not to wake the residents whose bedroom windows were feet away. In minutes they were back at the gate. Watch #3 gave the second all-clear. The gate swung open again, and a horde of people sprang to their feet from out of the darkness and bolted for the vehicles, cat carriers and pig bundles in their arms.

The pigs and their people filled Joe's van instantly. As soon as the side door slid shut, he backed out, turned around, and headed toward the gate. Watching him go, Valerie thought for a minute he'd forget to put on his lights, but he didn't.

Loading the cat carriers took longer. Each one had to be pushed into place in one of the wooden slots on the shelves. That done, about a dozen human beings squashed into place on the floor of the aisle between the racks. Valerie backed the van into the first driveway, turned to follow Joe, and flicked her headlights on. The vans were about two blocks apart.

There were high spirits in the back, yet for Valerie this was always the most harrowing time: having the animals, yet not having made a complete getaway.

As the convoy headed slowly out of the development, her fears were realized: a car snapped on its headlights and pulled out of a cul-de-sac. It was almost three o'clock in the morning, not a likely time for someone to pop out to the store. From her side mirror, Valerie couldn't make out what sort of car it was, but she knew there was a damned good chance it was a cruiser that had been parked somewhere in the development, passing quiet time.

Valerie pulled back the curtain behind the driver's seat and shouted at everyone in the back to be still and quiet. Their excitement evaporated.

"Possible cop car. Behind us," she said. She could see Joe's van a block ahead, driving so as not to arouse suspicion, stopping carefully at the stop signs that met him at every second block. Valerie knew he was doing exactly what she was doing: trying to drive so that he *seemed* sober, respectable, and lawful. By now, the officer had no doubt jotted down Valerie's tag number, "just in case." At least it wouldn't trace.

There was one last stop sign to go before the exit to Greenbelt Road. Valerie signaled the turn, slowed down and braked. "If I were in that cruiser," she thought, "I'd stop the van now, before it leaves the development." Joe pulled out. Now it was her turn. The street lights at the intersection showed a bank of lights on top of the car: it *was* a cruiser. Here goes, Valerie thought, pulling out into the highway. The cruiser turned, too, but the other way. It made a U-turn and headed back into the development.

"Jesus Christ!" Cheers and laughter came from the back of the van. They were home free!

They had raided a research facility that was involved not only in animal experimentation, but in intensive agriculture as well. Two for one. On Route 50, just before the entrance ramp to the beltway, Valerie's van stopped. One of the new kids opened the side door, carried the bag filled with their mud-caked shoes over to the big dumpster behind a convenience store, and tossed it in.

The Agricultural Center was remarkably quick to respond. "Pregnant women and AIDS patients at risk from released cats," their public relations department informed the press. "Stolen cats carry virus dangerous to human fetus," the press repeated. "Can it be treated?" asked reporters of the Agricultural Center. "No, that would be very difficult," they replied, "That's why the research was so valuable. Dr. Dubey was looking for a treatment."

PETA called a news conference, assembling a nurse, a mother with her newborn, and a pregnant woman to answer the reporters' questions. A PETA spokeperson's prepared statement read:

> We wish to counter the scare tactics being used to distract the public from the very real suffering of cats, pigs, and other animals used in USDA experiments.
>
> Whoever at the USDA has said that toxoplasmosis is not treatable should be fired. Toxo is not only easy to treat, it is easy to prevent. The USDA is covering up the fact that the true cause of toxoplasmosis is not these few cats, but improperly cooked meat— 25 percent of all pork and 10 percent of all lamb is infected with this parasite. Yet, the USDA doesn't warn people about that, it simply supports the system of intensive farming that causes such health hazards.
>
> The USDA claims that its cat research is vital and aimed at treating humans and animals. In the fifteen years Dr. Dubey has conducted these experiments he has never once attempted to investigate or conduct any treatment of any human or animal. His most important finding is that humans and cats should not eat uncooked horsemeat! His second most 'important' finding is that the greater the amount of infected tissue you force into animals, the greater their infection!
>
> The USDA's issuance of a 'National Alert,' alarming pregnant women by creating the impression that toxoplasmosis-infected cats from Beltsville are out there somewhere threatening their lives, is a standard trick. A trick taught at all the seminars on laboratory security in the last several years under the title, 'How to handle a break-in at your lab.' Researchers and public relations specialists are told to try to promptly turn the story into a general endorsement of the worth of animal experiments, and to raise doubts in the public mind about the danger of disease transmission from the rescued animals.
>
> This research was clearly targeted because it is cruel and worthless. We have received assurances from the people who entered

the Research Center that the cats are under veterinary care, showing that they were and remain fully aware of the medical needs of the animals. Cats with toxoplasmosis can easily be treated, and no pregnant woman will be asked to handle these cats' feces with her bare hands or to eat the animals. Therefore, no danger exists.

The African miniature pigs didn't stay small for long. In fact, they soon grew to about the size of Volkswagens.

The family whose fruit farm they live on would never stand for anyone to talk down to them, let alone for anyone to scald them, skin them, and use their bodies for BLT's. "Snork Maiden" is the grand dame of the herd. She leads the rest of them up to the farmhouse door. Most of them, except Rudi, who's really boisterous and impatient, stand by and wait while Snork bangs on the door with her leathery snout. One of these days she may tear it from its hinges. On a hot day, you can see Lily and Rudi rolling on their backs in their mud wallow, oinking their conversations, and having a ball; then running up onto the porch, their hooves pattering on the wood, demanding that someone stop work and open a package of their favorite oatmeal cookies.

It turned out that only eleven of the cats had been given toxoplasmosis; the others had not yet been injected with the parasite. After their treatment at the veterinary hospital, they joined the other cats in a basement recreation room converted into a comfortable interim home for them.

New York activists placed some of the cats by word of mouth and through ads. When they were down to seven, the owner of the house had become too fond of them to part company with any more.

While the USDA cats were sunning themselves in the light from French windows, batting at imaginary butterflies in the garden, and feeling love for the first time in their lives, NIH was having a series of closed-door meetings about how to deal with the animal rights movement.

In October, 1987, a memorandum was leaked to PETA. The memo contained a summary of an interagency discussion that had occurred a month after the USDA raid. It read:

The stakes are enormous. The animal rights movement threatens the very core of what the Public Health Service is all about.

The 'bunker' strategy is no longer tenable.

The health research community must participate in a more pro-active posture, working in concert with patient groups, voluntary health organizations, the American Medical Association, and other groups of health professionals. Wherever feasible, the research institutions should leave the 'out front' activities to the other groups. The PHS and its agencies should find some acceptable way to provide funding for some of these efforts and technical support for others.

Although it is important that we continue to work toward 'having our house in order,' we must realize that by making this our major focus, we tacitly accept the premise of the animal rights movement and play into their hands.

The pro-active posture should focus in two directions: [first] contemporary examples of health advances directly dependent upon animal research. Here we should draw liberally from those health areas that already enjoy wide public and congressional support, i.e. AIDS, dementia, schizophrenia, various childhood disorders, etc. We should draw up a list of such illnesses and the research upon which treatment is dependent, keeping in mind the existence of various specialized groups such as Danny Thomas and so forth. The example of the Juvenile Diabetes Association should be instructive.

A pro-active stance should [also] include a vigorous focus on the fundamental philosophical underpinnings of the animal rights movement, namely the moral equivalence between human beings and animals. This could be highlighted by some of the more outrageous quotes from Elizabeth Newkirk [sic] and Alex Pacheco, that dramatize how the movement's philosophy is based on a degradation of the concept of human nature.

Other strategies outlined in the memo included finding ways, through a National Institutes for Mental Health intramural program, to fund "fellowships in animal research advocacy" and find spokespeople "trained in the arguments of the animal rights people. Although most investigators are not interested in such advocacy and are not skillful at it, there are a few who would be interested if there were financial incentives."

Other developments included a legislative strategy that would ensure that all answers to questions by Congress "concerning what we are doing (or why we are not doing more) in a given area should include reference to the difficulties imposed by restrictive regulations and by the activities of animal activists."

The Department of Education was to be contacted, too, "concerning infiltration of high schools by the animal rights people." A "counter-educational effort" (that's an accurate description, Valerie thought) was to be mounted, in cooperation with the AMA.

The memo, which was written by Frederick Goodwin, M.D., then head of Intramural Research at NIMH, was carbon-copied to the head of the Foundation for Biomedical Research—a private interest group funded primarily by pharmaceutical and cosmetics companies that continue to use animals, and founded by Charles River Breeding Company, the world's largest commercial supplier of animals for experimentation.

Epilogue

The outer worlds follow a pattern of size,
Of content, rotation and lune;
On all points they follow a similar rule —
Save Pluto, the runaway moon.
The others were formed by a nebular law;
In place they were properly strewn;
Not one was an upstart, crashing the class —
Save Pluto, the runaway moon.

I n July of 1988, NIH took a bold step. In an attempt to thwart
a court ruling in favor of PETA's escalating legal battle to
gain custody of the surviving Silver Spring monkeys still
trapped at Delta, it issued a statement. The monkeys it had once
refused to accept from the Institute for Behavioral Research,
promised Congress never to experiment on again, and called "of
no scientific value," became — overnight — "experimental animals
of extremely high scientific value." *Not* to use them again, NIH
Director Dr. James Wyngaarden pronounced, "would be inhumane." To grant them a moment in the sunlight or fresh air or
access to a cage in which they could take two steps "would kill
them."

At about the same time, Paul, the old, pot-bellied warrior monkey with massive layers of scar tissue on his shoulders and down
his arms, died at Delta under mysterious circumstances, and his
body was promptly incinerated. The report from Tulane said that
Paul had lost over fifty percent of his body weight before succumb-
ing. Next to go was Billy, the timid monkey who had held on to
Alex's fingers so tightly and who, robbed of the use of his arms,
had to eat with his feet.

The Physicians Committee for Responsible Medicine (PCRM),

a newly formed organization of medical doctors opposed to "cruel and wasteful" animal experiments, raced into court to try to prevent NIH and Tulane from conducting invasive brain experiments on Billy in his final moments. The court denied Billy protection. "Science" prevailed and Billy's skull was removed under anesthesia. Electrodes were dipped into his brain over eighty times before he was allowed to leave a world that had treated him so wretchedly.

Now only Sara and Nero remained at Tulane. PCRM returned to the courts to charge NIH with scientific fraud, and PETA's case to win custody edged toward the U.S. Supreme Court. Everyone now knew that the cases had to do with principle; the monkeys had become pawns in the fight over whether people have the right to protect animals. Few believed any longer that Nero and Sara would ever feel a tree branch beneath their feet, reach for a leaf, or enjoy the light touch of a breeze and the smell of the outdoors. The only primate's touch they would ever feel would be from a white-coated primate who planned to kill them.

The risk of being arrested for past actions was now a factor of Valerie's everyday life. She knew from friends in the police department that the FBI was heavily involved in an effort to break the ALF apart and that they had a wiretap order for PETA's phones. When Ronnie Lee was arrested and his office ransacked, Valerie's name and address had been found. She knew this because she received a warning in the mail, postmarked Yorkshire and signed "M." Written exchanges between the ALF in Britain and any of its overseas contacts were out of the question. All mail was opened and read or read by machine, its postal jacket left undisturbed. Valerie had to plan ahead: if the boom dropped, there needed to be a self-sufficient East Coast ALF unit in place, a unit that would be unaffected if she were arrested.

With that in mind, she had given Joe a lot of responsibility during the planning and raid on the USDA. Valerie liked him and had sensed his potential from the day he came into her circle. He was sharp, sincere, willing to take risks, committed to the cause, and, thank God, neither tempestuous nor petty. She and Josh had discussed him, she had nurtured him, and they had both agreed that he'd make a good leader.

Valerie had learned a lot of useful things from her experience at the camp in England, and she wanted Joe to experience the sense of international unity and purpose it had instilled in her. She wanted him to get an infusion of animal liberation philosophy, as well as take the ALF's crash courses in practical skills, like electronics. She made arrangements to send him across the Atlantic, feeling a special sense of pride and delight that the next generation was "in the works."

A new grand jury sprang up in Maryland and was reportedly working in tandem with the FBI, the federal grand jury in California, and Scotland Yard. Valerie knew that on at least two occasions since the SEMA break-in, officers from Scotland Yard's unit assigned to ALF activities had visited the United States to meet with NIH representatives and with the FBI.

Sources close to the Maryland state's attorney reported that he felt he was a hairsbreadth away from nailing down what had happened at SEMA, and Miki broke the news to Valerie that Simba had been interviewed by the FBI. Luckily, they had not asked him the questions that, as a good Christian, he might have felt duty-bound to answer honestly. Miki theorized that the white FBI agents who questioned Simba were probably convinced that middle-aged black men didn't qualify as suspects in what the FBI thought was a "white" movement.

The FBI had fixed on a young white suspect who fit their stereotype, and they were confidently pursuing him. It seemed that Chuck, the new caretaker Valerie and Bear had encountered in the supply room at SEMA, was only a part-time worker in the lab. The rest of the time he attended law school. The FBI knew not only that the four chimpanzee babies had taken a permanent hike on Chuck's shift, but that Chuck's fiancee was employed by an animal rights organization. According to the "intelligence" coming to Valerie from the Rockville courthouse, the FBI was convinced that Chuck's fiancee had either told animal rights people about Chuck's job and that they had carried out the raid, or that she and Chuck had done it themselves.

The FBI didn't like the idea of some smart-ass would-be-lawyer committing a crime right under their noses. They made it clear to Chuck that he would never graduate, let alone practice law, unless he "came clean." The pressure must have proved too much for him. Perhaps he *had* been planning to get the chimpanzees out; perhaps his fiancee *had* told others. Whatever the rub, becoming a prime suspect in a federal felony case was more than he could bear. Chuck checked out of school and left for South America to teach English at a "poor school." If the FBI wanted to question Chuck further, they'd have to come up with something more concrete.

The attorney general's office in Maryland wasn't doing any better. An inspector general's car was discovered parked at the end of the PETA driveway late one night. The two men inside it had been making notes of who came and went from the office all day. A PETA director walked down the driveway and invited the men to come in and look around. Unprepared for the invitation, they said no. When the FBI learned about that, they had asked for someone's head on a plate.

More agents from the inspector general's plainclothes division kept getting spotted. Two agents turned up at PETA's news conference on the USDA raid. The men, both posing as "freelance" writers, were promptly exposed, and found themselves having their pictures taken, surrounded by smiling PETA employees, and answering questions from angry reporters who resented their ruse. A month or so later, another agent was unmasked at PETA's "Humanitarian Awards Gala" at the Willard Intercontinental Hotel. He was recognized by a PETA employee as one of the agents who had parked in the government car outside the PETA office. The PETA employee played the agent along, nagging him into spending more and more of the government's money on raffle tickets and Treasure Chest coupons, then loading him up with doggie bags of delicious vegan food and favors to take home to his family.

To add to the confusion, the FBI had also chosen as a suspect in the USDA raid a young man named Pete. He had just turned twenty and worked for a pest control company near the Beltsville Agricultural Research Center.

Pete's first "mistake" was to have a "Liberate Laboratory Animals" bumper sticker on his car. He'd picked it up at an exhibit on the National Mall that summer, and put it on his car to show his sympathies. By sheer coincidence, Pete had not shown up for work the morning after the USDA raid. The next day, one of the secretaries, aware of Pete's bumper sticker, asked him, jokingly, if he had liberated the cats.

Pete, who was attracted to this young woman, decided to play it for all the machismo it was worth. Whether he "confessed" his involvement or hinted at it, it was enough for the apple of his eye to call the police. The police notified the FBI, who sent agents to Pete's workplace, tore the seats out of his car looking for evidence (all they found was a marijuana cigarette), and hauled him in for hours of fruitless questioning.

The ALF had never met poor Pete.

Police work can be tough, and agents and cops vary as much as anyone else in the amount of brain power, intuitive sense, and effort they bring to a case. So far, luckily, the American ALF had drawn the Keystone Cops.

By April of 1989, Josh had honed his bomb-making skills. That month, the University of Arizona at Tucson was "remodeled" by three separate incendiary devices consisting of little more than a car battery, an alarm clock, and some fire starters. The device caused an estimated $288,000 of damage to its five-story administration building and to the microbiology and pharmacy labs.

The ALF spray-painted "Nowhere is Safe—ALF" on the walls and doors of the animal buildings before removing 1,231 animals: mice with open sores and wounds, many of whom had been dying slowly and messily from cryptosporidium (a diarrheal disease), rabbits, guinea pigs, rats, and tropical frogs. Valerie saw Josh afterward, and learned that much of the research on the approximately 82,000 animals the university used had been put on hold. Several of the research projects had been permanently wiped out.

"It shows how 'vital' they were," Josh said, "when they don't even dare apply to restart them."

The raid was the last straw for Alabama Senator Howell

Heflin. Encouraged by his agricultural and biomedical research constituents, he promptly introduced a bill making it a federal offense to burglarize or vandalize a research facility. As he toured the ruins of the Arizona lab, Heflin's aide announced to the press, "Researchers are beginning to feel that they are working under a state of siege." University president Henry Koffler was at his side to describe the university's plan to bolster security: double steel doors, a computerized entry system, full electronic surveillance, and twenty-four-hour patrols of armed guards for a total security tab of close to $1 million.

"This attack has destroyed the work of years of research," Koffler announced. "Whoever's responsible deserves the most severe punishment possible."

In the underground community, neither Koffler's comments nor Heflin's new bill were taken seriously. According to press reports, the university police department "found little to no evidence at any of the four crime scenes." Anyone involved in liberations, arson, and the cross-country transportation of rescued animals already knew they faced multiple felony charges that could imprison them for ten to twenty years per count. Making the offenses federal might entitle ALF members to a better-quality prison, but it was certainly no deterrent.

A few months after the Arizona liberation and fires, Joe and four other members of Valerie's newly formed unit hit Texas Tech University in Lubbock. The raid was the first in Texas and an attempt to break up experiments on cats conducted by a professor called John Orem.

Orem's experiments, which had been going on for fifteen years, involved connecting sleep-deprived cats to a recording device by bolting their heads into a steel clamp and putting metal rods into their ears and mouths so they couldn't move their heads. The bones were exposed around their eyes, and screws were threaded through holes drilled behind their eyes. Holes were cut into their windpipes. The cats were punished if they failed to learn to hold their breath whenever a tone sounded. Their punishment came from a blast of ammonium hydroxide, which made them salivate and burned their eyes.

"Gore-'em" Orem had carved his career out of cats' brains. Sleep deprivation was his specialty, and he had devised innumerable ways to keep cats awake: the "flowerpot method," in which he placed cats on a tiny wooden plank inside a water-filled drum, where falling asleep meant plummeting into the drink; by lowering the temperature in their room to below freezing; and by forcing them to keep running hour after hour on a treadmill that would not stop.

The night of the raid Valerie sat propped up in bed, listening to Sean's breathing and biting her fingernails, waiting for news.

When they called in, "Joe & Co." were jubilant. They had found five cats still alive, and got them all out safely before going back to destroy Orem's expensive electronic equipment and stereotaxic restraint devices. They also had removed the preserved brains of cats named "Fluffy," "Alfalfa," "Lady," "Pepe," and two dozen others. These they would bury in a field full of Texas wild flowers before coming back to Maryland. And, in three-foot-high letters sprayed on the wall of the emptied lab, they had written, "Don't Mess with Texas Animals."

The cats from Texas Tech included a three-legged tomcat. Joe gave Val the pleasure of naming him and she called him "Chester," after the Silver Spring monkey who got her into the ALF and stole her heart. This Chester had lost one of his legs during a laboratory "accident." There is a pit in his head where the electrodes have been removed, and he is on phenobarbital to control his seizures. He and the other four cats spent their recovering days with a long-time ALF benefactor, a strikingly elegant woman who buys and rehabilitates starved horses she finds at auctions. She was reluctant to see Chester leave for his permanent home because, she said, he is "a real man of a cat, all spirit and go."

The other cats, including a stumpy little orange tiger cat, barely grown, who had stunted legs that the vet could not explain, had recently arrived at the lab from a dealer who made his pickups at Texas pounds. They were too scared to adjust immediately to kindness; they'd never seen it and didn't quite believe it existed.

PETA went after Orem hard, criticizing the "grant gravy train"

365

that allowed him to collect money for things he'd be arrested for doing on the street. Officials at Texas Tech snatched up the National Association of Biomedical Research's media plan, claiming with barely a pause to catch their breath that Orem's experiments had "the potential to save babies' lives." Overnight, fifteen years of go-nowhere sleep deprivation experiments in cats became SIDS (Sudden Infant Death Syndrome) research for human babies.

As PETA's national director, the lot fell to me to fly out to Lubbock with Dr. Kenneth Stoller, a California pediatrician whose decision to speak out against waste and cruelty had already proved of enormous help to animal rights groups. Together, we held a news conference in which Dr. Stoller blew away the smoke Texas Tech was using to cover Orem's crude tests.

"Dr. John Orem has yet to produce a practical application," Dr. Stoller told reporters. "I have reviewed his published papers, and whatever he says he has been researching, it certainly is not SIDS. He has been playing with millions of taxpayer dollars over his career. Now he is playing with the emotions of SIDS families."

Dr. Stoller was joined by other physicians and veterinarians who had read Orem's papers. Dr. Suzanne Cliver denounced the experimenter's work as "among the most ghastly I have read. . . . I could find no justification whatsoever for carrying out this horrifying work. The gross insensitivity to the animals used is a profound embarrassment to the scientific community."

Dr. William Wittert wrote, "The research done by John Orem does not have any relationship to humans' Sudden Infant Death Syndrome. . . . The studies are extraordinarily cruel and the cats are . . . certainly subjected to extraordinary suffering."

NIH was getting madder by the minute. While Orem's research subjects licked their wounds and tried to heal, and the Texas animal rights groups gathered to discuss how to keep the pressure on Texas Tech, the lights were burning into the night at the Bethesda headquarters of the biggest grant-funding agency in the world. They needed to show solidarity with Orem, with Texas Tech, with animal experimenters everywhere, but they also needed to look concerned about animal welfare.

How about putting together a team of "investigators" who could fly out to Texas and find nothing wrong, no matter what? Yes, that would do nicely!

When the team was announced, it was no surprise. Adrian Morrison, Taub's old friend from the University of Pennsylvania, headed the list. Morrison and the other experimenters flew to Texas to meet Orem, who affected the style of a lanky, pipe-smoking cowboy. They compiled the draft of their report which would "exonerate" Orem. "It has been a terrible experience for Professor Orem," they wrote. "He spends his life looking over his shoulder now. The break-in came out of the blue to destroy him."

As Tina, Joe's Texas contact, stated in her news release on behalf of the ALF, "The experimenters will defend every atrocity. They will give assurances, make false claims, and call us terrorists. But who are the true terrorists? For the animals who have no voice, Frankenstein lives."

In January of 1990, Valerie had a chance to pay Adrian Morrison back. A student at the University of Pennsylvania thought Morrison had been "a bit too friendly" to his girlfriend. If the animal rights movement would like access to the old university building where Morrison worked, he could make a set of keys available.

Valerie got the tip through a student contact she had picked up after Eddie's graduation. She jumped at the opportunity. Morrison had not only tried to whitewash Orem's grisly deeds, but Valerie had never forgotten his disgusting attempt to make the jury disbelieve the incredible suffering of the Silver Spring monkeys. She and Edna decided it would only take the two of them to do the job. They didn't quite trust the student, but they thought the risk worth taking. If they were careful, they might only pick up a trespassing charge if they were caught going in, and if they were caught with Morrison's papers, Valerie figured petty larceny. The real value of the files wasn't monetary—it was in their content.

Tiger was deployed to check the place out two nights before Valerie and Edna went in. Tiger's girlfriend, dressed in a fur coat so as not to look like an animal rights activist, had strolled with him along the quadrangle of the target building. They were kissing against the red stone walls outside the archway leading into the quad, checking out the pedestrian traffic, when a white Buick appeared at the curb, the driver angrily blowing the horn at them.

Tiger and Debbie saw the woman passenger get out. The woman marched up to them, handed Debbie an anti-fur card, and said, "Do you know how many animals it took to make that coat?" Dumbfounded, Debbie muttered, "Oh, thank you, I'll think about it." The woman left.

Outside the quad, Valerie and Edna walked briskly through the old grill gates. Once inside the old building, Valerie stayed at the foot of the worn stone steps while Edna ran upstairs, found Morrison's office, and crowbarred open his file cabinets. Valerie could hear the noise of iron and crumpling tin above her as she watched through the glass door for signs of anyone coming their way.

Edna took a piece of orange chalk from Morrison's desk and scrawled "CAT KILLER" and "FIRST STRIKE FOR OREM AND TAUB" on his walls. She transferred from his files to her shoulder bag enough dirt to put Morrison on the front page of the *Village Voice*, and not for reasons he or his university wanted. She and Valerie walked casually to the car and pulled away. As soon as they hit the Schuylkill Expressway, Valerie turned on the dome light and began to read out loud to Edna from Morrison's papers. As they headed south on I-95 to Washington, they realized just how busy Morrison had been fighting animal rights.

Morrison had not only been active locally, stopping a humane education course at his own university, he had also kept a list of "trouble spots"—places and people being criticized for poor animal care or cruel research. Morrison had provided support to anyone who found himself or herself "persecuted" for animal abuse. The experimenters, including the University of Oregon's Barbara Gordon-Lickey and Richard Marrocco, were eternally grateful.

"Thank you once again," wrote Edward Taub, from his new position in the department of philosophy at the University of Alabama on August 2, 1989, "for very generously defending me. I am also touched by your saying that I am a 'good man'. . . . Your friendship and unstinting help over these long years is more than anyone has a right to expect. I think it says a great deal about the strength of your character, of your beliefs, and of your moral fiber . . . it is truly you who is [sic] a 'good man.'"

The *Village Voice* reporter, Jack Rosenberger, took copies of all the files and examined them for authenticity. When he was satisfied that they were what the ALF claimed, he called the researchers and Morrison himself and asked for their side of the story. By the time *Voice* readers finished reading Rosenberger's article, they knew what Morrison had been doing to cats for the previous twenty-five years: studying how they react to extreme temperatures before electrically burning out sections of their brains, exposing sleep-deprived cats to loud noises, and crushing cats' spinal columns with a jeweler's forceps.

Days after the article ran, a brown paper package addressed "Dr. Adrian Morrison" arrived at the front desk of the University of Pennsylvania veterinary school. Morrison knew he had ordered nothing, was expecting nothing, and noticed there was no return address or postage on the package. His hands sweating, he called the police.

The campus police sped to the scene, evacuated the veterinary building of all its human occupants and cordoned off the area. The bomb squad carefully took the package apart while students, anxious faculty members, and the press, who had picked the story up from the police wire, observed from a safe distance. The bomb squad opened the package and slowly and carefully took out its contents: a pair of women's bikini briefs.

Morrison was no longer comfortable at the university. When he went out in the morning to pick up the newspaper from his front lawn he noticed he was being watched by animal rights activists. The parcel had made him jumpy, too. He had already pulled his daughter out of her university classes and was wondering what to do. He decided to take a sabbatical to Italy to visit his old friend Dr. Luigi Parmeggiani, an animal experimenter at the University of Bologna.

The Italian anti-vivisectionists were waiting for him. Everywhere Morrison looked, he found his own caricatured face on posters all over the campus. "Wanted for Murder of Cats" read the caption beneath his red beard.

Morrison's "cavalry" came in the form of another NIH plan. Morrison was given a newly created position at NIH headquarters in Bethesda. He was to be director of laboratory animal care, a permanent, full-time spokesperson for an industry under constant attack. If Mohandas Gandhi was right, and "the greatness of a nation and its moral progress can be judged by the way it treats its animals," NIH's action did not speak highly of America. However, the ALF was pleased with Morrison's new appointment: at least he would not be doing any more cat experiments for a while.

Josh was married in the spring of 1989 aboard his boat off the coast of southern California. His daughter, Jessica, was born at Cedars Sinai Hospital a year later. Valerie sent Josh and his wife a copy of Dr. Michael Klaper's book on the benefits of a vegan diet during pregnancy and was pleased to note that the baby weighed eight pounds when she was born. According to Josh, she is never bothered with the gastric disturbances or the coughs, colds, and sniffles of cow's milk-raised babies. Valerie has seen her and says she's beautiful and strong. Josh promises he's going to make sure Jessica grows up to be the best liberationist a man could hope for!

Mandy is very old now. She has a new friend, "Lucky," courtesy of a medical student at Johns Hopkins University who couldn't bear to let him die. Lucky disappeared through a back door the morning he was scheduled to be used in a student surgery "show and tell." His energy helps keep Mandy alive.

Sean's business, Wildnear, is doing extremely well—well enough that the ALF has been able to buy Joe's cell an ID-making machine and a new van. Sean has also been able to pay for the services of the ALF's newest human resource: a whiz kid who has begun to hack into the computer systems of . . . well, you may read about it in the papers before long.

Ronnie Lee is scheduled for parole in September of 1992. In addition to revolutionizing the prison food services system in Britain (British prisons, like most airlines, now offer vegetarian or vegan meals), Ronnie has put his time in prison to good use, studying Italian, French, Spanish, and German. In 1990 he applied for and received approval for a government grant that will pay his food and lodging and allow him to attend university when he is released from prison. What he plans to do with this knowledge is a matter of broad speculation in police circles.

In the wake of a series of fire bombings, the Band of Mercy reemerged on the British underground animal rights scene in 1990. Its actions contrast drastically with the inflamed and anarchistic rhetoric of the British ALF Supporters' Group's newsletter, *Ark Angel*. The Band of Mercy's recent actions mark a return to the original, gentler ideas of liberation that first emerged in the 1800s.

In 1990, "game" bird farms and more fur farms were added to the ALF's target list in America. Since then, hundreds of minks and foxes, and even a few coyotes, have been rescued in "Operation Bite-Back." In one case in a small town in Pennsylvania, and another in upstate New York, no press was sought and no calling cards left. The raids were not claimed in either case because the ALF didn't want the local whistleblowers to have their homes burned down or their dogs poisoned. In Washington state, Michigan, and Oregon, the story was different: college students tipped the West Coast ALF off to state-funded mink research projects and the ALF released the researchers' papers after burning the non-animal buildings to the ground.

Valerie is retired from "active duty" now, for personal reasons she will not discuss, but she remains involved in financing, planning, and scouting for ALF actions. I will use her own words to close this story:

"Despite the combined efforts of all the wretched industries we abhor, the ALF is alive and well and growing. If people want to stop the ALF it is simple: *stop doing unspeakable acts to other-than-human beings!* For as long as there are Chesters and Isoldes and Berthas in the labs, having things done to them that human beings would not be allowed to do to their worst enemies in times of war, there will be an ALF. There will be an ALF for as long as tiny chicks feel the pain of that searing wire on their beaks and chained pigs dig hopelessly into the hard cement with their hooves; as long as foxes are killed with hot prods, and orphaned raccoons, whose mothers die in the traps, are left to starve in their dens; as long as there are terrorized animal victims of human injustice and callousness.

"You know the expression, 'All it takes for evil to triumph is for good people to do nothing.' Well, all it takes to get the animals out and stop the suffering is the will to do so. If you can find it in your heart to be part of this force for radical change, *please* get involved. Somehow. Perhaps what you have read will move you to pick a target and a few close friends, do your homework, and go for it.

Jeremy Bentham once wrote, 'The day may come when the rest of the animal kingdom may acquire those rights which never could have been withheld from them but by the hand of tyranny.' When enough of us stop being patient and polite and sitting quietly, the hand of human tyranny *will* be lifted. So, let's do it. Let's achieve it: Free the Animals!"

About the Author

Ingrid Newkirk is cofounder and president of People for the Ethical Treatment of Animals (PETA), the largest animal rights organization in the world. She is the author of *Kids Can Save the Animals! 101 Easy Things to Do, The Compassionate Cook, 250 Things You Can Do to Make Your Cat Adore You,* and *You Can Save the Animals: 251 Simple Ways to Stop Thoughtless Cruelty.* Newkirk has spoken internationally on animal rights issues, championing the cause of animal liberation to the public and teaching activists how to eliminate animal suffering in their own neighborhoods.